Principles of Busi

Edited by Brenda Barrett

THOMSON

LEARNING

Australia • Canada • Mexico • Singapore • Spain • United Kingdom • United States

THOMSON LEARNING

Principles of Business Law

The Thomson Learning logo is a registered trademark used herein under licence.

For more information, contact Thomson Learning, Berkshire House, 168–173 High Holborn, London, WC1V 7 AA or visit us on the World Wide Web at: http://thomsonlearning.co.uk

British Library Cataloguing-in-Publication Data
A catalogue record for this book is available from the British Library

ISBN 1-86152-575-3

First edition published 2001 by Thomson Learning

Typeset by LaserScript Limited, Mitcham, Surrey
Printed by TJ International, Padstow, Cornwall

Contents

Preface

This book has been written by lecturers all of whom have worked, and most of whom are currently working, in the law group at the Business School of Middlesex University. They are teaching on the LL.B., BA in Business Studies and other related undergraduate programmes, as well as postgraduate programmes in both law and management.

Each author has contributed one or more chapters, summarizing the material used in modules offered to students studying law, business or management in Middlesex University. It has been the objective of the contributors to produce a book that, within its covers, contains a sufficient outline of each of the law subjects needed to provide the prospective manager with a broad understanding of the legal framework within which business organizations operate in the United Kingdom.

It is believed that the book will serve as a basic text for undergraduates undertaking a programme in business studies. Such students may use the more general chapters, such as the first, introducing the legal system, and the chapters outlining contract tort and criminal law, in their first year. The more specialized topics such as employment law and intellectual property they may not fully utilize until their final year.

It is expected that this book will also be useful reading for those students on postgraduate management and other vocational programmes who either did not study law at undergraduate level, or studied so long ago as to benefit from a refresher course!

Brenda Barrett
June 2000

Table of Cases

EC CASES

Table of Statutes

Table of Regulations

Table of Directives

Notes on the Contributors

Brenda Barrett has spent most of her working life at what is now Middlesex University Business School. For many years she has taught tort to undergraduates and employment law to postgraduate students. Her research interest is occupational health and safety and on this subject she has published extensively and lectured throughout Great Britain and overseas. She is a barrister. Her doctoral thesis was on employers' liability.

Chris Chang is a principal lecturer in Middlesex University Business School. He teaches land law and equity and trusts. He obtained first class honours in LL.B. at what was then Manchester Polytechnic (now Manchester Metropolitan University). He is a member of the English Bar and an Advocate Solicitor of the High Court of Malaysia.

Penny Childs is currently a lecturer in law at the University of Plymouth. She was previously a principal lecturer at Middlesex University. She has extensive experience in teaching both criminal law and tort at both undergraduate and postgraduate level. She has also taught information technology law and is now also teaching aspects of business law. She has publications in the field of criminal law including a student text and a computer assisted learning package.

Penny English is a lecturer in law at Middlesex University, where she teaches EC law. She previously worked as an archaeologist. This has led her to develop research interests concentrating on the law relating to the ownership and protection of cultural property.

Stephen Homewood is a barrister. He is currently Chair of the Law Academic Group in Middlesex University Business School. He teaches public and environmental law to a range of programmes, including both undergraduate and postgraduate ones as well as professional courses. He has researched and published in these fields. His other interest is human rights. He also sits on the national council of the UK Environmental Law Association.

Martin Kleyman is a chartered accountant who spent his first two years after qualifying in the tax department of a medium-sized accountancy firm. He has lectured in tax to undergraduates and those seeking to pass professional examinations. As well as providing tax compliance and planning advice to various businesses, he also lectures at Middlesex University Business School in auditing and financial accounting as well as tax.

David Lewis is professor of employment law and Head of the Centre for Industrial and Commercial Law in Middlesex University Business School. His previous publications include *Essentials of Employment Law* (with Malcolm Sargeant) and *Discipline* (with Philip James).

Elvira Rubin was educated in Germany, but studied for her LL.B and other legal qualifications in London. She is a senior lecturer in Middlesex University Business School. She has wide experience of teaching company law, EC law and business law more generally to undergraduate students. She has also taught undergraduates in Germany, France and Spain.

Malcolm Sargeant now teaches employment law at Middlesex University Business School after some years in human resource and commercial management. He is co-author of *Essentials of Employment Law*, published by the Institute of Personnel Development, and is an active member of the Business School's Centre for Research in Industrial and Commercial Law. His doctoral thesis was on transfer of undertakings.

Patterson Simmons teaches a wide range of students, at both undergraduate and postgraduate level. Her subjects are business law, international trade and property law (including equity and trusts). Before joining Middlesex University she taught at Birmingham University and then at the Inns of Court School of Law. She has taught in France and Malaysia. She has also worked for a large multi-national company. Her first degree, taken at Berkeley (California) was in french literature. Her research interests are in international trade.

John Weldon teaches property law across the range from intellectual property to land law at Middlesex University Business School. His research interests span these subjects. He has also acted on behalf of the Council of Europe as an expert on property issues in Eastern Europe.

Peter Wilding is a lecturer in consumer law at Middlesex University Business School. Before joining the University he practised in London as a solicitor specializing in European and commercial law. His previous publications include 'Influencing the European Union', 'Securing Business Funding From Europe and the UK' and 'Standard Conditions in Commercial Contracts.'

Helena Wray is a lecturer in law at Middlesex University Business School. She teaches English legal system and public law. She is a solicitor and formerly practised in the City of London in the fields of aviation and commercial law. She also has interests in and has researched into the delivery of legal services and immigration law.

Part I
The Framework of
Business Law

Introduction to the legal system 1

Helena Wray

WHAT IS LAW?

> All of us are confronted with rules every day of our lives. Most of us make, interpret and apply them, as well as rely on, submit to, avoid and grouse about them ...
>
> *How to Do Things with Rules*, William Twining and David Miers,
> Preface to 3rd edition (Weidenfeld and Nicolson, 1991)

Laws are rules that are enforced in courts of law.

There are few aspects of human life that are not governed by legal rules. All businesses will inevitably encounter the law at some time. An understanding of the broad legal principles governing the work of businesses is important for the prospective business manager. On the other hand, laws change and knowledge becomes out of date. Equally important therefore is an appreciation of how law is made and changed. Such is the aim of this chapter.

Laws can be found in a number of places; Acts of Parliament, regulations, by-laws and judges' decisions are just a few. The relationships between these different sources of law are discussed below under 'Sources of law'.

Legal rules, no matter what their source, can also be divided into various types or classifications. Lawyers will often refer to these classifications. The courts used, the terminology applied, and the remedies available may all differ according to the classification of law in question. In this section are described some of the most important.

CRIMINAL AND CIVIL LAW

In *R* v *Great Western Trains* [1999] Great Western Trains Limited pleaded guilty in the Central Criminal Court to contravening the Health and Safety at Work Act 1974. The charge was brought after the Southall Rail Crash in 1997 in which seven people died. The company was fined £1.5 million.

In *Great Scottish & Western Railway Co Ltd* v *British Railways Board* [2000] an employee of the British Railways Board allowed a 'state coach', forming part of a luxury train known as the Royal Scotsman, to roll down a slope into the Royal Scotsman's dining car, causing over £1 million of damage. Under its agreement with the Royal Scotsman's owners, British Railways Board was liable to pay for the damage.

The distinction between criminal and civil law is one of the most important distinctions in the legal system. Criminal law aims at preventing and punishing behaviour considered damaging to society as a whole and cases are nearly always brought by the state. Civil law is concerned with enabling individuals to settle their private disputes and an action is brought by the individual or organization concerned. The popular view of criminal law is that it deals with individuals committing crimes. For the most part, that is true but, as the first example at the head of this section demonstrates, companies can be convicted of criminal offences.

The difference between criminal and civil liability is demonstrated by the two cases mentioned at the head of this section. In the first case, *R* v *Great Western Trains*, the actions of the railway company had resulted in several deaths and many injuries. Criminal proceedings were brought by the state and a fine imposed as there is a clear public interest in punishing such behaviour and preventing its reoccurrence. In the second case, where the consequences were less serious, it was for the injured party, Great Scottish and Western Railway Company Limited, to bring a civil action for damages.

Criminal proceedings are heard in different courts from civil law proceedings (see below, 'The courts and their functions') and the burden of proof (i.e. what the party bringing the action must prove to win its case) is different. A criminal case must be proved 'beyond reasonable doubt'. In a civil claim, the case is decided on 'the balance of probabilities'.

Civil and criminal proceedings use different terminology. In criminal law, the case is brought against the defendant by the prosecution and the decision is known as a verdict. The defendant is either convicted if found guilty or acquitted if found innocent. In civil law (depending on the type of proceedings), a claimant or applicant brings an action against a defendant or respondent. The decision is known as a judgment (or sometimes a decision or a ruling) and the defendant/respondent is said to be either liable or not liable. It is important to use the terminology correctly.

The same event may give rise to liability in both civil and criminal law. As well as its criminal liability for the Southall rail crash, Great Western Trains were under a liability in civil law to pay compensation to victims or their relatives.

PUBLIC AND PRIVATE LAW

In *R* v *Inland Revenue Commissioners ex parte Matrix Securities Ltd* [1994] Matrix Securities Limited claimed that the Inland Revenue was not entitled to withdraw an assurance previously given by letter that a certain scheme would attract tax relief. The House of Lords found that as the assurance had been given on the basis of inaccurate and misleading information, the Inland Revenue was entitled to withdraw it at a later date.

In *Home Office* v *Dorset Yacht Co* [1970] seven borstal trainees (young offenders) escaped from a training exercise near Poole Harbour. They stole a yacht, set it in motion and collided with another yacht which they then boarded. They caused considerable damage to the second yacht. The Home Office as employer of the borstal officers who had charge of the trainees was sued and ordered to pay compensation to the yacht's owners.

Public law is concerned with the duties and functions of public bodies and officials (government departments, civil servants, regulatory bodies, etc.). It includes both criminal proceedings and also applications for 'judicial review' brought against public bodies over the way they have exercised their powers. In a modern regulated environment, businesses have increasingly to deal with public law issues. The first example at the head of this section summarizes a public law issue decided through judicial review proceedings.

Private law is the law regulating the relationships of private individuals and businesses. It includes such areas as the law of tort and the law of contract. The second example is a well-known private law decision in negligence and is part of the law of tort.

It is not always easy to know whether a dispute is a matter of public law or of private law although the procedures differ for each. A claim in private law is often against private companies or individuals but may be against a public body acting in a private capacity such as employer or contractor. In the *Dorset Yacht* case, the Home Office was liable as its employees (the borstal officers) had negligently allowed the boys to escape and cause damage. The legal principle would be the same whether the negligent employee was employed by a government department or by a private company. In the first example, however, it was the actions of the Inland Revenue in carrying out its public duties that were (unsuccessfully) challenged.

INTERNATIONAL AND DOMESTIC LAW

In *Fothergill* v *Monarch Airlines* [1980], Mr Fothergill collected his baggage after a flight with Monarch Airlines and realized that the suitcase had been damaged. He promptly reported the damage to the airline. More than a week later he informed the airline that items were missing out of his suitcase. The liability of airlines for lost and damaged baggage is governed by the Carriage by Air Act 1961, which applies the provisions of the Warsaw Convention. Under the Warsaw Convention, an airline is liable for damage to baggage only if it is notified within seven days of receipt of the baggage. The House of Lords held that under the terms of the Convention, loss of items constituted 'damage' to baggage and the airline was not liable in respect of damage not reported within seven days. Mr Fothergill was not entitled to compensation for the missing items.

Domestic law is the law of a particular state or political unit. For businesses operating in the UK, this will mean the law of England and Wales or of Northern Ireland or of Scotland. The legal systems of other countries are, of course, also domestic law. Those who do business in France, have to comply with French domestic law.

International law governs the legal relations between states and takes the form of agreements between states or laws made under such agreements. These agreements are treaties although they are sometimes described as, for example, conventions. In the UK, treaties do not affect domestic rights and obligations until they are incorporated into domestic law by an Act of Parliament. Once this has happened however, international law may directly affect the position of individuals and businesses as Mr Fothergill discovered to his cost.

The next section considers the effect upon English law of two important international agreements, namely the Treaty of Rome (and amending treaties) the founding treaty of the European Union and the European Convention on Human Rights.

SOURCES OF ENGLISH LAW

Introduction

The principles of English law are not conveniently placed in one document but must be gathered from a diverse range of sources. It is a question not just of identifying the legal principles from amongst these sources but of prioritizing them where there is a conflict. Domestic and external sources of law are discussed separately as the effect of the latter is more complex.

Domestic sources

These are listed in descending order of importance i.e. the most important is legislation and the least important is custom. In the event of a conflict between them, those mentioned first will take priority over those further down the list.

Legislation

Legislation is law created by, or as a consequence of, an Act of Parliament. Of all the domestic sources, it is regarded as the most authoritative as it has been created by a democratically elected and accountable Parliament. If legislation conflicts with, for example, case law, the legislation will be given preference.

There are two types of legislation: primary and secondary legislation.

Primary legislation

> In *British Railways Board* v *Pickin* [1974] Mr Pickin claimed that an Act was invalid on the grounds that Parliament had been misled and that Parliamentary rules had not been followed. In 1968, Parliament had passed the British Railways Act removing rights from the owners of adjoining land to claim ownership of abandoned railways. Mr Pickin was, as a consequence, unable to claim ownership of a strip of disused railway line adjoining his property. The House of Lords refused to hear his claim on the basis that the courts had no power to disregard an Act of Parliament or to investigate the manner in which it had been passed.

Primary legislation is law made by Parliament. It is also known as statute law or an Act of Parliament. Acts of Parliament are passed by the House of Commons and, with rare exceptions, the House of Lords also approves them.

While it is going through the stages of obtaining Parliamentary approval, a statute is known as a 'Bill'. When it is ready to become law, it receives the 'Royal Assent' and becomes an Act of Parliament. An Act comes into effect immediately upon receiving the Royal Assent unless provided otherwise in the Act itself. Most Acts of Parliament state that they are to come into effect at a later date.

Great political and legal importance is attached to the doctrine of the 'supremacy of Parliament'. This is the doctrine that Parliament may make whatever laws it chooses and their validity may not be challenged in the courts or elsewhere (as Mr Pickin discovered in the case referred to at the head of this section). The only exception to this rule is in relation to EC law, discussed below.

While statute law is the most important source of domestic law, the meaning of the words contained in statutes is not always clear. The courts play a significant role in the interpretation of statutes. This is discussed below.

Secondary legislation

In *R* v *Secretary of State for Trade and Industry, ex p. Thomson Holidays* [1999] Thomson Holidays, tour operators, challenged the validity of regulations. A Monopolies and Mergers Commission Report had found that tour operators were forcing travel agents to limit the discounts offered for rival operators' holidays. This had the effect of distorting competition and keeping prices artificially high. The Secretary of State for Trade and Industry used powers under the Fair Trading Act 1973 to make regulations prohibiting tour operators from placing certain restrictions on travel agents. The Court of Appeal found that the regulations challenged went beyond the powers granted by the Fair Trading Act and were invalid.

In *Boddington* v *British Transport Police* [1998] Peter Boddington had been fined £10 for smoking in a railway carriage in which smoking was prohibited. He appealed on the grounds that the decision to ban smoking in all compartments went beyond the powers granted under the Transport Act 1962 to make by-laws regulating the use of the railway. The House of Lords held that Mr Boddington was entitled to challenge the validity of the by-law as a defence to a criminal charge but that, in the circumstances, the power to make and apply the by-law was not exceeded; the by-law was valid and the conviction should stand.

Secondary legislation is legislation made by a body or person under authority granted by Parliament through an Act of Parliament. Secondary legislation can take a number of different forms. Statutory instruments (sometimes in the form of rules or regulations) are made by Ministers. Orders in Council are made by the Privy Council. By-laws may be made by local authorities or public authorities. Sometimes the power to make secondary legislation in the form of codes of conduct or professional regulations will be granted to public or professional bodies such as the Law Society.

The significance of secondary legislation as a source of law is easily overlooked. For example, in 1999, Parliament passed 35 Acts of Parliament and 3491 statutory instruments. Secondary legislation governs many important aspects of everyday life. Businesses are bound by a wealth of secondary legislation governing matters from health and safety issues to employee rights following the take-over of a business.

Secondary legislation is used very frequently for a number of reasons including:

● Parliament's time is limited;

- technical or specialist knowledge may be required in the drafting of legislation so that the job can be done better by experts;
- secondary legislation is easy to amend so that it offers a degree of flexibility which primary legislation cannot.

However the widespread use of secondary legislation has been criticized principally for a lack of accountability. There is some Parliamentary scrutiny but the bulk and complexity of much secondary legislation make thorough Parliamentary control effectively impossible. The same factors can make it difficult for a business (or individual) to ascertain its legal position under secondary legislation.

As discussed above, the validity of an Act of Parliament cannot be challenged in the courts (except under EC law). The same is not true for secondary legislation. If secondary legislation is made in excess of the power to grant it contained in the primary legislation, it may be declared *ultra vires* and thus invalid by the courts. This is what happened in *Ex parte Thomson Holidays* and what Mr Boddington hoped would happen in *Boddington* v *British Transport Police*.

Case law

Case law is law made by judges. Over the centuries, judges, faced with situations for which there were no existing legal rules, adapted and extended pre-existing legal principles in order to meet the new situations. The evolution of this judge-made law has been bound up with the development of the doctrine of precedent described below.

Case law is always inferior to statute law. If there is a conflict between a statutory provision and case law, the statute will always prevail. There are two systems of case law: common law and equity. The reasons for having two systems of case law are historical and the principles of both equity and common law now apply in any court. As equity is a less significant source of law than the common law, it is dealt with here after common law. However, in the event of a conflict between equity and common law, the rules of equity will prevail.

Common law

In *Carlill* v *Carbolic Smoke Ball Company* [1893] the Carbolic Smoke Ball Company placed adverts in the press stating that anyone who contracted influenza after using the company's carbolic smoke ball, as instructed for a period of two weeks, would receive a reward of £100. They also stated that £1,000 had been deposited with a bank to show the company's 'sincerity in the matter'. Mrs Carlill bought a smoke ball, used it as instructed and duly caught the 'flu. She claimed £100. The company claimed that the advert did not give rise to a legal obligation and refused to pay. The Court of Appeal decided that she was entitled to the reward.

Common law is the original system of judge-made law. It is called common law because in the Middle Ages, it was applied across the country as against the local laws based mainly on previously existing custom. Major areas of law have been developed mainly through the common law, including the law of contract, the tort of negligence and many criminal offences. *Carlill* v *Carbolic Smoke Ball Company* was a case decided by the application of the common law principles relating to the formation of a contract.

While common law is always subject to statute law, limits on what Parliament can practically achieve in the time available mean that common law rules remain an important source of law. The principles established in the *Carlill* case still apply today where rewards are offered in advertisements. How common law rules evolve and are applied is discussed in the section below on the doctrine of precedent.

Equity

> In *Brownlow v G H Marshall Limited* [2000] Pamela Brownlow was, with her sister and brother, director and equal shareholder of a company, G H Marshall Limited, founded by their parents. She was also the company secretary. In 1997, she was removed from her posts and dismissed from the company. She brought court proceedings because she wanted her brother and sister to buy her shares. This they were unwilling to do. The court found that, in equity, there was an expectation that if any of the children were removed from the management of the company, the others would purchase his or her shares at a reasonable price. The court ordered that the shares be valued and that Mrs Brownlow's brother and sister buy them.

The principles of equity emerged in the Middle Ages because of problems associated with the rigidity of the common law and its inability to offer any remedy other than financial compensation (damages). As the example cited above demonstrates, equity is concerned with ensuring justice in the particular case. There are a number of equitable principles which the court will apply even where these may conflict with formal legal rights. Mrs Brownlow's brother and sister were under no common law or statutory obligation to buy her shares but it would have been unfair, in the circumstances, to have treated Mrs Brownlow as an ordinary shareholder. Because equity is concerned with individual justice, equitable remedies are only available at the discretion of the court. A rather quaint sounding, but important, equitable maxim is 'He who comes to equity must come with clean hands'. This means that those who seek equitable remedies must not themselves be guilty of misconduct in the case.

Equity, unlike the common law, will recognize rights in property other than those of strict legal ownership. It has been instrumental in the development of the law of trusts, mortgages and other areas of law where rights exist but are not reflected in the legal title to property. Without it, many modern businesses (particularly partnerships) would have to take a different form as would arrangements for the transfer of property upon death and many land transactions. Although much of the conduct of companies is now governed by statutes such as the Companies Act 1985, these statutes reflect the influence of equity in the development of company law particularly in relation to the duties of directors and the treatment of minority shareholders.

The courts will also apply a range of equitable remedies although, as previously noted, these are discretionary and may not be demanded as of right. Equitable remedies include injunctions (orders of the court prohibiting or, less frequently, requiring certain actions), specific performance (ordering the performance of a contractual obligation) and rescission (allowing for the termination of a contract in certain circumstances). A modern equitable remedy is the doctrine of 'equitable estoppel' which may prevent the enforcement of strict contractual rights.

Custom

> In *Egerton v Harding* [1974] cattle strayed from a common through gaps in a hedge into a garden where they caused damage. The garden's owner brought a claim for damages against the cattle's owner. The Court of Appeal dismissed her claim as there was a duty upon landowners arising under custom to fence their land against the common.

Local customs may impose obligations upon the owners of land or grant rights over privately owned land such as fishing rights. To be enforceable in law, a custom must have existed continuously and without challenge since 1189. Local customs are occasionally relevant in property transactions or disputes as in the example above.

Another type of custom is trade customs. These have evolved from the trade practices of merchants over centuries, for example the 'baker's dozen' is 13. Many of these customs have fallen into disuse or have been adopted into the common law or into statute. The courts may still refer to trade customs in order to determine the terms of a contract where the parties have not agreed terms to cover the situation in question. However, a trade custom will always be displaced by the express terms of a contract.

International sources of law

The UK is signatory to a wide number of international agreements and treaties which may affect the legal rights of businesses particularly those doing business abroad. There are two international agreements, however, which have been afforded a particular status in UK law so that they are of general application and act as sources of law. One of these is the EC Treaty as amended. This provides for the UK's membership of the European Union. The other is the European Convention on Human Rights.

The signature and ratification of a treaty do not, by themselves, change the domestic law of the UK. A separate Act of Parliament (the 'incorporating statute') is required if that is to happen. It is not sufficient therefore simply to look at the contents of an international agreement in order to determine its effect on UK law. The incorporating statute must also be considered.

EC law

> In *Litster v Forth Dry Dock and Engineering Co Ltd* [1989] regulations made to implement EC law protecting employees' rights upon the take-over of a business applied to persons 'employed immediately before the transfer'. Employers dismissed employees at 3.30 p.m. without notice or holiday pay and transferred the business at 4.30 p.m. They maintained the regulations did not apply as the employees were not in employment immediately before the transfer. The House of Lords interpreted the regulations to give effect to EC law and read the necessary words into the regulations to prevent the employers' obligations being evaded.

> In *R v Secretary of State for Transport ex p Factortame (No 2)* [1991] the House of Lords ordered that the relevant parts of the Merchant Shipping Act be suspended pending a decision on the legality of the Act's provisions. Each EC member state had

been granted quotas limiting the numbers of fish caught so as to preserve stocks. Parliament passed the Merchant Shipping Act 1988 because Spanish-owned vessels had reregistered as British in order to take advantage of the UK's fishing quotas. The Act required UK registered fishing vessels to have a genuine connection with the UK. The legality under EC law of the Act's requirements law was challenged. The statutory provisions remain suspended and unenforceable.

The European Union (formerly the European Community) was founded by the Treaty of Rome 1957 as amended by subsequent treaties and is a highly complex political and legal institution. The Treaty of Rome is incorporated into UK law by the European Communities Act 1972.

As a source of UK law, the law of the EU (usually known as EC law) is of vital importance. Wherever possible, domestic law must be interpreted so as to comply with EC law. An example of this is the *Litster* case. In the event of a direct conflict between EC law applicable in this country and UK domestic law, EC law prevails. This is what happened in the *Factortame* case above.

EC law is thus the supreme source of law in the UK and may override all domestic laws including, it would appear, validly enacted Acts of Parliament. It is only supreme however because Parliament, in passing the European Communities Act 1972 (ECA) consented to such supremacy. Such consent could, in theory, be withdrawn through the repeal by Parliament of the ECA. Such repeal would have enormous political and economic consequences entailing, as it would, the likely withdrawal of the UK from the EU but there is no legal obstacle to such a course of action.

European Convention on Human Rights

In *Saunders* v *UK* [1997] Ernest Saunders, director and chief executive of Guinness plc, was convicted of a number of offences connected with an unlawful operation causing a dramatic rise in Guinness' share price during a take-over battle. His conviction was partly based on the transcript of interviews carried out by inspectors appointed by the Secretary of State for Trade and Industry under powers granted under the Companies Act 1985. Under the Companies Act, it is a contempt of court to refuse to cooperate with the inspectors. The European Court of Human Rights found that Mr Saunders's right not to incriminate himself had been infringed and that the UK had breached Article 6 of the European Convention on Human Rights (right to a fair trial).

The status of the European Convention on Human Rights (the 'Convention'), as a source of UK law, is of some complexity. The Convention was established in 1950 and was intended to provide a means of safeguarding individuals against the abuse of basic rights such as the right to life, freedom from torture and so on. However, many articles of the Convention can have an effect on the day-to-day conduct of individuals and businesses. Employers, for example, may need to take account of, among others, Article 8, Respect for Private and Family Life, Article 10, Freedom of Expression and Article 11, Freedom of Assembly and Association.

Although the UK was a signatory, until very recently the Convention was not incorporated into UK law so that its provisions could not be enforced in the domestic courts. Mr Saunders could only bring his case in the European Court of Human

Rights. However, in 1998, the Human Rights Act was passed. Implementation of most of the provisions in this Act is due to take place in October 2000. Its effects upon the role of Convention law as a source of UK law will be significant:

- All primary legislation will be interpreted wherever possible to comply with the Convention. The courts may not overturn incompatible legislation but the higher courts may make a 'declaration of incompatibility' which will allow for incompatible legislation to be amended in Parliament by an expedited procedure.
- Secondary legislation will be subject to Convention rights and may be overturned by the courts if incompatible. The only exception will be when the incompatibility arises because of a requirement of the primary legislation that authorizes the secondary legislation.
- It will not be possible to bring an action against a private individual or company challenging existing common law or equitable principles on Convention grounds but, over time, such laws may be reinterpreted to comply with Convention rights.
- Public authorities and officials will be required to act in accordance with the law of the Convention unless prevented by primary legislation. These will include the statutory and regulatory bodies who oversee the conduct of businesses such as the taxation authorities, the Companies Registry and the Stock Exchange. Of particular relevance may be Article 6 which provides the right to a fair and public hearing in both civil and criminal proceedings. This was the basis upon which Ernest Saunders brought his case.

Private individuals and businesses will not be required to act in accordance with Convention law unless such law exists in a domestic form such as a statute or case law.

The implementation of the Human Rights Act 1998 is likely, for a period at any rate, to increase the uncertainty of our law. An awareness of this, coupled with good practical legal advice, is perhaps the best weapon for the prospective business manager.

THE COURTS AND THEIR FUNCTIONS

Courts exist to resolve disputes, provide remedies and punish criminal behaviour. To do this, a court needs to reach a decision on two issues. First, it needs to ascertain the facts of the case and, secondly, it needs to decide upon the law applying to those facts.

In most cases, it is the judge who decides upon questions of fact although in jury trials, that task is left to the jury. Evidence of facts is provided by witnesses, exhibits and sometimes in written statements. Questions of law are always decided by judges. Identifying the law is not an exact science. In most cases, unresolved questions of law revolve around one of two issues; the meaning to be attributed to the words of legislation or the identification of the applicable principles of common law or equity.

This section will summarize the principal courts in England and Wales and explain how they relate to each other. It will also explain two of the main functions of the courts in resolving disputes: applying the principles of common law and equity via the doctrine of precedent and determining the meaning of statutes (statutory interpretation).

The Court System

The principal division of our legal system into civil and criminal law is reflected in our court system with separate courts to deal with civil and criminal matters. Tribunals also deal with a range of matters and in particular frequently resolve administrative disputes with public bodies. English courts are arranged hierarchically so that the lower courts' decisions may be appealed to the higher courts. The decisions of the higher courts are binding upon the lower courts according to the doctrine of precedent. Figure 1.1 summarizes the hierarchy of the principal English courts.

The civil courts

County courts are the lowest civil courts (although a few civil matters, e.g. licensing applications are heard in the magistrates' courts). There are approximately 400 county courts in England and Wales. County courts are local courts; they only hear disputes having a connection with the area they serve.

County courts can hear most types of civil claim and, because proceedings are generally cheaper and less complex than in the High Court, government policy has encouraged a shift towards use of the county court: most claims for £50 000 or less are now heard there. Within the county court itself, there is a *small claims court* where most claims worth less than £5000 are heard under a simplified procedure with limited appeal rights. The Court of Appeal (Civil Division) hears most appeals from the county court.

The *High Court*, based mainly in London, is a superior court to the county court. Proceedings have, in the past, tended to be slower and more expensive but a High Court judgment has more authority as it can become a legal precedent. It now only hears claims worth £50 000 or above unless the matter is unusually complex. There are three divisions of the High Court; Chancery, Queen's Bench and Family Division. The subject matter of the claim will determine the division in which it is heard.

A civil claim can be started in either the county court or the High Court and may be transferred between them according to its value, its complexity, its importance and other factors. The parties themselves have less control than in the past over which court is used. Recent reform (see the section, 'Court proceedings' below) aim to make High Court proceedings faster and less complex.

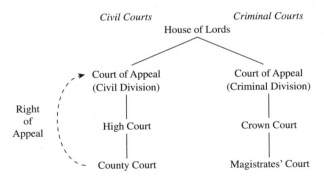

Figure 1.1 The hierarchy of the principal English courts

Appeals from the High Court are heard by the *Court of Appeal* (*Civil Division*). Rarely, an appeal can be made directly to the House of Lords. The Court of Appeal (Civil Division) is the principal appeal court in civil matters. As the House of Lords hears only a small number of cases, most appeals will be heard only in the Court of Appeal. Consent of the original trial judge is sometimes required. Most appeals are heard by three judges (known as Lord Justices of Appeal) and are decided by majority judgment.

Appeal to the *House of Lords* is possible only with the consent of either the Court of Appeal or the House of Lords. Most appeals are on points of law of general public importance. The full title of this final court of appeal is the Appellate Committee of the House of Lords which serves as a reminder that the judicial function is separate from the House of Lords' role as a political body. The judges are known as Lords of Appeal in Ordinary. There are usually five sitting at any one hearing and judgment is by majority.

Criminal courts

There are three categories of criminal offence. Summary offences (relatively minor) crimes may only be tried in the Magistrates' Court. Indictable offences (serious crimes such as murder or rape) may only be heard in the Crown Court. The third category is known as 'either way' offences and may be heard either before magistrates or in the Crown Court. At present, the magistrates may elect to send a case to the Crown Court for trial or the defendant may choose trial in the Crown Court. The government proposes to remove this choice from defendants.

The lowest criminal court is the *Magistrates' Court.* Most cases are heard by lay magistrates of which there are about 30 000 in England and Wales. Lay magistrates are unpaid and without legal training although they are assisted by legally trained Justices' Clerks. Of the criminal cases heard in England and Wales, 97 per cent are tried by magistrates. Appeals against conviction by magistrates are heard mainly in the Crown Court although certain types of appeal are heard in the Divisional Court of the Queen's Bench.

More serious criminal offences are tried in the *Crown Court* before a judge and jury. The function of the jury is to decide upon questions of fact while the judge rules on questions of law. Of the 3 per cent of criminal cases sent to the Crown Court, most result in guilty pleas heard by a judge alone, so that, despite the symbolic importance of jury trial, less than 1 per cent of all criminal cases are tried by jury. Appeals are usually to the Court of Appeal (Criminal Division) but sometimes to the Divisional Court of the Queen's Bench.

The *Court of Appeal* (*Criminal Division*) hears most Crown Court appeals. As in civil appeals, there are usually three judges with decision by majority. Leave of the trial judge or the Court of Appeal itself is required. The workings of the Court of Appeal (Criminal Division) have been subject to criticism in recent years following well-reported miscarriages of justice. Recent reform and the establishment of the Criminal Cases Review Commission may improve matters over the longer term. The importance of a fair and vigorous appeals system when an individual's liberty is at stake cannot be over-stated.

The *House of Lords* will hear only appeals on a point of law of public importance. Its role as an appeal court rectifying miscarriages of justice is limited.

Tribunals

Tribunals were created to provide a less formal means of resolving disputes and, in principle, the parties should not need legal representation. Modern tribunals, however, often deal with issues of considerable legal and factual complexity and research shows that parties who are legally represented tend to fare better. Tribunals are usually presided over by a legally qualified chair assisted by lay experts in the field concerned, although there has been a move recently towards greater use of legally qualified chairs sitting alone.

There has been an enormous growth of *administrative tribunals* in the past decades as one of the principal means of resolving disputes between the individual and state bodies. Examples include the mental health review tribunal and the lands tribunal. There are more than 2000 such administrative tribunals. Also very important are *employment tribunals*. They hear disputes between employer and employee on a wide range of issues including claims for unfair dismissal and discrimination. *Domestic tribunals* are tribunals set up by private bodies for their own internal purposes, for example, to act as the disciplinary committee of a professional body.

Most tribunals decisions may be appealed, either to a higher tribunal or eventually to the High Court but the right to appeal is not universal, particularly in the case of domestic tribunals. Regardless of appeal rights, the High Court may intervene if the rules of natural justice are not followed or the tribunal exceeds its powers.

Role of the European Court of Justice

Article 234 of the EC Treaty provides that any domestic court may refer a case to the European Court of Justice (ECJ) where a ruling on an EC law question is necessary to help it reach a decision. Thus any court may refer a case. Any court from which there is no further right of appeal must refer a case. The House of Lords is therefore obliged to refer cases where there is an outstanding EC law issue.

So far as its role under Article 234 is concerned, the role of the European Court of Justice is limited to settling the EC law issue referred to it. It does not decide the case itself but by establishing the correct EC law, enables the domestic court to give judgment. It is thus not a court of appeal. ECJ decisions on questions of EC law are binding on all English courts.

THE DOCTRINE OF PRECEDENT

A principal function of the courts is to decide what law applies when Parliament has not settled the question through legislation. Judges do this using the principles of equity and common law developed in thousands of cases over the centuries by the courts. The method which judges use to determine which of all these cases contain legal principles applicable to the case before them is called the 'doctrine of precedent'.

There are two key principles underpinning the doctrine of precedent. The first is that similar principles of law will be applied to cases with similar facts. The second is that courts lower in the court structure will be bound by decisions made by higher courts as to what those principles of law are. Decisions of the higher courts are binding when the 'material facts' in a subsequent case are substantially similar and the first court is in a position in the hierarchy of courts to bind the subsequent court.

What is binding is not the actual decision itself but the legal principle upon which the decision is based. This legal principle is known as the *ratio decidendi*.

The doctrine of precedent ensures a degree of consistency and predictability in the law. This is important for reasons of justice as similar cases should be treated alike. Also, if the parties to a dispute can predict the likely outcome of a court hearing, they are much more likely to settle the dispute themselves than if each party thinks they may win.

Three elements must be established for the doctrine of precedent to apply:

1 the material facts must be sufficiently similar;
2 the court which made the previous decision must be in a position to bind the present court;
3 the legal principle (*ratio decidendi*) of the previous case must be identified.

The establishment of these elements will now be considered in turn.

The material facts must be sufficiently similar

In *Donoghue* v *Stevenson* [1932] a woman suffered shock and gastroenteritis after drinking lemonade from an opaque bottle contaminated by the presence of a dead snail. The House of Lords held that a manufacturer owes a duty of care to the ultimate consumer of its products, where there is no opportunity for the consumer to inspect the product before using it.

In *Grant* v *Australian Knitting Mills* [1936] serious dermatitis had been caused by the presence in long underpants of an irritating chemical caused by negligent manufacture. The Privy Council (members of the House of Lords sitting as final court of appeal for other jurisdictions) followed *Donoghue* v *Stevenson* and found in favour of the purchaser.

In *Evans* v *Triplex Safety Glass Co Ltd* [1936] a car was fitted with a 'Triplex Toughened Safety Glass' windscreen. About a year after purchase, the windscreen cracked and disintegrated. The purchaser sued the manufacturer. The judge distinguished this case from *Donoghue* v *Stevenson* as there was no evidence that the defect had been caused during the manufacturing process and it was possible that inspection by Mr Evans might have revealed the defect.

Once the facts of a case have been determined, the judge has to decide if they are sufficiently similar to a previous case for that previous case to be binding. It is only the material facts which have to be similar; so trivial or unimportant differences should be ignored.

The first case is a famous one setting out the principles of the tort of negligence. In the second case, the court followed *Donoghue* v *Stevenson*. The court in *Grant* found there was sufficient similarity in the two situations (both concerned manufactured products in which the defect was not immediately apparent) to follow *Donoghue* v *Stevenson*.

In *Evans,* the court found the facts to be materially different from *Donoghue* v *Stevenson,* as, in this case, the defect could have occurred at any time and Mr Evans might have spotted it by examination. The court therefore distinguished this case from *Donoghue* v *Stevenson*.

The court which made the previous decision must be in a position to bind the present court

In *Miliangos* v *George Frank (Textiles) Limited* [1975] an English company, George Frank (Textiles) Limited, agreed to buy polyester yarn from a Swiss national, Mr Miliangos. The company did not pay and Mr Miliangos issued proceedings in London for payment in sterling. Between the time proceedings were issued and the date of the hearing, sterling had fallen in value against the Swiss franc by about a third. Mr Miliangos therefore wished to amend his claim so that it was expressed in Swiss francs. A previous House of Lords decision had held that judgment debts could only be given in sterling. The House of Lords overruled its previous decision to allow Mr Miliangos to claim the debt in Swiss francs.

Previous legislation governing anti-competitive practices required registration of agreements which restricted the parties' freedom of trade. In *Re Automatic Telephone and Electric Co Ltd's Agreement* [1965] the Court of Appeal had to decide whether the Registrar of Restrictive Trade Agreements had the power to order disclosure of documents relating to the restrictive agreements. By a majority of two to one, the Court of Appeal decided he did. Willmer LJ dissented from that decision. In a judgment given later on the same day, in a second case with similar facts, Willmer LJ followed the Court of Appeal decision in *Re Automated Telephone and Electric Co* even though he had dissented from that judgment at the time it was made.

Decisions of the House of Lords are binding on all lower courts. Following a Practice Statement in 1966, the House of Lords is no longer required to follow its own previous decisions although it will usually do so. The power to overrule its own previous judgments means that where decisions have become outdated or have been wrongly made, the problem can be rectified without waiting for Parliament to take action, which may involve a wait of many years.

On the other hand, because the House of Lords may sometimes change previously decided legal principles, the law is less certain and predictable than it might be. The principle of law applied in the overruling case is effective retrospectively, that is, it applies in all past situations as well as all present ones adding to the potential for uncertainty and disruption. There is a tension between the need for certainty and the requirements of justice. In the case of *Miliangos* v *George Frank (Textiles) Limited* the law was changed to enable it 'to keep in step with commercial needs' (per Lord Wilberforce). Changing the law might unsettle established legal precedents but to fail to do so would render the law inflexible and unresponsive.

The Court of Appeal is bound by decisions of the House of Lords. In the Civil Division it is bound to follow its own previous decisions:

1 where there are two previous conflicting Court of Appeal decisions, the Court of Appeal may choose which to follow;
2 where there is a subsequent House of Lords case which is inconsistent;
3 where the previous decision was given *per incuriam*, i.e. without taking account of a relevant legal principle.

In the case referred to above, the judge, WILLMER LJ, was obliged to follow a previous Court of Appeal decision even though he had disagreed with it when it was made.

The Criminal Division of the Court of Appeal, in addition to the exceptions above, may depart from one of its own previous decisions where this is necessary in the interests of justice. This reflects the importance of avoiding unjust criminal convictions, an importance outweighing the necessity for certainty in such instances. The High Court is required to follow House of Lords and Court of Appeal decisions. Most High Court decisions are not binding on other High Court judges although they are often followed. The Crown Court may sometimes be bound by High Court decisions as well as by Court of Appeal and House of Lords decisions. County courts and magistrates' courts are bound by High Court, Court of Appeal and House of Lords decisions. They neither bind themselves nor each other.

Note that all courts are required, under the European Communities Act 1972, to follow rulings of the *European Court of Justice* on questions of EC law.

The legal principle (ratio decidendi) *of the previous case must be identified*

> Talk of *finding* the ratio decidendi of a case obscures the fact that the process of interpreting cases is not like a hunt for buried treasure but typically involves an element of choice from a range of possibilities. (*How to Do Things With Rules,* Twining and Miers).

When a previous decision is a binding precedent, it is not the decision as such which is binding on the lower court but the legal principle upon which the decision was based, otherwise known as the *ratio decidendi*. It is necessary to be able to identify the *ratio decidendi* in order to apply it. This is not always a straightforward matter. Judgments may run to many pages and can be very complex. Judges do not usually aid the reader by signalling the whereabouts of the *ratio decidendi*. It is a question of reading and understanding the judgment as a whole.

Judgments frequently contain a number of different statements of law. Only a statement of law that is necessary to enable the judge to reach a decision is the *ratio decidendi*. Subsequent readers have to distinguish between statements which are *ratio* and other statements of law, known as *obiter dicta* or things said 'by the way'. Only the *ratio* is binding on a subsequent court.

Court of Appeal and House of Lords cases are heard by a number of judges who each give a judgment. Even where judges agree as to the outcome of a case, each may have different reason for the decision. It is not always possible to talk of a single *ratio* and there may not always be agreement as to what the *ratio* is.

Role of obiter dicta

> In *Hedley Byrne* v *Heller & Partners* [1963] advertising agents booked advertising time on behalf of a client. Concerned about the client's financial position, they sought a report from their client's bankers. They received and relied on a report said to be given 'without responsibility ...'. The clients went into liquidation. The advertising agent sued the bank. The House of Lords held there could be a duty to take care in making statements. However, in this particular case, there was an effective disclaimer of responsibility.

In *Henderson* v *Merrett* [1994] Lloyds' Names (wealthy individuals who ultimately underwrite insurance policies insured through Lloyds of London) sued their underwriting agents for negligently conducting their business leading to huge losses. The House of Lords found that the principle established in *Hedley Byrne* v *Heller* applied to negligently performed services.

While only the *ratio decidendi* is strictly binding, *obiter dicta* statements can be very persuasive particularly when made by the House of Lords. Many very important legal principles have developed through courts following *obiter dicta*.

For example, in *Hedley Byrne* v *Heller,* the House of Lords made important statements of law relating to the duty to take care when making statements of fact. In the event, the case was decided on a different basis because the defendant had effectively disclaimed any responsibility for the statement concerned. The statements regarding the duty of care in making statements were not essential to the decision and were *obiter dicta.* They have however been relied on in subsequent cases to develop the modern law relating to negligent misstatement and provision of services resulting in economic loss. In *Henderson* v *Merrett Syndicates,* the House of Lords applied the principle contained in the *obiter* statement in *Hedley Byrne* v *Heller.* In its turn, the principle in *Henderson* will now form a *ratio decidendi* to be applied in subsequent cases.

Obiter dicta include all judicial statements other than the *ratio decidendi.* As well as statements of law which are not necessary for the decision, statements of law made in a dissenting (minority) judgment or in relation to a hypothetical situation can all be *obiter dicta.*

Doctrine of precedent – conclusion

The doctrine of precedent seems to offer, by and large, stability coupled with slow evolution of the law. Judges themselves are mostly unwilling to be seen to be acting as law makers, perceiving their role as being to apply the law to be found in existing cases. Yet the process is a complex one which allows a degree of judicial flexibility and discretion:

- A judge has to decide whether the facts of a previous case are sufficiently similar as to be binding. If the facts are different (and it is rare that all material facts are the same), the judge may *distinguish* the previous case so that he or she is not obliged to follow it.
- There may be uncertainty as to what the *ratio decidendi* of a previous case is particularly when there is more than one judgment.
- There may be more than one relevant case of equal authority each decided upon a different basis. The judge may also take account of persuasive authorities such as *obiter dicta* particularly when from an authoritative source such as the House of Lords.
- A case with similar facts may not have previously come before a court so that the judge can rule only by analogy or by reference to general principles.
- A higher court may decide to overrule the precedent of a lower court and set a new precedent or the House of Lords (and, in limited circumstances, the Court of Appeal) may decide to overrule itself.

THE INTERPRETATION OF STATUTES

In *Fisher* v *Bell* [1961] a shopkeeper displayed a flick knife in his window. Under the Restriction of Offensive Weapons Act 1959, it was an offence to 'sell or offer for sale' any flick knife. In ordinary language, it would seem that the defendant was offering a flick knife for sale. However, in contract law, the term 'offer' has a particular meaning. The display of goods in a shop window is considered in contract law not to be an offer but an 'invitation to treat'. The defendant was acquitted.

In *Royal College of Nursing* v *DHSS* [1981] the Royal College of Nursing (RCN) brought a case to establish whether nurses could legally carry out a new abortion procedure. Section 1(1) of the Abortion Act 1967 prohibits the termination of a pregnancy except by a 'registered medical practitioner'. At the time the Act was passed, abortion was carried out by doctors. Later, there was developed a procedure in which the actual act which induced abortion could be undertaken by a nurse. The House of Lords decided that nurses could carry out the new procedure.

Legislation is viewed as the preferred means of creating law as it is made by a democratically elected Parliament and should reflect the priorities and concerns of society as a whole. Statutes are drafted by skilled Parliamentary draftsmen and are usually fairly detailed. In theory, the function of the judge is merely to apply the words of the statute to the situation before him or her. Such a view reflects the constitutional role of the judge as the interpreter of the law, not its creator.

The reality is somewhat more complex. Even the most precisely drafted legislation can give rise to ambiguities and multiple possible interpretations. The court is then required to decide which is the correct interpretation, 'correct', in these circumstances, being the interpretation giving effect to the intentions of Parliament. There are many ways the meaning of a statute may not be clear. For example, the meaning to be attributed to a word or phrase may not be clear. In *Fisher* v *Bell*, there was more than one possible meaning of the phrase 'offer for sale'. Parliament cannot necessarily foresee future technological or other developments. That was the problem in *DHSS* v *Royal College of Nursing*. These are just two examples of the types of problem that can arise. The courts spend about half their time deciding the meaning of legislation.

There are two broad approaches that may be taken. Each approach has the same aim, to give effect to the intentions of Parliament. However, each approach tackles the task in a different way.

The literal approach

The traditionally dominant approach in English law is the literal approach to interpretation. It assumes that the best way to ascertain Parliament's intentions is through the literal meaning of the words themselves. The relatively detailed and precise style of UK legislative drafting encourages such an approach and by restricting themselves to the words of the statute, judges are perceived to be respecting the supremacy of Parliament as law maker. However, a strict literal approach can give rise to an unlikely or unjust result.

The literal approach consists of three 'rules of interpretation' which judges will apply in order to determine the meaning of the statute; the 'literal rule' and two subsidiary rules, the 'golden rule' and the 'mischief rule'. While they are referred to as rules, they do not have any formal status. Rather they have evolved as terms to describe what judges do when faced with difficulties in interpretation.

The literal rule

In *Inland Revenue Commissioners (IRC)* v *Hinchy* [1960] Mr Hinchy had filed an incorrect tax return. Statute provided that where an incorrect return was filed, the individual should pay a penalty 'treble the tax which he ought to be charged under this Act'. The court had to decide whether this meant treble the total tax liability or treble the tax due on the income which had not been declared. The court applied the literal rule and found that Mr Hinchy had to pay three times his total tax liability notwithstanding that only a portion had been wrongly declared.

The 'literal rule' is the first rule which courts usually apply. They seek to interpret the statute according to the literal meaning of the words it contains. In most instances, this interpretation will be satisfactory and consistent with the requirements of justice. In some cases, however, the application of the literal rule will give surprising and even unjust results. In *IRC* v *Hinchy* the court gave effect to the literal meaning of the words even though it would seem doubtful that in so doing they were giving effect to Parliament's intentions. The literal rule has been frequently criticized for giving rise to apparent absurdities. It is also unable to resolve satisfactorily the problems which arise when words have more than one possible meaning or where other ambiguities arise. In these circumstances, the courts may choose to adopt one of two other rules of interpretation.

The golden rule

R v *Allen* [1872] concerned S57 of the Offences Against the Person Act 1861 which provided that the offence of bigamy was committed if a person already married should 'marry any other person during the life of the former husband or wife'. 'Marry' could, on a literal interpretation, mean 'to contract a valid marriage', which would render the offence impossible to commit as a bigamous marriage is never valid. The court decided that, in this context, 'marry' should mean 'go through a ceremony of marriage'.

In *R* v *Registrar General, ex parte Smith* [1991] an individual wished to take advantage of his right under s.51 of the Adoption Act 1976 to see a copy of his original birth certificate which would reveal the name of his birth mother. Although this right was not qualified under the terms of the Act, his application was refused. The applicant was a psychotic who had already killed twice and who was believed likely to harm his mother if he should trace her.

The golden rule may be used if the literal rule would give an absurd or unjust result. It may be applied in a narrow or wider version. The narrow application arises if a word carries more than one possible meaning in which case, the court may choose the least absurd. This is what happened in *R* v *Allen*. The wider application of the rule arises when the meaning of the statute is clear but to apply it would result in a socially undesirable result. This wider version was applied in *ex p. Smith*.

The mischief rule

> In *Corkery* v *Carpenter* [1950] the Licensing Act 1872 provided that anyone found drunk in charge of a 'carriage' could be arrested immediately. The defendant was drunk in charge of a bicycle. He could be arrested.

The mischief rule may be applied when the literal rule does not provide a solution. It allows the court to resolve ambiguities by reference to the 'mischief' which the Act was passed to remedy. It was first formulated in the sixteenth century in *Heydon's Case*.

The mischief rule was applied in *DHSS* v *Royal College of Nursing* referred to at the start of the section on statutory interpretation and in *Corkery* v *Carpenter* mentioned above.

Presumptions and rules of language

In addition to these major 'rules', there are a number of other presumptions to which judges may refer. For example, it is presumed that a criminal offence will only be created by unambiguous language. There are also rules of language governing, for example, the ways lists of objects will be interpreted.

Other aids to interpretation

The courts have always made use of materials contained within the Act itself (such as interpretation sections, preambles, schedules and so on) in order to interpret the statute. While the courts have always referred to dictionaries in order to determine meaning, there has been a recent tendency to allow recourse to a wider range of outside sources. Of particular significance here is the case of *Pepper* v *Hart* [1993] in which the House of Lords ruled that, in certain circumstances, *Hansard*, the record of Parliamentary debates, may be referred to in order to clarify an ambiguity.

In most cases, the literal rule is still applied whenever this gives a coherent result (even where this may be counter to the personal beliefs of the judge in the case). However, the courts have in modern times been increasingly reluctant to apply the literal rule if this would result in injustice or absurdity.

Both the golden rule (particularly in its broader application) and the mischief rule incorporate elements of a purposive approach although they only permit the court to look outside the literal meaning of the words in the event of ambiguity or absurdity. Critics of the wide use of these rules point out that they increase the discretion of the judge. On the other hand, the credibility of the justice system is likely to be undermined by the application of the literal rule where this results in rulings which, while technically in conformity with the law, are clearly counter to the intentions of Parliament, the very body whose wishes judges are committed to upholding.

The purposive approach

> In *Pickstone* v *Freeman* [1988] women warehouse operatives were paid the same as male operatives but less than male checkers who were doing equivalent work. They brought an equal pay claim using the male checkers as their comparators. Under the

Equal Pay Act 1970, their claim appeared barred even though the Act had been amended to give effect to EC law which would have permitted the claims to proceed. The House of Lords interpreted the words of the Act so as to comply with EC law.

The purposive approach takes, as its starting point, the legislative intention. It tends to be used in legal systems which, in contrast to the UK, adopt a more generalized and less detailed style of legislative drafting. Courts in many European countries take a purposive approach and both the European Court of Justice and the European Court of Human Rights adopt a purposive approach to the law which they apply, that is EC law and the European Convention on Human Rights. The increasing influence of these bodies of law upon UK law means that a purposive approach to interpretation is likely to become increasingly significant.

In interpreting EC law, UK courts follow judgments of the European Court of Justice including the purposive approach to the interpretation of EC law. Where there are EC law issues, therefore, the UK courts tend to adopt a purposive approach. The words of the Equal Pay Act were interpreted in *Pickstone* v *Freeman* to give effect to the legislative intention to comply with EC law. In *Litster* v *Forth Dry Dock* the House of Lords not only interpreted regulations but read in additional words in order to give effect to the legislative intention. While the effect of EC law upon the interpretation of statutes is significant, it is limited to those areas affected by EC law. The effect of the incorporation of the European Convention on Human Rights through the Human Rights Act is likely to be even more significant.

Upon implementation (due in October 2000 in England and Wales, already in effect in Scotland), all domestic legislation will be interpreted, so far as possible, to comply with those parts of the European Convention incorporated by the Act. This will apply to all legislation no matter when passed or for what purpose. In doing so, the courts will take into account the case law of the European Court of Human Rights including the European Court's purposive approach to interpreting the provisions of the Convention.

It is likely that some longstanding judgments on the meaning of legislation will, in due course, be revised in the light of the Human Rights Act. Nor will it only be legal questions specifically surrounding civil liberties or related issues which will be affected. Laws directly affecting businesses such as taxation, company law or financial regulation may well also be affected.

Conclusion to statutory interpretation

In *Jones* v *Tower Boot Co Ltd* [1997] Raymond Jones had been subjected to serious racial abuse by fellow employees. The employers claimed that these acts were not carried out 'in the course of employment' as required for a successful claim against the employer under S32 of the Race Relations Act 1976. The Court of Appeal accepted that these acts clearly did not occur in the course of employment according to the literal sense of the words. However, it would render the legislation meaningless if the employer were not to be held liable for their employees' actions in circumstances in which the employer did not take reasonable steps to prevent the abuse.

- The traditional approach to the interpretation of statutes in English law has always been to start with the literal meaning of the words themselves and only if this proves unsatisfactory to consider other factors including the purpose for which the statute was passed. The purposive approach, on the other hand, takes the legislative intention as its starting point.

- There appears to be an increased willingness in the courts to consider the purpose for which legislation has been passed. In part, this is connected to the growing importance of EC law in our legal system but can be seen as extending into areas where EC law does not apply. The purposive approach was adopted, for example, in *Jones* v *Tower Boot Co* referred to above.

- The implementation of the Human Rights Act 1998 is likely to increase the tendency to interpret statutes in accordance with the legislative purpose. Following implementation, all legislation will, in the first place, be interpreted purposively to comply with the European Convention on Human Rights. The literal approach will still be applied but will be subordinate to a purposive interpretation in accordance with the ECHR.

USING THE LAW

The final part of this chapter provides some practical information about the workings of the legal system. There will be three sections: the legal profession, courts proceedings and alternatives to the courts.

The legal profession

Most businesses use legal professionals at some stage, whether on questions relating to the organization and administration of the business, the acquisition and protection of its assets, its relationships with others or, unfortunately, as the result of a dispute. It is almost always worth paying for good legal advice at an early stage rather than having to deal with the consequences of any mistakes later on.

The English legal system is unusual, although not unique, in having a divided legal profession. Most lawyers are either solicitors or barristers although some may work as legal executives who assist solicitors in particular areas of work, often with a high degree of expertise. Both barristers and solicitors may work as employees of business organizations, advising and representing their employer on legal issues.

Solicitors and barristers need a law degree or equivalent postgraduate qualification. Both branches then undertake some further years of professional study and training.

Solicitors

Assuming that in-house lawyers are not being used, a firm of solicitors is the first point of contact for legal advice. Solicitors are sometimes compared to medical general practitioners because most firms of solicitors will deal with a range of legal issues on a day-to-day basis. However, solicitors are becoming increasingly specialized. A small high street practice is unlikely to be able to deal with large-scale commercial transactions but may be very effective at advising individuals or small businesses on their particular concerns. It is important to choose the right firm of solicitors for the type of work required and it is sensible to ask some searching questions about their expertise, fee structure and back-up support. Firms are becoming used to doing 'beauty parades' in which they are asked openly to compete against a number of other firms for work. On the other hand, a good relationship between a business and its adviser is also vital, so a degree of personal contact is advisable before a decision is made.

A solicitor can advise on many aspects of business such as incorporation or partnership agreements, employment matters, intellectual property rights and property matters. As well as advising clients, solicitors draft documents and represent their clients in negotiations and disputes. They also undertake the preparatory work involved in taking a dispute to court. Some solicitors will do courtroom advocacy.

Barristers

At some stage, a solicitor may suggest employing a barrister. In most cases, a barrister may only be instructed through a solicitor. There are far fewer barristers than solicitors (i.e. approximately 9000 in practice compared with 75 000 practising solicitors). They work as individuals within sets of Chambers with other barristers, mostly in London. Barristers tend to be specialists. They may be consulted when a particularly complex question of law arises which would be time-consuming or impractical for a more generalist solicitor to resolve. They are also used for court proceedings as barristers are trained in advocacy skills.

The divided legal profession has been much criticized particularly as it means that a client will often incur a double set of costs. Defenders of the system point out that the increase in costs may be less than first appears. Barristers generally have lower overheads than solicitors and can often undertake work in their specialist area more quickly and cheaply. Advocacy is a particular skill requiring a degree of practice which most solicitors, concentrating on non-litigious and pre-courtroom matters, do not have the time to develop. A good solicitor and barrister will work as a team bringing their particular skills and experience to the issue.

Nevertheless the future of the barristers' profession (known as the Bar) is uncertain. Solicitors are becoming a more specialized profession and can now acquire similar rights of audience (the right to perform advocacy) to barristers, lessening the justification for an independent specialist profession. There is a growing emphasis on resolving disputes in other ways than through the litigation process and on shortening and simplifying court hearings so that the skills of a solicitor in advising clients and negotiating settlements may become more prominent at the expense of a barrister's traditional advocacy skills. It is likely that there will always be a small independent Bar doing higher court advocacy and serving smaller firms of solicitors who do not have the resources to deal with all legal matters within the firm, but the size of that profession may decrease in future.

Court proceedings

The popular view of the lawyers' work sees the courtroom trial as central. In fact, the overwhelming majority of legal work is unrelated to litigation and even where disputes do arise, they are usually resolved before coming to court. Leaving aside claims for personal injury, of every 1000 court proceedings commenced, only three will reach trial. That figure does not take into account the disputes that are settled without proceedings ever being issued.

Most individuals and businesses dread litigation for several reasons:

- *Cost*: Legal fees are very high and may often exceed the amount of a smaller claim. Research carried out prior to the current reform programme found that in 40 per cent of cases where the amount claimed was less than £12 500, the fees exceeded the amount of the claim. Costs are unpredictable, particularly if a case goes to appeal. A party may win a case in the High Court and the Court of Appeal. If the opponent then appeals to the House of Lords and wins, it is likely to be awarded its costs for all three hearings. A party who has won two out of three hearings may thus have to pay two sets of legal costs for each of the three hearings. The government is attempting to address the issue of excessive costs through reform of the civil litigation process and conditional fee agreements.
- *Delay and loss of time*: Litigation has, in the past, frequently taken many years to resolve. This not only increases costs but causes added anxiety and loss of time for the parties. It is hoped that the current reforms will reduce delay.
- *Complexity*: Court proceedings are notoriously complex adding to delay and cost. Again, it is intended that the reform programme will reduce complexity.
- *Adversarial process*: Court proceedings are conducted in this country on an adversarial basis. This means that the parties argue their case before a neutral judge. Each party will present the best case possible and seek to undermine the case of the other side. Each side will have its own witnesses and experts and there is an emphasis on lengthy oral proceedings. The conduct of the proceedings has been traditionally left in the hands of the parties' lawyers who will use the court system tactically to obtain the maximum advantage for their client. The adversarial system has many undoubted advantages in terms of testing each side's evidence and legal argument but it also frequently has the effect of increasing hostility and destroying longstanding business relationships.

Government reform of the civil process

Following many years of criticism of the workings of the civil justice system, Lord Woolf was appointed in 1994 to investigate ways of making the system more efficient. His report was published in 1996 and in 1999, new Civil Procedure Rules were introduced to implement his reform programme. It is too early to predict just how effective the reform programme will be and further adjustments and amendments will undoubtedly have to be made. The general theme of the reforms is to ensure a system of justice that is affordable and practical. Key features include:

- *Tracking system*: each case is allocated by a judge to a particular track: small claims arbitration, fast track or multi-track, depending on complexity and value. The most complex and time consuming procedures are thus reserved only for the most complex or valuable cases.
- *Judicial case-management*: judges have more responsibility for managing the progress of cases in a number of ways such as by setting timetables or identifying key issues.

- *Limits are placed* on the time available to hear oral argument, on the witnesses that may be called, and on other aspects of the trial process.
- *Lawyers' fees* are fixed in many cases and lawyers are under an increased obligation to inform clients of the likely cost of the proceedings.
- *The civil court system is more streamlined*: the rules for the High Court and county court have been unified. A claim may be started in any court and transferred if necessary and forms now use simpler language.

Conditional fee agreements

Conditional fee agreements were first introduced to this country in 1995 and their scope and effectiveness have increased over the years to include most money claims. If a party to litigation enters a conditional fee agreement with a solicitor and loses the case, the solicitor will be paid nothing. If it wins however, the solicitor will be paid not only the usual fee, but an additional 'success fee' which will be paid out of damages if it cannot be recovered from the losing party. A party who loses the case is likely to be ordered to pay the costs of the other side. To guard against this possibility, a one-off premium is paid at the start of the case to an insurance company for a policy to protect against that eventuality.

While conditional fees allow litigation to be funded without risk to the client, they have been criticized as solicitors are likely only to agree to take those cases which they believe have a good chance of winning and which will result in payment. It is possible that more risky or uncertain cases may not find lawyers willing to take them on. If they do, the insurance premium against losing may be unaffordable or unavailable.

Alternatives to litigation

Problems with the civil justice system have led to the increasing use of methods of resolving disputes which do not involve the courts. Such alternative methods are known as Alternative Dispute Resolution or ADR. There are two types of ADR: adjudicatory and non-adjudicatory ADR.

Adjudicatory ADR

Adjudicatory ADR occurs where the parties to a dispute invite a neutral third party to rule on their dispute and agree to abide by the decision. The most significant form of adjudicatory ADR is *arbitration*. Arbitration is popular with businesses and many business contracts contain a clause requiring the parties to submit to arbitration in the event of a dispute. It is also frequently offered by trade organizations as a way of resolving consumer disputes. Arbitrators are often experts in the area of business concerned, avoiding the necessity of calling expert witnesses. Arbitration can take many forms from full hearings similar to court proceedings to decisions made on the basis of written documents only. The courts will intervene in an arbitration only to protect the principles of natural justice or occasionally to settle points of law. An arbitrator's award can be enforced through the courts. Arbitration is usually quicker and cheaper than court proceedings but this is not necessarily always the case.

Another form of adjudicatory ADR are the *Ombudsmen* schemes which investigate maladministration in various services. While they were initially created to investigate government services, the schemes have now been extended to a variety of sectors such as banking, insurance and legal services. A major limitation of the schemes is that they are concerned only with how a decision is reached not whether the decision is fair in itself. Another problem is that some businesses do not comply with the Ombudsmen's decisions.

Non-adjudicatory ADR

In non-adjudicatory ADR, the parties seek to agree a solution themselves. The role of the third party is to aid the parties in finding a solution not to impose one themselves. The principal forms of non-adjudicatory ADR are *mediation* and *conciliation*. A mediator will act as a go-between identifying the issues and communicating the concerns of each side to the other. A conciliator plays a more active role in suggesting possible solutions.

Mediation is often associated with family disputes but can also be used by businesses. For example, the Centre for Dispute Resolution based in London provides mediation services for businesses. Conciliation is often associated with industrial and employment disputes as the Arbitration and Conciliation Advisory Service offers a conciliation service in such cases.

Apart from time and cost, the advantages of mediation and conciliation are that they allow the parties to find their own solution to the dispute and that they reduce the hostility often caused by the adversarial nature of court proceedings. They are therefore particularly appropriate when it is important for the parties that they have a continuing business relationship despite the existence of a dispute.

However, they are not appropriate in all circumstances. If one party is much more powerful than the other or is not acting honestly then the formality and rigorous cross-examination characteristic of court proceedings may be necessary. The courts are also a more appropriate forum for deciding disputes which turn on a point of law or where it is important that a judicial precedent is established. While mediation or conciliation are usually cheaper than court proceedings, if they do not succeed then court proceedings may still be necessary at additional cost. The courts will enforce an agreement reached through mediation or conciliation but again at further cost.

One problem with ADR as a whole is that because lawyers may be unfamiliar with it, they do not always actively promote it to their clients. That may change in the future. The government is keen to encourage ADR where appropriate. For example, the Civil Procedure Rules allow proceedings to be stayed in order for ADR to be attempted.

PROGRESS TEST

1 Explain the differences and similarities between civil, criminal, public and private law.

2 Under what circumstances may the courts find that legislation is unenforceable? Will the implementation of the Human Rights Act make any difference to your answer?

3 When is a court required to follow a decision made by another court? Which part of the decision is binding?

4 What are the arguments for and against the universal application by the courts of the literal rule of statutory interpretation?

5 For what purposes do businesses need lawyers?

6 For what reasons might a business, even if it has a good legal claim, decide against starting legal proceedings?

2 Introduction to EC law and its relationship with English law

Penny English

WHAT IS EC LAW?

> By creating a Community of unlimited duration, having its own institutions, its own personality, its own legal capacity and capacity of representation on the international plane and, more particularly, real powers stemming from a limitation of sovereignty or a transfer of powers from the states to the Community, the Member States have limited their sovereign rights, albeit within limited fields, and have thus created a body of law which binds both their nationals and themselves. (Case 6/64, *Flaminio Costa* v *ENEL*).

This legal Community, then known as the European Economic Community (subsequently the European Community (EC) and now the European (EU) was created when six European countries (France, Germany, Italy, Belgium, the Netherlands and Luxembourg) signed the Treaty of Rome in 1957. Membership of the Community has now increased to fifteen, as the original members have been joined by Denmark, Ireland, the United Kingdom, Spain, Portugal, Greece, Sweden, Finland and Austria.

The aim of the Community was 'to lay the foundations of an ever closer union among the peoples of Europe' (Preamble of the EC Treaty). Initially, this integration was, as its original name suggests, primarily economic in its scope. The central objective has been to create a single market, unhindered by national frontiers. It is defined in Article 14(2) (ex Article 7a) EC: 'The internal market shall comprise an area without internal frontiers in which the free movement of goods, persons, services and capital is ensured ...'.

In order to fulfil its objectives it has established its own supranational institutions which have legislative and judicial powers (the Commission, Council of Ministers, European Parliament and European Court of Justice). Subsequent revisions of the EC Treaty (the Single European Act which came into force in 1987, the Treaty on European Union (the Maastricht Treaty) in 1993 and the Treaty of Amsterdam in 1999), have widened its objectives and more policy areas have been added, such as the environment, social policy and citizenship.

Whatever disagreement there may be over the future political direction of the Community, it is clear that business operates increasingly in a European context. This makes some knowledge of EC law of growing relevance. This chapter concentrates on some of the key principles which govern the way European

Community and UK law interact, in order to provide a framework for understanding the substantive areas of law affecting the business environment which have an EU dimension. First, can the European Union make laws about everything? If not, what can it make laws about? (the issue of competence). Secondly, what happens if these laws then conflict with national law? (the concept of supremacy). Finally, does EC law give rights to individuals, and if so, can they have these rights enforced through their national courts? (the doctrines of direct effect, indirect effect and state liability).

Three cases have been selected to illustrate these issues, which each arose out of disputes whose subject matter involved different aspects of the impact of EC law on business. As well as providing examples of the way EC law and domestic law relate to each other, they also demonstrate the way EC law affects us all, as employees, companies and consumers. The first Case C–84/94, *United Kingdom* v *E.U. Council (re Working Time Directive)* concerned the extent to which the Community regulates the working environment. The second example is not one case but a series of cases, the *Factortame* litigation, which arose out of restrictions on the rights of EU nationals to pursue their business in the territory of another member state. Finally, *Paola Faccini Dori* illustrates the extent to which individuals can rely on their rights under EC law, in this case a customer who wished to change her mind after having signed a contract.

Note on Treaty numbers

Confusingly the Treaty of Amsterdam, in attempting to make the EC Treaty more rational, has renumbered almost all of the Treaty Articles. The convention is to refer to the old numbering in brackets after the new number; e.g. Article 5 (ex Article 3b). Obviously, cases decided before the Treaty of Amsterdam use the old numbering.

THE ISSUE OF COMPETENCE

> The Community shall act within the limits of the powers conferred upon it by this Treaty and of the objectives assigned to it therein.

> In areas which do not fall within its exclusive competence, the Community shall take action, in accordance with the principle of subsidiarity, only if and so far as the objectives of the proposed action can not be sufficiently achieved by the Member States and can therefore, by reason of scale or the effects of the proposed action, be better achieved by the Community.

> Any action by the Community shall not go beyond what is necessary to achieve the objectives of this Treaty (Article 5 EC (ex Article 3b)).

What can the EU legislate about? As the quotation from *Costa* v *ENEL* above pointed out, the creation of the EC has resulted in a transfer of powers, within limited fields, from the member states to the Community. Since this means that both can make law, the first key issue to address is where the division between EU and the member states authority to legislate lies. As is clearly stated in the first part of Article 5, the Community can only act within the limits of the powers conferred on it by the Treaty. In order for any legislation passed by the Community to be valid, the EU must have competence to act in that area. The extent of its competence is to be found in the EC Treaty, which sets out the policy areas within which the states have agreed that the Community may act. Although the areas of EU competence have grown over the years, there still remain areas in which the member states retain full sovereignty (or *exclusive competence*) as well as areas where both the EU and the member states have competence to act (*concurrent* or *shared competence*).

Within the areas of shared competence, the principle of *subsidiarity* applies (second and third paragraphs of Article 5 (ex Article 3b)). This concept which has its origins in Catholic social philosophy, has since the Treaty of Maastricht to be taken into account for all Community legislation. It is a mechanism for deciding at which level action is more appropriate; in this context, the Community or member states. It is a term capable of having numerous definitions and has been used both by those advocating and those opposing EU action. As is clear from Article 5, subsidiarity regulates areas of shared or concurrent competence, that is areas where both the member states and the EU can legislate. It does not affect those areas where either the EU or the member states have exclusive competence. The extent of exclusive Community competence is not clear and writers disagree on this point.

There is a two-part test in Article 5: that the objectives cannot sufficiently be achieved by the member states and that by reason of scale or effects, these can better be achieved by the Community. Finally, the third paragraph states that the proposed action must not go beyond what is necessary to achieve its objectives. This idea of *proportionality*, originally derived from German administrative law, has become a general principle of EC law. A number of these general principles of law have been developed by the Court of Justice, such as fundamental rights and legal certainty which have become part of EC law.

If the Community does act, this must be based on a specific Treaty article. The European Court of Justice (ECJ) has sometimes been called upon to decide whether a piece of Community legislation has a correct legal basis and has made it clear that objective factors are decisive. Case C–300/89, *Commission v Council ('Titanium Dioxide')* concerned measures to control waste from the titanium dioxide industry. The Court was asked whether this should be considered an internal market measure, based on Article 100 EC (now Article 94) or a measure to protect the environment, in which case it should be based on Article 130s EC (now Article 175(1)). The Court said:

> It must first be observed that in the context of the organisation of the powers of the Community the choice of legal basis for a measure may not depend simply on an institution's conviction as to the objective pursued but must be based on objective factors which are amenable to judicial review. ... Those factors include in particular the aim and content of the measure.

It elaborated this argument further in Case C–155/91, *Commission v Council (Waste Directive)* where it added a second test: the *principal* aim and content of the measure has to be examined. Even if a measure has ancillary effects on another area, it is the main aim which determines its correct legal base.

In Case C–84/94, *United Kingdom v E.U. Council (Spain, E.C. Commission intervening) (re Working Time Directive)* the European Court of Justice was asked to decide whether the Community had legally exercised its authority to act when it passed the Working Time Directive.

Background

The EC had introduced a number of minimum requirements concerning the working environment in the form of the Working Time Directive (Directive 93/104 EC). The directive regulates the maximum number of hours that can be worked in a week as well as stipulating minimum rest periods and holiday entitlement. There is a degree of flexibility built into the rules; for example the maximum 48-hour week can be extended by agreement. They are also subject to a number of exceptions as they do not apply to various categories of employee: transport workers, fishermen, managing executives, seasonal workers, junior hospital doctors and others.

The UK government sought to challenge the legality of the directive in the European Court of Justice, hoping that the Court would annul the directive. The motivation for the challenge was political: the UK was questioning the right of the EC to legislate in this particular field. The Conservative government in the UK at the time considered that such things as working time should not be decided at the European level, but should be matters for member states to regulate as they saw fit. It took the view that this formed part of the terms and conditions of employment, which is something that in the UK has traditionally been settled between employers and employees, not by government. This limited role for the state contrasts with the system in many other European Union states, where there is far more government intervention and legislation to regulate industrial relations.

The UK's argument was that this unnecessary bureaucracy and over-regulation would be harmful to the country's global competitiveness. As Ian Lang, Secretary of State for Trade and Industry said in the House of Commons:

> We are determined to preserve the flexibility in labour matters that has been such an important element in the revival of our economy over recent years ...

> We reject the imposition on industry of unnecessary requirements that cannot but damage competitiveness and jobs, and we consider that the directive would be the thin end of the wedge that would lead to more such burdens (*Hansard. House of Commons Debates* 12 November 1996, Col 156).

The government had secured the UK's opt-out from that part of the EC Treaty known as the Social Chapter at the negotiations before the Maastricht Treaty (the Treaty on European Union, which came into force in 1993). The UK had been unwilling to accept an extension of Community competence in the social field, and opted out of these provisions, which were accepted by all the other member states. It was therefore wary of the possibility of what it saw as 'social engineering' being introduced by the back door. Its view was that the Directive was undermining the spirit of the opt-out as although it was purportedly a health and safety measure (an area in which the Community can legislate), the link with health and safety was tenuous. It considered the Directive was primarily intended to regulate social organization and promote job creation. The Social Chapter has now been incorporated into the main body of the EC Treaty by the Treaty of Amsterdam, which came into force in May 1999. This followed the election of a Labour government in the UK, after which the UK policy towards the Social Chapter changed.

Legal issues

In legal terms, the challenge was on a number of grounds. Two of these will be looked at here, as they relate directly to the question of the Community's competence to act: choice of legal basis and failure to comply with the principle of subsidiarity.

The Directive had been based on Article 118a EC, which clearly gives the Community competence to legislate on matters of health and safety:

1. Member States shall pay particular attention to encouraging improvements, especially in the working environment, as regards the health and safety of workers, and shall set as their objective the harmonisation of conditions in this area, while maintaining the improvements made.
2. In order to help achieve the objective laid down in the first paragraph, the Council ... shall adopt by means of directives, minimum requirements for gradual implementation, having regard to the conditions and technical rules obtaining in each of the Member States. Such directives shall avoid imposing administrative, financial and legal constraints in a way which would hold back the creation and development of small and medium-sized undertakings.
3. The provisions adopted pursuant to this article shall not prevent any Member State from maintaining or introducing more stringent measures for the protection of working conditions compatible with this Treaty (ex Article 118a EC (this is now revised to form Article 138)).

The first ground that the UK invoked was the question of the choice of the correct legal basis. It contended that Article 118a did not confer on the Community power to legislate on working time because it allowed it to act only within a narrow health and safety policy field (which it interpreted as meaning matters such as physical hazards in the workplace), not the broad social arena covered by the directive. It argued that there was no scientific link between health and safety and working time. Instead, as a general measure, the directive should have been based either on Article 100 EC (now Article 108) concerning the approximation of laws which 'directly affect the establishment or functioning of the internal market' or Article 235 EC (now Article 308), which allows the Community to act if specific powers are not given elsewhere in the Treaty.

Why did the UK contest the legal basis of the directive, if it accepted that the Community might have competence under another article of the Treaty? The answer lies in the legislative procedures used under the various articles of the Treaty. The Community uses a number of different procedures to enact legislation. Although these have been streamlined to some extent by the Treaty of Amsterdam, the legislative process remains complex. Each Treaty article prescribes the procedure to be used for measures based on that article. In this case, if the measure had been introduced under Article 100 or Article 235, the voting requirement in the Council would have been for unanimity. This would have allowed the UK successfully to block the measure if it had voted against it. However, Article 118a required a different voting procedure: qualified majority voting. Under this system of voting, the voting is weighted in accordance with the relative size of the member states, with the largest states having ten votes down to the smallest with two. A single member state is, under this system, not able to veto a measure. In fact, the UK had abstained from the vote. If the UK had been able to establish that the measure had been adopted under the wrong legal base, and it was subsequently reintroduced under Article 100 or Article 235, it would then have been able to ensure that it was not adopted at all by voting against it.

What did the Court have to say about the legal base of the Working Time Directive?

First, it looked at the wording of the article. It did not accept the UK's argument that it should be narrowly interpreted to cover only physical conditions and risks. It said that there was nothing to suggest that the concepts 'working environment, 'safety' and 'health' should be interpreted restrictively. Quite the reverse; that the wording favoured a broad interpretation to embrace all factors in the working environment which could affect the health and safety of a worker, including certain aspects of the regulation of working time. Next, it looked at whether Article 118a was the appropriate choice of legal base in this case. It reiterated that it was necessary for the choice of legal basis to be made on objective factors amenable to judicial review and that the principal purpose is paramount:

> Where the principal aim of the measure in question is the protection of the health and safety of workers, Article 118a must be used, albeit such a measure may have ancillary effects on the establishment and functioning of the internal market.

The Court found that the directive's principal aim *was* the protection of the health and safety of workers, rejecting the UK's assertion that the relationship between working time and the health and safety of workers was not justified. Even though it might have effects on employment levels and social conditions, this was not its principal aim. Therefore the Court concluded that it was correct to base the Working Time Directive on Article 118a.

The UK also claimed that the directive breached the principle of subsidiarity. Article 118a is a clear example of shared competence: the EC has competence to legislate, but member states are free to introduce more stringent measures should they so wish. As it is not an area of exclusive Community competence, the principle of subsidiarity needs to be considered. In the case of the Working Time Directive, the Court swiftly dismissed the UK's claim that the measure was not consistent with subsidiarity. The objective of Article 118a was to adopt minimum requirements so as to contribute, through harmonization, to achieving the objective of raising the level of health and safety protection. Unilateral action by the member states is not the way to achieve harmonization. Action at the Community level was the appropriate, indeed only, way to achieve this aim.

The Court dismissed the UK's other arguments and concluded that the measure (apart from one minor point) was legitimately introduced. The UK accepted the Court's decision (as it is obliged to do under EC law), and the provisions of the Working Time Directive have been transposed into UK law.

THE ISSUE OF SUPREMACY

> Member States shall take all appropriate measures, whether general or particular, to ensure fulfilment of the obligations arising out of this Treaty or

resulting from action taken by the institutions of the Community. They shall facilitate the achievement of the Community's tasks.

They shall abstain from any measure which could jeopardize the attainment of the objectives of this Treaty. (Article 10 (ex Article 5) EC).

What happens when EC law and national law conflict? A clear principle has been established that EC law should have *supremacy* over national law. In case of conflict with national law, EC law prevails. The Treaty itself does not make the doctrine of the supremacy of EC law explicit, although it can certainly be argued that it is implied in the 'loyalty' article of the EC Treaty, Article 10 (ex Article 5). It has been for the European Court of Justice, as in many other areas where the court has fleshed out the bare bones of the Treaty, to make the situation plain. There is a practical logic to this concept: were EC law not to prevail but in individual member states national law could apply irrespective of EU provisions, the whole coherence and uniformity of the law would break down. As the Court said in Case 6/64, *Costa* v *ENEL*, Community law:

> cannot be overridden by domestic legal provisions, however framed, without being deprived of its character as Community law and without the legal basis of the Community itself being called into question.

The ECJ has held that the principle applies to national constitutional provisions as much as to ordinary Acts of Parliament: Case 11/70, *Internationale Handelsgesellschaft mbH* v *Einfuhr- und Vorratstelle für Getreide und Futtermittel*:

> the validity of a Community measure or its effect within a Member State cannot be affected by allegations that it runs counter to either fundamental rights as formulated by the constitution of that State or the principles of a national constitutional structure.

National courts have a duty to set aside national law which is in conflict with EC law: Case 106/77, *Amministrazione delle Finanze dello Stato* v *Simmenthal SpA*:

> a national court which is called upon, within the limits of its jurisdiction, to apply provisions of Community law is under a duty to give full effect to those provisions, if necessary refusing of its own motion to apply any conflicting provision of national legislation, even if adopted subsequently, and it is not necessary for the court to request the prior setting aside of such provision by legislative or other constitutional means.

The following series of cases illustrates the question of conflict between national and Community law:

- Case C–213/89, *R* v *Secretary of State for Transport ex parte Factortame Ltd. and others* (*Factortame I*)
- Case C–221/89, *R* v *Secretary of State for Transport ex parte Factortame Ltd. and others* (*Factortame II*)
- Case C–246/89, *Commission* v *United Kingdom*
- Cases C–46, 48/93, *Brasserie du Pêcheur SA* v *Federal Republic of Germany* and *R* v *Secretary of State for Transport, ex parte Factortame Ltd. and others* (*Factortame III*)

Background

The UK had introduced measures in the Merchant Shipping Act 1988 imposing nationality and residence requirements for the registration of British fishing vessels. This was introduced to prevent the practice known as 'quota hopping', whereby fishing quotas allocated to the UK under the common fisheries policy could be exploited by fishing vessels, which although flying the British flag, had little genuine link with the UK. These quotas had been introduced in response to the dwindling fish stocks in Community waters. Ninety-five fishing vessels, mostly Spanish-owned, which had previously been registered under the British flag were unable to retain this registration under the new rules.

Legal issues

> Within the scope of the application of this Treaty ... any discrimination on grounds of nationality shall be prohibited (Article 12 EC (ex Article 6)).

> restrictions on the freedom of establishment of nationals of a Member State in the territory of another Member State shall be prohibited.

> Freedom of establishment shall include the right to take up and pursue activities as self-employed persons and to set up and manage undertakings, in particular companies or firms (Article 43 EC (ex Article 52)).

EC law is clear: individuals and companies should be able to pursue their business anywhere in the European Community free from discrimination on grounds of nationality. Was the Merchant Shipping Act contrary to Article 12 (ex Article 6) and in particular Article 43 (ex Article 52) EC? The fishing vessel owners brought a case in the High Court alleging that this was the case. The High Court sought a *preliminary reference* from the European Court of Justice, because it needed clarification on points of EC law. This procedure is laid down in Article 234 (ex Article 177). This allows a national court, when it needs a ruling on the interpretation or validity of a point of EC law in order to decide a case before it, to ask for this clarification by way of a preliminary reference. Once the ECJ has answered the national court's questions, the matter is returned to the national court to decide the case on the facts before it. It is then the national courts which apply and enforce EC law. It is not only through this route that breaches of EC law by the member states come to the attention of the ECJ. Under the provisions of Article 226 (ex Article 169), the Commission can bring an action against a member state if it is in breach of Community law. It did so in this case: Case C–246/89, *Commission* v *United Kingdom*.

While the original reference of the UK Court to the ECJ was pending, further events made another reference necessary. The Spanish fishermen stood to go out of business while the Merchant Shipping Act was in force. What they needed was a temporary injunction to ensure that by the time the case was finally decided it would not be too late to be of any use. The House of Lords agreed that they did stand to suffer irreparable harm if interim relief was not granted, but that the British courts have no power to suspend an Act of Parliament and that a common law rule prohibits the granting of an injunction against the Crown. So another Article 234 (ex Article 177) reference was made to the ECJ.

In reply, the ECJ held, in case C–213/89, *R* v *Secretary of State for Transport, ex parte Factortame (Factortame I)* that the national rule which prohibited the granting of an injunction against the Crown had to be set aside if it prevented the granting of interim relief. The logic behind this was to ensure the effectiveness of EC law, something that the Court is constantly striving to ensure:

> any provision of a national legal system and any legislative, administrative or judicial practice which might impair the effectiveness of Community law by withholding from the national court having jurisdiction to apply such a law the power to do everything necessary at the moment of its application to set aside national legislative provisions which might prevent, even temporarily, Community rules from having full force and effect are incompatible with those requirements, which are the very essence of Community law.

The decision had a considerable impact in the UK, since it seemed to some that the European Court of Justice was undermining the constitutional principle of the sovereignty of Parliament. However, as Lord Bridge clearly expressed when the case returned to the UK, there was nothing here that was not inherent in Community law already:

> Some public comments on the decision of the Court of Justice, affirming the jurisdiction of the courts of member states to override national legislation if necessary to enable interim relief to be granted in protection of rights under Community law, have suggested that this was a novel and dangerous invasion by a Community institution of the sovereignty of the United Kingdom Parliament. But such comments are based on a misconception. If the supremacy within the European Community of Community law over the national law of the member states was not always inherent in the EEC Treaty it was certainly well established in the jurisprudence of the Court of Justice long before the United Kingdom joined the Community (*Factortame Ltd* v *Secretary of State for Transport (No. 2)* (1991)).

When the question of the compatibility of the UK statute with EC law was decided, parts of it were, not surprisingly found to be contrary to EC law: Case C–221/89, *R* v *Secretary of State for Transport, ex parte Factortame Ltd and Others (Factortame II)*. It was held to be inconsistent with Community law for there to be a nationality requirement for the owners and operators of fishing vessels registered as British, although it was permissible to have rules which ensured that the vessels were managed and controlled from within the UK.

THE ISSUE OF STATE LIABILITY

> It must be held that the full effectiveness of Community rules would be impaired and the protection of the rights which they grant would be weakened if individuals were unable to obtain compensation when their rights are infringed by a breach of Community law for which a Member State can be held responsible (Cases C–6/90 and C–9/90, *Francovich and Bonifaci* v *Italy*).

Can there be a remedy for breaches of EC law by the member states? Rights are of little use without corresponding remedies. The individual will have won a hollow victory if the court has only been able to establish that his or her rights have been infringed without taking steps to remedy this wrong. The ECJ has always sought to ensure that Community law is effective: a key element in the effectiveness of Community law (or indeed any system of law) is the provision of suitable remedies. The Court established in *Francovich* that the government of a member state, if it is in breach of its obligations under EC law, is liable to pay damages to an individual who has suffered loss resulting from that breach. The exact scope of the provision was not entirely clear. The basic conditions for the principle of *state liability* had been established but a number of points were left unanswered about its wider implications.

The Spanish fishing fleet had been illegally prevented from fishing UK waters during the period when the provisions of the Merchant Shipping Act were imposed. Could they claim damages for losses they had incurred during this time? Again the question was referred to the ECJ. It was joined together with another case which concerned importing beer into Germany from France which raised the same legal issues: Cases C–46/93 and C–48/93, *Brasserie du Pêcheur SA* v *Federal Republic of Germany* and *R* v *Secretary of State for Transport, ex parte Factortame and Others* (Factortame III). The reply from the ECJ listed the three conditions which have to be met for the principle to apply: the rule of law infringed must be intended to confer rights on individuals; the breach must be sufficiently serious; and there must be a direct causal link between the breach of the state's obligation and the damage suffered by the individual. It went on to give some guidance as to what constitutes 'sufficiently serious'.

When the case returned to the House of Lords, *R* v *Secretary of State for Transport, ex parte Factortame Ltd and Others (no. 5)* (1999), it was held that the conditions for liability were met. The Treaty did confer rights on individuals, the breach by the UK government was sufficiently serious and this did cause loss to the owners of the fishing vessels who were unable to reregister their boats. The UK government will now have to pay damages to those who suffered losses as a result of the infringement of their rights as Community nationals by the Merchant Shipping Act; a measure which the government knew at the time was likely to be in breach of the Treaty.

THE ISSUE OF DIRECT EFFECT

the Community constitutes a new legal order of international law for the benefit of which the states have limited their sovereign rights, albeit within limited fields, and the subjects of which comprise not only Member States but their nationals. Independently of the legislation of the Member States, Community law therefore not only imposes obligations on individuals but is also intended to confer on them rights which become part of their legal heritage (Case 26/62, *NV Algemene Transporten Expedities Onderneming van Gend en Loos* v *Nederlandse Administratie der Belastingen*).

When can EU rights be relied upon in the national courts? This groundbreaking judgment early in the life of the Community established that the EC Treaty confers rights on individuals. Traditionally, an international treaty (and the EC Treaty is one) does not do this. The Court is therefore making a profound statement about the nature of EC law: that what has been created is a new form of international law which does have the effect of conferring rights on individuals which become part of their legal heritage. These rights can therefore be relied on in national courts in the same way as national law. The Court went on to set some practical conditions for this principle of *direct effect* to apply (slightly modified by later cases). Essentially it is a practical test. Is the provision of EC law clear and precise enough for a court to be able to apply it?

A distinction can be drawn between *vertical* and *horizontal* direct effect. Vertical direct effect arises when the relationship is between an individual (or company) and the state. This was the situation in *Van Gend*: contrary to a provision in the EC Treaty (ex Article 12 (now Article 25)), an import duty had been increased. Since it was the state which was imposing the duty on private individuals and companies, the relationship was a vertical one. The Court held in a subsequent case (Case 43/75, *Defrenne* v *Société Anonyme Belge de Navigation Aerienne*) that Treaty articles may also give rise to direct effects in a horizontal relationship, that is between two private individuals or companies. Gabrielle Defrenne was able to rely on her rights under the EC Treaty in ex Article 119 (now Article 141), which established the principle of equal pay against her employer, a private company.

The above cases concerned the direct effect of Treaty articles. It was not clear until later cases whether this principle of direct effect would also apply to secondary legislation. The EC Treaty empowers the institutions to pass legislation. We have seen one example in the first case study in this chapter; the Working Time Directive. Such secondary legislation can take three forms: *regulations, decisions* and *directives*.

Regulations automatically come into force in every member state without anything further needing to be done. There is clearly no problem with them. Having entered into the national legal system, they can be relied on in the same way as domestic legislation. Decisions differ from regulations in that they are not addressed to everyone but apply to those member states, undertakings or individuals to whom they are addressed. As they are automatically applicable there is again no problem.

The problems arise with directives. These differ from the other two types of binding Community law in that they do not automatically enter into national law. They have to be implemented by the member states (*transposed* into national law). This is not to say that they are any less binding than regulations or decisions but they are binding as to the end result to be achieved while leaving the means and form of achieving that end up to the member state. This allows for more flexibility for member states to take into account local conditions and ways of doing things. Each directive will include a time limit; within that time (usually about two years) the member state should bring in (or amend) national legislation which gives effect to the provisions of the directive. This system can lead to problems. If a member state has transposed the directive correctly and fully and on time, there is no problem. The individual can simply rely on it in the same way as any other national laws. That the law was passed in order to fulfil the requirements of an EC directive is irrelevant and invisible. It is where the directive has not been transposed at all, or has been transposed but incorrectly or incompletely, or has left some ambiguities that the individual may want to rely directly on the rights in the directive.

Case 41/74, *Van Duyn* v *Home Office* was the first case where the ECJ was asked to decide whether an individual could rely on the direct effect of a directive. The Court held that directives could be directly effective (provided, like directly effective Treaty articles, they are sufficiently clear and precise). Ms Van Duyn's case was against the state (she wanted to rely on the provisions of a directive to challenge the UK's refusal to allow her to enter the country); she was in a vertical relationship. Therefore this case established that directives could have vertical direct effect. It was not clear whether they could also have horizontal direct effect until Case 152/84, *Marshall* v *Southampton and South-West Hampshire Area Health Authority (Marshall I)*. This case was also an example of a vertical relationship, so the provisions of the directive in question could be relied upon. The Court took the opportunity, however, to explain its logic and why the direct effect of directives should be restricted to vertical direct effect.

> The binding nature of a directive, which constitutes the basis for the possibility of relying on the directive before a national court, exists only in relation to 'each Member State to which it is addressed'. It follows that a directive may not of itself impose obligations on an individual and that a provision of a directive may not be relied upon as such against such a person.

As the directive is addressed to the member state, which has a duty to implement it, the state cannot be allowed to benefit from its own failure to act to fulfil its obligations. This distinction between vertical and horizontal direct effect seems harsh on employees in the private sector who would not, if they found themselves in a similar situation, be able to rely on the provisions of a directive. The distinction was not without its critics. In the following case, the Court was asked to reconsider its position: Case C–91/92, *Paola Faccini Dori* v *Recreb Srl*.

Background

Paola Faccini Dori signed up, outside Milan railway station to purchase an English language correspondence course. She subsequently changed her mind and sent a registered letter to the company saying that she wanted to cancel the contract. An EC directive (Directive 85/577) on the protection of the consumer in respect of contracts negotiated away from the business premises (such as 'doorstep selling') had been brought in by the Community. Its purpose was to improve consumer protection in this area. Generally in these situations, the consumer is at a disadvantage as it is the trader who initiates the negotiations for which the consumer is wholly unprepared and taken by surprise. In most such cases the consumer is not in a position to be able to compare the quality and price of the offer with competing products. The directive aimed to redress the balance by giving customers the right to a cooling-off period of seven days with respect to such contracts. However, the directive had not been implemented into Italian law. Would she nevertheless be able to rely on the rights the directive gave her?

As an individual in dispute with a private company and therefore in a horizontal relationship, following *Marshall,* Paola Faccini Dori would not be able to rely on rights in an unimplemented directive. The ECJ was not willing to reconsider and stood by its previous opinion, stating:

> The effect of extending [direct effect of directives] to the sphere of relations between individuals would be to recognise a power in the Community to enact obligations for individuals with immediate effect, whereas it has competence to do so only where it is empowered to adopt regulations.

If she could not rely on the direct effect of the directive, was there any other mechanism that might be able to ensure that she could enjoy her EC rights? The Court, in *Faccini Dori,* referred to another possibility. To help fill the gaps created by the limitations on the application of the principle of direct effect, the Court has developed another principle, that of *indirect effect*. Sometimes called the 'interpretative obligation', this obliges national courts, as a consequence of their obligation to ensure the effectiveness of EC law, to interpret national law in the light of relevant EC law whether or not it has direct effect. It was first discussed in Case 14/83, *Von Colson and Kamann* v *Land Nordrhein-Westfalen*:

> The Member States' obligation arising from a directive to achieve the result envisaged by the directive and their duty under Article 5 [now Article 10] of the Treaty to take all appropriate measures, whether general or particular, to ensure the fulfilment of that obligation, is binding on all the authorities of Member States including, for matters within their jurisdiction, the courts. It follows that, in applying the national law and in particular the provisions of a national law specifically introduced in order to implement Directive No. 76/207, national courts are required to interpret their national law in the light of the wording and purpose of the directive in order to achieve the result referred to.

Where, as was the case in *Von Colson*, the national legislation does not adequately transpose the provisions of a directive, the national courts will have to give effect to the purpose of the directive indirectly, by interpreting national law in the light of the directive. Subsequent cases have built on *Von Colson*, notably Case C–106/89, *Marleasing* v *La Comercial Internacional de Alimentatión* and Case C–334/92, *Wagner Miret* v *Fondo de Garantia Salarial*. These cases make it clear that when applying national law, whether it has been adopted before or after the directive, the national court must interpret that law, as far as possible, in the light of the wording and purpose of the directive. There are however, still some uncertainties as to the scope of this principle. Indirect effect cannot always be utilized; there may be no relevant national legislation to interpret, or it may be impossible to interpret it to give effect to EU rights. In that case, as the ECJ indicated in *Faccini Dori*, the remedy may be to use the principle of state liability, discussed above in the context of *Factortame*.

PROGRESS TEST

Imagine that the EC has issued a directive (fictitious) which provides that all teachers and lecturers should have a 6-month period of paid leave every 3 years.

1 The UK government was opposed to the measure, but was outvoted in the Council of Ministers. What grounds might they try to use in order to have the directive declared invalid?
2 The directive had not been implemented in the UK, although the time limit for doing so had expired. Jane, a teacher, wanted to exercise her right under the directive and take paid leave. Might she be able to rely on the directive in such circumstances? If so, what conditions would need to be satisfied?
3 The UK later passes a statute in order to implement the provisions of the directive. It states that 'Teachers and lecturers who are British nationals shall be entitled to paid leave'. Pierre, a French national, has been a lecturer at an English university for the past 10 years. When he applied for paid leave, he was refused on the grounds of his nationality. Could he challenge the UK statute as being incompatible with EC law? What is the status of a national law which conflicts with EC law?

The structure of the organization: company law

3

Elvira Rubin

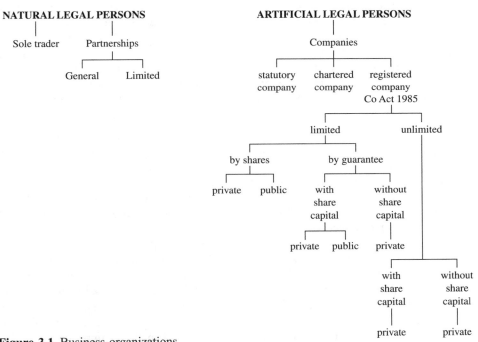

Figure 3.1 Business organizations

WHAT IS A BUSINESS ORGANIZATION?

There are three main ways of running a business organization:

1 *Sole trader*: a person may operate a business on his or her own account.
2 *Partnership*: in *Khan and Another* v *Miah and Others* [1998] the parties involved had decided to operate a restaurant as a partnership. They opened a joint bank account for themselves as 'partners'. They bought premises and equipment. They quarrelled and the partnership was dissolved. Some time later the restaurant was opened. The parties claimed to be entitled, as partners, to 50 per cent of the business profits up to the date of the dissolution of the partnership. In the Court of

Appeal, Lord Justice Roch said, that the 'actual' carrying on of business activity, not the necessary preparation for it, marks the beginning of a partnership. Consequently a partnership did not exist until the restaurant business was actually being carried on and by then the plaintiffs were no longer involved in the business.

3 *Company*: in *Salomon* v *Salomon & Co Ltd* [1897] Mr Salomon converted his sole trader business of leather merchant into a limited company by registration as 'Salomon & Co Ltd' under the Companies Act 1862. He sold his business as 'a going concern' to the new company of which he became the major shareholder and managing director. His wife and five children held one share each. The company paid for the business partially in shares, debentures and cash. Thus Mr Salomon, as a debenture holder, became also a secured creditor (see under loan capital). Soon the company experienced financial difficulties and had to go into liquidation. After Mr Salomon's debentures had been discharged out of the assets of the company no funds were left to pay the unsecured creditors. It was argued that Mr Salomon and the company were one, that the company was his agent and that he personally was responsible for the debts of the company. The House of Lords held: the company was duly registered, there had been no fraud since the shareholders had been properly informed, the business now belonged to the company and no longer to Mr Salomon, the company was not his agent and he was not responsible for the company's debts.

> Lord Macnaghten: 'The company is at law a different person altogether from the subscribers to the memorandum; and, though it may be that after incorporation the business is precisely the same as it was before, and the same persons are managers, and the same hands receive the profits, the company is not in law the agent of the subscribers or trustees for them. Nor are the subscribers as members liable, in any shape or form, except to the extent and in the manner provided by the Act'.

No one form of business organization is better. The choice depends on the individual requirements of those setting up and running the business. Deciding factors would include the preferred degree of control over the business, the capital available or needed in the future, the extent of personal liability for the business, the degree of publicity required by law, tax considerations. Each type of business organization creates different legal consequences for those involved in the running of or dealing with the business. A person may start his commercial career as a sole trader. When more capital is required the business may be converted into a partnership or a company.

SOLE TRADER

Someone who starts a business often begins as a sole trader. The organization is owned entirely by the sole trader and operated on his or her own account. When conducting the business the trader is the business and is personally subject to the general law and pays personal income tax on the profits of the business. The business and the sole trader are one in law. As a consequence he or she has unlimited liability for the debts and obligations of the business to the full extent of his or her personal assets.

No formal legal requirements need to be completed to set up in business as a sole trader. However, careful consideration must be given to the choice of business or trade name if this is different from the name of the sole trader. The Business Names Act 1985, ss. 2 and 3, prohibit the use of names that imply a connection with the government, a local authority or are sensitive words unless permission has been obtained from the Secretary of State, the relevant government department or body. Section 4 of that Act requires that the name of the sole trader and address for service of documents is stated: on all business letters, written orders for goods and services to be supplied to the business, invoices and receipts, and written demands for payment of debts. It must also be displayed at the business premises.

There are no minimum capital requirements. Any funds needed may be raised against personal security. The business accounts do not need to be in a particular format and there is no need to disclose financial records to anyone but the Inland Revenue. When the value of goods and services provided by the business exceed a certain level VAT is payable.

The sole trader normally controls, manages and operates the business him- or herself. A sole trader enters into contracts in his or her own name and thus may sue and be sued personally. Business decisions can be made quickly without having to consult with others. However, lack of expertise may lead to personal financial loss. Since he or she also bears unforeseeable risks such as theft or fire there should be adequate insurance cover. The appointment of an accountant or auditor is not required. A sole trader may decide to engage the help of his or her family or to hire employees to lighten the workload.

Section 268 of the Insolvency Act 1986 requires any person, including a sole trader, to satisfy a statutory demand for payment for a sum in excess of £750 within a period of three weeks. If such a demand is not met the creditor may take steps to obtain a declaration of bankruptcy under the Insolvency Act 1986. That is to say the court may make a bankruptcy order and appoint an insolvency practitioner who will realize the person's business and personal assets and pay the creditors in the prescribed order. The bankruptcy order may then be discharged automatically or by the court. The assets available do not include tools of the trade, clothes and personal effects. The insolvent or bankrupt sole trader may also come to a voluntary arrangement with his creditors.

PARTNERSHIP

> Partnership is the relation which subsists between persons carrying on a business in common with a view to profit (Partnership Act 1890, s.1(1)).

'Persons' in this context includes any human and artificial legal persons such as companies. Minors may be partners. However, until they reach the age of 18 some contracts may not be enforceable against them.

A partnership is an unincorporated association of persons. Business includes every trade, occupation or profession, so long as it is legal. The business created by the partners is called 'the firm'. It has neither a legal existence of its own nor its own separate legal personality. The partnership cannot in its own name own property and employ persons or create a floating charge over its undertaking.

In *Sadler* v *Whiteman* [1910] FARWELL LJ said:

> In English law a 'firm' as such has no existence; partners carry on business both as principals and agents for each other within the scope of the partnership business. The firm name is a mere expression, not a legal entity.

The existence of partnership is established as a question of fact by analysing all the circumstances in the light of section 1.

A partnership is the result of an agreement between two or more persons. The Companies Act 1985 s.716, limits the number of partners in a partnership to 20 but certain professional persons such as solicitors, accountants, stockbrokers may form larger partnerships.

There are no formalities needed to form a partnership. The agreement may be made orally or in writing and may even be implied, if the intentions of the Partnership Act 1890 s.1 are satisfied. It is, however, advisable that the intended partners seek legal advice and draw up a proper partnership agreement suited to their individual needs. The terms of this agreement may later be changed by unanimous consent. The existence of the partnership does not depend on this document actually having been signed by the partners. A partnership does not have to be registered anywhere, consequently it can come into existence by implication. The partnership agreement should specify:

- duration of the partnership;
- amount of capital invested by each partner and if interest is to be paid;
- how the profits are to be shared and paid;
- entitlement to a salary and vacation;
- which partners are responsible for the management;
- who may sign cheques;
- amount to which a partner may commit the partnership without approval of the others;
- provision for death or retirement of a partner.

In the absence of a partnership agreement any disputes will be settled according to the provisions of the Partnership Act 1890.

The Limited Partnership Act 1907 allows the formation of a 'limited' partnership. There must be at least one general partner with unlimited liability but the remaining partners may by the agreement be made liable only to the extent of their capital contribution for the debts of the business. A limited partnership must be registered with the Registrar of Companies and provide the names and extent of liability of the limited partners. Consequently this type of partnership can never be created by implication. The limited partnership is not very often used as a type of business organization.

Carrying on business

In *Keith Spicer Ltd* v *Mansell* [1970] two persons decided to go into business together and form a company. Before incorporation one of the two ordered goods (which were not paid for) for the business. The claimants then sued Mr Mansell, the other, for the price of the goods arguing that the two were partners. The Court of Appeal held that Mansell and his associate were not partners but company promoters.

For a partnership to exist the 'persons' must be 'carrying on' business with a view to profit. 'Carrying on' means the actual conduct of the activity for which the partnership is formed. Contracts in the preparing stage of a partnership are not partnership contracts. (See also *Khan* v *Miah*, above.)

The Partnership Act 1890, s.2 contains rules for determining the existence of a partnership. A person does not necessarily become a partner by taking a share of the profits. There must be an intention of making and sharing the profits achieved by the business. Thus, co-ownership of property with shared profits does not automatically create a partnership. Nor does the granting of a loan to a partnership, repayable out of business profits, necessarily make the lender a partner.

The firm has neither a legal existence of its own nor its own separate legal personality. The partners are fully liable without limit for the debts and obligations of the firm. The partnership cannot in its own name own property and employ persons or create a floating charge over its undertaking. The partners may choose any name they like for the business, either their own names or a trade name. The provisions of the Business Names Act 1985 apply (see also sole trader, above). A partnership does not have perpetual existence: the Partnership Act 1890 makes it a 'partnership at will', meaning that any partner can terminate it by giving notice to his or her partners. The partnership agreement may provide against this happening.

The legal relationship between the partners

This is governed by the Partnership Act 1890 ss.19–31. The relationship between the partners is based upon a contract and upon 'utmost good faith and confidence'. However, partners are free to regulate their relationship as they wish, as long as this reflects the essential quality of the partnership. If there is no partnership agreement any disputes will be solved according to the Act.

The Act says that every partner is entitled to take part in the management of the partnership business. Any variation of this type of management structure should be expressly stated in the partnership agreement.

The partners acquire a number of rights. They:

- share equally in the capital, profits and losses of the firm; sharing in proportion to their individual contribution is a matter of agreement;
- cannot be employed by the partnership; a salaried partner, depending on the circumstances, may be considered a mere employee, although he or she is able to bind the firm and is liable for the debts of the firm (this is partnership by representation);
- have no automatic right to remuneration for acting on behalf of the firm unless otherwise agreed;
- have the right to be indemnified for expenses incurred when acting on behalf of the firm in the ordinary course of business;
- are entitled to participate in the management of the firm unless otherwise agreed;
- have the right to inspect the books.

Decision making, unless otherwise agreed, is by:

- *simple majority* for ordinary matters connected with the business;
- *unanimity* for the
  - introduction of a new partner,
  - expulsion of a partner,
  - change in the constitution and nature of the business.

Duties of the partners to each other

The partners owe each other contractual duties, reflected in the Partnership Act and fiduciary duties. They must:

- render true accounts;
- provide complete information on all aspects of the partnership;
- account for any personal benefits obtained;
- avoid conflict of interest.

They must not:

- make any secret profits;
- compete with the business of the firm;
- use confidential information elsewhere.

Partnership property

The partnership property, that is to say, any property originally brought into the partnership, any property acquired for the purposes and in the course of the business and property bought with the firm's money must be applied exclusively for the purposes of the firm. Partners who put personal property at the disposal of the firm should ensure that it is clearly identified as such, otherwise it might become absorbed as partnership property. The partners may, subject to the partnership agreement, assign their shares in the partnership by way of mortgage, sale, etc.

Liability of the partners to outsiders

The partners are unlimitedly liable to outsiders for the obligations of the firm. Contractual obligations result in joint liability (i.e. a liability shared between partners may be imposed upon one of them) and tortious obligations are joint and several (i.e. where liability is shared between partners, a partner may be held liable for part or the whole of the debt). (Partnership Act 1890, ss.5–18). The Civil Liability (Contribution) Act 1978 has largely done away with the distinction between joint and several liability. Proceedings may now successively be brought against jointly liable persons, despite an earlier judgment against others.

Contractual liability

In *Cox* v *Hickman* (1860) Lord Cranworth said: '... the liability of one partner for the acts of his co-partners is in truth the liability of a principal for the acts of his agent'.

In *Mercantile Credit Co Ltd* v *Garrod* [1962] two men, in partnership, operated a garage business. They had expressly excluded buying and selling cars. When one of them bought a car, based on s.5, the partnership was nevertheless liable to pay for it, because purchase of the car was an act for 'carrying on in the usual way business of this kind'.

The power of a partner to bind the firm and his other partners is based on the law of agency and the Partnership Act and depends on the partners' authority. The partners are simultaneously principal, agent for the firm and agent for each other.

The partners may have:

- actual authority;
- implied authority;
- usual authority;
- apparent authority.

The existence of actual authority is a question of fact. The Partnership Act, s.5 is the starting point for considering whether, as a question of fact, a partner can bind the firm in other circumstances. A partner can *only* bind the firm for the 'purposes of the business of the partnership' and only if doing an act 'for carrying on the usual way of the business of the firm'. He cannot bind the firm if 'he has no actual authority and the outsider knows this or does not know or believe the person with whom he is dealing is a partner'. Crucial here are the type of partnership business and the usual way of conducting it.

By s.6 a partner is deemed to have acted as the firm's agent if he or she entered transactions in the firm's name or in relation to the firm's business. But by s.7 a partner cannot, without express authority, bind the firm by acts that are not apparently connected with the firm's ordinary course of business. He or she will then be personally liable. Unless prohibited, partners in a trading firm have extensive usual authority. But they may not bind the firm by deed, compromise a debt, submit to arbitration or give guarantees in the firm's name.

Section 14 provides for partnership by 'holding out' or by 'apparent' authority. When a person represents her-/himself or knowingly allows her-/himself to be represented, either verbally, in writing or by conduct, as a partner of the firm he or she may become liable as a partner.

Retiring partners should ensure that their names no longer appear in connection with their former partnership.

Liability of incoming and retiring partners

By s.17 an incoming partner is normally only liable after having become a partner. To avoid future liability a retiring partner must give notice of leaving the firm (s.36). *Actual* notice must be given to those who have dealt with the firm and who knew him to be a partner. *Notice, actual or in the London Gazette* should be given to those with no previous dealings with the firm, but knew her or him to be a partner.

Dissolution of the partnership

In the following instances partnerships are dissolved (ss.32–44):

- without the involvement of a court:
  - after expiration of a fixed term,
  - after completion of a venture,
  - by any partner giving notice to the other partners of dissolving the firm if duration of the partnership is not fixed,
  - bankruptcy, death or change of partnership share of one of the partners,
  - mutual consent,
  - illegality;

- with a court order on application by any partner:
    - mental disorder of a partner under the Mental Health Act 1983,
    - where a partner is no longer able to perform his or her partnership duties,
    - if a partner conducts her- or himself prejudicially to the business,
    - if the business can only be carried on at a loss,
    - if the court is of the opinion that it is 'just an equitable' to dissolve the partnership.

On dissolution the partnership property, including goodwill, is sold. Any debts and obligations are paid out of the proceeds. The partners are usually proportionally liable in case of insufficient funds. Surplus funds are usually proportionally divided amongst the partners. Under certain circumstances a receiver or manager may be appointed to wind down the affairs of the partnership. The authority of each partner may continue insofar as it may be necessary to wind up the affairs of the partnership.

COMPANY

The legal status of the company: the consequences of incorporation

In *Lee (Catherine)* v *Lee's Air Farming Ltd* [1961] Mr Lee formed a company to operate his business of crop spraying. He was the controlling shareholder, the managing director and chief pilot. The company insured itself against liability to pay compensation in case of accident to its employees. Mr Lee was killed in an air crash while working for the company. Mrs Lee then claimed compensation from the company under the insurance. It was argued that she was not entitled to any compensation because of the close relationship between Mr Lee (as both employer and employee) and the company. It was held that Mrs Lee was entitled to compensation because Mr Lee as a worker was in law a distinct person from the company he had formed.
(See also *Salomon* v *Salomon & Co Ltd*, above.)

It is important to understand the legal status of a company and the consequences of incorporation because the majority of businesses are corporate entities. Initially a business person may conduct his or her business in his or her own name, as a sole trader, but as the business thrives he or she is likely to seek corporate status for the enterprise. Businesses achieve corporate status by incorporation and registration as either public or private companies, limited by shares. To become incorporated they have to follow the procedures set out in the Companies Act currently in force, and once incorporated they will be governed by the rules set out in this legislation. Following the incorporation of the company it will be managed by directors and is likely to employ people to work for it. This section will set out the statutory framework.

The case of *Lee (Catherine)* v *Lee's Air Farming Ltd* [1961] provides a relatively modern example of the principle established over 100 years ago in *Salomon* v *Salomon & Co Ltd* [1897]. The House of Lords considered that Mr Lee could function simultaneously as managing director (controlling mind of the company) and an employee of that company. The company he had formed was a separate legal entity.

Adverse consequences of incorporation

In *Macaura* v *Northern Assurance Co Ltd* [1925] Mr Macaura owned a timber estate, which he sold to the company he had formed. He insured the timber against fire in his own name. When the timber was destroyed by fire the insurance company successfully claimed that he had no insurable interest as a shareholder. The proper person to insure the timber would have been the company itself.

In *Re Lewis' Will Trust* [1985] Mr Lewis had made his will in 1964 leaving his freehold farm and premises to his son. After 1961 the farm was transferred to a company of which Mr Lewis was the major shareholder. Upon Mr Lewis's death his will could not be executed as intended because at the time of his death Mr Lewis no longer owned the farm. He only owned shares in the company to which he had transferred the farm. The shares, not having been expressly bequeathed, were divided between Mr Lewis's son and daughter.

These two cases demonstrate that a businessman who is considering changing the status of his business so that it trades as a limited company should take careful account of the consequences of doing so! If he fails to do this, there may be consequences that are not intended.

The status of the company

As a legal entity separate from the human persons who have formed it a company can carry out the following activities.

- A company can sue and be sued in its own name: it can incur its own debts and liabilities.
- It can incur liability in tort for the wrongs done by its officers and employees acting on its behalf in the course of its business. This is an application of the principle of 'vicarious liability' (explained later in this book in the chapter on tort).
- A company can be convicted of committing a crime where the crime is an offence of strict liability. The company can even be convicted of an offence requiring a 'state of mind' when a senior employee has actually committed the crime. The actual wrongdoer must, however, be a person who is sufficiently senior for the law to regard him or her as the 'directing mind and will' of the company. It is possible, but not normal, for a company to be made liable for manslaughter. (See the chapter on criminal law.)
- It can make contracts. On the other hand a shareholder can neither enforce nor benefit from a contract made by the company.
- It can issue debentures. These are long-term loans secured by the assets of the company, they are explained more fully later in this chapter.
- A company can enjoy perpetual succession. This means that a company can continue to exist even if all the shareholders have died. Its existence is not dependent on the composition of the body of shareholders.

The concept of 'limited liability', when a company is of the category known as a 'limited liability company', refers only to the liability of individual shareholders. The company itself is fully liable, without limit to the full extent of its assets.

Lifting the veil of incorporation

There are situations when the law, as set out in statutes, or decided by the courts, disregards the separate legal personality of the company. In these situations the law is said to 'go behind the veil of incorporation' that is go behind the corporate form and impose liability on the directors or individual members (shareholders) of the company. In English law there is no comprehensive rule as to when this may happen. The privilege of the separate legal person may not be misused for purposes of fraud, the avoidance of legal obligations, default on tax liability or the commission of crimes.

Statutory piercing

Companies Act 1985

The following sections of this Act expressly provide for lifting the veil of incorporation:

- Section 24: this applies only to public limited companies (the meaning of public in this context is explained below). If the number of members falls below two and the remaining member carries on the business for more than 6 months, he or she will become personally liable for the debts of the company.
- Section 117(8): the officer/s of the company will become liable for a fine if they start trading or exercise borrowing powers before the certificate of incorporation has been issued and, in the case of a public company, the trading certificate has not been obtained. The trading certificate must be obtained within the 21 days prescribed by the Act.
- Section 394(4): an officer of the company, or person acting on its behalf, will become personally liable for transactions made without the proper name of the company displayed on letters, official publications, bills of exchange, promissory notes, cheques or orders for money or goods. This is particularly important where the company operates (as it is legally entitled to do) under a trading name that differs from the name under which it was registered upon incorporation.
- Section 458: personal criminal liability will arise for fraudulent trading, whether or not the company is being wound up.
- Section 23: a subsidiary cannot be a member of its holding company.
- Sections 227–230: companies in a group of companies or subsidiaries must comply with the requirements to produce individual accounts of these companies as well as group accounts.

Insolvency Act 1986

If in the course of winding up it appears that any business of the company has been carried on with intent to defraud creditors of the company or creditors of any other person, or for any fraudulent purpose ... then the court on the application of the liquidator may declare that any persons who were knowingly parties to the carrying on of the business in the manner above-mentioned are to be liable to make such contribution (if any) to the company's assets as the court thinks proper. (The Insolvency Act s.213).

This Act imposes personal liability upon directors or other company officers in respect of corporate activities.

The Insolvency Act applies only when the company is in the process of being wound up and the liquidator has doubts regarding the behaviour of company directors or officers. The liquidator will check into the affairs of the company for up to 2 years prior to the company being wound up. Upon his or her findings he or she may apply to the court for civil sanctions so that the persons in question will be ordered to contribute personally to the assets of the company.

Section 213 (above) is concerned with fraudulent trading. In *Re Patrick & Lyon Ltd* [1933] Ch 786 it was judicially stated that 'actual dishonesty involving moral blame' needs to be established. Such a situation may arise when the business of the company is carried on despite the realization that there is no reasonable prospect of paying the creditors.

Section 214 deals with wrongful trading and has greatly affected the position of directors. Wrongful trading occurs when a director of the company, before the company goes into insolvent liquidation, does not take every step to protect the interests of the company's creditors when he knew or ought to have known that there was no reasonable prospect of the company avoiding insolvent liquidation. Thus, this section imposes a statutory duty towards creditors. The director/s is/are compared to a reasonably diligent person with the 'general knowledge, skill and experience that may reasonably be expected of a person carrying out the same functions as carried out by that director'. The court considers what such a person would have done in like circumstances.

To protect themselves against the application of s.214, company directors must be fully aware of the company's financial situation and the company's activities. Any concern about the company's financial situation should be voiced at the first possible opportunity, like at a board meeting. Then every step, such as seeking professional advice or stopping trading, should be taken to minimize potential loss to the company's creditors.

Judicial piercing

The following cases are illustrative of situations in which the courts have intervened to prevent the separate legal entity of a company being utilized for improper purposes:

A company has been formed for fraudulent or improper purposes or is a facade to avoid legal obligations

In *Jones* v *Lipman* [1962], in order to avoid completion of the sale of a house, a company was formed for the purpose of conveying the house to it. The intention was that after the house had been transferred to the company the original purchaser would be unable to claim it. The court ordered specific performance of the original contract because it recognized the improper purpose for which the company had been formed.

As a matter of public policy

In *Daimler Co Ltd* v *Continental Tyre and Rubber Co Ltd* [1916] a company was registered in England, although all its officers and all its members, apart from one, were German. After the outbreak of World War I the company sued another English company for moneys owed to it. The defendant company refused to pay arguing that to do so would be to trade with the enemy. The defendant asked for the claim to be struck out. The court looked behind the corporate veil and established that those in actual control of the company were 'enemy aliens' and therefore the company itself should be regarded as such.

Agency

In *Smith, Stone & Knight Ltd* v *Birmingham Corporation* [1939] the court had to consider the relationship between a holding company and its totally owned subsidiary. The court established the criteria to determine when an agency relationship between such companies will exist so that they should be treated as one entity. Whether there will be an agency relationship will depend on such facts as who is in control, who makes the financial decision, who benefits from profits made.

Groups of companies

Sometimes the courts have been prepared to look at a group of companies as a whole and disregard the separate legal personality of each company in the group, considering it as a single legal and economic unit, carrying on a 'single' business. However, recent case law shows that the courts are now less prepared than they were formerly to do this. Nevertheless it remains possible that a parent company may be held liable for obligations of its subsidiaries as its 'shadow director' (see below, under directors). It may also be liable if it has given a contractual promise to cover the subsidiary's obligations.

Preparing to form a company

The role of the promoter

In *Emma Silver Mining Co Ltd* v *Lewis* (1879) it was said that 'a promoter is someone who is involved in giving instructions for the preparation and registration of the memorandum and articles of association; obtaining directors, issuing a prospectus, negotiating underwriting contracts or contracts for the purchase of property by the company and procuring capital. Someone who allows others to form a company and to raise the necessary capital on the understanding that he will profit from the operation is also a promoter.'

A promoter is a person who intends to form a company. Very often the promoter will intend to sell an existing business (often the promoter's own) to the company. This is what Mr Salomon did (see *Salomon* v *Salomon & Co Ltd* cited at the beginning of this chapter). The promoter is not an agent of the company, since the company has yet to be incorporated. However the promoter stands in a fiduciary relationship to the company. Whether or not someone is a promoter will be decided as a question of fact and not of law. Someone acting in a purely professional function, such as a solicitor of accountant, is not a promoter.

Duties owed by the promoter

The promoter owes to the company to be formed:

- equitable fiduciary duties;
- common law duties;
- statutory duties.

Fiduciary duties

> In *Gluckstein* v *Barnes* [1900] it was held that disclosure of profits must be made by the promoter to an independent board of directors.

> In *Salamon* v *Salomon* [1897] it was held disclosure might be made to existing or intended shareholders.

The promoter must not make any secret profit out of the promotion and must disclose any interest, which he or she has in the transactions entered into. There are two situations, which may arise:

1 A person, not yet acting as a promoter, having purchased an asset, later becomes the promoter of a company and sells that asset to the company. In this situation the promoter does not owe a fiduciary duty to the company in relation to this transaction and any profit made is legitimate. He or she must, however disclose to the company his or her interest in the asset.
2 On the other hand if a person who is already acting as promoter purchases an asset with the intention of selling it to the company, then a fiduciary duty is owed to the company and the interest in the asset must be declared. The company may claim any secret profit made on the resale of the asset to the company.

Common law duties

The promoter must abstain from deception and must exercise reasonable skill and care.

Statutory duties

The promoter must observe the formalities necessary for incorporation, as prescribed by the Companies Act and by the Financial Services Act 1986 the promoter may be responsible for the correctness of the contents of the prospectus.

Remedies where the promoter is in breach of duty

The following remedies may be sought where a promoter is found to be in breach of his or her duty.

- Rescission of the contract – Rescission means that the company returns the asset to the promoter and the purchase price will be recovered. If the promoter has sold to the company a personal asset and has not disclosed his or her interest therein, the contract may be rescinded. Rescission may occur provided the company has not given cause to believe that it intends to affirm the contract, after having found out about the non-disclosure or misrepresentation and provided rescission is still possible. Rescission may no longer be possible if the parties cannot be put back into their original position or if a third party has acquired rights.

- Recover from the promoter the difference between the purchase price and the true market value of the asset – if the promoter had acquired the asset before becoming a promoter of the company there was no fiduciary relationship at the time and any secret profit may be retained.
- Recover from the promoter the secret profit made by the promoter if he or she was already a promoter at the time when he or she acquired the asset with the intention of selling it to the company.
- Sue the promoter for damages for breach of fiduciary duties.
- Sue the promoter in the tort of negligence for breach of the duty of care.
- Sue the promoter for fraud under the tort of deceit.
- Sue for misrepresentation under the Misrepresentation Act 1967 ss.2(1) and/or 2(2).
- Those who have acquired securities in the company on the basis of inaccuracies or omissions in the listing particulars or prospectus may sue the promoter as well as officers of the company responsible for their contents under common law or under the Financial Services Act 1986.

Remuneration and expenses of the promoter

In *Re English & Colonial Produce Ltd* [1906] it was held that even if the memorandum and articles of association contained provisions for the remuneration of the promoter, the company is still not bound to pay.

A promoter is not automatically entitled to any pay from the company. He or she must have an express contract with the company.

Pre-incorporation contracts

A pre-incorporation contract is a contract entered into before the company is actually incorporated. Very often it is the promoter who will enter into such contracts.

Who is liable under a pre-incorporation contract?

In *Kelner* v *Baxter* (1866) the contract was signed: 'on behalf of . . . . The company to be incorporated'. It was held that the promoter was personally liable.

In *Newborne* v *Sensolid (Great Britain) Ltd* [1954] the contract was signed 'Leopard Newborne (London) Ltd', followed by the signature of Leopard Newborne. It was held that the promoter was not liable because a non-existent person, the company yet to be formed, cannot sign a contract.

According to the common law liability depended on how such a contract was signed, as the cases given above demonstrate. The situation is now governed by the Companies Act 1985, s. 36C:

> A contract which purports to be made by or on behalf of a company at a time when the company has not yet been formed has effect, subject to any agreement to the contrary, as one made with the person purporting to act for the company or as agent for it, and he is personally liable on the contract accordingly.

Therefore a person who enters into a pre-incorporation contract is in a vulnerable position since he or she will be personally liable, regardless of the way the contract is signed unless there is an express statement to the contrary (see statement by Lord Denning in *Phonogram Ltd* v *Lane* [1981]). The intention to shift liability away from the promoter cannot be implied.

There is a practice of creating companies without there being an immediate specific purpose for doing so. Such companies may be purchased 'off the shelf' by a business person having a need for a company. The question of liability for pre-incorporation contracts will not arise with off-the-shelf companies, since these companies already exist when the business person acquires them.

The company cannot ratify pre-incorporation contracts. After the company's formation a new contract will have to be made, and the old contract will be discharged. This procedure is called novation.

Formation of the company

In English law there are three types of company. The category into which a particular company falls depends on the mode of its incorporation:

- *The statutory company* – This type of company is formed by the promotion of a private Act of Parliament and was formerly used for public utilities. Friendly societies, building societies or insurance companies may be formed in this manner.
- *The chartered company* – This type of company is formed by Royal Charter and is rare today, unless the purpose of the company is education, a charitable or other public purpose.
- *The registered company* – This is the most common type of company for business organizations and is formed by registration under the Companies Act 1985, or earlier legislation. The relevant law governing these companies is mainly found in the Companies Act 1985 and case law.

Classification of registered companies

It may be useful while reading this section to refer back to Figure 3.1.

The unlimited company

The advantage of this type of company is that it is not required to publish its accounts and thus could be attractive to professional persons. But there is the disadvantage that the members have unlimited liability.

The limited company

A company may either be limited by guarantee or limited by shares.

In a company limited by guarantee the members have guaranteed to contribute to the assets of the company up to a specified amount, in the event of the company being wound up. Since 1980 this type of company can no longer be formed with a share capital and thus it is not suitable for commercial purposes.

A company limited by shares is the ideal business organization to overcome the disadvantages of the partnership, namely lack of separate legal personality and therefore unlimited liability of the individual partners. Here the liability of the members is limited to the amount unpaid on their shares, whereas the liability of the company itself is unlimited, to the full extent of all of its assets. However there is a price to be paid for these advantages:

- there are statutory incorporation requirements;
- there are increased legal formalities;
- accounts must be published through the Registrar of Companies;
- there are administrative expenses;
- the management is no longer in the hands of the incorporators and/or shareholders, unless they are also appointed as directors.

The company, as an artificial legal person, distinct from its members, has perpetual existence until it is dissolved. As an artificial person, a company can:

- own property;
- open a bank account;
- employ people;
- enter into contracts;
- lend and borrow money;
- sue and be sued.

The shareholders, through their shareholding, own the company, but it is most important to realize that the company itself owns all of its assets. It is of the utmost importance to business persons to be fully aware of this fact. It means, for example, that if someone who operates a supermarket as a company takes home the ingredients for a meal, without paying for them, that person, though in one sense the owner of the business would nevertheless be stealing from the company. Many company directors have had to face legal actions, and even prison sentences for not knowing and observing this distinction between their personal property and the property of the company.

The business of the company is conducted by the board of directors or other company officers and is subject to control by the shareholders.

Companies limited by shares may be either *public* or *private* companies, depending on the company's capital requirements and how it intends to raise this capital.

The public limited company

Section 1(3) of the Companies Act defines a public company as a company limited by shares (i.e. with a share capital) the memorandum of which states that it is a public company. Such a company may offer its securities, that is its shares and debentures, to the public: thus it is able to raise large amounts of capital.

A public company must have at least two shareholders, two directors, a company secretary, an auditor (see below) and a minimum share capital of £50 000 of which at least a quarter must be paid up (i.e. £12 500). Public companies are subject to stringent legislative controls regarding the maintenance of their capital.

The private limited company

A private limited company needs only one shareholder, one director, a company secretary and an auditor (unless it is defined as a 'small' company). There is no minimum capital requirement. A private limited company is prohibited from offering its securities to the public and can generate capital only through private investors. Thus the amount of capital that can be raised is limited.

This type of company is often chosen when a sole trader or a partnership needs to expand, but may also be first choice when setting up in business because of the limited liability of the shareholders and the possible tax advantages. However, on initial incorporation with very little capital the concept of limited liability is mostly illusory. When such a company wants to raise a loan from a bank its directors will usually be asked to provide a personal guarantee for this loan.

The Companies Act has introduced accountancy exemptions for private limited companies. Small companies may file abbreviated accounts and medium companies may abbreviate their profit and loss account but shareholders must be presented with a full account. The rules on capital maintenance for private companies are more relaxed. So also are the rules on pre-emption rights and on the requirements to hold formal meetings.

Single member companies

Since the Companies (Single Member Private Limited Companies) Regulations 1992, made to comply with the EC harmonization programme, it is possible to form a company with only one member. This member may also be the director. However this type of company still needs the services of one other person – to act as company secretary – because a single director may not simultaneously function as director and company secretary.

Under the Companies Act public companies may re-register as private companies and private companies may re-register as public companies.

Registration of the company

Where to register

In order to register a company a number of documents must be registered with the Registrar of Companies. The address to which this documentation has to be delivered differs according to the jurisdiction (England and Wales or Scotland) in which the company will have its registered office.

Registration fee

The normal fee is £20, but for same day registration it will be £200.

Registration procedure

The following documents have to be sent to the Registrar of Companies:

- *Companies form 10* – This requires a statement of the first director/s and company secretary/ies and intended situation of the company's registered office.
- *Companies form 12* – This requires the statutory declaration of compliance with the Companies Act regarding registration. A solicitor, a director or the company secretary, must make this declaration.
- *Companies form PUC1* – This requires a statement of capital.
- *Memorandum of Association* – The content of this document is personal to the company, but in practice will be in largely standard format. It has to cover the matters required by statute. These are mainly concerned with the relationship of the company to the outside world; such matters as the type of the company, the share capital, its division into shares and the objects of the company.
- *Articles of Association* – The Articles of Association may again be personalized for the individual company or those of Table A of the Companies Act may be adopted. The Articles have to deal with the internal organization of the company. They must cover such matters as class of shares, rights of shareholders, meetings of the company, voting rights of members, the payment of dividends and the responsibilities of the directors.

When these procedures have been satisfactorily completed the Companies Registry will issue a certificate of incorporation.

Off-the-shelf companies

If speed is of the essence, there is the option of buying a company that is already registered, but non-active. All that needs to be done is to transfer the shares to the new shareholders and advise the Registrar of Companies of the appointment of new directors and a secretary. It may be desirable to change the name of the company, its memorandum of association and its articles to suit specific needs. The advantage of off-the-shelf companies is that they eliminate the problems associated with pre-incorporation contracts.

Starting to trade

A private company may start trading immediately it has its certificate of incorporation. A public company must first obtain a trading certificate. This must be obtained within 21 days of incorporation.

The Memorandum of Association

The Companies Act, s.2 sets out the matters, which must be contained in the Memorandum. There are six compulsory clauses, they deal with:

1 name;
2 registered office;
3 objects;

4 liability;
5 capital;
6 association.

The name

The name of a private company must end with either 'Limited Company' or 'Ltd'. Public companies' names must end with 'Public Limited Company' or 'Plc'. The choice of name is otherwise wide open, provided: the name chosen is not a name already on the index of names maintained by the Registrar of Companies; is not prohibited by legislation (e.g. Red Cross); does not indicate a connection with the government; the Crown, a professional body, etc. In such instances permission must be obtained from the Secretary of State or the relevant body. A name that is too similar to one already used by another company may lead to an action for the tort of passing off, at the instance of the other company. There will be liability for 'passing off' if there is a possibility of confusing the public.

The Business Names Act 1985 requires that the company's name be printed on all company stationary, cheques, etc. and must also be prominently displayed at all business premises. The company's name may be changed by special resolution of the members.

The registered office

The registered office does not need to be the company's trading office. It could be solicitors' offices. The registered office's address must be in England, Wales or Scotland, dependent on where the company has been incorporated. It is the location at which documents can be served.

The objects of the company

The objects clause states the activities in which the company may engage, now and in the future. The purposes of the objects clause is to inform prospective shareholders, so that they may decide whether they want to invest in a company engaged in those activities. It also allows third parties intending to deal with the company to establish the contractual capacity and powers of the company.

The contractual capacity of the company was at common law limited to the extent of its objects clause and any contracts entered into beyond these objects will be void and *ultra vires* (i.e. beyond the powers of the company). Historically *ultra vires* contracts could not be ratified by the company.

The common law rule was established by case law.

In *Ashbury Railway Carriages and Iron Works* v *Richie* (1875) the company, formed to make railroad wagon and rolling stock, entered into a contract with Richie to build a railroad in Belgium. This contract was held to be *ultra vires* the company and Richie was not able to get paid for the work done.

To avoid the application of the *ultra vires* doctrine and the involvement of the courts in determining what was ancillary to the main object of the company, it became usual to draw up very detailed objects clauses and to insert independent objects clauses. Memoranda drawn up in this way stated that each clause should be interpreted as being a separate object.

Third parties dealing with the company were also liable to be caught by the 'constructive notice' doctrine. Under this doctrine, since the memorandum and articles are, through registration, made public documents, anyone dealing with the company is deemed to know their content, whether or not they have actually been read by the third party in question.

The force of the *ultra vires* rule has been greatly reduced by the need to comply with an EC directive. Changes in the British law were introduced by the Companies Act 1989, to amend the Companies Act 1985. The position is now that the company is able to adopt a new form of objects clause and operate as a 'general commercial company'. It may operate thus where the company's memorandum states that the object of the company is to carry on business as a general commercial company. Under the Companies Act 1985, s.3A the objects clause should state:

a. the object of the company is to carry on any trade or business whatsoever, and
b. the company has power to do all such things as are incidental or conducive to the carrying on of any trade or business by it.

Such clauses, since they are interpreted objectively, should however be accompanied by an additional clause stating that the directors may engage in associated activities. The advantage of this new clause is that the problem of *ultra vires* no longer arises. But, there is a danger as far as the shareholders are concerned: the directors may now effectively engage the company in any activity they choose.

Alteration of the objects clause

Under the Companies Act, s.4 a company may, by special resolution, freely change its objects clause. Section 5 of the Act allows holders of at least 15 per cent of shares, or a class of shares, to apply to the court, within 21 days from the resolution, asking the court to exercise its power to cancel, amend or confirm the alteration.

Contractual capacity of the company

Section 35 of the Act does not abolish the *ultra vires* doctrine, but it is now largely ineffective *vis-à-vis* third parties. Neither the company nor a third party can question the validity of a contract entered into by the company on the ground that the contract is beyond it objects clause.

A shareholder may, once he or she is aware of intended *ultra vires* activities by the company, apply to the court for an injunction to stop the company from pursuing such activity, provided the company is not yet under any legal obligation in relation to these activities. In practice, shareholders normally become aware of such plans only after they have been initiated and then an injunction is no longer available.

However, the directors of a company have a statutory duty to observe the limitations imposed upon them by the company's constitution, that is the memorandum and/or the articles. Should they act in disregard of these limitations they become personally liable for any losses the company may suffer. The shareholders may now, by special resolution, ratify such a contract and by a second special resolution absolve the directors from any liability.

Limitation of liability

The memorandum must state that the liability of the shareholder is limited; in a company limited by guarantee the extent of the guarantee must be stated.

Capital

The capital clause states the amount of capital the company is authorized to issue. In practice this may differ from the issued share capital: the company may not wish to issue all the capital it is authorized to issue. The clause states the number of shares that may be issued and the par value (i.e. nominal value) of each share, but not the type or class of shares. Share capital in English companies may now be in a foreign currency.

Association

The association clause states that the subscribers (that is the persons signing the document) wish to incorporate and each subscriber must take at least one share.

Articles of Association

A company limited by shares may register articles regulating the internal affairs of the company. If it fails to do this Table A of the Companies Act will apply. It is advisable that the articles be composed according to the company's own needs. By s.9 of the Act the articles may be changed by special resolution. There are, however, some restrictions on making such changes.

- *At common law* – the change must be bona fide and for the benefit of the company as a whole.

  In *Greenhalgh* v *Ardene Cinemas Ltd* [1951] this was held to mean 'not the company as a commercial entity distinct from its corporators, but the corporators as a general body'.

- *By interpretation of the statute* – while s.9 creates a statutory right, which may never be taken away, however, weighted voting rights (vote weighted according to shareholding) may render a change ineffective. Weighting is, according to case law, permissible. Since it does not categorically take away the right, it simply renders it impossible to be exercised.

Can changing the articles result in a breach of contract?

Whether changing the articles leads to breach of contract depends on how the original contractual right was created. A contract based solely on the articles is, by its very nature, different from an ordinary contract and is changeable without the permission of the individual concerned. Statute allows for such a change. Where rights are only conferred by the articles, a change in the articles does not result in liability for breach of contract. However, if there is also a separate contract, a change of the articles may result in a breach of that separate contract.

The result is that any person taking up a position as an officer of a company, based merely on the articles needs to realize that the appointment may be terminated or altered at any time without a right to compensation. Therefore an appointment to office based on the articles should be supported by a separate contract.

Legal effect of the Memorandum and the Articles

Section 14 of the Companies Act provides that the memorandum and the articles, once registered, constitute a contract between each member and the company and the members between themselves. Members can only enforce this contract in their capacity as members and not as outsiders, such as in a professional capacity. Damages for breach of contract are not recoverable since this would result in a reduction of the company's capital.

The management of the company

Who manages the company?

In *John Shaw & Sons (Salford) Ltd* v *Shaw* [1935] GREER LJ said 'A company is an entity distinct alike from its shareholders and its directors. Some of its powers may, according to its articles, be exercised by the directors, certain other powers may be reserved for the shareholders in general meeting. If powers of management are vested in the directors, they and they alone can exercise these powers. The only way in which the general body of the shareholders can control the exercise of the powers vested by the articles in the directors is by altering the articles, or, if opportunity arises under the articles, by refusing to re-elect the directors of whose actions they disapprove. They cannot themselves usurp the powers which by the articles are vested in the directors any more than the directors can usurp the powers vested by the articles in the general body of shareholders.'

The company, being an artificial legal person, needs humans to act on its behalf, that is the directors and shareholders. The distribution of powers between them, subject to the provisions of the Companies Act, depends on the articles of association. As the shareholders own the company they may run it. Since this is impracticable Article 70 of Table A allows the shareholders to delegate the powers of management to the board of directors collectively. By Article 72, the directors may in turn delegate powers to a 'managing director' who executes the instructions of the board. The shareholders may however, by special resolution, influence the directors' course of action.

The Companies Act and the Insolvency Act have preserved for the shareholders certain residual rights, exercisable only by the shareholders. These are to:

- alter the Memorandum of Association;
- alter the Articles of Association;
- alter the share capital;

- remove directors;
- appoint and remove auditors;
- put the company into liquidation;

In addition, the following restrictions are placed on directors of the company:

- director's powers to allot shares must be authorized by ordinary resolution or the articles;
- directors must observe pre-emption rights, but this is relaxed in the case of private companies.

By Table A of the Companies Act shareholders have powers to:

- fix rights attached to new issues of shares;
- affect a variation of these rights;
- appoint directors;
- declare dividends within the percentage recommended by the directors;
- capitalize profits and reserves.

Powers exercisable concurrently by the directors and shareholders unless kept exclusively in the domain of the directors are:

- appoint additional directors;
- fill casual vacancies on the board of directors;
- fix remuneration of the managing director.

If the powers are concurrent, a members' resolution will prevail over the directors' own decision.

The power to commence litigation on behalf of the company lies with the directors. Only if the directors make no decision may the shareholders decide otherwise.

The directors

Who is a director?

In this Act 'director' includes any person occupying the position of director, by whatever name called (Companies Act s.741(1)).

In relation to a company, 'shadow director' means a person in accordance with whose directions or instructions the directors of the company are accustomed to act (Companies Act s.741(2)).

Whether someone is a director is a question of fact and not of law. A public company must have at least two directors and a private company at least one.

Appointment of directors

First directors are named in the articles and in the Memorandum; subsequent directors are appointed by ordinary resolution at the annual general meeting. Directors of a public company must be voted on individually unless previously otherwise agreed: otherwise the appointment will be void. Even if the procedure of appointment has been faulty, the act of the directors concerned are valid.

The general rule that directors cannot be appointed over the age of 70 can be easily bypassed by the available exceptions.

To protect a company both against directors abusing their privileged and advantageous position to their own advantage, and from possible very high compensation payments, the Companies Act has established protective measures and disclosure requirements.

Duration of directors' appointments

If a director's service contract is for more than 5 years, without any provision for termination by notice, for any reason, or only under special circumstances, approval must be obtained from the shareholders in general meeting. In the absence of such approval, the contract is still valid but is deemed to contain a clause entitling the company to terminate on reasonable notice. Directors' service contracts are open for inspection by the shareholders.

Remuneration of directors

Directors, as managers of the company, are not automatically entitled to remuneration, unless this is specified in the articles. However, someone appointed 'managing director' is a servant of the company and remunerated according to the contract of service.

Directors may sometimes be required to acquire shares in their companies within a specified time of their appointment. Any shareholdings by the directors in the company must be disclosed.

Vacation of office

Directors normally retire each year by rotation but are eligible for re-election.

Under the Companies Act ss.303 and 304 directors may be removed from office by the shareholders by ordinary resolution before their term of office has expired even if the articles provide otherwise. But the directors must be given 28 days' notice of such an intended resolution and they are entitled to be heard on the resolution at the meeting. A director dismissed under this section is nevertheless entitled to compensation. Since this may be rather costly to the company the exercise of this right needs careful consideration. This statutory right under s.303 may never be excluded but may become ineffective by weighted voting rights.

The Companies Act contains provisions to protect the assets of the company from being stripped by unscrupulous directors. Should directors intend to buy from or sell to the company any personal assets the transaction, if over a prescribed value, needs approval by the shareholders. Also, loans to directors by the company are only permissible in limited circumstances, unless the company is a bank. Furthermore, directors are required to disclose to the company, which could be via the board of directors, any personal interest they have in any contract that the company intends to enter into and they are not entitled to vote on this contract.

In addition to the shareholders' powers to dismiss directors, disqualification from holding the office of director may be by order of the court.

Company Directors Disqualification Act 1986

In *Re Sevenoakes Stationers (Retail) Ltd* [1991] Ch 164 a director, who was a chartered accountant, had honestly, but negligently failed to keep proper accounts and file the accounts of companies under his control and had created debts for the companies knowing that they were experiencing financial difficulties and was disqualified for 5 years for being 'unfit' as director.

Persons may be disqualified from being involved or concerned in the management of companies for two categories of conduct.

- *Disqualification for general misconduct* – This may be by:
  - conviction for indictable offences in connection with the promotion, formation or liquidation of companies and receivership or management of the company's property; persistent breaches of companies legislation (failing to file the required documents with the registrar of companies);
  - fraud under s.458 of the Companies Act; and
  - summary conviction for failing to comply with companies legislation.
- *Disqualification by reason of unfitness to hold office of director* – This applies to persons who have been directors or shadow directors of a company which has at any time become insolvent and their conduct was such as to make them unfit to be directors and to persons who have acted as directors while being undischarged bankrupts.

The maximum time for disqualification is 15 years.

Directors' duties

To whom are the duties owed?

Directors, besides being agents of the company, owe three types of duties. These duties are owed to the company itself and not to the shareholders unless take-over negotiations are in progress. No duty is owed to creditors of the company as long as the company has good financial standing. Once monetary difficulties arise creditors as well are owed a duty under the Insolvency Act. The duty owed to employees imposed by the Companies Act is merely to have regard to their interests but cannot be enforced by the employees.

Directors, when passing a vote as directors, must do so in the interest of the company; but when they vote as shareholders they may vote in their own interests.

Types of duties owed

Common law duties of care and skill

The standard of care required in practice was established in *Re City Equitable Fire Insurance Co Ltd* [1925]. It was held that a director has no need to exhibit in the performance of his or her duties a greater degree of skill than may reasonably be expected from a person of his or her knowledge and experience. He or she is not bound to give continuous attention to the affairs of the company, nor bound to attend all board meetings. In the case of duties that may properly be left to some other official, a director is, in the absence of grounds of suspicion, justified in trusting that official to perform such duties honestly. Failure to exercise these duties will result in liability for negligence.

Since there is no qualification or expertise required to become a director no professional standard exists. The courts apply a subjective test and a person performing at his or her best, as he or she honestly believes, is normally not in breach. Recent case law indicates a more stringent attitude of the courts, particularly in respect of executive directors. Persons with professional qualifications, non-executive directors included, will now have to display a higher standard and their own knowledge and expertise may be taken into account. The degree of standard of care required was also considerably raised by s. 214, IA relating to wrongful trading by directors of companies in insolvent liquidation. The test, both subjective and objective, is:

> what conclusions would have been drawn and what steps would have been taken by a reasonably diligent person, with the general knowledge, skill and experience that may reasonably be expected of a person carrying out the same functions as by that director with the general knowledge, skill and experience of that director (see *Norman* v *Theodore Goddard* [1991]).

In recent case law this test has been accepted as being the general standard of care required.

The company may, by ordinary resolution, ratify a breach of duty and the director, in his or her position as a shareholder, may thus ratify his or her own breach. By the Companies Act s. 310, a company may indemnify and insure directors against any liability to the company for negligence, default, breach of duty and breach of trust, including the cost of criminal and civil proceedings if they are successfully defended.

The court may relieve a director from liability if, in all the circumstances, he or she has acted honestly and reasonably. (s.727)

Fiduciary duties

> In *Regal (Hastings) Ltd* v *Gulliver* [1942] 1 AC 554 a company which owned a cinema intended to form a subsidiary to acquire two more cinemas with the intention to sell the three cinemas. Since the company financially was not in a position to provide all the capital, the directors and friends subscribed for shares and the cinemas were bought. Then the two companies were sold at a profit. The former directors were sued by the new shareholders for the profits made on the sale of their shares because they had obtained them from an opportunity coming to them as directors. It was immaterial that the company itself had lost nothing since it had been unable to make the investment itself.

Directors have the following fiduciary duties:

- *To act in good faith in the interest of the company* – directors are not trustees of the company since the assets of the company are not vested in them. But they do stand in a fiduciary position to the company. As such, directors must act in good faith in the interest of the company and not of individual shareholders. Again a subjective test is applied and a breach is not ratifiable.

- *Not to put themselves into a situation of conflict of interest* – this rule, again, is to prevent directors from taking advantage of their position for their own benefit, in particular taking for themselves commercial opportunities open to the company.

A director who takes from his or her former company, after resignation a 'maturing opportunity', even if the company would not have been able to secure that opportunity for itself and has not suffered any loss, is nevertheless accountable to the company for any profits made. While such a breach may be ratified, English law is not clear on the position of a director when the company has actually sanctioned that he or she may take up an opportunity that it does not want or cannot afford. It is still undecided whether that director is in breach of his or her fiduciary duty.

Directors may not profit from contracts entered into with their companies unless that interest is disclosed. Breach of this duty does not require fraud or dishonesty. The requirement to disclose to the company in general meeting has been relaxed. It is now permissible, subject to the articles, that disclosure is made to the board of directors.

In addition, there are the following further fiduciary duties:

- *Not to use their power for an improper purpose* – directors who use their fiduciary powers for purposes other than those for which they were given will exceed their authority and are liable accordingly, even if these powers are used in the interest of the company. Again an objective test is applied.

  In *Howard Smith Ltd* v *Ampol Petroleum Ltd* [1974] the directors of a company involved in a hostile take-over and also needing additional capital issued new shares, thereby reducing the majority to minority shareholders and providing more funds. This was an improper use of power because the main purpose was to decrease the majority shareholding and shares may only be issued to satisfy the need for capital.

  Breach of this duty is ratifiable.
- *Not to fetter their discretion* – directors must at all times be free to make decisions and vote as they think is best. They may not enter voting agreements.

Statutory duties

Conflicts of interest may also arise when directors enter into contracts with their companies. A number of statutory provisions protect the company against the self-interest of the directors.

- *Companies Act 1985.* Compensation for loss of office must not be net of tax. Compensation for loss of office due to the company being wound up or in a take-over (but not bona fide payments as damages for breach of contract); substantial property transactions with the company all need approval. The power to grant loans to directors is severely restricted.
- *Insolvency Act 1986, ss.213 and 214.* Fraudulent and wrongful trading. When a company is in financial difficulties – and eventually goes into insolvent liquidation – the directors' prior conduct is subject to scrutiny by the liquidator.
- *Criminal Justice Act 1993.* This Act, applicable only to listed companies, concerns insider dealing. It replaces previous legislation and imposes criminal liability.

Directors may not use 'inside information' for their own benefit or pass it on to others, since this could destroy confidence in the stock market and be greatly disadvantageous to shareholders.

- The Department of Trade and Industry (DTI) has great powers of investigation.
- *Cadbury Code.* This applies only to listed companies and lays down guidelines for the allocation of power on the board of directors. It provides:

> There should be a clearly accepted division of responsibilities at the head of a company, which will ensure a balance of powers and authority, such that no one individual has unfettered power of decision. Where the chairman is also chief executive, it is essential that there should be a strong and independent element on the board, with a recognised senior member.

Company secretary

Every company must have a company secretary. A sole director may not also be the company secretary.

The directors usually appoint the secretary. They may also fix his or her term of office. The company secretary is an employee of the company. Recent case law has elevated him or her to the position of officer of the company and has awarded him or her authority to enter into contracts on the company's behalf in administrative matters. Any other powers must be delegated to him or her. The company secretary's main function is to keep minutes of meetings and to submit the required documents to the registrar of companies. The secretary of a public company must have the required qualifications for office, whereas anyone can be the secretary of a private company.

The shareholders

How does one become a shareholder?

- by subscribing for the original issue of shares;
- by acquiring shares at a later stage;
- by transfer;
- as personal representative of a deceased member;
- by operation of law;
- by reconstruction of the company.

Meetings of shareholders

There are three types of meetings:

1 *Annual General Meetings* (AGM) 21 days' notice in writing;
2 *Extraordinary General Meeting* (EGM) 14 days' notice in writing, 21 days for special resolutions, 28 days for dismissing directors;
3 *Class Meetings.*

The Companies Act, the Memorandum and the Articles govern the convening, conduct of, voting at and quorum for meetings.

All companies must hold AGMs with no more than 15 months intervals between them. If AGMs are not called any member may apply to the DTI which may give the necessary direction. Private companies may elect to forgo the holding of AGMs. The directors may also call EGMs. Shareholders with the required voting rights may request to call an EGM which must then be called by the directors within the prescribed time.

Types of resolutions

There are three types of resolutions which may come before shareholders' meetings, each requiring a particular majority before it can be passed: (the term 'majority' is with respect to those members present and voting)
1 ordinary – passed by simple majority;
2 extraordinary – passed by $\frac{3}{4}$ majority
3 special – passed by $\frac{3}{4}$ majority on 21 days' notice.

Voting

Voting may be by show of hands of those present and does not reflect the true shareholding; one hand–one vote. It may also be by poll, either in person or by proxy, where the number of votes reflects the number of shares held; one share–one vote.

Quorum

The required quorum for shareholders' or directors' meetings is usually two but may be fixed by the articles. In exceptional circumstances a quorum of one has been approved by the courts. In single member companies it is obviously only one.

Minutes and registers

Minutes must be kept for directors' and shareholders' meetings. This requirement is particularly noteworthy for single member companies where the same requirement applies. A single shareholder/director may assume that, since he or she is holding a meeting with him- or herself, as he knows everything that is happening it need not be recorded. But keeping proper minutes may protect the single member/director from being accused of improper conduct or improperly dealing with the company's assets.

By statute a company is required to keep certain registers at its registered office which are open to inspection such as: register of shareholders, register of substantial shareholding, register of charges.

Shareholders' remedies for maladministration

As has been shown, directors owe a number of duties to the company and shareholders may vote in their own interest. But what can shareholders, whether the majority, minority or individuals do when these duties are not observed or when the majority exercise their voting rights to the detriment of the minority?

The Common Law

> In *Foss* v *Harbottle* (1843) it was held that the company is the only proper litigant, since the directors' duties are owed only to the company, and that the majority rule prevails, thereby reinforcing the principle of the separate legal personality of the company.

Another reason for this decision was to prevent a multitude of legal actions by individual shareholders and to avoid court orders from becoming ineffective since the majority, in most cases, could ratify the action complained of.

Common law exceptions

There are three exceptions to this general rule:

1 A shareholder may bring a *personal* action when his personal rights, as conferred by the Companies Act or by the constitution of the company, are infringed.
2 A shareholder may bring a *representative* action. Here a shareholder sues on behalf of himself and other shareholders.
3 A shareholder may bring a *derivative* action. Here the right to sue for 'fraud on the minority' is derived from the right of the company against those in control.

It is self-evident that those who have perpetrated fraud on the minority are not going to sue themselves in the name of the company.

To be liable for 'fraud on the minority' more than negligence is required. The shareholder/s must show that:

● what was taken for themselves actually belonged to the company. This would apply to personally buying assets from the company or selling personal assets to the company at a profit;
● that the benefit passed to those against whom the claim is made;
● those who profited by this transaction were those in control of the company.

Inequitable use of majority power

Case law has established that use of majority voting power to the disadvantage of the minority is a question of equitable principles and does not need to be considered as an exception to the rule in *Foss* v *Harbottle*. It is usually difficult for minority shareholders to establish an exception to the general common law rule. In most cases it is impossible to prove *locus standi*.

Statutory exceptions

The Companies Act 1985, s.459 provides a remedy, upon successful petition to the court, to shareholders, personal representatives and holders of shares by operation of law for 'unfairly prejudicial' conduct and omissions, actual or proposed, towards them in their capacity as shareholders. The plaintiff's own conduct, even if open to criticism, does not entail disqualification from seeking a remedy under this section.

If the court is satisfied that there was 'unfair prejudice' an order may be made to

● regulate the conduct of the company;

- restrain the doing or continuing of certain acts;
- authorize civil proceedings in the name of the company;
- order the majority to buy out the minority (proper valuation of the shares may prove difficult);
- forbid the alteration of the memorandum or articles without court authorization.

The Insolvency Act 1986, s.122, provides a rather drastic remedy. It allows the court, upon application by the disgruntled shareholder, to make an order that the company should be wound-up if it is 'just and equitable' to do so. To be granted this remedy the shareholder's own conduct must not be open to criticism. This remedy is mainly sought in the case of small companies – quasi-partnerships, where all communication and confidence have broken down, expectations to participate in the management are dashed or severe restrictions on the transfer of shares are imposed.

The company and its obligations

Contract

The company's contractual capacity

Section 35 of the Companies Act has removed 'lack of corporate capacity' as a ground for invalidating the company's contracts thereby making the *ultra vires* rule mostly ineffective for outsiders. But it still operates internally.

The directors' contractual capacity

> In favour of a person dealing with a company in good faith the power of the board of directors to bind the company, or authorise others to do so, shall be deemed free of any limitations under the company's constitution (Companies Act s.35A).

Since the company is an artificial legal person it can only operate by giving authority to human persons, usually the board of directors, to act as agents on its behalf. Thus the law of agency becomes applicable.

The authority of the directors derives from the constitution of the company (usually Article 70) and the shareholders. The limitations under the constitution include limitations deriving from resolutions of the company and from agreements between the members of the company or any class of shareholders. Here as well, the shareholders may stop unauthorized acts by injunction, provided no legal obligations have as yet arisen or they may ratify the activity. Because of the new s.35 of the Companies Act, normally a third party is no longer prevented from enforcing a contract with the company. He or she may, however, suffer because of the lack of capacity of the company's agents.

In order to enforce a contract where lack of authority is claimed the third party will have to prove:

- 'dealing' with the company – dealing now covers commercial as well as charitable acts, – and
- having acted in 'good faith' – notice of any limitations on the directors' authority does not by itself constitute 'bad faith'. It seems that actual knowledge and

understanding of the contents is required. Nevertheless the courts may argue that the third party should have been more alert.

Where a third party has acted in good faith he or she may assume that the board of directors is free from any limitations to act and to confer authority on others. The question then remains: did the other act within the authority conferred?

Types of authority of an agent

- *Actual authority* is authority specifically given by the board of directors to either an individual director or some other company officer.
- *Implied authority* may derive from the actual authority. It may also arise from the conduct of the parties or from the circumstances of the case.
- *Apparent authority* may arise where there is no actual authority. (Apparent and implied authority are not mutually exclusive.)

The third party has to prove that:

- a representation of the agent's authority was made to him or her – the representation is usually by conduct such as allowing someone to act in a particular way;
- the representation was made by someone with actual authority, such as the board of directors;
- reliance on that representation.

The third party will not be able to establish apparent authority if he or she knew or had reasons to believe that the agent of the company had no authority.

The indoor-management rule

In *Royal British Bank* v *Turquand* (1856) the Bank made a loan to a company in the course of winding-up. By a bond, signed by two directors, the company agreed to repay the loan. According to the company's articles such loans had to be authorized by the company in general meeting but no such resolution had taken place. It was held that the company had to repay the loan because the bank was entitled to assume that the authorizing resolution had taken place. There was no need to verify if such a resolution had taken place.

An outsider is entitled to assume that internal procedural requirements have taken place. This rule applies to a procedurally defective appointment of directors, but does not apply if no appointment at all has taken place. (Under s.285, acts of directors with a defective appointment are still valid.)

The *Turquand* Rule does not apply if the third party:

- knows of the failure to comply;
- is aware of facts which would cause a reasonable man to investigate and discover the non-compliance;
- under the circumstances, should have investigated filed documents, thereby discovering the non-compliance.

In addition the Turquand Rule does not apply to forgeries.

If the company is contracting with its own directors, persons connected with its directors or companies in which its directors have an interest, the company may avoid these contracts where the board has exceeded its powers as given in the company's constitution, when entering into contracts with any of the above mentioned parties (s.322).

Third parties, who have not acted in good faith, and thus not satisfying s.35A, will be bound by their transactions.

The capital of the company

A company can raise capital in two ways:

1 *Share capital* – i.e. by issuing shares, or
2 *Loan capital* – either short-term (e.g. obtaining overdrafts or other credit) or long-term (debentures).

Share capital

What is a share?

In *Borland's Trustee* v *Steel Bros. & Co Ltd* [1901] it was held that: 'A share is the interest of a shareholder in the company measured by a sum of money, for the purpose of liability in the company in the first place, and of interest in the second, but also consisting of a series of mutual covenants entered into by all the shareholders inter se.'

Shares are transferable to another person. The transfer of shares is regulated by the articles and may be restricted in private companies. Shares of public companies are usually freely transferable. Companies must issue a share certificate and maintain a register of shareholders.

Classes of shares

Companies may have one or several classes of shares with different rights attached to each class:

- *Ordinary shares* or equity shares usually confer one vote per share. Entitlement to a variable dividend arises only after it is declared by the directors. In a winding-up these shareholders are entitled to the remaining assets of the company, after all claims by creditors and preference shareholders are met. There may also be ordinary non-voting shares.
- *Preference shares* have a fixed dividend to be paid when declared, before the ordinary shareholders, and may grant preferential claims to any surplus capital on a winding-up.

The class rights may be varied according to the company's own internal procedures and the requirements of the Companies Act.

Issuing shares

Section 80 provides that directors may issue shares only if they are authorized to do so by the articles or by ordinary resolution of the shareholders. Private companies may give this authority by elective resolution. An allotment of shares without the proper authority is still valid but the directors are liable to a fine.

Section 89 creates pre-emption rights. A new issue of equity shares must first be offered to the existing shareholders in proportion to their shareholding. Private companies may vary or permanently dispense with pre-emption requirements but public companies may only vary them. An allotment in breach of pre-emption rights is still valid. Shareholders who have suffered a loss as a consequence may sue the company and the officer/s responsible for the loss suffered.

Payment for shares

To prevent watering-down of the company's capital, shares may not be issued at a discount. At least the nominal value of the shares must be paid. Shares issued at a discount are still valid but the shareholder is liable to the company for the discount. A company does not have to demand payment in full; it may choose to request payment in stages at a later time. It is permissible for companies to accept non-cash consideration, including goodwill and know-how. Private companies may accept as payment an undertaking to work or perform services for the company. Even if the actual value is not that of the nominal value of the shares the courts will not intervene provided it is not fraudulent. For public companies the rules are much stricter. Any non-cash consideration must be independently valued by an expert, within 6 months prior to allotment (ss.99–115).

Any share premiums (i.e. difference between the price paid and the nominal value) must be paid at the time of the allotment and must be paid into a share premium account. It is treated as capital. The company may use the share premium to issue bonus shares, pay preliminary expenses or expenses on issues of shares or on redemption of debentures (s.130).

Capital maintenance

The company's capital, being security for creditors, must be preserved. Legislation therefore provides a number of rules for the protection of this capital with some exceptions for its reduction or the purchase by the company of its own shares (ss.135–181).

Reduction of capital

A company may, with the authority of the court, reduce its share capital if it is authorized to do so by the articles and a special resolution. The court will give its approval if the reduction is not prejudicial to the company's creditors and fair to its shareholders. The Registrar of Companies must be notified of such a reduction.

The reduction may be effected in three ways:

1 extinguishing or reducing liability on partly paid shares;
2 cancelling paid-up share capital which has been lost or is not represented by available assets;
3 paying off part of the paid-up share capital out of surplus assets.

Redeemable shares

If the company requires capital for a specified time only then it may issue redeemable shares, with the intention of buying them back later.

The company can only issue redeemable shares if it is authorized to do so by its articles, it also holds non-redeemable shares, if the shares are fully paid-up and redeemed in cash, and the terms of redemption provide for payment on redemption. The date for redemption must now be fixed before the issue. The financing of redeemable shares may be out of either distributable profits or proceeds of a new issue of shares made for that purpose. However, private companies may redeem partially out of capital. Any premium payable on redemption must be paid out of distributable profits. After redemption the shares are treated as cancelled. The power of private companies to redeem out of capital must be contained in the articles and a special resolution must have been passed. In order to exercise the power to redeem out of capital the directors must make a statutory declaration that the company will be able to pay its debts and carry on business for at least one more year. Any member or creditor may object to the court against payments out of capital within 5 weeks of the resolution and any objections must be notified to the registrar. The court may cancel or confirm the resolution.

Purchase of the company's own shares

Generally, a company cannot purchase its own shares but it may wish to do so in certain circumstances where the Companies Act provides an exception to the general rule. The Companies Act distinguishes between the types of purchase and not the types of shares.

A company may make a *market purchase*. This normally applies only to listed shares and is a purchase on a recognized investment exchange. Here the vendor of shares and the purchase price are not known. Authority for this purchase must be given by ordinary resolution and must specify the number of shares to be purchased, the minimum and maximum purchase price and the date by which this authority expires. The authority may be varied, revoked or renewed. Payment for the shares must be made out of distributable profits and the Registrar must be informed of such a purchase.

The alternative is an *off-market purchase*. Here shares are purchased otherwise than on a recognized stock exchange or on a recognized stock exchange but not subject to that exchange's marketing arrangements. The vendor and the price of the shares are known. The company will have a contract with the vendor. The purchase and the terms of the contract must be authorized by special resolution. The authorization may be revoked or varied.

A written contract must be available for inspection by the shareholders and the contract must disclose the vendor's name and purchase price. The company may also enter into 'contingent' contract to be executed at a later date. If for some reason the company is not in a position to honour its contract there is no liability to pay damages since that would result in a reduction of share capital. Specific performance may be available.

Financial assistance for purchase of own shares

It is a criminal offence for a company and any officer of it, to give financial assistance, either directly or indirectly, either before or after, for the acquisition of its own shares. Financial assistance includes gifts, guarantees, securities, loans that would reduce the net assets of the company. But there are exceptions to this rule. Financial assistance by the company, either before or after the acquisition, is permissible:

- whether or not its principal purpose was for the acquisition of the shares, provided it was for an incidental part of some larger purpose of the company and was given in good faith in the interest of the company;
- when a company lends money in the ordinary course of its business;
- when it falls into some other exceptions.

The 'principal purpose' requirement will be assessed as a question of fact. Case law indicates that the courts do not freely accept this as a defence. However, this provision will most likely allow management buy-outs by employees, but not by directors.

Private companies may provide financial assistance for the acquisition of their own shares, provided this does not reduce the net assets of the company or is made out of distributable profits.

Dividends

Since dividends are a distribution of the company's profits they may only be paid out of distributable profits and not out of capital. Anyone receiving an unlawful distribution is liable to repay it to the company. The right to a dividend arises only if and when declared by the directors.

Loan capital

The second principal method for a company to raise capital is via loan capital. Trading companies have an implied power to borrow for the purposes of the business and give a security for the loan.

Debentures

These are loans creating a right against the company. The document evidencing the loan is called a debenture. It stipulates the terms of the loan. A debenture holder becomes a 'secured creditor', having rights over 'unsecured creditors' in the event of the company's liquidation.

Charges

A charge is the security for the loan and may be over the company's fixed or permanent assets (i.e. buildings) or floating or changing assets (i.e. stock in trade).

Fixed charges may be legal or equitable, floating charges are only equitable. The company may not dispose of assets that are subject to a fixed charge without the lender's consent. The company may however, without the lender's consent, deal with the asset under a floating charge in the ordinary course of its business. A floating charge can be disadvantageous for a lender: since the asset under it is a changing asset, so is its value. The lender may also lose his or her right as secured creditor over preferred debts or if the charge has been registered in contravention of the Insolvency Act, s.245. Fixed charges normally have priority when made over the same asset as floating charges, even if created later. Therefore protective clauses may be incorporated into floating charges giving them priority over later created charges. Such clauses are only valid if the later chargee is actually aware of them.

Crystallization of floating charges

Crystallization occurs when the charge ceases 'to float' over the class of assets under it and it becomes fixed over the assets. Only then is it possible precisely to ascertain the value of the assets charged. In certain circumstances crystallization occurs automatically. It may also occur upon events specified in the debenture.

Registration of charges

Section 396 contains a list of registerable charges. A charge must be registered, either by the company or the lender, with the registrar within 21 days of its creation, or it will become void against the liquidator, but the indebtedness of the borrower remains and the lender becomes an 'unsecured creditor'.

Information required for registration of a charge

The following information must be provided: the date of creation of the charge, the amount secured, short particulars of the property charged, the name of the chargee. Upon registration a certificate of registration will be issued. This is conclusive evidence that the formalities for registration have been observed.

The court may allow registration out of time or a rectification of the particulars given, if the error was 'accidental or inadvertent or not prejudicial to the position of creditors and shareholders or that it is just and equitable to do so'.

Insolvency and liquidation

A company may be dissolved either because it is in severe financial difficulties and no longer able to pay its debts or because the shareholders are no longer interested in it.

Inability to pay debts

A company is deemed to be unable to pay its debts:

> if a creditor owed a sum exceeding £750 has served on the company a written demand in the prescribed form at the company's registered office and the company has not paid the sum for three weeks (Insolvency Act 1986 s.123).

The person dealing with the affairs of a company in financial decline must be a qualified 'insolvency practitioner' such as a solicitor or accountant. There are several ways of dealing with a company that is in financial difficulties. Besides liquidation alternative methods to liquidation were introduced by the Insolvency Act 1986 with the aim of saving the company:

- receivership;
- voluntary arrangements;
- administration orders.

Receivership

In the event of a company being unable to honour its obligations under a debenture or if the assets under the charge are in jeopardy, a receiver may be appointed by the chargee or the court. The function of the receiver is to realize the assets charged to satisfy the creditors' claim. The receiver's duty is to the chargee and not to the company. In case of a floating charge over the whole undertaking of the company the receiver is an administrative receiver (i.e. receiver and manager) and has wide powers of management so that he or she may keep or sell the company as a going concern. Even after a receiver has been appointed it is still possible to petition for a winding-up petition. The receiver remains in charge of the assets in his or her care. Once his or her work is finished the liquidator will take over (Insolvency Act 1986, ss.28–49). Receivership often results in liquidation of the company.

Voluntary arrangements

Voluntary arrangements are informal compromises, without the involvement of the court, between the company's creditors and the company with the aim of saving the company. A proposal for voluntary arrangements may be made by either the directors of the company, the liquidator or administrator. A nominee is appointed to assess the merits of the scheme proposed. If he or she considers the scheme practicable he or she applies to the court for preliminary approval. Once the proposal is approved by a meeting of creditors and members, the scheme is binding on the company and all the creditors. The decision of the meetings may be challenged within 28 days. The scheme is put into effect by a supervisor who may be the same as the nominee. A considerable disadvantage of such arrangements is that they are not binding on secured or preferential creditors. However, nevertheless, these schemes have gained considerable popularity (Insolvency Act 1986 ss.1–7).

Administration orders

The purpose of administration orders is not to enforce a security but to facilitate a moratorium, binding on all the creditors, in respect of the debts of a company in financial difficulties.

The court may make an administration order upon application of the company, its directors, its creditors or all or any of them if it is satisfied that the company is likely to become unable to pay its debts. The aim of such an order could be: to save the company as a going concern; to approve a voluntary arrangement; to sanction a scheme of arrangement under s.425 (see Chapter 13 on mergers and take-overs); or a more advantageous realization of the company's assets than would be effected by a winding-up. Such orders will not be made once the company has gone into liquidation, if the company is an insurance company or an administrative receiver has been appointed and a debenture holder does not consent. Between a presentation of application and the making of such an order, the company cannot be wound up by resolution or order, no securities may be enforced without the approval of the court and no other proceedings may be commenced or continued without the sanction of the court. The administrator has wide powers of management. Once the administrator has fulfilled his or her function and the company is still a going concern, the directors of the company will take over. Alternatively, the administrator will be released when liquidation is the only possibility (Insolvency Act 1986 ss.8–7). It appears that this procedure enjoys a certain popularity.

Liquidation and dissolution

During liquidation or winding-up, the directors' powers are at an end. The liquidator, in the name of the company, concludes the company's business, realizes its assets and distributes the proceeds amongst the creditors and, in case of any surplus, the shareholders. A company may be wound up either voluntarily by the shareholders or creditors or compulsorily by an order of the court (162, Insolvency Act 1986 ss.73–162).

A *members' voluntary winding-up* can take place only if the company is still solvent, a statutory declaration to that effect has been made by the directors and upon a special resolution or extraordinary resolution. The liquidator is appointed by the members.

A *creditors' voluntary winding-up* occurs when the liquidator is of the opinion that the company is unable to pay its debts in full. A creditors' meeting is called where they may nominate a liquidator and a liquidation committee.

A *compulsory winding-up* is effected by an order of the court on petition by the company, the directors, any creditor/s, contributory, the official receiver, Secretary of State, together or separately. On a winding-up order all actions with or against the company are stayed.

Dissolution of the company

Three months after the registrar of companies has been informed of the completed winding-up of the company and duly registered this, the company will be dissolved.

PROGRESS TEST

1 What types of business organizations are available in English law and what are their main distinguishing features?
2 By what means is a company limited by shares created and what are the consequences of incorporation?
3 ABC Limited was registered to carry on the business of manufacturing electric typewriters. The Board of Directors decided to change its activity to making computers. Mr Smart, one of the directors, entered into a contract with X Ltd to purchase 5000 mini-tower cases. Can X Ltd enforce this contract?
4 Mr Stewart is offered the position of director in Grow Ltd. Before he accepts he wants to know his legal position as a director. Advise him.
5 What are the options open to a company in financial difficulties?
6 Is a registered company free to use its capital as it pleases?

4 Civil liability of business organizations 1: Contract

Patterson Simmons

WHAT IS AN ENGLISH CONTRACT?

In *Re Cory, Kinnaird* v *Cory* (1912) the deceased had promised to donate over £1000 towards the completion of Central YMCA's project to build a memorial hall but died before he did so. Central YMCA alleged that the promise was contractual and could be enforced against the deceased's estate that assumed his legal obligations when he died.

The *Concise Oxford Dictionary* defines a contract as 'a written or spoken agreement between two or more parties, intended to be enforceable by law'. The definition refers to only two of the three major components of an English contract: an agreement reached between the parties and their intention to make that agreement legally binding. The definition omits the third essential component, consideration. Consideration is what each party gives to the other in exchange for the other's promise to him. Consideration is an important ingredient of an English contract. It is what gives it the nature of a bargain. In *Re Cory* the deceased's promise was gratuitous. Central YMCA had given no consideration to the deceased in exchange for it. There was no contractual promise that Central could enforce.

FORMATION OF THE CONTRACT

The agreement

In *Fisher* v *Bell* [1961] the defendant shopkeeper exhibited in his shop window a flick knife with a price tag attached. He was prosecuted for 'offering for sale' an offensive weapon contrary to statute.

In *Hyde* v *Wrench* (1840) the defendant offered to sell his farm to the claimant for £1000. The claimant said that he would purchase it for £950. After the defendant refused to sell at that price, the claimant said he would accept to buy for the original price of £1000.

The formation of a legally binding agreement is based on the presumption that it is made when the parties' minds are at one on all the important terms and the terms are complete and precise. The agreement is presumed to be made when the terms offered by one party to the agreement (the offeror) have been accepted exactly and without ambiguity by the other (the offeree) and the acceptance has been 'communicated' to the offeror. In *Fisher* v *Bell* the shopkeeper had not made an offer. In *Hyde* v *Wrench* acceptance of the offer did not occur.

An offer

An offer presents terms to the offeree in a way that indicates an unequivocal willingness on the part of the offeror to be bound by them if the offeree accepts them exactly. An offer is not 'an invitation to treat' which is a statement that may look like an offer, but which merely invites offers to be made. It is intended to start negotiations that may lead to an offer. In *Fisher* v *Bell* the shopkeeper had not committed the statutory offence alleged as the goods displayed in his window with price tags were invitations to treat and not offers for sale. The customer usually makes the offer to buy to the shop as demonstrated by *Pharmaceutical Society of Great Britain* v *Boots Cash Chemists (Southern) Ltd.* [1953]. The self-service shop had not committed an offence as it had sold the prohibited drug at the cash desk where the qualified chemist accepted the customer's offer to buy the goods by taking the customer's money and exchanging it for the goods.

Advertisements, circulars, price lists, quotations are usually treated as invitations to treat, not offers. The presumption can be rebutted by evidence of a contrary intention on the part of the advertiser. Lord Parker in *Partridge* v *Crittenden* [1968] took the view, for example, that an advertisement of goods by its manufacturer could possibly be construed as an offer, as the manufacturer would be in a position to supply more goods to satisfy demand if many persons answered the advertisement. Advertisements of a reward or a payment in return for some action requested are an accepted exception to the usual presumption. The case of *Carlill* v *Carbolic Smoke Ball Co.* [1893], discussed in relation to consideration, is an example of such an advertisement. The advertisement of a payment in exchange for an act was an offer that Mrs Carlill accepted by conduct.

Acceptance of an offer

Acceptance must accord unequivocally and precisely with the terms of the offer. A reply altering one or more terms of the offer is not an acceptance of it. It is a counter-offer, the effect of which is to cancel the offer so that it no longer exists and to replace it with the new counter-offer. It, in turn, has to be accepted before a binding agreement is made. In *Hyde* v *Wrench* the purported acceptance to buy the farm for £950 was a counter-offer. It cancelled the original offer to sell for £1000 so that the original offer no longer existed at the time when the claimant tried to accept it.

When businesses make contracts, there may be a series of counter-offers during negotiations until one is finally accepted unequivocally and exactly by the other party. Each business may wish the contract to be concluded on its own terms of business set out on a standard form included in its correspondence. The exchange of these forms is sometimes referred to as 'the battle of forms'.

A request for information is not to be confused with an offer or counter-offer. Information is merely being sought and neither the request nor the reply is intended to have legal effect. Before an offer or counter-offer is made, a question might be asked such as what the lowest price of sale would be. A reply, stating the lowest price, would not constitute an offer. It merely answers the query.

When does acceptance take effect so that the contract is formed?

In *Entores Ltd* v *Miles Far East Corporation* [1955] the issue disputed was when and, consequently, where, an acceptance by telex of an offer to supply goods became binding. For the claimant to sue the defendant, an American company, in an English court on the contract, the contract had to have been made in England. Whether it had depended on when acceptance took place.

In *Adams* v *Lindsell* (1818) the defendant sent a letter to Adams offering to sell woollen fleeces and asking for an acceptance to be sent by course of post. Although Adams posted his acceptance on the same day that he had received the letter making the offer, the defendant's letter reached him later than the defendant had expected. In consequence, the defendant also received the letter of acceptance later than expected and had already sold the fleeces to someone else.

The general rule is that acceptance must be communicated or notified to the offeror. For instantaneous means of communication this was interpreted in *Entores* v *Miles Far East Corporation* to mean when the acceptance is received by the offeror. On the facts of the case acceptance was communicated when the message appeared on the claimant's telex machine at its London office. The contract had been made in England.

In *Brinkibon* v *Stahag Stahl* [1983] it was thought that telex acceptances should usually be deemed to have been communicated to the acceptor at the time when they are received on the offeror's telex machine provided this is during office hours. However, as telex arrangements in businesses vary, no universal rule could cover all situations and cases should be resolved by reference to the intention of the parties, by sound business practice and by the judgment of the court as to where the risks should lie.

It is likely that acceptance by facsimile and e-mail will be approached similarly.

An exception to the rule that communication of acceptance takes place when it is received is the postal rule which applies to acceptance by letter or telegram. The rule is that acceptance is effectively communicated when the letter of acceptance is properly posted or the telegram sent by the post office. In *Adams* v *Lindsell* acceptance became effective when Adams posted his letter of acceptance to Lindsell and not when Lindsell received it. Lindsell broke that contract by selling the fleeces to someone else after the first contract had been made.

Can an offer be withdrawn and, if so, when is the withdrawal effective?

In *Byrne & Co* v *Leon Van Tienhoven & Co* (1880) the offeror sent a letter on 8 October withdrawing an offer that he had sent by letter the week before. On the same day (11 October) as the offeree received the offer, he sent a telegram of acceptance, followed by a letter of acceptance sent by post a few days later. The offeree did not receive the letter of withdrawal until much later on 20 October.

The withdrawal of an offer is possible if it is communicated to the offeree (i.e. received by him or her) before the contract is made. If it is not, it will not be effective. In *Byrne* v *Van Tienhoven* communication of the withdrawal was received after the contract had been made. The contract was formed when the telegram accepting the offer was submitted to the post office. The contract had therefore been formed before the offeree received the communication of the withdrawal. The withdrawal was ineffective.

The offer can be effectively retracted, even if the offeror has not himself informed the offeree of his change of mind, as long as the offeree knows of it through a reliable source.

Are the terms of the agreement certain and complete?

An agreement without clarity and precision of its vital terms (e.g. price, nature, size and quantity of goods) will not usually be legally binding. The court will endeavour to uphold business agreements despite some apparent uncertainty or vagueness of the terms, if it possibly can. Therefore, if the agreement itself provides some mechanism for giving precision to the terms, the agreement is likely to be upheld. For example, the price of land in a sale agreement vaguely described as 'the market price' can be ascertained by referring to prices on the market for similar land. A previous course of dealings between the parties, the usual practices of the trade in which the parties are engaged, and statute may also assist in clarifying the term presumed to have been intended by the parties. If the court, by resorting to such methods, still is unable to find sufficient certainty in the terms, the agreement will not be legally binding.

Consideration and privity of contract

In *Carlill* v *Carbolic Smoke Ball Co.* [1893] the proprietors of the Carbolic Smoke Ball, a medicinal preparation, offered to pay £100 to anyone who caught influenza after using it according to its instructions. Mrs Carlill, bought and used the preparation as instructed, but contracted influenza.

In general promises that are not supported by consideration are unenforceable in English law unless the promise is in a deed which is recognized in law as being equivalent to consideration. Consideration is often described as the price paid (in a broad sense of the term) by the promisee (the person to whom a promise is made) for the promise of the promisor (the person making the promise) and at his or her request. Consideration can be either an act performed or a promise given at the request of the other party and in exchange for the promise.

Contracts are described as unilateral when one party only makes a promise in return for the act he or she requests of the other. When the act has been performed, the promise becomes binding, as the performance is good consideration for the promise. This type of consideration is called 'executed', as it has been performed at the request of the promisor and in response to his or her promise. There was a unilateral contract between Mrs Carlill and Carlill Smoke Ball Co. She could enforce the company's promise as her purchase and use of the product was consideration executed in return for the promise.

Most contracts, however, are bilateral; that is promises are exchanged between the parties. A promise to do something is made by one party to the other in return for the other party's promise in return to do something. For example, I promise to pay you £400 if you promise to give me your computer: you promise to give me your computer if I promise to pay you £400. This kind of consideration is called executory because the promises are to carry out acts at a future time.

> In *Re McArdle* [1951] a mother had built an extension to her house, so that her son could live there. He later promised her that he would leave his share of the house to her other children in return for her having built the extension.

Both executed and executory consideration are good consideration in the eyes of the law and are enforceable. 'Past' consideration is not usually binding. Past consideration is an act done by a promisee to whom a promisor later makes a promise in return for it, but which, when performed had neither been requested by the promisor nor done in exchange for his or her promise. The subsequent promise is not binding on the promisor, as the promisee's past act was not performed in consideration of it. In *Re McArdle* the son's promise could not be enforced, as the extension was not built by his mother at his request in exchange for his promise to her. Her act was past consideration.

An exception to the rule that past consideration is not good consideration may arise from the circumstances in a commercial context where an act requested is done and a promise to remunerate the act is implied at the time of performance. A subsequent express promise to pay a certain amount may be interpreted as merely specifying the amount of the earlier implied promise. This was the logic applied in *Re Casey's Patents, Stewart* v *Casey* [1892] where the previous working of a patent was good consideration for the promise.

Consideration is good if it has some economic value, although the value need not be adequate. In *Chappell & Co Ltd* v *Nestle Co Ltd* [1960] a small amount of money and two chocolate bar wrappings were requested by Nestle in exchange for its promise to provide a popular record. Although the wrappings and money would not usually be considered adequate for a pop record, their economic value was sufficient consideration in the eyes of the law.

Some kinds of promises or actions may not be recognized as real or sufficient because the promisor or performer is already obliged by law to do them. Consequently the promise or action will not be given or done for the other party's promise. In *Collins* v *Godefroy* (1831) the promise of the defendant to pay the claimant money if the claimant acted as the defendant's witness in court was not binding because the claimant had already been subpoenaed as a witness.

For the same reason, the promise to perform an existing contractual obligation owed to the other contractual party is not usually sufficient consideration for a further promise by the other party. In *Stilk* v *Myrick* (1809) the crew's promise to sail the ship home after two desertions was not sufficient consideration for the captain's promise to pay them extra as they had already promised him to sail home and to put up with the usual emergencies of a sea voyage. Doing something or promising to do something that goes beyond the existing contractual duty can be good consideration for a further promise of the other contracting party as it was in *Hartley* v *Ponsonby* (1857). The crew's contractual promise to sail the ship home did not include doing so in hazardous circumstances. Promising to return in such circumstances was good consideration for the captain's promise to pay extra.

The actual performance of an existing contractual obligation may sometimes be good consideration for a further promise by the other contractual party where the performance causes the promisor to receive a practical benefit from someone else. In *Williams* v *Roffey Bros & Nicholls (Contractors) Ltd* [1991] the actual completion on time by Williams of his carpentry obligations under a contract with Roffey Bros, after Roffey Bros had promised to pay him extra if he did it, enabled Roffey Bros to avoid a penalty payment that would have been recoverable under another contract with someone else.

Consideration is usually provided directly by the promisee. Williams indirectly provided the benefit received by Roffey Bros as the performance of his contract caused the benefit to be received. Consequently Williams' performance of his existing contractual obligation to Roffey was good consideration for Roffey's further promise to pay Williams extra.

An exception to the rule that a promise needs to be supported by consideration is the equitable doctrine of promissory estoppel. A promise to forgo a contractual obligation for which no consideration has been given may be enforced by a party that relies on it to his or her detriment, if it would be inequitable for the promisor to go back on his or her promise. The equitable defence of promissory estoppel may be allowed against a promisor who tries to go back on his or her promise in these circumstances.

> In *Beswick* v *Beswick* [1968] Mrs Beswick, in her capacity as widow of the deceased, Mr Beswick, was unable to enforce her nephew's contractual promise to her husband to pay her an annuity when her husband died.

Closely associated with the notion of consideration is the doctrine of privity of contract. This doctrine provides that only the parties to the contract can sue and be sued on the contract. The parties alone have provided consideration for their promises. Under the doctrine, a non-party, often termed a third party, cannot sue on the contract even if it is made for his or her benefit. By reason of this doctrine, Mrs Beswick, as third party to the contract between her husband and nephew, could not sue on it even though it was intended to benefit her. The law recognizes various exceptions to the doctrine that could circumvent the rule. Mrs Beswick was able to rely on one of these to have the nephew's promise enforced.

The doctrine has recently been restricted by statute. The Contracts (Rights of Third Parties) Act 1999 specifically provides that third parties to a contract may sue on a contract made for their benefit if the parties to the contract so permit.

Intention to form legal relations

> In *Rose and Frank Co* v *J.R. Crompton Bros. Ltd* [1923] an English manufacturer and the claimant agreed that the claimant would act as sole agent for the manufacturer in the United States. A document, purporting to be a record of the parties' intentions, stated that the parties pledged to honour the arrangement in good faith but that it was not intended to be a legal agreement subject to the jurisdiction of the courts.

In *Balfour* v *Balfour* [1919] a husband and wife agreed that the husband would pay his wife maintenance of £30 a month and that she would apply it for that purpose. The wife sought to enforce her husband's promise.

A necessary element of an English contract is the intention on the part of the parties for the agreement to be legally binding. An agreement without that intention does not constitute a legal relationship between the parties. As parties rarely express their intention, the courts make presumptions, based on inferences that reasonable people would draw from the conduct and words of the parties and the nature and context of the agreement. Agreements made in a commercial context are usually presumed to be legally binding whereas those made in a domestic or social environment are presumed not to be. Contrary evidence can rebut the presumptions. Although the parties entered into a commercial arrangement in *Rose and Frank Co* v *J.R. Crompton Bros. Ltd* their expressly stated intention that it was not to be legally binding was upheld by the House of Lords. The domestic agreement between spouses in *Balfour* v *Balfour* was presumed not to have been intended by them to be legally binding. The husband's promise could not be enforced.

Form

In *Mountstephen* v *Lakeman* (1871) the claimant, a builder, was employed by the Local Board of Health to lay sewers in the town. The defendant, chairman of the Local Board of Health, orally instructed the claimant to connect various house drains to the sewer. The claimant agreed to do so if the Board or the defendant undertook to pay him. The defendant orally agreed to see that he was paid. The Board denied having any contract with the claimant and the defendant alleged that his promise to guarantee the Board's debt was not in the correct form and consequently was unenforceable.

Some, but not all, contracts must be in a particular form or comply with certain formalities to be valid. A conveyance of a legal estate in land or a grant of a lease for more than 3 years, for example, are required to be made by deed. A deed is a formal written document, signed by the individual making it and who has an intention to make the deed; the maker's signature is witnessed; and the deed is delivered to the other party. Contract law considers a deed to be equivalent to consideration so that, even if the parties to it have not given consideration, they can enforce it.

Some types of contract need not be by deed but need to be in writing for their validity or, in some instances, enforceability. Bills of exchange, promissory notes, a contract of marine insurance, and the sale or disposition of an interest in land are examples of contracts that must be in writing to be valid. Some regulated consumer credit agreements and regulated consumer hire agreements under the Consumer Credit Act 1974 have limited enforceability unless executed in writing.

Other contracts, such as a contract of guarantee, may be oral but there must be some written evidence of them for their enforcement. A signed memorandum of their important terms will usually suffice. In a contract of guarantee the promisor undertakes to discharge the main debtor's debt if the latter fails to do so. In *Mountstephen* v *Lakeman* the defendant's argument did not succeed. His promise did not guarantee the debt of the Board (the principal debtor). Had it done, the argument would have been successful because there was no evidence in writing of the oral agreement. Instead it was a contract of indemnity whereby the defendant assumed sole liability to the claimant for the payment by the Board in any event. As such, the contract could be oral. The defendant was liable to pay the claimant. The claimant could sue the defendant accordingly.

Many contracts, like a contract of indemnity, need not be in any particular form. They can be completely oral; or a combination of writing and verbal terms; or a series of written documents. An oral or written document may incorporate a document by reference, that is by simply referring to it and stating that it is part of the contract. For example, a verbal contract of sale by telephone may refer to the conditions of sale of one of the parties thereby incorporating those terms into the contract. A contract can also be inferred by conduct of the parties.

Illegality and public policy

In *Anderson Ltd* v *Daniel* [1924] a vendor of artificial fertilizers delivered the goods without the necessary invoice stating their chemical composition which was a statutory requirement.

In *Esso Petroleum Co Ltd* v *Harper's Garage (Stourport) Ltd* [1968] Harper had entered into exclusive purchase agreements with Esso for its motor fuel in respect of its two garages: one to last for just over 4 months and the other for 21 years. It also undertook other covenants. The 21-year agreement was contained in a mortgage of the garage to Esso for that period and was irredeemable until its expiry.

Contracts may be void for illegality as well as on the grounds of public policy. Examples of illegal contracts are those forbidden by statute or the manner of performance of which is forbidden by statute. For instance, gaming and wagering contracts are rendered null and void by the Gaming Act 1845. Other illustrations are the several statutes forbidding agreements that encourage certain types of restrictive trade practice such as the Resale Prices Act 1976 that prohibits collective price maintenance agreements. Rather than outlawing the type of contract itself, statute may prohibit the way in which it is performed. In *Anderson Ltd* v *Daniel* statute had defined the sole manner of performance. Performance was illegal as the claimant had not followed the specification and consequently could not recover the price of the delivered fertilizers.

In deciding whether a statute with a vague provision prohibiting or disapproving of a type of contract clearly implies Parliament's intention to outlaw the contract, the courts consider the purpose of the statute. If the purpose is to protect the public or a class of persons in the public from such contracts, a prohibition is more likely to be intended. If the statute specifies penalties for infringement that assists the aim of the statute, it is less likely that Parliament intended the type of contract to be outlawed. *Archbolds (Freightage) Ltd v S Spanglett Ltd* [1961] illustrates the court's approach. Although an unlicensed vehicle was used in the performance of a contract of carriage, the contract was not illegal because the purpose of the statute in question was other than to control the way goods were transported by their owners and the penalties prescribed for the use of unlicensed vehicles adequately reinforced the statutory purpose.

Other contractual situations may be illegal, not by statute, but by previous case law, often for reasons of public policy. Examples are contracts that contain an unlawful purpose, such as to commit a civil wrong, a crime or to perpetrate a fraud, or a purpose contrary to good morals. A case illustrating an agreement with an immoral element is *Pearce* v *Brooks* (1866) where the claimants were unable to recover the money for hire of an ornate coach to a prostitute knowing that she was to use it in her trade. Contracts damaging to the interests of the state, including those injuring the good relations of the state with foreign states, are illegal. In *Foster* v *Driscoll* [1929] an agreement to send whiskey to be smuggled into the United States when prohibition laws were in force there was unenforceable. Other illegal contracts are those which prejudice the administration of justice by perverting its course or abusing the legal process.

If a contract is overtly unlawful, immoral or damaging to the interests of the state, neither party, however innocent, can enforce it. If it was intended to be overtly for, or to be exploited for, one of those purposes it cannot be enforced by the party intending to exploit it in that way, nor by the other party if he or she knew of that intention. A party who did not know of the other's intention can enforce it. Generally a person cannot recover money or property which he or she has already transferred under an illegal contract, but there are exceptions.

Contracts that are void (a nullity; invalid) on grounds of public policy are those that prejudice marriage, that oust the jurisdiction of the courts to hear the case, and those in restraint of trade.

The public policy on which the doctrine of restraint of trade is based is the practical effect of such a restraint curbing a person's freedom to work or trade. The doctrine protects that public interest. A contract in restraint of trade that on first impression is void may be valid and enforceable if the complainant can show that, at the date of the contract, it satisfied the double test of reasonableness: that is that it was reasonable between the parties and that the defendant had not established that it was unreasonable in the public interest. A valid restraint of trade can be enforced by injunction restraining its breach.

An exclusive dealing agreement is a type of contract in restraint of trade and void unless it satisfies the double test of reasonableness. Although both agreements in *Esso Petroleum Co Ltd* v *Harper's Garage* would seem at first sight to be void in restraint of trade, the 4-year agreement was upheld as a reasonable requirement to provide adequate protection to Esso's legitimate interests: that is maintaining a stable country-wide system of distribution and sustaining a sequence of sale outlets. Therefore it was reasonable between the parties and it was also not unreasonable in the public interest. The 21-year agreement, however, was void. It was unreasonable between the parties, as the length of the agreement was not necessary to protect Esso's interests.

As well as exclusive purchase agreements, exclusive service agreements may be in restraint of trade if unnecessarily oppressive unless they fulfil the reasonableness tests. Such an agreement entered into by a young song-writer and his publishers in *Schroeder Music Publishing Co Ltd* v *Macaulay* [1974] was held to be void and not reasonable because the publisher was given the sole right to publish the writer's songs but had no obligation to do so. Other agreements in restraint of trade are those restricting the occupation of an employee or partner after leaving their employment or partnership. A purchase agreement of the goodwill of a business that restricts competition by the vendor with the new business is also in restraint of trade.

OPERATIVE MISTAKE AND VITIATING FACTORS

In *Cundy* v *Lindsay* (1878) a rogue, Blenkarn, ordered goods by post from Lindsay, signing his letter in such a way as to convey an impression that he was Blenkiron & Co, a well-known business on Wood Street. Believing that to be the case, Lindsay entered the contract and sent the goods to 'Messrs Blenkiron', at the premises that Blenkarn had hired on Wood Street. Blenkarn resold the goods to an innocent purchaser, Cundy. Lindsay sued Cundy for conversion (a tort), claiming that he still owned the goods.

In *Derry* v *Peek* (1889) a statutory right to run trams by steam had to be obtained from the Board of Trade. The Company directors, believing that consent would be granted to the plans they had submitted to the Board, stated in the prospectus of their company that the company had this right. In reliance on the statement, the respondent bought shares in the company that was wound up after consent was refused.

Both cases concern misleading information conveyed to a person whose decision to enter the contract or the purported contract is influenced by it. The cases exemplify different factors at work preventing a genuine meeting of the minds of the parties. In *Cundy* v *Lindsay* an operative mistake prevented a contract forming between Lindsay and Blenkarn. Lindsay did not consent to enter an agreement with Blenkarn. Their contract was void from the start and had no legal effect. In *Derry* v *Peek* a misrepresentation did not prevent the formation of the contract but rendered it voidable, that is capable of being set aside or rescinded by the innocent party. The cases show that an operative mistake and an active misrepresentation have different legal consequences.

Mistake

In *Cundy* v *Lindsay* one of the parties was mistaken as to the identity of the other party, a reasonable person in the circumstances would also have been mistaken and the other party knew of the mistake. Consequently no binding contract was reached to pass the ownership in the goods from Lindsay to the rogue. As a result the rogue could not pass title in the goods to Cundy. In sale contracts made face to face rather than by letter, it is presumed that the two parties intended to contract with each other, despite any mistake which the seller might have made as to the creditworthiness of the rogue-buyer who presents a worthless cheque. A mistake of this kind would be of the quality or attributes of the other person, not his or her identity, and a voidable contract would be formed. Ownership in the goods would pass under it to the rogue, who in turn could pass the ownership to an innocent purchaser as in *Phillips* v *Brooks Ltd* [1919]. This consequence would be prevented if the original seller rescinded the contract with the rogue before the second sale. The basis for rescission would be fraudulent misrepresentation, not operative mistake.

Contracts may be void for mistake in cases where the parties are at cross-purposes other than in mistaken identity cases. For example, where one party, but not the other, is mistaken about the essence of the subject matter or about an essential term of the contract and a reasonable person would have also been mistaken by reason of the ambiguity of the circumstances, the contract may be invalid. Contracts were void in

Scriven Bros & Co v *Hindley & Co* [1913] where the seller made a successful bid for tow at an auction thinking it was hemp and in *Hartog v Colin and Shields* [1939] where the seller intended to offer goods at a set price per piece in accordance with previous negotiations and trade custom, but mistakenly had offered it at the set price per pound.

Moreover, a fundamental mistake shared by the parties as to the possibility of performance or the existence of the subject matter of the contract may render the contract void. Nevertheless, predicaments which arise are not usually solved by the principle of fundamental mistake where the contract itself provides a solution or the law has allocated the risk to one party or the other. In *Couturier* v *Hastie* (1856) both parties were mistaken that the grain being sold existed when in fact it did not. The contract provided that the buyer did not bear the risk in the event of the non-existence of the goods. For this reason judgment on whether the contract was void for mistake was not necessary. Although statements in case law have suggested that a shared fundamental mistake as to the quality of the contract (i.e. that the contract was essentially different from the matter it was thought to be) would render a contract void, the actual decisions in important cases have not born this out. In *Bell* v *Lever Bros Ltd* [1932] and in *Solle* v *Butcher* [1950], the contracts were not void for fundamental mistake as to quality.

If a contract mistakenly signed is radically different in substance or in kind from the one that the signatory thought he or she was signing and the signatory proves that he or she exercised reasonable care in signing the contract, the contract will be void. Genuine consent to the contract will be lacking. He or she can plead, 'It is not my deed', as a defence to a claim on the contract. The defence is hard to prove and rare. It was unsuccessful in the major case, *Saunders* v *Anglia Building Society* [1971], where an old lady, believing that she was making a gift of her house to her nephew, signed a deed transferring the house to his friend. The two deeds were held not to be radically different in nature as both divested her of the house so that the transferee could raise money on it. It was also held that she had been careless in signing the deed without reading it first, although she had broken her glasses.

Misrepresentation

In *Bisset* v *Wilkinson* [1927] a vendor of land, who had never grazed sheep on it, stated to the purchaser, who wanted to use it for sheep-grazing, that the land could hold 2000 sheep. In fact the land could not.

In *Dimmock* v *Hallet* (1866) a vendor of farmland asserted that the farms had tenants, but failed to disclose that the tenants were giving up their tenancies.

In *Attwood* v *Small* (1838) the purchaser of a mine used his own agents to verify the statements of the vendor as to the earning potential of the mine.

Operative mistake is exceptional. Misrepresentation is a more prevalent factor that vitiates consent. Most types of misrepresentation render the validly formed contract voidable (capable of being rescinded by the misrepresentee). A misrepresentation is defined as an important misleading statement of fact made during pre-contractual negotiations that has not become a term of the contract but which induces the party to whom it is made (the misrepresentee) to enter into a contract with the person making it (the misrepresentor).

The statement in *Bisset* v *Wilkinson* was held not to be misrepresentation as it was not a statement of fact, but was merely an opinion. Exaggerated sales talk, statements of intention or of law, like opinions, are not statements of fact and will not normally be misrepresentations. Had, however, the vendor in *Bissett v Wilkinson* previously used the land for grazing sheep, the vendor would have made a statement of fact. Even if the statement had been given as an opinion, if, in the context of the circumstances, the opinion implied that the vendor had reasonable grounds for holding it, the opinion would have become a misrepresentation.

Exceptions exist to the general rule that non-disclosure of important facts does not amount to misrepresentation. Silence distorting a statement of fact is a misrepresentation as in *Dimmock* v *Hallet*. A misrepresentation will also arise where changed circumstances convert a true assertion into a false one and the misrepresentee is not informed of the change prior to the contract. In contracts of utmost good faith, such as insurance contracts, where the insured fails to make full disclosure of all material facts, insurers can rescind the contract.

Reliance is an important component. The misrepresentee has to be induced into the contract by the misrepresentation. In *Attwood* v *Small* the purchaser could not sue the vendor for misrepresentation, as he had not relied on the vendor's statements. However, where the statement of the misrepresentor is one reason, amongst others, which persuades the misrepresentee to contract, it will suffice. The misrepresentee is not required to do what the purchaser did in *Attwood* v *Small*, namely to check the truth of the statements made by the misrepresentor. The misrepresentee's failure to investigate does not excuse the misrepresentor from liability. LORD JUSTICE JESSEL said in *Redgrave* v *Hurd* (1881):

> If a man is induced to enter into a contract by a false misrepresentation it is not a sufficient answer to him to say, 'If you had used due diligence you would have found out that the statement was untrue ...'.

Remedies for misrepresentation

In *Esso Petroleum Co Ltd* v *Mardon* [1976] the estimated throughput of petrol for the filling station that Esso gave to Mardon induced Mardon to enter into a tenancy agreement with Esso for the station.

In *Whittington* v *Seale-Hayne* (1900) an honest representation by the defendants that the premises were in a sanitary state induced poultry-breeders to lease them from him. The lease required the claimant to execute any work required by the public authorities. By reason of the premises' insanitary condition, the public authority required the drains to be replaced; the manager fell ill; the poultry were unable to breed or died. The claimant sued for lost stock and profits, a wasted breeding season, rent paid and medical expenses.

The type of misrepresentation determines its remedy. Although case law refers to fraudulent and innocent misrepresentation (honest belief in the truth of the misrepresentation whether reasonable or not), two types of innocent misrepresentation are distinguished: innocent made negligently and wholly innocent. For clarification textbooks often categorize these as fraudulent, negligent and wholly innocent misrepresentation.

The misrepresentation in *Whittington* v *Seale-Hayne* was made wholly innocently, that is with honest belief and reasonable grounds for that belief. The remedies available were an indemnity and rescission. An indemnity differs from damages in that it only covers expenses arising necessarily from the contractual obligations. Consequently the defendants could only recover rents, rates and the repairs required by the lease but not other losses. The court may exercise its discretion to order damages instead of rescission (Misrepresentation Act 1967 s.2(2)) if the opportunity to rescind has not been lost.

However, the misrepresentation in *Esso Petroleum & Co Ltd* v *Mardon* was negligent, that is it was made with honest belief but no reasonable grounds for that belief. The principles of negligent misstatement in tort, established in *Hedley Byrne Co Ltd v Heller & Partners Ltd* [1964], were applied in *Esso Petroleum* to a contractual context. By reason of the misrepresentation the misrepresentor and misrepresentee had contracted together, unlike negligent misstatement cases where reliance often leads to a contract with a third party. As in *Hedley Byrne*, the misrepresentee must prove that the misrepresentor owed him or her a duty of reasonable care when making the statement by reason of the special knowledge and skill of the misrepresentor and his or her reasonable foresight of the misrepresentee's reliance. Mardon could show that Esso owed him a duty of reasonable care, which Esso breached, resulting in Mardon's losses under the contract. If a claim for misrepresentation is brought under these principles, damages will only be recovered for loss reasonably foreseeable at the time of breach. Damages will be calculated according to the 'out of pocket rule', the aim of which is to put the misrepresentee in the position that he or she would have been in had the misrepresentation not been made.

An alternative means of suing for negligent misrepresentation is under s.2(1) of the Misrepresentation Act 1967, which requires the misrepresentor to disprove his or her negligent misrepresentation. The burden is discharged only by showing both honest belief and reasonable grounds for it up to the time of contracting. In *Howard Marine and Dredging Co Ltd* v *Ogden & Sons (Excavations) Ltd* [1978] the misrepresentor could not discharge the burden. It was not reasonable to rely on information in the Lloyds Register rather than checking the actual carrying capacity of the two barges in the actual files of the company. Under s.2(1) the loss that can be covered is assessed as if the misrepresentation had been made fraudulently. Rescission is also available. Suing under the Misrepresentation Act is more advantageous to the misrepresentee than suing under *Esso Petroleum* and *Hedley Byrne*.

Derry v *Peek*, a fraudulent misrepresentation case mentioned above, defines the mental states necessary for fraud in the tort of deceit. A false statement is made fraudulently if the maker knows it is untrue, does not believe it to be true or makes it recklessly, not caring if it is true or not. The state of mind is difficult to prove. Damages under the tort of deceit are recoverable for all actual damage or loss directly arising from the misrepresentation. The damages are measured by the 'out of pocket rule'. Rescission is also available.

Rescission enables a misrepresentee to set the contract aside. Rescission brings the contract to an end and the parties restore each other to their original positions. The misrepresentee recovers what he or she provided under the contract and gives back what he or she obtained. The other party does the same. The contract exists until it is rescinded. There is no right of rescission if restoration of the parties to their pre-contractual positions is impossible. It is also lost where the misrepresentee has affirmed the contract after learning of the power to rescind; where a reasonable amount of time has elapsed, or where an innocent purchaser in good faith buys goods from a seller who obtained them under a voidable contract.

Duress and undue influence

Duress and undue influence are other vitiating factors that render a contract voidable. The remedy is rescission. Duress consists of threats inducing a contract between the threatening and threatened parties. The relevant threats include personal violence or economic duress (threats to goods, a business or to breach a contract). Undue influence arises where a party exerts unfair and improper influence over another to enter a contract.

TERMS OF THE CONTRACT

Express terms

In *Dick Bentley (Productions) Ltd* v *Harold Smith (Motors) Ltd* [1965] the claimant purchased a Bentley car from a car dealer, Harold Smith, in reliance on the untrue, but honestly made, representation that the car had only done 20 000 miles since being fitted with a new engine and gear box.

In *Oscar Chess Ltd* v *Williams* [1957] the defendant, during the negotiation for the part-exchange of his Morris car with the claimant, a car dealer, honestly stated that his car was a 1948 model. He had based his information on the car's logbook which unknown to him had been previously falsified.

The content of a contract consists of terms. These are mainly the promises exchanged expressly by the parties. It is sometimes a problem determining the scope of the expressed promises. Some may have been made during the pre-contractual negotiations and never become terms of the contract; others may have become part of the contract.

Representations are pre-contractual statements, whether oral or in writing, made during negotiations that lead to the formation of the contract. In some circumstances the court will draw an inference that the representation was intended to become a term of the contract. If false, this will be a breach of contract. A mere representation, one that has not become part of the contract, if false, may be a misrepresentation. The courts may need to determine whether a representation has become a term or not because the remedies for misrepresentation and breach of contract are different. The scope of the contractual obligations is not always clear. Various assurances may be given during negotiations and not expressly referred to when the contract is made. Questions may arise as to whether pre-contractual statements have become contractual terms or remain mere representations.

Case law indicates when the circumstances of cases are more likely to infer that a representation was intended by the parties to be a term. In the *Dick Bentley* and *Oscar Chess* cases above, the ability of the parties to ascertain the truth of the representations was a determining factor. In *Dick Bentley* an intention that the representation as to the car's mileage was intended to be a contractual term was deduced from the fact that the seller, a car dealer, who should have known or could have found out the history of the car (e.g. by writing to its maker), made the representation. In *Oscar Chess*, on the other hand, the evidence that the seller was a private person with no special knowledge of the car and the buyer was a car dealer, in at least as good a position as the seller to ascertain the age of the car, inferred that the representation was not intended to become a contractual promise. It remained a mere representation.

These factors act only as guides in determining the parties' intentions. Inferences may be drawn from other circumstances also. The longer the time lapse between the representation and the formation of the contract or the seller's invitation to the buyer to check the representation, the less likely it is that the parties were likely to have intended the representation to be a term.

If the whole contract is reduced to writing, all its express terms will usually be in the written document. Representations that have not been included will normally not be deemed to form part of it. Although the 'parole evidence' rule provides that extrinsic evidence, oral or otherwise, is not admissible to add to, vary or contradict the terms of the written contract, exceptions exist. The court may consider that the written document is not the whole contract and that a pre-contractual oral assurance was so important to the contract, that it forms part of the contract. In *Evans J. & Son (Portsmouth) Ltd v Andre Merzario Ltd* [1976] although an oral representation made during negotiations was not included in the written agreement, the Court of Appeal held that it was nevertheless a contractual term because it was the only basis on which the claimant would enter the contract. The claimant only consented to enter the contract of carriage if its machinery, shipped in containers, would be stowed below deck. As the containers were carried on deck and some fell overboard, the claimants could sue for breach of contract.

Collateral contracts

In *City and Westminster Properties* (1934) *Ltd* v *Mudd* [1959] the claimants inserted a clause in the written lease of a lock-up shop which restricted its use to trade purposes only. During negotiations the claimants had, however, orally assured Mudd that they would not object to his living on the premises if he signed the lease as it was, which he did. Mudd lived on the premises. When the claimants sought to forfeit the lease for his breach of the lease, Mudd successfully relied on the collateral contract as a defence.

An oral statement preceding a subsequent written contract of which it forms no part and may even contradict, may not be a mere representation but may be a collateral contract. A collateral contract is a separate contract from the main contract, consisting of a clear oral promise intended to be legally binding, the consideration for which is the other party's entry into the main contract.

Implied terms

In *Hutton* v *Warren* (1836) a farm tenancy agreement contained no express obligations of the tenant farmer or landlord after the tenant had given notice to quit. Although the tenant farmer continued to plough and sow the arable land until the end of the tenancy, was the landlord obliged to reimburse him for the use of his seeds and labour during that period?

Liverpool City Council v *Irwin* [1976] concerned a tower block of flats, occupied by families, all of whom were dependent on the use of the common parts of the building which had been vandalized and were in need of repair. There was no mention in either the contracts or conditions of tenancy about who was to maintain the common parts, although the Council had reserved these parts of the building to itself. The defendants refused to pay their rent in protest at the state of the common parts.

In *The Moorcock* (1889) it was agreed that the respondent's steamship should be moored alongside the appellant's jetty. When the tide ebbed the ship sustained damage when she settled on a ridge of hard ground. Nothing was expressly stated about the care expected of the wharfingers in providing a safe berth.

Implied terms widen the scope of the terms in a contract

In each of the cited cases, certain terms were not expressed but were implied into the contracts in question, but for different reasons. In *Hutton* v *Warren* contractual obligations were implied by local custom that the tenant should work the arable land until the end of the tenancy and the landlord should reimburse the tenant farmer for his seeds and labour during the period of notice. In *Liverpool City Council* v *Irwin* the court implied an obligation on the landlord to take reasonable care to keep in reasonable repair and usability common parts of the building. Courts will imply terms into contracts if they are a necessary incident of the type of contract in question. Tenancy agreements of high-rise blocks of flats with common parts necessitate the implied term. A different criterion was used to imply a contractual term in *The Moorcock*. The court presumed that the parties, had they thought about the peril when contracting, would have expected the wharfingers to promise to take reasonable care to ascertain that the bottom of the river at the jetty was in a safe state so it would not damage the ship. Where a term would have obviously been intended by the parties in order to give business efficacy to a contract, the court will imply the term.

Terms are also implied by statute. The Sale of Goods Act 1979, as amended by the Sale of Goods and Supply Act 1994, is an example of a statute which inserts (by ss.12–15) certain terms into contracts for the sale of goods, in this case for the protection of the purchaser. Other statutes similarly imply terms into contracts of hire purchase, contracts of hire, and contracts analogous to sale contracts where ownership in goods is transferred to another person, such as contracts for work and materials.

Both implied and express terms can be broken.

Exemption clauses or terms

In *L'Estrange* v *Graucob (F) Ltd* [1934] the claimant signed a written contract to buy an automatic machine which turned out to be defective. In small but legible printing the contract exempted the seller from this liability. The claimant had not read the contract, nor had the small print been pointed out to her, nor did she know what she was signing. Would the seller be protected?

In *Olley* v *Marlborough Court Hotel Ltd* [1949] the claimant and her husband booked and paid in advance for their stay at the hotel. Afterwards they went to their room where they saw a notice on the wall excluding the liability of the hotel proprietors for the loss or theft of property belonging to hotel guests. During their stay, Mrs Olley's fur coat was stolen from their room. Could the proprietors avoid their liability to Mrs Olley by relying on the exclusion clause in the notice?

An exemption clause is a term of the contract inserted for the protection of the defendant. It purports to exclude or limit the defendant's liability for breach of contract, for misrepresentation or other liability such as negligence. It will protect him or her from liability if he or she can show that it is a contractual term; that it covered the damage that occurred and is valid. A clause in a written contract will be binding on the party signing the contract, even if that party is unaware of the clause. This was the principle on which the decision in *L'Estrange* v *Graucob* was based. The claimant was bound by the contract that she signed even though she had not read it. The defendant was protected from liability for breach of contract by the clause. An exception to this rule is made if the clause in a signed contractual document is misrepresented. For example, if a clause in the written document is wide but misrepresented as narrow, the clause will be ineffective except to the extent of the misrepresentation. In *Curtis* v *Chemical Cleaning and Dyeing Co Ltd* [1951] a signed contract excluded the cleaners' liability for damage howsoever caused to garments left to be cleaned. The claimant's wedding dress was stained while being cleaned. As the cleaners had told her before signing the document that the clause only excluded their liability for damage to beads and sequins, the clause did not protect the cleaners from liability for the stain.

If the clause is not in a signed contractual document, but is contained in a notice, order form or ticket whether the clause or notice is contractually binding will depend on whether reasonable notice of it was given prior to or at the time of contracting. In *Olley* v *Marlborough Court Ltd* because the notice was communicated after the contract was made, when guests had gone to their rooms, the hotel could not rely on it to exclude its liability. Exceptionally the court may imply an exemption clause into a contract when the express notice of it is communicated too late, if a consistent course of dealings was established between the parties and similar clauses had been previously used.

The clause will not be effective if it is contained in a document that a reasonable person would not expect it to be in, such as a receipt. In *Chapelton* v *Barry UDC* [1940] an exemption clause in a ticket for a deck chair given after payment of its hire was ineffective for that reason.

Reasonable notice must be drawn to the clause. The Court of Appeal in *Parker* v *South Eastern Rly* (1877) stressed that an objective assessment is required to determine reasonable notice. Would a reasonable person in the circumstances have been aware of the clause? It is immaterial if the actual claimant did not know of it. Whether he or she was blind, illiterate or just could not be bothered to read it is irrelevant. In the case the claimant was given a paper ticket when he paid to leave his bag valued at £24 at the station cloakroom. The front of the ticket said: 'See back'. The reverse side indicated that the defendant would not be responsible for packages exceeding the value of £10. The Court of Appeal returned the case to the lower court. The appeal court held that liability of the defendant would be limited by the clause only if the trial court found that the railway company had given reasonable notice of the term.

What constitutes reasonable notice varies depending on the nature and importance of the notice. More attention would be expected to be drawn to a notice exempting or limiting liability for an unusual, high-risk danger than a less serious or more usual one. Consequently details such as whether the notice is in small or big print, faded or in bold red letters may be relevant.

Where an exemption clause forms part of the contract, whether it was intended to cover the damage or loss that occurred is a question of construction. Any ambiguities in the clause are interpreted against the party relying on the clause. Liability, therefore, can only be excluded or modified by clear words. Even where the breach of contract brings the contract to an end, its exemption clause may still have effect if it precisely covers the liability. In *Photo Production Ltd* v *Securicor Transport Ltd* [1980] the exemption clause in the contract purported to exempt the defendant, Securicor, from liability for any injurious act by its employees unless the act could have been foreseen and avoided by due diligence on the part of the defendant. As one of the Securicor patrolmen deliberately started a fire at the factory, the damage and its circumstances were covered by the clause enabling the defendant to escape liability. The construction of the clause is mainly of importance only where two businesses with more or less equal bargaining strength, as here, negotiate terms. In consumer contracts or in standard term contracts, even if the clause is construed to cover the circumstances which occurred, the Unfair Contract Terms Act 1977 may render it either void or subject its validity to whether the clause is fair and reasonable in the circumstances.

The court's supervisory role on the use of exclusion clauses was insufficient to protect the weaker contractual party from their increased use by businesses at the expense of the consumer. Such terms are frequently found in standard form contracts pre-formulated by one party only on its own terms. The other party has power only to accept or refuse the contract. Consumers, for example, often have to contract on standard form contracts. To control the unfair use of exclusion clauses Parliament passed the Unfair Contract Terms Act 1977 which applies mainly to clauses which seek to exclude or limit business liability. Business liability attaches to things done in the course of business or from the occupation of premises used for business purposes of the occupier (s.1(3)). Business includes a profession and the activities of any government department or local or public authority (s.14). It does not generally apply to contracts between private parties. Section 2 controls the avoidance of liability caused by negligence. Terms which exclude liability for death or personal injury resulting from negligence are void (s.2(1)); clauses or notices which exclude or restrict other liability for negligence are subject to whether they are reasonable (s.2(2)). For the purposes of the Unfair Contract Terms Act 1977 negligence includes express and implied contractual terms to take reasonable care or exercise reasonable skill in performing the contract. Section 3 controls the avoidance of liability for breach of contract where one of the parties is dealing as a consumer (i.e. he does not make the contract in the course of business or hold him- or herself out as so doing and the other does and the goods sold are those ordinarily supplied for private use or consumption) or is dealing on the other party's written standard terms of business. Except insofar as it is reasonable, in these circumstances, the other party cannot exclude or restrict its liability for breach of contract; nor claim to be entitled to perform the contract in a substantially different way from that anticipated by the contract; nor claim to be entitled not to perform the whole or any part of its contractual obligation. Certain contracts are excluded from the effect of ss.2 and 3, such as contracts of insurance. Section 6 governs the avoidance of liability arising from the statutory implied terms.

In respect of exemption terms in the Unfair Contracts Term Act 1977, reasonableness means a term that is fair and reasonable to include in the contract, having regard to the circumstances which were, or ought reasonably to have been, known to or in the contemplation of the parties when the contract was made (s.11). The party seeking the protection of the term must show that it satisfies the test of reasonableness. The clause as a whole must be shown to be reasonable in relation to the contract as it is rather than the particular application of it in the case in question. In *Smith* v *Eric Bush: Harris* v *Wyre Forest District Council* [1990] some of the considerations in assessing whether the requirement of reasonableness was discharged were considered. They include the equality of the parties' bargaining power; whether the task covered by the exemption was difficult or dangerous; the practical consequences of the decision on the parties; and the question of insurance. With regard to reasonableness and the exclusion of the statutory implied terms between businesses in s.6 account is taken of the guidelines set out in the Schedule 2 of the Unfair Contract Terms Act 1977 as well as these matters.

The Unfair Terms in Consumer Contracts Regulations 1999 replace but are similar to earlier Regulations giving effect to an EC Directive whose object was to harmonize law within the European Union on unfair terms in contracts between consumers and sellers or suppliers. They regulate more than exemption clauses. They control terms in consumer contracts that have not been individually negotiated if they are unfair, namely not drafted in good faith and cause a significant imbalance in the parties' rights and obligations under the contract to the detriment of the consumer.

TERMINATION

In *Taylor* v *Caldwell* (1863) the defendants agreed to let the claimants the Surrey Gardens and Music Hall on certain specified days for a series of grand concerts and fêtes. After the contract was made but before the first day of the concert, the Music Hall was destroyed by fire through no fault of either of the parties.

In *Barber* v *NWS Bank Plc* [1996] the respondent bank was a finance company which had bought a Honda car from a dealer to sell to the appellant on a conditional sale agreement. Several months later the appellant wished to sell the car to pay off the balance owing to the bank from the proceeds of sale. Discovering that the Honda was also the subject of a previous finance agreement with a different finance company, the appellant purported to terminate the conditional sale agreement with the bank.

A contract can be terminated by various means. It will come to an end when the parties have performed all their contractual obligations or when the parties agree to end it. Either frustration or breach of contract may also terminate it. In *Davis Contractors Ltd* v *Fareham UDC* [1956] the doctrine of frustration was declared as automatically terminating the contract whenever the law recognizes that, without fault of either party, a contractual obligation has become incapable of being performed because the circumstances for its performance would render it a thing radically different from that which was undertaken by the contract. In *Taylor* v *Caldwell* the subsequent destruction and unavailability of the Surrey Gardens and Music Hall, the intact existence of which was essential to fulfil the contractual purpose, rendered the contract totally impossible to perform. The doctrine of frustration applied. Even where performance may technically be possible after fundamental changes of circumstance, the changes may frustrate the contract if its performance would be radically different. However on the facts of *Davis Contractors Ltd* v *Fareham*, the unforeseen shortage of labour and materials did not render the performance of a building contract radically different, despite the substantial delay and cost caused by them. Death or personal incapacity of a party on whose personal performance the contract depends, supervening illegality, or the destruction of a basic assumption on which the parties contracted are recognized events which may frustrate the contract.

The Law Reform (Frustrated Contracts) Act 1943 provides remedies applicable where frustration occurs. Before the frustrating event, sums paid are recoverable, and sums still to be paid cease to be payable. A party, who has already conferred a valuable benefit on the other, may be compensated. The frustration of the contract releases both parties from performing any further obligations arising under the contract after the frustrating event.

Frustration can constitute a defence, a lawful excuse, for a breach of contract. Breach of contract may also bring a contract to an end if the breach is repudiatory. When a party to the contract fails to perform one or more obligations completely or precisely without lawful excuse, the party is in breach. In *Barber* v *NWS Bank Plc* the contract contained an implied term that the bank had title to (ownership in) the Honda to sell it to the appellant. By entering into the conditional sales agreement without lawful excuse for not having title to sell, the bank was in breach of that agreement.

Traditionally the courts have classified terms of the contract as minor or subsidiary terms (warranties) or as major or essential terms (conditions) according to the presumed intention of the parties at the time they made the contract. The remedies available for the breach of terms depend on their classification. A breach of a warranty entitles the injured party to sue for damages (money compensation) only. Both parties must nevertheless continue to perform the contract. The breach of a condition, on the other hand, gives the injured party a choice of remedy. The injured party can affirm the contract and sue for damages; or can accept that the breach has repudiated the contract and terminate the contract as a consequence; if any damage is suffered, the injured party can also sue for damages. Parties may express their intentions in the contract or the court may ascertain them by inference from the nature, purpose and circumstances of the contract. Statute or previous case law may facilitate the determination. In *Barber* v *NWS Bank Plc* the broken term was held to be a condition. It was essential: the contract would have been inoperable without it. By reason of its breach the appellant was able to terminate the contract as well as to recover the full amount of the deposits and instalments already made.

If the broken term is not a condition, it will not necessarily be a warranty unless the wording of the contract indicates that this was the intention of the parties. The court may treat it as an innominate or intermediate term. The approach of the court to innominate terms is not based on the presumed intention of the parties when they made the contract. The question instead is whether the nature and effect of the breach which has occurred deprive the injured party of substantially the whole benefit which it was intended that the injured party should obtain under the contract. If this is the effect of the breach, the injured party can terminate the contract; if it is not, damages only are the remedy. In *Hong Kong Fir Shipping Co Ltd* v *Kawasaki Kisen Kaisha Ltd* [1962] the claimants sued the defendants for trying to terminate the contract for breach of a term that the ship was to be 'in every way fitted for ordinary cargo service' for a period of 24 months. The Court of Appeal refused to classify the term as a condition. It treated it as an innominate term and focused on the consequence of the breach on the contract as a whole. The provision of an unseaworthy ship by the claimant, causing the ship to be held up for 20 weeks, was not a breach which sufficiently deprived the defendant of substantially the whole benefit which it had contracted for. The ship was still available for use for 17 of the 24 months. Consequently the defendant's remedy would only be damages.

A breach may be anticipatory where a party specifies in advance an intention not to perform a major term of the contract. The other party has a choice. He or she may either treat the contract as discharged and sue for damages immediately without waiting for the actual date when performance is due or ignore the warning, continue to insist on performance and only if the obligation is breached when due, pursue the appropriate remedy at that time.

REMEDIES

> In *Victoria Laundry (Windsor) Ltd* v *Newman Industries Ltd* [1949] a boiler which the defendants had agreed to sell to the claimants was delivered 5 months after the agreed date. The claimants, who were launderers and dyers, sued for damages to cover the loss of profit that they alleged would have been made had the boiler been delivered on time. It would have been used to extend the business and for lucrative dyeing contracts with the Ministry of Supply.

Damages, the usual remedy for breach of contract, are money compensation for the damage or loss caused by the breach. They are awarded only where the damage or loss was caused by the breach and is not too remote. The main test for remoteness of damage in contract law is the rule in *Hadley* v *Baxendale* (1854). It was stated that loss is not too remote if it may fairly and reasonably be considered as either:

(i) arising naturally, i.e. according to the usual course of things, from the breach of contract or

(ii) may reasonably be supposed to have been in the contemplation of both parties at the time the contract was made as the probable result of the breach of it.

The parties need not actually contemplate the damage in the normal course of things because the knowledge that everyone is taken to know will be imputed to the parties in the first part of the rule in *Hadley* v *Baxendale*. Knowledge possessed by the parties at the time of contracting includes knowledge of special circumstances beyond those in the normal course of things. This is the knowledge referred to in the second part of the rule. In *Victoria Laundry (Windsor) Ltd* v *Newman Industries Ltd* damages could be recovered for the loss of normal profits in increasing the business because that loss was in the usual course of things but the loss of the lucrative dyeing contracts was too remote and not recoverable. The defendants had no special knowledge of these contracts at the time the contract was made and could not have contemplated that loss as a result of the delay. In *Koufos* v *C Czarnikow Ltd, The Heron II* [1967], the House of Lords considered the degree of risk of damage required to be in the reasonable contemplation of the parties for it not to be too remote. The damage required is that which is 'liable to result'. There must be a 'serious possibility' or 'real danger' that it will result.

Damages are awarded to compensate the claimant for the loss or damage suffered by reason of the breach. Where there has been no loss, damages will only be a nominal sum. Damages for breach of contract are usually quantified to put the claimant in the same position, as far as money can, that he or she would be in, had the contract been performed as the parties had agreed. The compensation is for loss of bargain or expectation. In some situations, however, damages compensate for reliance loss, that is expenditure incurred in reliance on the contract but wasted by reason of its breach. Damages for reliance loss aim to put the claimant in the position he or she would be in had the contract not been made. Damages for negligent and fraudulent misrepresentation are also calculated according to the 'out of pocket rule', which purports to put the claimant in the position that he or she would have been in had the misrepresentation not been made. Where relevant and not too remote, damages may additionally cover personal injury, damage to property, physical inconvenience and even distress or disappointment. In *Jarvis* v *Swans Tours Ltd* [1973] for example, the damages covered mental distress and disappointment caused to the claimant by the loss of enjoyment and pleasure of the package holiday that he had booked with the defendant.

The injured party cannot recover for loss that he or she could have avoided and is expected to take reasonable steps to mitigate (minimize) his or her loss as far as reasonably possible. If the injured party does not minimize the loss, a deduction is made in the calculation of the damages as though the loss had been minimized.

Damages that the court assesses, like those above, are called unliquidated damages. Sometimes parties agree to liquidated damages. These are a predetermined sum or a way of calculating it that the contract expressly states should be paid in the event of breach.

Termination of the contract for repudiatory breach should not be confused with rescission, a remedy available for most types of misrepresentation. The differences between them are mainly due to their historical development in distinct courts. Rescission is an equitable remedy. It retrospectively sets the contract aside from the beginning. The parties are restored to their positions prior to the contract. If restoration is not possible rescission is barred and will not be available as a remedy. The common law courts developed rules for termination of contract. Termination brings the contract to an end at the time it is terminated so that outstanding obligations under it need not be performed. The injured party may refuse to pay for the defective performance of the party in breach. Where there has been a total failure of consideration he or she may reclaim the money that he or she paid the party in breach. The latter may have to pay damages for loss suffered by the injured party by reason of the breach. The party in breach is obliged to complete any obligations which were due at the time of termination but which have not yet been carried out. He or she, however, will usually not need to perform obligations arising after termination, although he or she may be liable to pay damages for the loss caused to the injured party by not completing the contract.

Specific performance and an injunction are equitable remedies that may be awarded at the discretion of the court in circumstances where damages would be inadequate. A decree of specific performance is a court order to the defaulting contractual party to carry out obligations under the contract. For example, specific performance is available for a contract to sell or lease land because land is considered to be of unique value. Damages would not compensate for a refusal to sell or lease land. An injunction may be ordered by the court to restrain a party from acting in breach of a negative contractual term. An example of where such an order was used is *Warner Bros Pictures Inc* v *Nelson* [1937]. An injunction was granted restraining the defendant, the film actress Bette Davis, from breaking an undertaking in her contract of service not to work in film or stage productions for another company for one year.

A remedy for breach of contract must be brought within 6 years from the time the action accrued (usually when the breach occurred); otherwise, the defendant will have a defence to the claim under the Limitation Act 1980.

AGENCY

In *Watteau* v *Fenwick* [1893] Humble, who was employed by Fenwick to manage his public house, was expressly prohibited from purchasing cigars on credit. Watteau, unaware of the existence of Fenwick or any restrictions imposed on Humble, supplied the latter on credit with cigars.

In *Freeman & Lockyer (a firm)* v *Buckhurst Park Properties (Mangal) Ltd* [1964] a person who had not been appointed as managing director of a company, although the articles of association of the company gave it the power to make an appointment, nevertheless acted as a managing director with the knowledge and consent of the board of directors. The company denied liability on a contract that the 'acting' managing director had entered with a firm of architects, alleging that no actual authority had been given for him to contract on its behalf.

Agency, a particular application of contract law, is an essential feature of the business world. It is fundamental to the operation of partnerships and companies and many other business relationships. Agency is a legal relationship between two persons, one acting as an agent and the other as a principal, in which the agent, if authorized to enter into transactions with third parties on behalf of the principal, generates a legal relationship between the principal and the third parties. The principal can sue and be sued on such contracts.

The agency relationship may arise by agreement, between the principal and agent, by ratification or by necessity. The actions of an unauthorized person purporting to act as agent for someone, might be subsequently adopted (or ratified) by that person. Ratification retrospectively authorizes the agency. An agent is usually, however, appointed expressly by contract. It is not necessary that the express agreement is contractual as all that is required for actual authority to be conferred on an agent is the desire of the principal that a particular person should act as agent and the consent of that person to do so. An agency agreement may also be implied. The conduct and relationship between the parties establish that one has the actual authority of the other to act on behalf of the other. An explicit agreement usually specifies the tasks that the agent has authority to engage in and may even restrict the use of the authority in certain ways. One of the duties of an agent is to follow the lawful instructions of the actual authority given by the agency agreement with reasonable care and skill. The agent will be liable to the principal for any breach of them. The agent will also be liable to the principal for breach of his or her fiduciary duties, mainly to act in good faith and to not let personal interests conflict with those of the principal; not to make undisclosed secret profits from the position as agent.

Incidental, usual or ostensible authority may extend the agent's actual authority. Like actual authority, all of these bind the principal on the contract entered into on his or her behalf by his or her agent. An agent is presumed to have incidental authority to perform tasks which are subsidiary, but necessary, incidents of the task authorized by actual authority. An agent is presumed to have usual (or customary) authority which, by custom or usage, agents have in the particular trade or profession of the agent, or who occupy the particular office or post of the agent. An agent with actual authority, might, depending on the circumstances, also have incidental or usual authority. Therefore, even where an agent has broken the express terms of the agreement with the principal, the principal is still liable to the third party on the contract entered into by the agent by reason of the agent's usual authority. For this reason in *Watteau v Fenwick*, Fenwick was liable to Watteau for the unpaid cigars bought by Humble, despite Fenwick's express instruction to Humble not to buy cigars on credit, because it was usual for managers of public houses to purchase goods on credit. The usual authority of Humble bound Fenwick to Watteau. None the less as between the agent and principal, usual authority will not excuse the liability of the agent to the principal by reason of the breach of instructions.

Ostensible (or apparent) authority arises when a principal represents or holds out to a third party someone who is not his or her agent, as being his or her agent, or someone who is an agent with restricted authority to do a task, as having authority to act, and the third party relies on that representation. Should the third party know that the agent has no authority, the third party will be unable to sue the principal on the contract. Ostensible authority applies most frequently where the principal has terminated or restricted the actual authority of a validly appointed agent or has never appointed that person as his or her agent. Representation or holding out includes tacitly permitting a person to act in a certain way. In *Freeman & Locker (firm) v Buckhurst Park Properties (Mangal) Ltd* the action and knowledge of the Board of Directors condoned the actions of the managing director and held him out as an agent of the company (the principal) with authority to enter into the contract with the firm of architects (the third party). The circumstances gave rise to the ostensible authority of the managing director and the company was liable to the firm of architects on the contract.

Whether a principal is disclosed or undisclosed is also relevant to the legal positions of the parties. A disclosed principal is one that the third party knows exists, although the third party may not know his or her identity. The third party knows that the person he or she is dealing with is acting as an agent. A disclosed principal can sue and be sued on a contract entered into by his or her agent. A principal is undisclosed if the third party does not realize that he or she is dealing with an agent, that is does not know there is a principal. An undisclosed principal can sue the third party. As the agent and the undisclosed principal will have joint liability, the third party can elect to sue either. In *Watteau* v *Fenwick*, Fenwick was an undisclosed principal because Watteau had not realized that Humble was acting as an agent. Watteau chose to sue Fenwick rather than Humble.

A person who is not an authorized agent and who represents him- or herself to be an agent to a third party who relies on the representation, will be liable for breach of warranty of authority, unless the third party knows or ought to know that he or she has no authority. Liability will be imposed whether the person holding him- or herself out as an agent knows he or she has no authority, or whether he or she believes, honestly and reasonably, that he or she has authority, but does not. In *Yonge* v *Toynbee* [1910], an agent who had acted for his principal was liable for breach of warranty of authority because, unknown to him, the agency had terminated by reason of the insanity of his principal.

The Commercial Agents (Council Directive) Regulations 1993, implementing an EU directive, regulates the activities of commercial agents in Great Britain. A commercial agent is defined in Regulation 2 as 'a self-employed intermediary who has continuing authority to negotiate the sale or purchase of goods on behalf of another person (the "principal"), or to negotiate and conclude the sale or purchase of goods on behalf of and in the name of that principal.' The contractual relationship between a principal and a commercial agent, which hitherto was not regulated by special legislation, has been profoundly affected by the regulations. Certain rights and duties of the agent and the principal with respect to each other are implied into every commercial agency agreement with greater protection given to commercial agents than they have under the general law of agency.

PROGRESS TESTS

1 On Monday Martha advertised the business's photocopy machine in the newspaper for £250 giving her business telephone number and address and indicating that the business closed on Wednesday afternoons. After seeing the advertisement, Ali went to look at the copier to see if it would be suitable for his business. He told Martha that he would buy it for £150. Martha would not sell it for less than the advertised price. In case she changed her mind, Ali gave Martha his business and e-mail addresses. On Tuesday he rang to ask if her business would accept payment by cheque. She replied that it would. On Wednesday afternoon Ali e-mailed Martha saying that he would buy the copier for the advertised price. Before closure, Martha sent Ali a note saying that she had changed her mind and would sell him the copier for £150 after all. Her letter arrived on Ali's desk on Thursday morning at 9.30 a.m. Martha read her e-mail from Ali at 9 a.m. the same morning. A letter that Ali had posted to Martha on Wednesday evening confirmed his e-mail message. Martha did not receive that letter until 10 a.m. Thursday. Is there a contract between Martha and Ali and if so, when was it made and what were its terms?

2 Samson, a mini-cab driver, promised Ralph, a regular customer, to drive him to Glasgow from London and back at the weekend for £15 in exchange for the new customer that Ralph had introduced to the mini-cab business last month. Ralph happily agreed, promising to pay £15. In Glasgow Samson refused to drive Ralph back unless Ralph agreed to pay Samson an extra £50. Ralph promised to do so and Samson drove Ralph back to London. Are Ralph's promises contractually binding?

3 When Van Ltd negotiated the hire of three company vans to Fred for his removal business, its representative said that the vans each had the carriage space of 1600 cubic feet. He added that the vans could probably carry a load of 20 tons maximum, although the vans' documents were silent on the matter and nothing so heavy had ever been transported in the vans before. Although Fred was invited to have the vans inspected and to look at the documentation if he wished, he decided not to delay entering the contract by asking his garage specialist to confirm the

information. The contract caused Fred's business financial difficulties as the vans, in fact, had only 1100 cubic feet of carriage space and the capacity for bearing only 10 tons. Although the representative had honestly recollected the carriage capacity, he had not checked the documentation before entering into the contract with Fred on behalf of Van Ltd. Will Fred have any remedy against Van Ltd for the information given to him during negotiations, which induced Fred to make the contract with Van Ltd?

4 Stanley went shopping. At a garden shop he bought an expensive hosepipe. After paying, the shop assistant gave him a printed paper to sign. On the front it said: 'See back' He did not read the small print on the back as he had left his glasses at home. He asked the shop assistant to explain what it said to him. She told him that the seller would not be liable for soiled items bought; however, the back actually stated that the seller would not be liable for 'any defective products whatsoever sold'. Stanley signed the paper. He then went to the hardware shop to buy nails. At the entrance was a large notice in bold letters, stating: 'The owners and occupiers of these business premises are not liable for any damage to customers howsoever caused'. While Stanley was searching for nails in an open bin, a rusty and dirty nail tore his finger badly and another ripped the sleeve of his jacket. His finger became infected and had to be amputated. He had to buy another jacket. The first time Stanley used the hosepipe, it split. Can Stanley sue the garden shop for breach of contract and if he can, would the shop be able to rely on its exclusion clause in its defence? If Stanley sued the hardware shop for negligence, could it rely on its notice excluding liability in defence?

5 Smoke Ltd, a manufacturer of cigars and cigarettes, entered into a contract with Tobacco Farm Ltd whereby the latter was to ship in good condition 15 tons of tobacco leaves from Virginia, USA to Smoke Ltd in Liverpool. On arrival one third of the cargo had deteriorated and would have to be used by Smoke Ltd in the manufacture of a cheap variety of cigarettes for which demand was small. Smoke Ltd had planned to use three-quarters of the tobacco for cigars, its more expensive product, and one-quarter for a good brand of cigarette. Can Smoke Ltd terminate the contract (i.e. reject the cargo and not pay) and sue for damages, or can it only sue for damages? If, as a consequence of the breach, Smoke Ltd lost profits on its sales as well as a valuable supply contract with a gentleman's club, would the damages cover these losses?

5 Civil liability of business organizations 2: Tort

Brenda Barrett

WHAT IS TORT?

In *Bradford* v *Pickles* [1895] Mr Pickles wanted Bradford Corporation to buy his land. So he sunk well shafts and drew off water that would otherwise have 'percolated in undefined channels', beneath the surface, into the Corporation's reservoir. The House of Lords found that Mr Pickles had committed no tort.

In *Donoghue* v *Stevenson* [1932] two ladies went into a café and one bought the other a bottle of ginger beer. The bottle contained the remains of a snail and the lady, who drank some of the ginger beer before finding the snail, was ill. The House of Lords held that the manufacturer would have to pay compensation if the presence of the snail was due to his negligent conduct.

These two cases may help to explain why the question 'What is tort?' is not easy to answer! Tort is a grouping of judicial decisions. There are few Acts of Parliament. Academics struggle to identify what the cases have in common. Compare these authoritative statements:

> A civil wrong for which the remedy is a common law action for unliquidated damages, and which is not exclusively the breach of a contract or the breach of a trust or other merely equitable obligation (Salmond).

> The law of tort determines when one person must pay another compensation for harm wrongfully caused (Weir).

These two authorities, Salmond and Weir, agree on a number of aspects.

- *The function of tort is to provide compensation.* Compensation normally takes the form of unliquidated damages (i.e. the amount is decided by the court). But the situation is more complicated than this! First, there are situations where a person may be liable even though no damage has been suffered; for example walking on a concrete path on private property. Alternatively a person may suffer loss but get no redress. Also, in addition to, or as an alternative to awarding damages, a court may issue an injunction (i.e. order a wrongdoer to discontinue an activity that is unlawfully causing harm). If Mr Pickles had committed a tort the court would almost certainly have required him both to compensate the Corporation and to stop abstracting water.

- *Actions for tort are brought in civil courts.* The object is to compensate a victim not to punish a wrongdoer. However the same incident (e.g. a car crash) may result in both a prosecution in a criminal court and a civil action in tort. The shopkeeper who sold, and/or the manufacturer who produced the ginger beer that made Mrs Donoghue ill, might perhaps have been prosecuted for marketing an unwholesome product.
- *Tort includes a number of distinct areas of liability, themselves known as torts.* Important examples are negligence, trespass, nuisance and defamation. Most torts have been recognized for hundreds of years. The extent to which there can be tortious liability beyond the boundaries of these 'nominate' torts is not clear. In *Bradford* v *Pickles* the House of Lords did not extend liability: in *Donoghue* v *Stevenson* it did, creating negligence as another nominate tort.

Weir and Salmond are not necessarily in agreement on the following aspects, however.

- *Relationship to contract.* Salmond suggested tort operated within a different framework from contract. The problem before their Lordships in *Donoghue* v *Stevenson* was whether the appellant was entitled to compensation in tort when she had no remedy in contract because she had not herself paid for the ginger beer.

  Weir's statement, more recent than Salmond's, does not mention the difference between contract and tort. In practice it is not always clear whether a person can sue in tort for what is really a breach of contract. For example, if Mrs Donoghue had bought the ginger beer for herself she would have been able to sue the shopkeeper who sold it to her for breach of the contract of sale; but it is not certain that she could have sued him in tort. In fact she ignored the shopkeeper and sued the manufacturer. Had she been the purchaser she might have sued the shopkeeper in contract and the manufacturer in tort. In *Grant* v *Australian Knitting Mills* [1936] the House of Lords found both the shopkeeper and the manufacturer of underwear could be liable to the purchaser whom it caused dermatitis.
- *The boundaries of tort.* Salmond distinguished tortious liability from other forms of civil liability, but neither author addressed whether all damage suffered will be recoverable. Uncertainty about this accounts for much litigation.
- *Neither quotation mentions the interests protected.* They are:
  - *Person*: the greatest number of actions are for compensation for personal injury. The most important function of the tort of negligence is compensation of people who have suffered accidental injury.
  - *Land*: the torts of trespass and private nuisance enable occupiers of land to protect their interests.
  - *Economic loss*: in recent years there has been uncertainty about whether economic loss is recoverable in tort. Some writers consider that the treatment of economic loss is a major difference between contract and tort. The person who suffers a breach of contract may well claim for loss of the profit that would have followed if the contract had been honoured: the person who sues in tort will rarely get damages for loss of future income.
  - *Reputation*: the tort of defamation enables a person to protect his or her reputation.

OF WHAT SIGNIFICANCE IS TORT TO A BUSINESS?

An enterprise, its managers and employees, could all be at risk of liability in tort. In reality the person who has most resources is the one likely to be sued. This, and the rule of vicarious liability (explained below) means that most litigation will be against the organization itself (often a corporate body) rather than the persons it employs.

The likelihood of the organization being sued is increased by insurance. The existence of insurance cover ensures that the successful litigant will obtain compensation, but knowledge that liability will be met encourages litigation! The employer is required to insure against liability for accidents to its employees in the course of their employment (Employers' Liability (Compulsory Insurance) Act 1969). Section 143 of the Road Traffic Act 1988 has the practical effect of requiring employers to insure vehicles (other than the employee's own car) driven by their employees while at work. Most enterprises will also have insurance to cover any liability for accidents suffered by persons other than employees.

Only the areas where there is a particular risk of liability being incurred in tort by business organizations will be considered here. Liabilities are likely to be incurred by the business as an employer, a manufacturer of products, an occupier of land and buildings and an operator of vehicles. Some special topics are covered in other chapters.

GENERAL PRINCIPLES OF LIABILITY

In *Bolton* v *Stone* [1951] the defendant's cricket ball hit the claimant. As she did not prove the defendant had been negligent she obtained no compensation.

Two important general principles need to be considered:

Strict and fault liability

The rule is that the claimant always bears the burden of bringing evidence to satisfy the court that there is a case for the defendant to answer.

In torts of *strict liability* the claimant makes out a case by showing that the defendant has, by his or her conduct, caused something unlawful to occur. In these torts the defendant will then be liable unless he or she can establish a defence. Thus, in the tort of defamation the claimant has only to show that the defendant published a defamatory statement about the claimant for the defendant to be liable unless he or she can establish a defence: for example the defendant might escape liability by proving the statement was true.

To make out a case in torts where liability depends on *fault*, the claimant must prove both that the defendant has caused the unlawful situation and that the defendant was blameworthy. The type of conduct, or state of mind, that is regarded as blameworthy varies from tort to tort:

- in *deceit* the defendant must have acted *wilfully or recklessly*;
- in *trespass to land* and *person (battery)* the defendant must have *intended to act* (though not necessarily intended either to break the law or to cause injury to the claimant);
- in *negligence* the defendant's conduct must have been negligent.

A bad motive does not normally make conduct unlawful. That was why Mr Pickles was not liable to Bradford Corporation. The Corporation did not own the water Mr Pickles took out of the ground: so he did nothing unlawful in abstracting it. That his action was *malicious* was irrelevant.

There are two important exceptions to the general rule that malice does not make otherwise lawful conduct actionable.

1 If two or more people make an agreement to cause harm to another they will be liable for the tort of *conspiracy* unless their purpose is to further their own legitimate interests. So if Mr Pickles had made an agreement with Mr Sauce to draw off underground water they would have been liable for conspiracy, unless they needed the water for their own business.
2 In the tort of private nuisance, liability is for unreasonably interfering with neighbours' enjoyment of their land. The principle is that neighbours should live and let live. Therefore defendants will be liable for nuisance if they do something that is on the margins of what is tolerable, but act merely to annoy the claimant. For example a property developer who fired guns at the boundary between his property and that of the claimant in order to put the claimant fox farmer out of business, was liable for nuisance (*Hollywood Silver Fox Farm* v *Emmett* [1936]).

Vicarious liability

In *Mersey Docks & Harbour Board* v *Coggins & Griffith (Liverpool) Ltd* [1947] one organization hired a crane and its driver to another. While carrying out the contract the driver caused someone to be injured.

In *Rose* v *Plenty* [1976] a boy was injured while helping a milkman. The milkman's employer had forbidden him to employ boys to assist him in his work.

Vicariously liability describes the situation where someone is made liable for the wrongdoing of another person. Employers may be vicariously liable for torts committed by their employees in the course of employment.

There are two criteria that have to be met for the employer to be liable for the wrongdoing of the worker:

1 the worker must be the employee of the employer;
2 the employee was in the course of his or her employment when the wrong was committed.

The worker must be the employee of the employer

To satisfy this first requirement the worker must have the status of employee and the worker's contract must be with the employer. These requirements will be discussed in turn.

The worker must have the status of employee

When one person works for another there will normally be a contract governing their relationship. According to the nature of the contract the worker may be either an employee or an independent contractor. In the past employers were described as 'masters' and employees as 'servants': even today an employee is said to work under a contract *of service*. An independent contractor works under a *contract for services*. The employee has a personal contract with the employer. In a contract of service the employee is a part of the employer's organization and normally has an ongoing relationship with the employer in return for a regular wage. The independent contractor has a separate business organization and its contract with the employer is for the performance of a particular task, though this task may be ongoing, as, for example, where the employer has 'contracted out' the provision of some service, such as running the works' canteen. The independent contractor may have its own employees. The difficult situations are those where the independent contractor only provides his or her own labour, as a 'self-employed' person.

Determining whether the 'self-employed' worker is really an employee has proved difficult. The law requires that employers comply with a system whereby income tax and social security contributions are deducted before paying the wages to employees, but this system is not always honoured. Judges have sought without success for a simple test by which employees may be identified. In recent times they have accepted 'the multiple factor' approach suggested in *Ready Mixed Concrete (South East) Ltd* v *Minister of Pensions and National Insurance* [1968].

In this case MCKENNA J, had to consider a very complex contract, which gave the employer a great deal of control over their lorry driver's activities. He nevertheless decided that the driver was an independent contractor because the contract required him to purchase his own vehicle, thus giving the worker a valuable business asset.

His Lordship stated that a contract of employment exists if:

(i) The servant agrees that, in consideration of a wage or other remuneration, he will provide his own work and skill in the performance of some service for his master.

(ii) He agrees, expressly, or impliedly, that in the performance of that service he will be subject to the other's control in a sufficient degree to make that other master.

(iii) The other provisions of the contract are consistent with its being a contract of service.

If the first two criteria are met the worker is likely to be an employee. An important consideration will be whether the worker is paid a regular wage or only paid for work actually done: the worker who is paid, even if idle, is likely to be an employee.

The worker's contract must be with the employer

In the *Mersey Docks and Harbour Board Case* it was agreed that the crane driver was of the status of employee. The question was which organization was his employer. The two employers had agreed that if the man had an accident when doing the work the organization that was borrowing the crane would be responsible. The House of Lords held that the contract between the organizations could not transfer the man's contract of employment from one employer to the other. The contract of employment remained with the *general* employer, and that employer, rather than the *particular* employer using him at the time of the accident, should be *vicariously liable* for the accident.

The employee was in the course of employment

The employer will only be liable for the wrongs that the employee commits during the course of employment. In *Rose* v *Plenty* the milkman's employer was liable for the injury caused to the boy by the milkman's negligent driving of the milk float. Although the milkman was disobeying express orders when he employed the boy to help him, the work being done was delivery of milk. Delivery of milk was what the employee was employed to do and doing it was for the benefit of the employer. The decision in *Rose* v *Plenty* is typical of the broad approach to whether an employee is in the course of employment. In *Smith* v *Stages* [1989] two employees, whose base was in the Midlands, were sent to do a job in Wales: they were allowed to claim their rail fare as expenses and wages for the time they were travelling. They chose to travel home together in a car. The driver had an accident and the claimant (passenger) was injured. The House of Lords held that when the accident occurred the men were in the course of their employment because they were in paid working time. Again in *Lloyd* v *Grace, Smith & Co.* [1912] solicitors were found liable for the act of their managing clerk who fraudulently persuaded a client to convey her cottages to him. The solicitors certainly did not benefit from the act of their employee; but they had put him in a position where the client might legitimately trust him. On the other hand an employer will not necessarily be liable if an employee assaults someone, even if the employee does so while looking after his or her employer's interests. (E.g. in *Warren* v *Henlys Ltd* [1948] a garage was not vicariously liable when their petrol pump attendant struck a customer apparently leaving without paying.)

Vicarious liability is strict liability: even faultless employers can be liable. In practice it may be difficult to distinguish the employer's personal liability from its vicarious liability for the fault of the employee. In *Carmarthenshire County Council* v *Lewis* [1955] a small boy caused a fatal accident when he escaped from a school playground on to the road while his teacher was looking after another child. The House of Lords held the County Council, who employed the teacher, was liable personally for this accident. The fault was not in the teacher (if it were the Council would have been vicariously liable): the problem was that the employer operated a system that asked more of the teacher than one person could achieve.

Vicarious liability is a form of joint liability. Although the employer is liable the employee remains personally liable. However the claimant will rarely sue the employee, unless the employee is a driver or a professional person, such as a doctor, who has insurance cover.

LIABILITY FOR CAUSING PERSONAL INJURY

In *Letang* v *Cooper* [1965] the claimant suffered injury when the defendant ran over her legs while she was sunbathing. The Court of Appeal held that she could not obtain compensation unless she could show that the defendant either intended to injure her or acted negligently.

In *Re F* v *West Berkshire Health Authority* [1990] the House of Lords permitted doctors to sterilize a mentally subnormal woman for whom pregnancy would have been injurious. The doctors feared that without judicial authority they might have been liable for battery.

In *John Lewis & Co Ltd* v *Tims* [1952] the claimants were suspected of shop lifting. They were kept in the store detective's office until a manager could be informed.

With very few exceptions, such as statutory liability for defective products, the claimant will not succeed in claiming compensation for personal injury without showing that the defendant either acted negligently or intended to make contact with the claimant's body. The claimant therefore has to bring the action in either negligence or trespass to person (battery). *Letang* v *Cooper* established that the claimant could not sue for battery where the physical contact between claimant and defendant was neither intentional nor negligent. *Bolton* v *Stone* [1951] (above) established that the claimant could not sue in public nuisance for personal injury without proving negligence. *Read* v *Lyons* [1947] (explosion of ammunition) similarly established that the claimant could not rely on the form of strict liability established by *Rylands* v *Fletcher* (1868), in personal injury litigation.

Assault and battery

In *Re F* the doctors thought it necessary to go to court before performing surgery because battery is committed by intentional contact with the claimant's body made without the claimant's consent, however well-meaning that contact may be. In this case the woman was not capable of giving consent. In the case of a person of normal mental capacity, surgery cannot lawfully be performed without consent of the patient, except in an emergency where the patient is unable to consent and there is not time to get judicial authority. It is not open to patients to assert they have suffered battery if with hindsight they consider they would not have consented to an operation if they had realized the risks entailed. In these circumstances the patient must show that it was negligent of the doctor to have withheld information about the risks (*Sidaway* v *Bethlehem Royal Hospital* [1985]).

From this short account it will be clear that, surgery apart, battery is primarily concerned with physical attacks such as fights. It is closely associated with assault. Assault is committed by putting a person in fear that they are about to suffer battery. Employers are very often corporate bodies, unable to commit battery. An employee, such as a security guard, who attempted to evict or arrest a trespasser or a thief might commit battery if the force used were more than the circumstances justified.

False imprisonment

The tort provides a remedy for those who have been imprisoned when there is no reason to suppose they have committed any arrestable offence. However the Police and Criminal Evidence Act 1984, s.25 gives citizens a power of arrest where there is reasonable cause to believe an arrestable offence is being or has been committed. In *John Lewis* v *Tims* the store had not committed the tort as they had held the claimants only so long as was necessary to investigate the situation. In *Herd* v *Weardale Steel, Coke and Coal Co.* [1915] miners went on strike while underground, during a shift and the employer refused to bring them back to the surface before the end of the shift. The House of Lords again held this was not false imprisonment: the men had contracted to be underground. For there to be false imprisonment the claimant must be prevented from moving elsewhere. In *Bird* v *Jones* (1845) the claimant was unable to cross a bridge because the defendant had obstructed it: there was no false imprisonment – the claimant could have used another route.

The tort of negligence

Organizations are liable to be sued for negligence in respect of personal injury suffered by their employees, other workers or members of the public.

In the famous case of *Donoghue* v *Stevenson* [1932] LORD ATKIN said:

> You must take reasonable care to avoid acts or omissions which you can reasonably foresee would be likely to injure your neighbour. Who, then, in law is my neighbour? The answer seems to be – persons who are so closely and directly affected by my act that I ought reasonably to have them in contemplation as being so affected when I am directing my mind to the acts or omissions which are called in question.

The case was concerned with the specific question of whether a manufacturer owed a duty of care to the consumer. Nevertheless LORD ATKIN's words have been deemed to establish a general principle that a duty of care is owed to those who are sufficiently close to a person to be affected by that person's conduct. Closeness, or proximity, in this context is not entirely a matter of space and time. The consumer, for example, might be many miles away from the manufacturer and might not obtain the product for a considerable time after it left the manufacturer's premises.

To succeed in an action for negligence the claimant must prove:

1 the defendant owed him a duty of reasonable care;
2 the defendant broke that duty by negligent conduct;
3 the defendant's conduct caused the claimant to suffer foreseeable damage.

The duty issue

By 1970 LORD ATKIN's neighbour principle had become so well established that LORD REID could say in *Home Office* v *Dorset Yacht Co Ltd* (a case concerning damage to property):

> *Donoghue* v *Stevenson* may be regarded as a milestone, and the well-known passage in Lord Atkin's speech should I think be regarded as a statement of principle. It is not to be treated as if it were a statutory definition. It will require qualification in new circumstances. But I think that the time has come when we can and should say that it ought to apply unless there is some justification or valid explanation for its exclusion.

The duty is to take reasonable care in all the circumstances. Generally no liability is incurred by failing to act, unless some previous action has created a duty situation. Thus it is no tort for a person to stand and watch a child drown in a shallow pond, *unless* the child has been entrusted to that person's care. What has to be done will vary according to the situation. An exception is that in industrial injury cases it was established before *Donoghue* v *Stevenson,* and confirmed by the House of Lords in *Wilsons & Clyde Coal Company* v *English* [1938], that the employer's duty to employees is threefold. It is 'the provision of a competent staff of men, adequate material, and a proper system and effective supervision'. This historic formula is still honoured, but in practice employer's liability differs little in law from other forms of liability for negligently causing injury to another.

Breach of duty

> In *Scott* v *London and St Katherine Docks Co* (1865) sacks of sugar fell from the defendants' crane on to the claimant.

> In *Roe* v *Ministry of Health* [1954] two patients entered hospital for minor surgery and emerged permanently paralysed from the waist downwards because the anaesthetic with which they were injected had been contaminated with disinfectant.

Now that it is rarely in dispute in personal injury litigation that the defendant owed the claimant a duty of care the focus has shifted to the breach issue. Whether the defendant has broken the duty of care is a matter of fact, established by evidence.

The burden of proving that the defendant has been negligent falls on the claimant, but the claimant cannot be expected to know exactly how the defendant operates. Therefore if the claimant has shown that there is evidence of negligence the court will be sympathetic unless the defendant can show it was not negligent. This rule that the burden of proof may shift to the defendant because 'the thing speaks for itself' is often expressed in Latin as *res ipsa loquitur*. In *Scott* v *London and St Katherine Docks Co* (1865) ERLE CJ stated the rule thus:

> There must be reasonable evidence of negligence, but where the thing is shown to be under the management of the defendant, or his servants, and the accident is such as, in the ordinary course of things, does not happen if those who have the management of the machinery use proper care, it affords reasonable evidence, in the absence of explanation by the defendant, that the accident arose from want of care.

Interestingly, in this case the defendants persuaded the court that they were not at fault!

In *Roe* LORD DENNING, in the Court of Appeal, considered that the facts spoke for themselves, but no liability was attached to the hospital. Investigation after the accident suggested that the anaesthetic had become contaminated when the ampoules in which it was contained were sterilized, because the glass tubes had hairline cracks. The court considered that the danger of contamination occurring in this way was not *foreseeable* and so the hospital had not been negligent. However the court warned that now the risk had become known it would certainly be negligent for any hospital to allow another such accident to occur.

As the House of Lords pointed out in *Qualcast* v *Haynes* [1959] a decision that has been reached on the evidence in a particular case does not create precedents for future cases. So in the *Qualcast* case their Lordships refused to hold that a decision that an employer had been negligent in failing to advise a trainee to use protective clothing meant an employer was negligent in failing to order an experienced worker to wear protective boots.

The authorities in relation to breach of duty are statements as to the criteria by which a defendant's conduct will be objectively evaluated. The leading authority is

Blyth v *Birmingham Waterworks Co* (1856) where ALDERSON B described negligent conduct as:

> the omission to do something which a reasonable man, guided upon those principles which ordinarily regulate the conduct of human affairs, would do, or doing something which a prudent and reasonable man would not do.

This formula means little today since 'the man in the street' is rarely sued for negligent conduct, unless he caused an accident while driving a car! Now that most defendants are experts, either professionally qualified practitioners or corporations, what is expected is the standard of the reasonable expert. So the medical practitioner is expected to observe the standards of responsible, reasonable and respectable fellow practitioners, whether administering treatment (*Bolam* v *Friern Barnet Hospital Management Committee* [1957]) or informing the patient as to risks involved in treatment (*Sidaway* v *Board of Governors of the Bethlehem Royal Hospital* [1985]). Even the learner driver (covered by insurance!) is expected to drive to the standard of the qualified driver (*Nettleship* v *Weston* [1971]).

Where the defendant is an industrial enterprise failure to follow industry standards will certainly be negligence. Indeed those standards may not be sufficient: the judge may declare that the industry is negligent. In *Cavanagh* v *Ulster Weaving Co. Ltd* [1960] a worker on a building site fell when crossing a roof, with no handrail, while wearing rubber boots. Their lordships were not persuaded that the victim's employers had not been negligent to allow this, even when there was evidence that this sort of behaviour was common place in the construction industry! In addition *Roe's* case makes it clear that organizational systems and procedures need to keep pace with scientific and technological progress.

Damage

> In *Barnett* v *Chelsea & Kensington Management Committee* [1969] a night watchman went to the defendant's hospital complaining of vomiting. He was told to go home. Later that day he died of arsenic poisoning.

> In *Hughes* v *Lord Advocate* [1963] employees of the Post Office left unattended an open manhole covered by a canvas shelter. Paraffin lamps surrounded it. A boy took a lamp, entered the shelter and stumbled into the manhole. The lamp exploded and the boy was badly burned.

The third factor that the claimant has to prove in the tort of negligence, is that the defendant's conduct has caused the claimant actionable damage.

If the claimant cannot show that the defendant *caused* the damage suffered, then clearly the defendant will not be liable. The question is, 'Would the claimant have suffered the injury *but for* the conduct of the defendant?' The hospital was not liable in *Barnet's* case although they had been negligent in not admitting the deceased. This was because he died from poisoning which they did not cause and if they had admitted him to hospital they would not have been able to provide treatment to counteract the effect of the poison.

Even if the defendant has caused events but for which the claimant would not have been injured, the defendant will not necessarily be liable for the damage suffered by the claimant. Following the ruling of the Judicial Committee of the Privy Council in

The Wagon Mound [1961], a property damage case (fire following negligent oil spillage by ship), the defendant will only be liable for damage that is a foreseeable consequence of the negligent conduct. In *Hughes* v *Lord Advocate* the House of Lords held that the Post Office was liable for the injury suffered by the boy as a consequence of the negligence of their employees. It was foreseeable that an inquisitive child would suffer personal injury in the situation: it was not necessary to liability for the exact sequence of events to be foreseeable.

While the defendant's negligent conduct may set in motion a series of events that lead to the claimant's injury it may be that some or all of the damage suffered by the claimant is too *remote* in law for the defendant to be liable for it. For example the *chain of causation* may be broken by the action of the claimant him- or herself or another person. In *McKew* v *Holland & Hannen & Cubitts (Scotland) Ltd* [1969] the claimant injured his knee in an accident at work: for this injury the defendants, his employers, were undoubtedly liable. While he was convalescent he climbed a steep staircase where there was no handrail, lost his balance, fell and broke his ankle. The House of Lords held that his employers were not liable for the broken ankle: the claimant's action in climbing the stair had broken the chain of causation.

Liability for causing psychiatric injury

In *Wilkinson* v *Downton* [1897] as a practical joke the defendant told the claimant that her husband had been badly injured. The shock made the claimant very ill.

In *Dulieu* v *White* [1901] a pregnant barmaid was so shocked when, due to the defendant's negligence, horses burst into the premises where she was working that she suffered a miscarriage.

In *McLoughlin* v *O'Brian* [1983] the claimant was taken by a neighbour to the accident ward of a hospital. There she saw the 'aftermath' of a serious road accident in which members of her family were involved.

In *Wilkinson* the defendant was found liable because his intentional conduct had caused the injury. The injury having followed from the defendant's words, the judge relied on the tort of deceit to support his decision.

Since *Dulieu* v *White* courts have awarded damages to those who have suffered nervous shock where by negligent conduct the defendant has caused an accident and given the claimant reasonable cause to fear that he or she will suffer personal injury. In the twentieth century a lot was learned about mental illness, its causation and the forms it takes. In *Page* v *Smith* [1996] the claimant's car was in collision with another car, due to the other driver's negligence. The claimant was not physically injured but claimed to have suffered mental illness as a result of the accident. The House of Lords found that the claimant was a 'primary' victim, that is a person at risk of suffering physical injury in the accident in question. They held that in these circumstances there was no distinction between physical and mental illness and if the claimant could prove the accident had caused him mental illness the defendant would be liable. Compensation is not normally allowed to any claimant who has not shown the symptoms of shock caused by the traumatic event. The claimant usually claims to have suffered post traumatic stress disorder.

The difficult cases are those in which the claimant is only a 'secondary' victim, that is someone who witnesses a catastrophic event, or its immediate aftermath and suffers shock as a result, though never personally in danger of physical injury. In these cases the defendant, whose negligence caused the catastrophe, will only be liable to compensate the claimant if there are ties of love and affection between the claimant and those who have suffered physical injury. So in *McLoughlin* v *O'Brian* the lorry driver whose negligence had caused the accident was held liable to the claimant, who was the wife and mother of the victims. *Alcock* v *Chief Constable of South Yorkshire Police* [1992] concerned the disaster in which 95 spectators were crushed to death at the Hillsborough Football Stadium. The House of Lords held that the negligent defendants were not liable to claimants who had lost loved ones, but had merely watched events on television. These secondary victims had not been physically present at the catastrophe or its immediate aftermath. Again in *White* v *Chief Constable of South Yorkshire Police* [1999] the House of Lords found against police officers who had been on duty at the stadium. Even if these officers were rescuers (people to whom the law is sympathetic in cases of physical injury) they were not entitled to compensation unless they were in physical danger or had personal ties of love and affection with the victims.

In *White* the majority of their Lordships did not consider the officers had a special status because they suffered psychiatric injury from witnessing in the course of their employment a catastrophe caused by their employer's negligence. There is a growing number of cases, starting with *Walker* v *Northumberland County Council* [1995], in which an employer has paid compensation to an employee who has suffered mental illness caused by the employer negligently permitting the worker to be stressed over a period of time by work overload. These cases are interesting because they are a departure from the tradition that shock is an essential element in liability for psychiatric injury.

Occupiers' Liability

In *Roles* v *Nathan* [1963] self-employed chimney sweeps were working on a central heating system. An expert told them, and the occupier of the premises, that they must not work when the boiler was alight and the 'smoke hole' open. On Friday night, when she believed the sweeps had left, the occupier lit the boiler. The following morning the sweeps were found dead by the open smoke hole.

The Occupiers' Liability Act 1957 was intended to clarify the common law rather than to impose new statutory liability on occupiers of premises for the safety of their visitors. Before the Act the common law recognized several categories of visitors and the occupier's *legal* duty differed according to the category. The Act provides the occupier owes a 'common duty of care' to all his or her visitors (s.2(1)). This duty is 'to take such care as in all the circumstances of the case is reasonable to see that the visitor will be reasonably safe in using the premises for the purposes for which he is invited or permitted by the occupier to be there.' (s.2.(2)) The Act paralleled the developments in the 'duty issue' that were at that time occurring in the tort of negligence generally. The tort has continued to develop and the Act contains more qualification and explanation than might be considered necessary were Parliament legislating on this subject today. On the one hand the Act spells out that the occupier must be prepared for children to be less careful than adults, but on the other the occupier may expect workers to 'appreciate and guard against any special risks' of their work (s.2(3)). So in *Roles* v *Nathan* the occupier was not liable to the widows of the chimney sweeps: they ought to have realized the dangers of inhaling fumes.

The occupier will not escape liability by warning the visitor of a danger, unless it is possible for the visitor to take steps to avoid it (s.2(4)). Thus it must, for example, depend on all the facts whether a notice 'mind your head' will discharge any duty the occupier might have where the roof is low! If the warning notice does not control the risk and it cannot be avoided, the visitor will not be deemed to have accepted it. On the other hand the occupier will not be liable for dangers created by an independent contractor whom he or she has employed, unless he or she has negligently failed to ensure the contractor is competent and has carried out the work properly (s.2(4)(b)).

The Occupiers' Liability Act 1984 imposes upon the occupier duties to people other than lawful visitors (principally trespassers). Under this Act the occupier owes a duty to take reasonable care for the safety of these persons in relation to dangers which the occupier reasonably believes to exist, provided he or she has reasonable grounds to believe there is someone in the vicinity. The occupier may discharge the duty by giving a warning of the danger or discouraging people from taking the risk. An adult who ignores a clear warning or takes an obvious risk (e.g. walks down a railway track) will be deemed to have accepted the risk.

While a warning notice may alert a person to a danger and so discharge the occupier's liability, the Unfair Contract Terms Act 1977, s.2(1) provides that no business may by contract or notice exclude or restrict liability for death or personal injury resulting from negligence. This section has a general relevance to all personal injury litigation based on negligence (for example it is not clear whether an employee can agree to work excessively long hours, see *Johnstone* v *Bloomsbury Health Authority* [1992]) but it is especially relevant in the context of occupiers' liability. The notice 'Patrons use this car park at their own risk' may correctly remind 'patrons' that the occupier will not be liable for the negligent driving of other 'patrons'. It would be unlikely to exempt the occupier from liability to the patron who sprained her ankle because the surface of the car park was very uneven!

Defences

> In *Froom* v *Butcher* [1976] the claimant car driver was injured in an accident caused entirely by the negligence of the defendant. The victim was not wearing a seat belt.

> In *Dann* v *Hamilton* [1939] the claimant was injured in an accident caused by the drunken driver of the car in which she was a passenger.

There are two principal defences to the tort of negligence. Both may be used as defences to some other torts.

Contributory negligence

Since the Law Reform (Contributory Negligence) Act 1945, where the claimant has proved that damage has been caused by the defendant, the defendant may plead that the injury is partly attributable to the fault of the claimant. If the defence is successful the judge will apportion the blame. So if two cars crash and both drivers are equally at fault, the claimant driver will be awarded 50 per cent of the damage he or she has suffered (subject to any offset necessary to satisfy a counterclaim by the other driver). In *Froom* v *Butcher* the claimant was held to be contributorily negligent in not wearing his seat belt. His failure to wear it did not cause the accident but was the reason why his injuries were severe: therefore his damages were reduced.

Volenti non fit injuria (assumption of risk)

A person who has consented to the risk of injury suffered is barred from obtaining any compensation. The courts are reluctant to allow this defence. In *Dann* v *Hamilton* it was held that a passenger who accepts a lift knowing the driver to be drunk does not accept the risk of injury in an accident the driver may cause. (In *Owens* v *Brimmel* [1977] it was held that the passenger's conduct might be contributory negligence.) The defence rarely succeeds where the claimant is an employee, for in *Smith* v *Baker* [1891] the House of Lords drew the distinction between a worker knowing there is a risk and agreeing to take it – a worker who refused would probably lose his job.

TORTS RELATING TO PROPERTY

Land

> In *Anchor Brewhouse Developments* v *Berkley House (Docklands Development)* (1987) the defendants used tower cranes for the purpose of developing their site. The boom of the cranes swung over the properties of the claimants.

> In *Hunter* v *Canary Wharf Ltd* [1997] the claimants lived in houses near to the Canary Wharf development. They alleged that during the development they had suffered from dust caused by building a new road and that the development interfered with their reception of television.

Apart from the tort of negligence, there are two principal torts concerned with the protection of interests in land: trespass and nuisance.

Trespass

Trespass is committed by direct interference with possession of land, by entering on the land, or going under it or over it. The claimant does not have to show that the defendant's trespass has caused damage. In the *Anchor Brewhouse* case the claimants claimed that the booms of the cranes were trespassing over their property and sought injunctions to prevent the continuance of the trespass. The defendants pleaded that even if there were an infringement of air space, and this were a trespass, the claimants ought not to be granted injunctions because they were suffering no damage and the use of the cranes was essential to the development of the site. The judge held that, although injunctions cannot be demanded as of right, there was so much case law in favour of these claimants that injunctions had to be granted.

The tort is committed against the person entitled to possession of the land, so a landlord can trespass by entering premises let to a tenant, unless the tenancy agreement authorizes him to enter. On the other hand persons occupying land cannot by their unauthorized presence deprive the owner of his or her right to vacant possession. In *Portland Managements Ltd* v *Harte* [1977] the claimants purchased properties and found them to be occupied by persons they believed to be squatters. Being unable lawfully to evict them without going to court (see Criminal Law Act 1977 s.6) they brought an action claiming the residents were trespassing. The Court of Appeal held that once the claimants had shown their ownership of the land the burden shifted to the defendants to show they had a legal right to possession.

Trespass to land is not a crime; damage caused by trespassers may be! Police officers and representatives of the public utilities are not entitled, by virtue of their official position, to enter onto private property. Representatives of electricity, gas and water companies have statutory authority to enter in an emergency. The Police and Criminal Evidence Act 1984 s.16 enables police, who have obtained a warrant, to enter premises to search for the persons or articles specified in the warrant. Under s.17 they may enter without a warrant to arrest a person for an 'arrestable offence' (broadly an offence which could carry five or more years' imprisonment) or to prevent a breach of the peace.

Nuisance

This tort takes two forms: public and private. A public nuisance, at common law, is something that 'materially affects the reasonable comfort and convenience of life of a class of Her Majesty's subjects' (See *Att. Gen* v *PYA Quarries* [1957]). It is only actionable as a tort if the claimant shows he or she has suffered damage over and above that suffered by the rest of Her Majesty's subjects. The claimant need not have an interest in land.

Private nuisance may be brought by a claimant to protect the value of his or her land when the defendant has unlawfully interfered with the claimant's enjoyment of that land. Nuisance occurs when there is an 'escape' from the defendant's land of something, such as noise, smell, smoke or vibration. Normally nuisance is committed by a course of conduct, rather than an isolated incident. It is immaterial that the defendant has acted without negligence. The claimant must have an interest in the land where the nuisance is suffered: some of the claimants in the *Canary Wharf* case found that merely living at premises did not give a sufficient interest in land to win an action in nuisance. The claimant will not succeed unless damage has been suffered, but the damage may take the form of either damage to the property itself, as by smoke and dirt (*St Helen's Smelting Co* v *Tipping* (1865) or loss of amenity. In the *Canary Wharf* case their Lordships agreed that interference with television reception could be loss of amenity and therefore a nuisance, though on the facts they did not consider that interference caused by a building did amount to a nuisance. When claiming for loss of amenity the claimant cannot expect a better standard than the location of the property warrants. A judge once remarked: 'What would be a nuisance in Belgrave Square would not necessarily be so in Bermondsey' (*Sturges* v *Bridgman* (1879)). The *Canary Wharf* case clarified that nuisance does not provide a remedy for someone who has suffered personal harassment at a property without having any rights in that property.

In *The Wagon Mound* [1961] case the Privy Council held that in the tort of *negligence* a claimant could only claim compensation for damage that was foreseeable (requiring evidence that it was foreseeable that spillage of oil on to the sea would cause fire damage). In *Cambridge Water Co* v *Eastern Counties Leather plc*

[1994] chemicals used by the defendant had seeped a distance underground, over a long period of time, to pollute the claimant's well. The House of Lords held that in *nuisance* (as in negligence) only foreseeable damage could be claimed. Therefore the claimants obtained no compensation because the sequence of events was unforeseeable. Possibly in some situations a claimant might be denied damages but granted an injunction to prevent further damage. An injunction would not have been appropriate in the *Cambridge* case since it would not have prevented further pollution.

Goods

In *Hollins* v *Fowler* (1875) brokers bought and re-sold some cotton. They did not know that the person from whom they bought it had no right to sell it.

In *Perry* v *British Railway Board* [1980] the defendant withheld delivery of the claimant's steel because rail workers sympathized with striking steelworkers.

Remedies available for torts related to goods are governed by the Torts (Interference with Goods) Act 1977. The statute was necessary largely because goods are transferred frequently and it may be necessary in litigation to determine the rights of all the people involved in a chain of events. The Act aims to get all parties to court at the same time. Section 3 gives the court discretion to decide whether to award return of the goods and/or damages. The Act sets out a procedure by which a person, like a shoe repairer, may sell unclaimed goods and recover any money properly spent on them.

The Act applies to a range of torts, including trespass, negligence and conversion, but the claimant has to rely on case law to establish which, if any, tort has been committed. In business transactions the tort most usually in question is conversion. This tort is committed by a person selling, using or destroying goods without the right to do so. Ownership of goods is very hard to prove; so the burden is on the claimant to prove a better right than that of the defendant. Conversion is a tort of strict liability, thus it may be committed by an innocent defendant, like the cotton broker in *Hollins* v *Fowler*. It can also be committed by someone who, like the railway in *Perry* v *BR Board*, detains goods without a right to do so.

LIABILITY FOR CAUSING ECONOMIC LOSS

In *Derry* v *Peek* [1889] a prospectus incorrectly stated a company had authority to run trams on steam power. Without this authority the company shares had little value.

In *Hedley Byrne* v *Heller & Partners Ltd* [1964] a bank negligently stated that a customer was creditworthy.

Frequently, in economic loss claims incorrect statements have been made. Many cases concern situations where the claimant and defendant are nearly, but not quite, in a contractual relationship.

In *Derry* v *Peek* the House of Lords held that the company's directors were not liable in the tort of deceit to shareholders who relied on the prospectus, because the directors had not acted wilfully or recklessly. After that it was believed that there was little prospect of getting compensation in tort for incorrect statements until, in *Hedley Byrne*, the House of Lords held that a person making a statement may owe a duty of care to the person receiving it. This opened the way for liability for negligent misstatements. In *Hedley Byrne* the bank escaped liability because when providing the reference they had expressly stated that they would not accept liability. Nowadays such an exclusion of liability may be considered unreasonable and therefore invalid under the Unfair Contract Terms Act, s.2(2).

Following *Hedley Byrne* the courts developed principles on which a defendant may be liable for negligent misstatements. The defendant must have made the statement in a business rather than a social context: he or she must have accepted responsibility for the statement and the claimant must have been entitled to rely on it.

Sometimes it is not clear whether the defendant's negligence has been in making an incorrect statement or in negligently collecting the evidence (e.g. conducting a survey) on which the statement is based. In *Smith* v *Bush* [1990] the House of Lords held that surveyors can be liable for negligent surveys on which the purchaser of property has relied, even though the surveyor was under contract with the mortgagee rather than with the purchaser seeking to obtain the mortgage. In *White* v *Jones* [1995] the majority of the House of Lords went further and imposed liability on solicitors who had failed to alter a will in accordance with client's instructions. They found that because the solicitors had assumed responsibility and then failed to act they were liable to those who would have inherited under the revised will.

In some cases the claim may fail because the economic loss is too remote a consequence of the negligent conduct. In *Spartan Steel & Alloys* v *Martin* [1973] the defendants' negligence caused the electricity supply to the claimants' factory to be cut off. This caused metal in the claimants' furnace to solidify, damaging the furnace and preventing the manufacture and sale of the products in it. The claimants were able to recover for the damage to the furnace and for the loss of profit they would have got by selling the goods actually being manufactured when the breakdown occurred. They were not able to recover for the loss of profit on goods they might have made in the period while the furnace was being repaired: this future loss was deemed to be too remote.

In recent years courts have only imposed a duty of care on a defendant in cases where the claimant and defendant are 'neighbours', the damage suffered was foreseeable *and* it would be 'fair, just and reasonable' to impose the duty. So in *Caparo Industries plc* v *Dickman* [1990] the accountants who had prepared an auditor's report, for a shareholders' meeting, as company law required, were not liable to people who relied on the report when purchasing shares. The House of Lords held that even if the accountants had negligently misrepresented the company's position it would not be fair, just and reasonable to say they owed a duty to each and every actual and prospective shareholder individually.

Similarly in *Murphy* v *Brentwood* [1991] their Lordships held that, even if a local authority had negligently certified that the foundations of a house were satisfactory, it did not owe a duty of care to the purchaser of the house.

A claimant may sue in tort where contract would be the more appropriate way to litigate. The courts are not usually sympathetic to such claimants. One reason the claimant prefers tort may be that contract law does not offer a satisfactory remedy. In *The Nicholas Heron* [1996] owners of a ship's cargo blamed the loss of the ship and its cargo on the negligence of a surveyor who had deemed the ship seaworthy. The House of Lords held it would not be just fair and reasonable to make the surveyor liable in tort to the cargo owners as the Hague Rules provided appropriate remedies in contract. Another reason the claimant may sue in tort is that the party to the contract is not creditworthy. The courts will not normally allow claimants to choose the more creditworthy defendant unless, as in the misstatement cases, they show they have specially relied on the defendant. In *Muirhead* v *Industrial Tank Specialists Ltd* [1986] the contractor who had supplied a fish tank to the claimant became bankrupt, but the claimant was unable to claim in tort from the firm who manufactured the electric pump for the tank, for the economic loss suffered when the pump failed. This claimant was unable to establish it had relied on the defendant.

The result of the case law is that a claimant is much more likely to recover for economic loss attributable to negligent misstatements than for economic loss caused by conduct.

LIABILITY FOR CAUSING DAMAGE TO REPUTATION

In *Sim* v *Stretch* [1936] the defendant sent a telegram to the claimant which said: 'Please send [Edith's] possessions and the money you borrowed, also her wages . . .'

In *Spring* v *Guardian Assurance* [1995] an employee sued his former employers for negligent misstatement when they provided an incorrect reference to a prospective employer.

Defamation

Defamation is the tort principally relied upon for the protection of reputation. Defamation is the publication of a statement that lowers a person in the estimation of right thinking members of society generally. The claimant has to prove three things:

1   The statement was published. A statement written by the defendant and sent to the claimant in a sealed envelope would not be published: there must be communication to a third person.
2   The statement could be understood to refer to the claimant. A defendant could be liable, even if he or she intended to write about a fictitious person, if a reasonable person might believe the claimant was the person referred to. In *Hulton* v *Jones* [1910] when a newspaper intended to write a story about the dubious adventures of a fictitious character called Artemus Jones, they were liable to a real person of that name.
3   The statement was capable of causing people to think less of the claimant. In *Sim* v *Stretch* the House of Lords found that the words in the telegram were not reasonably capable of bearing a defamatory meaning. Similarly in *Byrne* v *Deane* [1937] the Court of Appeal found that no reasonable person would think less of a person because it was said that he had reported illegal gambling to the police.

There are a number of defences. The defendant may plead justification: a defamatory statement is assumed to be untrue, but the defendant will avoid liability by proving it was true. Some situations are covered by absolute privilege: for example no action for defamation may be based on a statement made in Parliament. Others situations are covered by qualified privilege. For example, an employer will not be liable for a defamatory reference published only to someone, like a prospective employer, who has an interest in receiving it, unless the person defamed can show it was written out of malice. It may also be possible for the defendant to plead the words were fair comment on true facts. The Defamation Act 1996, ss.2–4 gives the defendant the opportunity to avoid litigation by admitting the defamation and offering to publish a correction and apology, together with making payment of suitable compensation, but this statutory defence is not available to a defendant who has been negligent.

If the statement is published in permanent form (i.e. libel, which includes broadcast statements) the claimant does not have to prove damages. If no loss has been suffered the court will only award nominal damages. Since defamation cases are heard in the High Court before a jury they are very expensive to fight. Claimants are usually well-known public figures. The defendant is often a newspaper. Juries have frequently awarded inappropriately large sums as damages. For example in *Esther Rantzen* v *Mirror Group Newspapers* [1994] the Court of Appeal reduced an award from £250 000 to £110 000. The judge will nowadays advise the jury of the sum that might be appropriate. An objective is to ensure that awards are not disproportionate to awards for personal injury.

Negligent misstatements

In *Spring's* case the House of Lords held that the tort of negligence could be used to provide compensation for damage caused by an incorrect reference. The disadvantage of suing in negligence is that the claimant will have to show that the reference caused damage.

This final case provides yet another example of the extent to which liability for negligence has largely superseded other forms of tortious liability.

PROGRESS TESTS

Now that you have studied this chapter prepare answers to the following questions. You may not find the exact answer in either the chapter or by further reading, because it may be that no court has considered the facts set out here. However you should find within the chapter the framework within which the situation would have to be considered.

1 Albert has spent the week away from home because his employer has required him to work over 100 miles away from where he lives. He has been allowed expenses for lodgings and for travel. When he was driving home in his own car after finishing the work he negligently knocked over and injured a pedestrian. Would his employers be liable to the pedestrian?
2 Betty has suffered a nervous breakdown. She has had to work particularly hard because her employer has had a lot of new work. It has been quite stressful because the computer system has been unreliable. All this has occurred at a time when Betty's mother has needed a lot of care and attention because she has had to undergo surgery for cancer. Would Betty's employers be liable for her illness?
3 Claude was seeking a new job and named his employers as a referee. Claude was interviewed but did not get the job. When he sought feedback as to why he had been unsuccessful the organization to whom he had applied told him he had been given a poor reference. Would Claude be able to get any redress from his employers?

4 Donaldson supplied Easygo with wood. Easygo used the wood for floorboards in the workshop they were fitting out under contract with Firepower. Firepower had a contract with Grandee to build them a new head office. The wood turned out to be inferior and the floorboards warped. Consequently Firepower defaulted on the contract which required the head office to be completed before the end of the year. Could Firepower sue Donaldson for the economic loss suffered because the contract they had with Grandee has not been honoured?

5 Harvey Ltd have a processing plant that needs a constant supply of clean water. They have been assured that water from their well is satisfactory for their purpose, but to be doubly sure they have installed a water purifier to treat the water taken from the well. One Sunday, when the plant is closed, the purifier is taken away by Instance Debt Collectors who wrongly believe it is one of the plants on their 'blacklist' as having outstanding loan debts on hire purchase contracts. When the purifier is not working it emerges that the well water has been polluted by petrol that has seeped into the well from a local petrol station operated by Jetswift. Consequently Harvey are unable to operate their plant. Would Harvey be able to successfully sue either Instance or Jetswift?

6 Civil liability of business organizations 3: Property law

Chris Chang

INTRODUCTION

> The only estates in land which are capable of subsisting or being conveyed or created at law are
>
> (a) an estate in fee simple absolute in possession;
> (b) a term of years absolute
>
> (The Law of Property Act 1925, s. 1(1))

English law recognizes two categories of property: realty and personality – that is land and chattels. This chapter is concerned with the law relating to land, otherwise known as real property. For a business to function effectively and efficiently, it is essential to have appropriate premises from which to operate. Even so-called 'virtual' or 'internet' companies need premises to store their computer equipment and house their staff. It is therefore a necessary evil that businesses need to have some knowledge of land law in order to be aware of their rights and liabilities in respect of the premises from which they operate.

The focus of the chapter is on the rights and obligations of the freehold owner and the lessee in respect of business premises.

Section 1(1) of the Law of Property Act 1925 (LPA 1925) cited above, provides that there are two main types of legal estates in land; namely the freehold title and the leasehold title. They must be conveyed (passed from one person to another) or created by deed (LPA 1925 s.52). These are the best forms of title that exist in land law. There are other types of estates in land that are only recognized in equity but businesses should avoid these.

FREEHOLD TITLE

A business may own the freehold title of the premises from which it operates. In such a case, it has absolute ownership to the premises, recognized by English law, and subject to the covenants and encumbrances contained on the title, mortgagee's rights and planning laws. It cannot normally be deprived of the premises. The land may also benefit from easements over neighbouring properties.

Covenants

In *Tulk* v *Moxhay* (1848) the seller of land imposed a covenant on the purchaser to keep the land and maintain it in an 'open state'. The defendant subsequently bought the land and wanted to build on it. An injunction was granted restraining the defendant from doing so. The court stated that the defendant could not use the land in a way that was inconsistent with the contract made by his predecessor of which he had notice.

In *Austerberry* v *Oldham Corporation* (1885) the defendants were owners of land that had had a road built on it by a previous owner. The previous owner had covenanted that he would build and maintain the road. An application was made to enforce the covenant against the defendants. The court decided that the covenant was not enforceable against the defendants because the burden of a covenant does not run with the land.

It is often the case that the title contains covenants or restrictions on the land. The most common of these are:

- covenants not to use the premises for immoral or illegal purposes;
- covenants not to remove support for the adjoining property in the case of a semi-detached or a terraced property;
- to keep the property in repair.

The covenants will bind the original covenantor and covenantee on the basis of privity of contract. The covenants are usually made for the benefit of a piece of land (the benefited land) and will impose a burden on another piece of neighbouring land (the burdened land). Difficulties arise where the burdened land has been transferred to someone who was not a party to the contract containing the covenant. In such a case, whether the transferee is bound depends on a number of factors.

First, it depends on whether it is a positive or restrictive covenant; that it to say it depends on whether the covenant requires action to be taken or merely prohibits something being done. The general rule is that a positive covenant is not binding on subsequent owners of the burdened land and cannot be enforced against them as seen in *Austerberry* v *Oldham Corporation* (1885) and followed in *Rhone* v *Stephens* [1994]. There are a number of exceptions to this, the most notable being the rule in *Halsall* v *Brizell* [1957]. This rule allows the enforcement of a positive covenant against the subsequent owners of the burdened land where the subsequent owners wish to make use of the benefit from the covenant. For example, the obligation to maintain a road will be enforced if the subsequent owners of the burdened land wish to make use of the road as well. Other exceptions include having a chain of indemnities, by the grant of a lease and by creating an estate rent charge.

Secondly, restrictive covenants will be enforceable against subsequent owners of the burdened land in some circumstances (*Tulk* v *Moxhay* (1848)). They will be enforced provided that:

- the covenant is one that touches and concerns the land;
- the covenant has been intended to run with the land; and
- the burden of the covenant has been transmitted to the subsequent owners of the burdened land by entry on the title (in the case of registered title) or by registration as a land charge (in the case of unregistered title).

A covenant that touches and concerns the land is one that benefits the land as opposed to providing a personal or commercial benefit. Most covenants are intended to run with the title of the burdened land because LPA 1925 s.79 automatically deems that to be the case provided that the conveyance does not make an express statement to the contrary.

Thirdly, for the owner of the benefited land to be able to enforce the covenant, the covenant must also have been attached to the land by assignment, annexation or under a building scheme.

If the business is subject to the burden of covenants, the business will have to ensure compliance with them. In the event of a breach of a restrictive covenant, those with the benefit of the covenant will be able to enforce the covenant by way of an injunction to restrain the breach of covenant and/or obtain damages. In the case of a positive covenant, the suitable remedy will be specific performance or a mandatory injunction to compel performance and/or damages.

Easements

> In *Re Ellenborough Park* [1956], on a sale of various plots of land surrounding Ellenborough Park, the purchasers were given the 'full enjoyment of the pleasure ground'. This grant was subject to the purchasers making a contribution for the upkeep of the park, a condition similarly imposed on other persons who had been granted such 'easements'. The Court of Appeal decided that this was a valid easement.

Easements are generally rights enjoyed by a landowner over someone else's land. Examples of easements are a right of way, a right of support, a right of light. An easement can even be a right for cars to be driven across, to store things on, install satellite dishes or television aerials. In order for a right to be recognized as an easement, the characteristics of an easement as laid down in *Re Ellenborough Park* [1956] have to be satisfied. These are that:

- there must be both a dominant and a servient tenement – i.e. there must be a piece of land that benefits the land (the dominant tenement) and a separate piece of land that is subject to the easement (the servient tenement);
- the easement must accommodate the dominant tenement – this means that the easement or right must be one that benefits the land as land and does not merely provide a personal or commercial benefit to the land owner. For example in *Hill* v *Tupper* [1863] the right to let out pleasure boats on a canal was held not to be a right that accommodated the dominant tenement.
- there are different owners of the dominant and servient tenements – by definition, an easement is a right over someone else's land and therefore there must be separate owners of the two tenements;
- the easement must be capable of being the subject matter of a grant – the right must be a right that has been or is capable of being recognized as an easement. There is no definitive list of easements but many rights have been recognized as being easements and hence it is a case of looking at precedents to determine whether the right claimed has previously been recognized by the courts as being an easement. If it has not, it is a question of persuading the court to extend the existing categories of easements by analogy. In *Dyce* v *Hay* (1852) the court noted

that the categories of easements were not closed and will expand with the changes that take place in society.

Apart from satisfying the requirements in *Re Ellenborough Park*, the easement must have also been granted or reserved either expressly or impliedly. Easements can be granted in the following ways:

- Express grant or reservation – usually in the deed of conveyance.
- Implied grant arising from necessity – for example, in the case of land locked land where an easement is implied over the vendor's land in order to reach the public highway (*Nickerson* v *Barraclough* [1980]).
- Implied grant in order to give effect to the common intention of the parties – an easement would be implied if it were necessary so that the property could be used for the purpose which the parties intended (*Wong* v *Beaumont Property Trust* [1964]).
- Easements arising under the rule in *Wheeldon* v *Burrows* (1878) – where quasi-easements used by the vendor prior to the conveyance that are continuous and apparent and necessary for the reasonable enjoyment of the land are regarded as an easement benefiting the purchaser.
- Implied reservation – the law allowing the vendor impliedly to reserve easements for itself over land that is being conveyed to the purchaser is strict. Only easements of necessity or in order to give effect to the common intention are implied. To allow other easements would be to allow the vendor to derogate from his grant.
- Deemed easements under LPA 1925 s.62 – this section provides for the transfer of existing easements to the purchaser upon a conveyance of the land. It also has the effect of converting permissive rights into easements where the two pieces of land were in separate ownership and the land having the benefit of the permissive right is then conveyed to the purchaser (*Wright* v *Macadam* [1949]).
- Prescription – it is possible to presume an easement has been granted from long user of a right provided that the use has not been by force, nor exercised either secretly or with permission. The law on prescription covers rights that can be acquired at common law, through the doctrine of lost modern grant and under the Prescription Act 1832.

Other rights and encumbrances

There are other rights and encumbrances that affect the ownership of land. These include:

- Profits a prendre – this is a right to take something which is part of the land or take something off the land that is capable of ownership at the time that it is taken. The law on this is similar to that relating to easements. Examples of profits include the right to take gravel or sand and the right to hunt or fish on the land. They are acquired in the same way as easements and one of the differences from easements is that profits can exist 'in gross'. That means that the person with the benefit of the profit does not have to own neighbouring land.
- Rentcharges – this is periodical payment charged on the land of the grantor. An estate rentcharge is one that is intended to secure the performance of positive obligations in respect of the land. As a result of the Rent Charges Act 1977, new rentcharges, with one or two exceptions, can no longer be created.

LEASEHOLD LAND

In *Street* v *Mountford* [1985] S granted M the right to occupy some rooms for £37 per week subject to 14 days' notice. The written agreement stated that M was granted a licence that did not give her a protected tenancy under the Rent Acts. The court decided that as she had exclusive possession of the premises, she had a lease and not a licence.

In *Lace* v *Chantler* [1944] a lease was granted for the duration of the war. The court held that the lease was void, as the duration was not ascertainable at the time of the grant.

Organizations may conduct their business from premises under a lease or a sublease. A lease is essentially a grant of an estate in land for a fixed term of years with exclusive possession. The estate can be for any fixed duration – from a few days or months to 999 years, but not indefinitely. A grant for an indefinite period will be regarded as a freehold. More importantly, the lease must give the lessee exclusive possession of the premises in order for it to be a lease; otherwise the grant will only be a licence which is not a proprietary interest. Exclusive possession means possession of the premises to the exclusion of all others including the lessor – *Street* v *Mountford* [1985]. Other requirements for a valid lease include a fixed commencement date, that the premises that are the subject matter of the lease are fixed and defined and the parties have the requisite capacity to enter into the transaction.

Most commercial leases are for longer than a few months. Commonly such leases are for 15 years or 25 years although there is no strict rule as to how long they should be, provided the lease is for a fixed duration of time – *Lace* v *Chantler* [1944]. Such leases normally have a clause providing for rent review at 5-year intervals with a break clause at the same time. This means that the rent can be increased at that time by the lessor but the lessee can also terminate the lease at the same time. Normally, the lessee would not be able to terminate the lease except at these intervals. There is case law on the interpretation of such rent review clauses but this will not be considered here.

Covenants in leases

The lessor normally imposes covenants in the lease binding on the lessee. Such covenants include covenants:

- not to assign, sublet or part with possession of the property without the consent of the lessor, whose consent shall not be unreasonably withheld;
- to pay the rent and service charges on the due date;
- to keep the premises in good tenant like condition, fair, wear and tear excepted;
- to use the premises only for specific types of businesses;
- not to alter or change the appearance of the premises.

The lessee must ensure compliance with these covenants. In the event of a breach of covenant by the lessee, the lessor has a range of remedies available to it or him. The remedies available depend on the type of breach, which will be considered in the next section.

It should also be noted that the lease could impose obligations on the landlord either expressly or by implication. These includes the following obligations:

- to give quiet enjoyment – that the lessee is put into possession of the premises and will not be physically disturbed by the lessor or those deriving title under him or it;
- not to derogate from the grant – that the lessor will not do anything that makes the premises less fit for the purpose for which they were let;
- to repair.

It may be appropriate at this point to consider what the obligation to repair entails. Depending on the lease in question, it may impose an obligation to repair on either the lessor or the lessee. In some cases, the obligation to repair is implied by law. However, the tenant's obligation to repair is usually an express covenant in the lease. It is a question of degree whether the work that needs to be done can be regarded as 'repair'. For instance, in *Lurcott* v *Wakely and Wheeler* [1911] the court decided that the replacement of an entire wall amounted to 'repair'. In contrast, in *Brew Brothers* v *Snax Ltd.* [1970], where the work required was building new foundations for the building, this was held to go beyond 'repair'.

In the context of the lessee's obligation to repair, it is common to find an exception for 'fair, wear and tear'. This exempts the lessee from liability arising from ordinary usage of the property and the effects of nature. For example, if a roof slate is blown off the roof by a thunderstorm, the lessee is not obliged to replace the slate. However, the lessee may be liable for consequential damage resulting from the loss of the slate. For example, if because of the missing roof slate, rainwater comes in and damages the ceiling, the lessee would then be obliged to repair the ceiling.

Where the lease is silent on the obligation to repair (which is rare in a properly drafted commercial lease), as a general rule, there is no implied obligation to repair imposed on the lessor (*Lane* v *Cox* [1897]). In the case of residential properties, the law does impose obligations in some instances, for example, under ss.8 and 11 of the Landlord and Tenant Act 1985. However, liability for commercial leases may arise under statute, for example, under the Defective Premises Act 1972, and the general law of negligence (*Cavalier* v *Pope* [1906]).

Breach of covenant for payment of rent

In *United Dominion Trust* v *Shellpoint Trustees* [1993] a mortgagee was regarded as within the definition of lessee under the County Courts Act 1984 and was entitled to apply for relief from forfeiture for non-payment of rent. However, as the application for relief was more than 6 months after the date of the execution of the possession order, the mortgagee was barred from claiming relief.

In *Maryland Estates Ltd.* v *Bar Joseph* [1999] the court held that the County Court could grant relief from forfeiture for non-payment of rent if all the arrears were paid by the tenant.

In the case of a breach of covenant for payment of rent, the lessor has various remedies including suing for damages or commencing distress proceedings. Distress is an ancient remedy and involves a direct action by way of self-help. In this case, the lessor will enter onto the premises (either in person or via a bailiff – *Law of Distress Amendment Act 1888* s.8 and take possession of the lessee's belongings. These are held for 5 days under a procedure known as 'walking possession'. Items such as clothing and the lessee's tools of the trade must not be taken. If the rent arrears and all costs are paid up within the 5 days, then possession of the belongings will be released. Otherwise, the belongings will be sold in order to recover the rent arrears and costs. Although this is an ancient remedy, it is still available in England and Wales. Some uncertainty surrounds whether the remedy will be available when the Human Rights Act 1998 comes into force. The remedy could be regarded as violating the right to a fair trial and the right to have peaceful enjoyment of possessions.

Alternatively, the lessor can forfeit the lease. It is important to note that the lessor does not have an automatic right to forfeit the lease. In order for the lessor to be able to forfeit the lease, whether for non- payment of rent or otherwise, there must be a forfeiture clause in the lease. Essentially, this is a clause that gives the lessor the right to enter the property and determine the lease upon a breach of covenant.

Before the lessor can forfeit a lease, it needs to make a formal demand for rent. An archaic procedure whereby the demand has to be made on the day it fell due between the hours of sunrise and sunset at the premises (*Duppa* v *Mayo* (1669)), this is often excluded in modern leases with the words 'whether formally demanded or not'. However, lessors normally issue a formal demand in order to give the lessee another opportunity to pay the arrears before court action is commenced. If the lessee still fails to pay the arrears, then the lessor can forfeit the lease. A lessor normally commences an action (essential in the case of residential property – Protection from Eviction Act 1977 s.2) for possession of the property either in the High Court or County Court depending on the amount of the claim. Although technically, in the case of a commercial lease, the lessor can take possession and hence forfeit the lease by re-entry, this must be done peacefully and without force (Criminal Law Act 1977, s.6 as amended by the Criminal Justice and Public Order Act 1994 s.72). It is inadvisable to forfeit the lease by re-entry where the lessee is still in occupation unless the lessee voluntarily gives up occupation. There are proposals for the removal of the right of re-entry as a means of forfeiting the lease and replacing it with a requirement that forfeiture can only take place through a court order.

If the lessee pays the rent arrears, interests and legal costs prior to the trial of the action, the lessee will be entitled to relief from forfeiture of the lease as seen in *Maryland Estates Ltd.* v *Bar Joseph* [1999]. If the lessee pays the amount due within 6 months of the date of the execution of the possession order, the court has the discretion to grant relief from forfeiture. The grant of relief for forfeiture is lost if a third party has entered into possession of the property or the application for relief is outside the 6-month period (*United Dominion Trust* v *Shellpoint Trustees* [1993])

Breach of other covenants

In *Expert Clothing Service & Sales Ltd.* v *Hillgate House* [1986] the court was asked to consider whether the breach of a covenant to reconstruct the property within a specified time period was capable of remedy when the reconstruction had occurred outside the time period. The court decided that the breach of covenant in this case was capable of remedy.

In *Savva & Savva* v *Hussein* [1997] the court decided that a breach of covenant not to make alterations was capable of remedy.

Where there is a breach of other covenants, apart from payment of rent, the lessor has various remedies available. These include an injunction to restrain the breach, damages and exceptionally specific performance to compel performance of the covenant. In the case of a repairing covenant, it is rare for the court to grant a specific performance order against the tenant. However, in *Rainbow Estates Ltd.* v *Tokenhold Ltd.* [1998] the court granted an order for specific performance of a tenant's repairing covenant. The court was prepared to make the order because the circumstances were such that there was no provision in the lease for re-entry for breach of covenant nor was there any provision in the lease allowing the lessor to enter onto the premises in order to undertake the repairs.

Forfeiture

The most important of these remedies is the right to forfeit the lease for breach of covenant. Forfeiture for breach of covenants other than payment of rent is in accordance with LPA 1925 s.146. The procedure here attempts to give the lessee another opportunity to rectify or remedy the breach before the lease is forfeited. LPA s.146 requires the lessor to serve a notice on the lessee stipulating:

- the breach complained of;
- requiring that the breach is remedied, if it is capable of remedy; and
- payment of compensation, if required.

Under this procedure the court is given the discretion to decide whether to grant relief from forfeiture (LPA 1925 s.146(2) and (4)). It should also be noted that the lessor could waive his or her right to forfeit the lease, if he (or she) or it does something that acknowledges the existence of the lease after he or it has had knowledge of the breach. The difficulty with the procedure is determining whether the breach is capable of remedy, when relief will be granted and whether the lessor has waived his or her right to forfeit.

The question of whether a breach is capable of remedy is a difficult one. Essentially, this is a question of fact in every case. It is important to get this right otherwise, if the lessor stipulates in the notice that the breach is incapable of remedy when in fact it is, then the s.146 notice is defective and will render the possession proceedings defective as well. In *Expert Clothing Service & Sales Ltd.* v *Hillgate House* [1986] the court decided that the breach of the covenant to build within a specific time period was capable of remedy. The reason for this was because the landlord suffered no irretrievable damage. Compare this decision with *Scala House and District Property Co Ltd.* v *Forbes* [1974] where the court held that a breach of a covenant against subletting was incapable of remedy. In the latter case, the court suggested that breach of a negative covenant was irremediable. The current practice is to decide the issue of remediability by looking at the facts and circumstances of the case. These include the nature of the covenant and the court then decides whether in fact the breach is one that is capable of remedy rather than looking at whether the covenant is positive or negative in nature. For example, *Savva & Savva* v *Hussein* [1997] concerned a negative covenant but the court nevertheless decided that the breach was capable of remedy. A similar approach was taken in *Billson* v *Residential Apartments Ltd.* [1992] where the court doubted whether the breach of a covenant not to make alterations was incapable of remedy.

A breach of covenant not to use the premises for immoral purposes has been regarded as an irremediable breach because it attaches a stigma to the property – *Rugby School (Governors)* v *Tannahill* [1935] – but see *Glass* v *Kencakes* [1966].

It should also be noted that in the case of a breach of covenant to repair, the Leasehold Property (Repairs) Act 1938 is applicable. This only applies to leases for 7 years with at least 3 years left to run. The effect of this Act is that the lessee can issue a counter notice within 28 days of service of the notice under s.146. Once the counter notice is served, the forfeiture proceedings cannot continue until leave of court is obtained. The purpose of this piece of legislation is to protect lessees from unscrupulous lessors seeking to take possession of the property towards the end of the lease so that it would not be subject to a renewal of the lease.

Relief from forfeiture

Under the s.146 procedure, the court has the power to grant relief from forfeiture to the lessee and sub-lessee, if there is one. In s.146(2), the court is asked to have regard to the 'proceedings and conduct of the parties . . . and all the other circumstances'. In *Shiloh Spinners* v *Harding* [1973] the court made it clear that in exercising its discretion under s.146(2) regard should be had to the willfulness and gravity of the breach and the disparity between the value of the lease and the damage caused by the breach. The last point was considered in *Van Harlem* v *Kasner* [1992] where the court suggested that it would have been prepared to grant relief to the lessee because of the disparity in value of the lease and the damage caused, if the breach had not been waived.

Where there is an innocent sub-lessee but the head lease is being forfeited, it can be harsh on the sub-lessee. The court can grant the sub-lessee relief from forfeiture under LPA 1925 s.146(4). The sub-lessee may apply for relief from forfeiture and if the relief is granted, the sub-lessee will become the immediate lessee of the lessor but only for the duration of the remainder of the sub-lease.

Waiver

A lessor can be deemed to have waived his or its claim to forfeiture of the lease, where he or it does something which acknowledges the continuance of the lease after the lessor has knowledge of the breach of covenant. For example, if the lessor is aware of the lessee's breach of the covenant not to make alterations and demands rent, this would be deemed to be a waiver of the right to forfeiture. In *Iperion Investments* v *Broadwalk House Residents* [1992] the lessor knew that alteration works had been done in breach of covenant but continued to demand and accept the rent. The court decided that the lessor could not forfeit the lease as he had waived his right to do so. Knowledge of the breach can also be imputed to the lessor via his or its agents. For instance, in *Metropolitan Properties Co Ltd* v *Cordery* [1980] the court decided that the knowledge of the porter at the property that there had been a breach of covenant could be imputed to the lessor.

Assignment of leases and transferability of obligations

In *Centrovincial Estates Ltd* v *Bulk Storage Ltd* [1983] a lease was granted for a term of 21 years. The rent was to be reviewed after 14 years. The defendant lessee assigned the lease and the assignee of the lease agreed to an increase in the rent. The assignee then defaulted in the rent and the plaintiff (who was an assignee of the lessor) sued the defendant for the rent arrears. The court decided that the lessee remained liable after the assignment and accordingly the original lessee was liable to pay the rent arrears.

Where the business is the original lessee of the property and decides not to continue running its business at the particular property, unless there is a break clause in the lease, it cannot terminate the lease. Where the lease permits the assignment or subletting of the property, the business can assign or sublet the premises. Assignment of the lease must be by deed (LPA 1925 s.52).

It is often the case that leases contain clauses that prevent the assignment, parting with possession or subletting of the property. There are two types of such covenants:

- an absolute covenant – where the lessor may refuse consent to the assignment, parting with possession or subletting even though his or her refusal is unreasonable.
- a qualified covenant – this is where the covenant states that the assignment, etc. cannot take place without the consent of the lessor.

In the case of the qualified covenant, the Landlord and Tenant Act 1927 s.19 implies into this covenant the proviso that the consent will not be unreasonably withheld. The court in *Houlder Bros* v *Gibbs* [1925] stated that the lessor's reasons for refusal must relate to:

- the character or personality of the intended assignee; or
- the proposed use of the premises.

This approach has been criticized in *Viscount Tredegar* v *Harwood* [1929], where their Lordships thought the approach in *Houlder Bros* v *Gibbs* [1925] was too narrow. However, this was merely an *obiter dicta* and later decisions have followed the approach in *Houlder Bros* v *Gibbs* [1925]. *In Bickel* v *Duke of Westminster* [1977] a lessor's refusal of consent was held to be reasonable because the assignee would secure statutory rights that were not in existence at the time of the lease. In *Bickel*, the Court referred with approval the decision of the court in *Houlder Bros* v *Gibbs* [1925].

The lessor must give his or her decision whether he or she consents to the assignment, etc., within a reasonable time – Landlord and Tenant Act 1988. Examples of reasonable refusal to consent to the assignment include the unsatisfactory references of the assignee (*Shanly* v *Ward* [1913]), and possible interference with future development of the area (*Pimms Ltd* v *Tallow Chandlers Co* [1964]).

In the case of leases created after 1 January 1996, the parties can stipulate in the lease the grounds upon which it is reasonable for the lessor to withhold consent to an assignment of the lease.

An important aspect of the assignment of the lease is whether the original lessees remain liable for breaches of covenants committed by assignees. In the case of leases granted prior to 1996, the enforceability of the covenants is based on privity of contract. The consequence of this is that the lessor may enforce all the covenants against the lessee throughout the duration of the lease even though the lessee may have assigned the lease and the assignee may have agreed to an increase in rent. The original lessee remains liable as seen in *Centrovincial Estates Ltd* v *Bulk Storage Ltd.* [1983] and *Selous Street Properties Ltd.* v *Oronel Fabrics Ltd.* [1984]. The original lessee can always get an indemnity from the assignee under LPA s.77, but more often than not, the assignee is bankrupt, insolvent or cannot be found.

This can cause unfairness as seen in *Centrovincial Estates Ltd.* v *Bulk Storage Ltd.* The original lessee has been subjected to a more onerous obligation (the higher rent) without his knowledge or consent. As a result of this, the Landlord and Tenant (Covenants) Act 1995 was enacted. The Act generally applies to leases created after 1995. Under s.5 of this Act, the lessor cannot sue the original lessee for breach by subsequent assignees under the lease. However, the original lessee could be made liable for the first assignee. Before the lessor allows the assignment of the lease, the lessee would be asked to guarantee that the assignee will comply with the covenants in the lease. By doing so the lessee becomes liable for the first assignee's actions. This takes the form of an authorized guarantee agreement. The 1995 Act makes it clear that the original lessee's liability is only in respect of the first assignment and no further. Any attempt to extend the original lessee's liability beyond the first assignment is void – s.25. It must be stressed that this does not apply to leases created before 1 January 1996; it only applies to leases created after that date.

The 1995 Act also introduced provisions to deal with pre 1 January 1996 leases where the liability of the original lessee is for the whole duration of the lease. The usual problem with assignees is the non-payment of rent or service charges. The Act overcomes this by introducing a requirement that should the lessor wish to pursue a claim against the original lessee for payment of arrears, the lessor must notify the lessee of the arrears within 6 months from the date they first accrue. This rule applies to all leases whether created before or after 1 January 1996. The rationale for this is to enable the original lessee to take remedial action before the arrears build up to unmanageable amounts.

The liability of assignees *vis-à-vis* the covenants in leases which are created before 1 January 1996, is only liable for covenants that touch and concern the land. In *Spencer's Case* (1583) the court decided that a covenant to build a wall was not a covenant that touched and concerned the land and therefore did not bind the assignee's successors in title. Lessors are likewise only bound by covenants that touch and concern the land: this is embodied in LPA, ss.141 and 142. Where leases have been created after 1 January 1996, all covenants pass with the assignment and there is no need to establish that the covenant is one that touches and concerns the land.

REGISTERED AND UNREGISTERED TITLE

In England and Wales, there was until relatively recently a dual system of title; namely:

- unregistered title;
- registered title.

In the case of unregistered title, ownership of land was evidenced by title deeds. The owner had to show the transfer of title from his predecessors to him in order to establish good title. If the deeds were lost or destroyed then the owner could not prove title. There was no central register for ownership of land. All land in England and

Wales is now subject to compulsory registration of title. That means that when there is a dealing with property, whether by sale, mortgage, lease, gift or otherwise, if the land is held under unregistered title, the parties have to apply to convert the title into registered title (Land Registration Act 1925, s.123). However, until there is a dealing with the property, there is no obligation to convert to registered title although the authorities are encouraging land owners to convert where possible.

In the case of registered title, there is a central register proving ownership of title and encumbrances affecting the land, for example, restrictive covenants and easements should appear on the register. The exception to that is overriding interests, which do not appear on the register and can bind the subsequent owners of the land.

It is important to bear this in mind because some of the types of interests discussed here, which affect ownership of land, such as easements and covenants, will only bind subsequent owners of the land if the proper procedures for protection of such rights are followed. As a business, rights such as the benefit of an easement to park cars on adjoining land, are important and hence the need to ensure the proper procedures have been followed to ensure continued enjoyment of such rights and interests.

PROGRESS TESTS

1 Timothy and Helene have signed an agreement entitled a 'licence' for the small shop on the High Street where they run their newsagents' business. The duration of the licence was for five years. Although the licence states that the lessors have the right to occupy the premises together with Timothy and Helene, they have never done so. The lessor, XYZ Ltd is now claiming to be entitled to evict them without any reasons even though there are three more years to run on the licence.

Can they be evicted?

2 XYZ Ltd is the freehold owner of a shop located on the High Street. It has discovered that the owner of the neighbouring shop intends to demolish it and to build a ten-storey block of flats in its place. There is a covenant on all the titles for the shops on the High Street that restricts the use of the premises for anything other than commercial purposes.

Can XYZ Ltd object to this and prevent the neighbour from building the flats?

3 Rose is the freehold owner of a shop. She granted a 25-year lease to Ben who started a business selling toys there. The lease stipulated that the lessee is not permitted either to alter the premises or sublet them without the consent of the lessor. Rose has discovered that Ben has recently sublet the premises to Connie who now runs a manicure shop there. Connie has built numerous cubicles in the shop and has painted the front of the shop bright purple.

Can Rose do anything about this?

7 Criminal liability and business organizations

Penny Childs

WHAT IS THE DISTINCTION BETWEEN CRIMINAL AND CIVIL LIABILITY?

> If a person drives a mechanically propelled vehicle on a road or other public place without due care and attention, or without reasonable consideration for other persons using the road or place, he is guilty of an offence (Road Traffic Act 1988 s.3 (as substituted by Road Traffic Act 1991 s.2)).

Criminal and civil liability differ in that a crime is a public wrong rather than purely an interference with a private right. Whilst it is possible for the same incident to give rise to both criminal and civil liability, the consequences of being found guilty of a crime or liable for a civil wrong may differ because it is said that the purposes of the two branches of law differ. Criminal law is primarily concerned with punishment of the offender whilst civil law is primarily concerned with compensating the victim. The liability created by the Road Traffic Act 1988 s.3 is criminal. The punishment is a fine and penalty points and there is a discretion about whether to disqualify the driver. A road accident that gives rise to criminal liability for careless driving might also give rise to a civil action by a victim in tort. In this situation, liability would not arise for the tort of breach of statutory duty, but might arise, for example, in the tort of negligence. The consequence of such an action would be an award of damages payable to the victim of the accident.

Civil actions are generally brought by applicants/claimants (the 'victims') whilst the majority of criminal actions are brought on behalf of the state through the Crown Prosecution Service. Some prosecutions are brought by other public officers. For example, offences under the Health and Safety at Work Act 1974 are enforced by a separate regulatory agency (the Health and Safety Executive). There is also some scope for a private prosecution by victims. In a civil action, the decision about whether to sue a defendant is entirely a matter of choice for the applicant whilst in criminal law, a prosecution may be brought (or not) irrespective of the wishes of the victim. Some other fundamental differences between civil and criminal actions lie in the burden of proof, the procedure and the court structure.

Many crimes (like the crime of careless driving) derive from statute and indeed most of those applicable to businesses will be statutory. Some statutes define the elements of the crime whilst others simply declare conduct to be a crime but leave its definition to the common law. In any case, interpretation of a statute is for the judiciary. A few crimes derive solely from common law as do general principles, including most defences. Crimes are divided into those triable only on indictment, only summarily and those triable either way. The more serious, indictable, offences are tried in the Crown Court by jury whilst summary offences, which are all statutory, like careless driving, are tried in the Magistrates' Courts without a jury.

The relevance of criminal liability in an organizational context

When considering offences that may be committed *against* a business, offences against the person will be of no relevance. There is scope for an organization to be the 'victim' of an offence against property and some of the most likely offences will be outlined at the end of the chapter.

The position is different when considering the liability that an organization incurs for *committing* a crime. A corporation, for example, can be tried for any crime except murder and treason. Most liability incurred by organizations falls into the category of strict liability. There is however scope for liability for fault based crimes through the doctrines of vicarious and corporate liability. One area that has caused concern, and has recently led to recommendation for reform, is the liability that an organization may face for activities or failures that cause the death of employees or others. The legal position in cases of corporate killing is one that should be of particular and current interest to business enterprises. However, before examining these areas, it is necessary to understand the basic structure of criminal liability.

THE NATURE OF CRIMINAL LIABILITY

> In *Fagan* v *Metropolitan Police Commissioner* [1969] Mr Fagan accidentally drove onto a policeman's foot and then refused to move after this was drawn to his attention.

It is a principle of the common law that an act does not make a person guilty of a crime unless his or her mind is also guilty. So Mr Fagan could not be guilty purely in respect of the act of driving onto the policeman's foot because the crime charged (assault) also requires proof of a guilty state of mind which Mr Fagan did not have at that time. The common law position is expressed in the maxim: '*actus reus non facit reum nisi mens sit rea*'. *Actus reus* is Latin for wrongful conduct and *mens rea* means guilty mind. This principle needs further explanation and it must be remembered that there are exceptions to it (especially under legislation) where liability is imposed without proof of a guilty mind.

Wrongful conduct

> In *R* v *Pittwood* (1902) a railway gatekeeper forgot to shut the gate and a person crossing the railway track was killed by an oncoming train. The gatekeeper was found guilty of manslaughter.

Criminal liability does not only arise in respect of acts done by the defendant. Whilst an act is the most common form of an *actus reus*, many crimes can also be committed by omission and some simply by an event or state of affairs (sometimes called 'status offences'). What amounts to the *actus reus* of an offence depends on the definition of the crime. For example, the *actus reus* of theft is defined as *appropriation of property belonging to another,* whilst that of manslaughter is *conduct causing the death of a human being.*

Many statutory offences are defined in terms of an omission to act. An example is failing to submit a tax return. It is also possible to be guilty of other offences, which do not specify an omission, by failing to act when under a duty to do so. A legal duty to act may be imposed by a statute or a contract or because of a special relationship between the defendant and victim, a voluntary assumption of a duty to care for the victim or because the defendant created a dangerous situation. Mr Pittwood was found guilty of manslaughter by omission because he had failed in his duty to act arising under his contract of employment. A similar issue arose in *Fagan* namely whether Mr Fagan could be guilty for failing to remove his car from the foot, by which time he had a guilty mind. The court decided that a crime like assault could not be committed by pure omission. However, Mr Fagan was found guilty on the basis that his conduct was an act (remaining on the foot) which continued up to and including the time he formed a guilty mind.

Some crimes require that the defendant's conduct bring about a result. For example, homicide requires proof that the conduct caused death. In these cases, the prosecution must also prove a causal link between the conduct and the result. Proof of causation in criminal law is similar to that in tort. The prosecution must prove 'but-for' cause and an unbroken chain of causation, generally established by showing that the defendant's conduct was the operative and significant (not sole) cause of the result.

Guilty mind

The state of mind required for conviction will also be found in the definition of the crime. It may be intention, recklessness or a special mental state, like dishonesty. Liability for some crimes may also be incurred through negligence (an objective form of fault). These types of fault liability will be examined later because the maxim *actus reus non facit reum nisi mens sit rea* has exceptions which are particularly relevant for organizational liability. These are crimes of strict liability where liability arises without proof of a guilty mind in respect of some, often central, part of the *actus reus.* Since many of these crimes are regulatory in nature and deal with matters of 'public welfare' they govern what are, commonly, business activities.

STRICT LIABILITY

In *Gammon Ltd* v *Attorney-General of Hong Kong* [1985] the company carried out building works in Hong Kong. Charges were brought under the local Building Ordinance for materially deviating from the approved building plans thereby operating in a way likely to risk injury or damage. The company pleaded that it did not intend to deviate from the plans in a material way and did not intend to cause a risk of injury or damage.

In *Pharmaceutical Society of Great Britain* v *Storkwain Ltd* [1986] retail chemists were charged under the Medicines Act 1968 with supplying drugs on forged prescriptions. The prescriptions purported to have been signed by a Dr Irani. The pharmacists, who had taken reasonable care, were deceived by the forgery and did not know that the signatures were false.

Most major crimes require proof of *mens rea* and all common law crimes require *mens rea* except public nuisance, contempt of court, criminal libel and outraging public decency. Where a statutory offence does not expressly require *mens rea*, whether or not it is a crime of strict liability is a matter of statutory interpretation. The courts have always held that where a statute is silent on the matter, 'there is a presumption of law that *mens rea* is required' and the presumption is strongest where the offence is 'truly criminal' in nature: *Gammon Ltd*. However, the Privy Council in this case confirmed that the presumption may be displaced but only if 'this is clearly or by necessary implication the effect of the statute' and only where 'the statute is concerned with an issue of social concern, and public safety is such an issue'. In *Gammon*, the court decided that since the purpose of the Ordinance was to regulate building sites and to protect public safety, the offence was strict and did not require proof that the company knew the deviation was material or that there was a risk of injury. Similarly in *Storkwain*, because the offence was concerned with public safety, the company was convicted despite lack of fault on its part. This is the effect of imposing strict liability. The defendant's state of mind is irrelevant and so (in the absence of any defence) it was no excuse that the pharmacist did not know or realize the possibility that the prescriptions were forged. It was not even a defence that nothing more could be done to prevent the offence occurring or that reasonable care had been taken (the pharmacist had, in fact, telephoned the number on the prescription but was deceived by the person answering).

The decision about whether to impose strict liability is affected by a number of factors:

- the wording of the statute;
- the subject matter of the offence;
- the nature of the penalty;
- effective promotion of the object of the statute.

The wording of the statute

In *Alphacell Ltd* v *Woodward* [1972] a company manufactured paper and its process produced effluent which ran into settling tanks with an overflow channel into a river. It had a pumping system that should have prevented an overflow and it regularly inspected the pumps. However the pumps became obstructed by vegetation and polluted water entered the river without the company's knowledge. The company was charged with causing polluted matter to enter a river contrary to the Rivers (Prevention of Pollution) Act 1951 s.2.

In *James & Sons Ltd* v *Smee* [1955] a company owned a lorry and trailer which was used without the brake cables being reconnected after the trailer had been uncoupled. The company was charged with permitting a vehicle to be used with defective brakes contrary to the Motor Vehicles (Construction and Use) Regulations 1951. This made it an offence to 'use or cause or permit to be used' a motor vehicle in contravention of the regulations.

If a *mens rea* word is used in part of the statute being considered but is absent from the part in question, this may lead to the inference that the omission is deliberate and that therefore Parliament intended strict liability. In *Storkwain* various sections in the

Medicines Act 1968 expressly provided for *mens rea* but the section under consideration did not and so strict liability was inferred. However, this is not always the case. For example in *Lim Chin Aik* v *R* [1963] (a case concerning illegal entry into Singapore), the fact that the word 'knowingly' was used in a number of sections of the relevant Ordinance, but not in the section being considered, was not enough to render the offence one of strict liability.

Some words are construed as implying *mens rea* whilst others are strict. The words 'sell' and 'use' do not import *mens rea* whilst 'knowingly', 'procure' and 'suffer' do. Thus in *James & Son Ltd* if it had been possible to charge the company with 'using' the vehicle, strict liability would have been incurred. However, the position is not so clear in other cases. The word 'cause' has been interpreted as imposing strict liability when used in the context of pollution but not in the context of causing another to commit an offence. Thus in *James & Son Ltd* the employer would not have been liable if charged with 'causing the use' because that would have required proof of *mens rea* (knowledge that the braking system was defective). However in *Alphacell* the company was guilty despite lack of fault on its part because its system design had caused the pollution. The imposition of strict liability was further confirmed by the fact that the word 'knowingly' was used in the context of 'permitting' pollution but did not appear in front of the word 'cause'. The word 'permit' in itself has been construed as strict in some contexts, for example 'permitting a vehicle to be used without insurance', but not in others. So in *James & Son Ltd,* the company was not guilty because 'permitting the use' required proof of knowledge of the defect which was not established. However, in *Vehicle Inspectorate* v *Nuttall* [1999] the owner of a coach business was prosecuted for 'permitting' his drivers to drive for too long without a break. The House of Lords held that knowledge that the drivers were doing so was not required and the owner could be liable for 'permitting' the activity by failing to take reasonable steps to prevent drivers from doing it.

The subject matter of the offence

In *Hobbs* v *Winchester Corporation* [1910] a butcher had sold meat that was unfit for human consumption. He was not aware of its condition nor could he have discovered it by any examination that he could reasonably have been expected to make.

In *St Margaret's Trust Ltd* [1958] a car dealer and customers misled a finance company about the price of cars being sold. As a result the finance company advanced over 50 per cent of the actual purchase price thereby contravening the Hire Purchase Order in force at the time.

The terms used to describe the types of offence most likely to be construed as strict include those dealing with matters of 'social concern'; 'public health or safety': *Gammon*; 'public welfare': *Lim Chin Aik*; 'regulatory offences'; 'quasi-criminal' offences: *Storkwain*; acts that 'are not criminal in any real sense but are acts which in the public interest are prohibited under a penalty': *Sherras* v *De Rutzen* [1895] (a case involving the sale of alcohol where the relevant licensing offence was held to require proof of *mens rea*).

The prevailing view is that the consequences of these offences is likely to be so damaging and widespread that the public interest outweighs the interest of the defendant. It is on this basis that offences dealing with consumer and public safety have regularly been held to be strict liability. For this reason, the butcher in *Hobbs* was guilty because the offence related to public health and safety. The fact that *Alphacell* involved pollution, which could have grave social consequences, was used to justify the conclusion that the offence was strict. *St Margaret's Trust* demonstrates a different type of 'social concern'. The finance company was guilty despite lack of fault because of the economic climate at the time. DONOVAN J, said:

> The object of the order was to help defend the currency against the peril of inflation which, if unchecked, would bring disaster on the country.

Offences that have been held to be strict on this basis include those dealing with food and drink (such as offences under the Food Safety Act 1990); licensing offences; drug offences; inflation; health and safety; product safety; and trade descriptions (under the Trade Descriptions Act 1968). Strict liability is often imposed for regulatory, summary, offences where the legislation is aimed at corporate activity precisely because of the difficulty in establishing *mens rea* on the part of a corporation (discussed further later).

The nature of the penalty

The more severe the penalty the more likely the crime will be viewed as 'truly criminal' and a requirement of *mens rea* implied. Regulatory offences which only carry a fine are more likely to be strict.

Effective promotion of the object of the statute

In *Wings Ltd* v *Ellis* [1985] a travel agency published a travel brochure which contained a false description. Once discovered, it was corrected in future brochures. The company was prosecuted under the Trade Descriptions Act 1968 s.14(1)(a) when someone read an uncorrected brochure.

It is frequently said that strict liability will only be imposed if it 'will be effective to promote the objects of the statute by encouraging greater vigilance to prevent the commission of the offence': *Gammon*. This according to the Privy Council in *Lim Chin Aik* means that:

> there must be something [the defendant] can do ... by supervision or inspection, by improvement of his business methods ... which will promote the observance of the regulations.

In *Wings* the company was found guilty even though it had done its best to prevent reliance on the brochure on the basis that liability would promote the purpose of the statute and encourage greater vigilance in respect of trade descriptions.

Statutory defences

In *Smedleys Ltd* v *Breed* [1974] there was a caterpillar in a can of Smedleys' peas. Smedleys had canned 3 500 000 tins of peas in 1971 with only three other complaints. The caterpillar had not been discovered in the processing system because it was the same colour, size and weight as a pea (and probably as nutritious as a pea).

> Smedleys was prosecuted under the law, as it was then, set out in the Food and Drugs Act 1955 and raised the statutory defence that the presence of the insect was an 'unavoidable consequence of the process of . . . preparation'.

All the ordinary defences to criminal liability apply to strict liability (for example, automatism, duress). Moreover it was confirmed in *Alphacell* that in the case of causing pollution, for example, defences such as Act of God or interference by a trespasser would apply. Moreover, it is now common for statutes which create strict liability to provide special defences. Where there is such a defence, it may be taken to imply that the offence was therefore intended to be one of strict liability.

The following are examples of common types of statutory defence.

- Proving that the defendant neither knew of nor was negligent about a particular element of the offence. An example is Misuse of Drugs Act 1971 s.28 which provides a defence to possession of drugs if the defendant didn't believe, suspect or have reason to suspect that the substance was a controlled drug.
- Proving that the offence was due to some 'other' cause (for example, a mistake, the default of another or an accident) and that the defendant took all reasonable precautions and exercised due diligence to avoid the commission of the offence. An example can be found in Trade Descriptions Act 1968 s.24(1) and was pleaded in *Tesco* v *Nattrass* which is discussed under corporate liability. Another example is in the Video Recordings Act 1984 and was pleaded in *Tesco* v *Brent* which is discussed under vicarious liability.
- Proving that the defendant took all reasonable precautions and exercised all due diligence to avoid the commission of the offence. An example can be found in Reg 14 of the General Product Safety Regulations 1994 and the Food Safety Act 1990 s.21.

However, in *Smedleys* whilst the defendants had taken all practical precautions to prevent the presence of the caterpillar there was no such defence to the crime charged. The defence available required proof that the presence of the caterpillar was unavoidable and the court held that it was 'avoidable' and Smedleys was guilty.

FAULT-BASED LIABILITY

Intention

> In *R* v *Hancock & Shankland* [1986] during the national miners' strike, two striking miners pushed a concrete slab over a bridge onto a motorway. They either intended to block the road or simply to frighten another miner who was travelling to work in a taxi. In fact the slab hit the taxi and the driver was killed.

Where an offence is not one of strict liability, *mens rea* or negligence will be required for liability. Serious offences are often only satisfied by proof of intention. For example, murder requires proof of intention to kill or intention to cause grievous bodily harm. There may be evidence of such an intent if the defendant personally realized that death or grievous bodily harm was a virtually certain consequence of the conduct. Hancock and Shankland, who may not have realized this, were found not guilty of murder because of a misdirection but they were convicted of manslaughter (which does not require proof of such an intent).

Subjective recklessness

In *R* v *Cunningham* [1957] the defendant broke into a gas meter. Gas escaped and partially suffocated someone. Mr Cunningham had not intended this to happen. He was charged with maliciously administering a noxious thing.

Most offences are satisfied by proof of recklessness as well as intention. Such offences include, for example, manslaughter and criminal damage. Mr Cunningham was acquitted because of a misdirection. The crime required, at least, proof of subjective recklessness which involved proving that he, personally, realized a risk of injury but carried on regardless.

Objective recklessness

In *R* v *Caldwell* [1982] the defendant set fire to a hotel but claimed that he was so drunk that he had not realized that his conduct ran a risk of endangering life. He was charged with aggravated arson.

A minority of offences is also satisfied by 'objective' recklessness although this is probably restricted to criminal damage and arson contrary to the Criminal Damage Act 1971. Mr Caldwell was found guilty of arson because he had been objectively reckless by failing to consider a risk which would have been recognized as obvious and serious by a reasonable person.

Special mental states

In *R* v *Flynn* [1970] a cinema manager 'borrowed' £6 from his employer as an advance on his wages, leaving an IOU in the till.

Some crimes require proof of a special mental state. Examples include theft contrary to the Theft Act 1968 s.1, and obtaining property by deception contrary to the Theft Act 1968 s.15 which require proof of dishonesty. Mr Flynn was not guilty of theft because he honestly believed that his employer would consent to him taking the money in the circumstances.

Negligence

In *R* v *Adomako* [1995] a patient died when a locum anaesthetist failed to notice that his ventilation tube had become disconnected.

Some crimes are satisfied by proof of negligence. In manslaughter, the negligence must be very serious (gross) to give rise to liability. Mr Adomako was charged with manslaughter and the House of Lords held that it was necessary to prove a breach of a duty of care which was so grossly negligent as to be considered criminal.

FAULT-BASED CRIMES AND ORGANIZATIONAL LIABILITY

In *Attorney General's Reference (No 2 of 1999)* [2000] GWT, a railway company, was prosecuted for manslaughter following the death of seven people in the Southall rail crash.

It should be apparent that organizational liability for an offence is difficult to establish where the crime requires proof of *mens rea* since this generally involves proof of a personal state of mind on the part of an individual. There is, however, the possibility of organizational liability incurred through the acts and subjective state of mind of those employed by or involved in the running of the organization. This arises through the operation of vicarious or corporate liability. The possibility of liability for objective fault (negligence or objective recklessness) could be more easily applied to organizations. It would take little stretch of the imagination to say, for example, that an organization has policies or practices that fall far below the standards to be reasonably expected of such an organization. This could amount to gross negligence. However criminal law is still based on the notion of individual responsibility and an organization can only be liable for a fault-based crime if someone within the organization can be identified as the wrongdoer for whom the organization may be held corporately liable. Therefore, had a prosecution for manslaughter been brought against the National Health Service Trust that employed Mr Adomako it would have been necessary to establish his liability first (or that of some other person working for the Trust). Then the relationship between that person and the corporation would need to be examined to determine whether it gave rise to parasitic liability. This is illustrated by *Attorney General's Reference (No 2 of 1999)* where personal liability for manslaughter was rejected and the need to establish fault on the part of an individual for whom GWT could be held responsible was affirmed. The methods for imposing liability on a human or corporate employer will now be examined.

Participation in crime – personal liability

In *R* v *British Steel plc* [1995] two sub-contractors were employed by British Steel on a labour only basis. They were employed to move a steel platform under the supervision of a company employee. One of the contractors died when the platform collapsed. The company was prosecuted under s.3(1) of the Health and Safety at Work Act 1974 for having failed in their duty 'to conduct [its] undertaking in such a way as to ensure, so far as reasonably practicable' that the contractor was not 'exposed to risks to . . . health and safety'.

Liability for many regulatory crimes arises in respect of a particular status (such as being an employer of a workforce or an owner of a vehicle). These offences may be committed by any individual or corporate body with the relevant status. For example, the employer's duties imposed by the Health and Safety at Work Act 1974 are personal and liability arises for a breach of the duty by the employer (human or corporate). So the offence charged in *British Steel* could be committed by the company failing to set up a safe system of work. However, frequently, the question is whether an employer can be liable for the act or omissions (and even states of mind) of employees. Thus the question that arose in *British Steel* was whether the actions of its employee who supervised the work could render the company liable for a breach of its personal duty. Ultimately, the company was liable. Companies were also personally liable in *R* v *Associated Octel Co Ltd* [1996] and *R* v *Gateway Foodmarkets Ltd* [1997] which also involved prosecutions under the Health and Safety at Work Act 1974.

Participation in crime – vicarious liability

> In *Seaboard Offshore Ltd* v *Secretary of State for Transport* [1994] the defendant company's ship set sail before the Chief Engineer had familiarized himself with the engines. The engines were flooded due to an error on the engineer's part. The company was prosecuted for failing to take reasonable care to ensure that the ship was operated in a safe manner.

Generally a person is not vicariously liable for the crimes of another. Thus in *Seaboard*, the House of Lords held that the wording of the statute meant that the owners or charterers of a ship could only be guilty of the offence if they 'personally' failed to take all reasonable steps in the circumstances of the case. They could not be held liable for a failure on the part of the engineer. It was, however, noted in the case that, if it had an unsafe system, the company could be liable (as owner or charterer) for failing to ensure the safe operation of a ship. It would not also be necessary to establish the liability of a natural person since this would be personal liability (as above).

There are exceptions where vicarious liability is imposed. Two common law offences, public nuisance and criminal libel, can be committed vicariously but most such liability arises from statutory offences. This may be by express statutory provision but more commonly it is implied by statutory interpretation. There are two methods for imposing vicarious criminal liability: extensive construction and delegation.

Extensive construction

> In *Coppen* v *Moore (No 2)* [1898] an assistant in one of the defendant's six shops sold a ham misdescribed as 'Scotch ham'. The misdescription occurred without the shop manager's knowledge and contrary to the defendant's specific instructions not to describe the hams by place of origin.

> In *Tesco Supermarkets Ltd* v *Brent London Borough Council* [1993] a cashier in Tesco sold an 18 classified film to a 14-year old. Tesco was prosecuted under the Video Recordings Act 1984 and raised the statutory defence that it did not know, nor had reasonable grounds to believe, that the buyer was under age.

In some statutory offences, the courts will construe the conduct of one person (an agent) as the conduct of another (the principal). This method of imposing vicarious liability only applies to strict liability offences. *Mens rea* cannot be imputed in this way. Three conditions must be satisfied for liability to arise: the verb in the offence must be capable of being construed extensively; the act must be committed by an agent or employee; and it must have been committed in the course of employment or agency.

Verbs that have been held to be capable of extensive construction include 'use', 'cause', 'sell' and 'supply'. So for example, an employer uses a vehicle when an employee or agent drives or otherwise uses it: *Green* v *Burnett & Another* [1955] (a case of driving a van with defective brakes) and a company causes pollution when it is caused by an employee. In *Coppen* v *Moore* the employer was guilty of selling the ham through his employee. He was 'the seller although not the actual salesman'.

Liability arises even where the employer specifically prohibits the activity and so it was no defence in *Coppen* that the shop owner had expressly forbidden description of the hams by origin. Since selling was an authorized act (albeit done in an unauthorized manner) it had occurred in the course of the employee's employment and so the defendant was guilty. In *Tesco Supermarkets* v *Brent*, Tesco was guilty of supplying the video and could not rely on the statutory defence because the cashier did have reason to believe that the buyer was under age. This case can also be taken to illustrate the fact that a corporate body can be vicariously liable in the same way as a human employer.

Delegation

In *R* v *Winson* [1969] the defendant was the director of a number of limited companies which owned licensed clubs. A manager was appointed to run each club. One manager was responsible for the sale of alcohol to people who were not club members in breach of the Licensing Act 1964.

In *Vane* v *Yiannapoullos* [1965] the defendant licensee of a restaurant was in the basement of the premises when his employee, a waitress, sold alcohol to persons not having a meal. The sale was in breach of the restaurant licence and the defendant was charged with 'knowingly' selling alcohol to persons not covered by the licence.

Vicarious liability imposed through the delegation principle depends purely on whether delegation has taken place. The relationship between the parties may therefore be one of employer and employee, principal and agent, partner and partner or just delegator and delegate. Unlike extensive construction, the principle allows the acts and also the *mens rea* of the delegate to be attributed to the delegator. Thus the company director in *Winson* was found guilty of the offence of 'knowingly' selling alcohol to persons not covered by the licence, even though he had not personally made the sale and did not know that it had happened. He had delegated control over the club to the manager and so was vicariously liable for both the manager's acts and *mens rea*.

Whether there has been 'effective' delegation or not is a question of fact. In *Vane* v *Yiannapoullos* the licensee was not guilty because the House of Lords decided that delegation had not taken place. He had not handed over 'all effective management' to the waitress and had not 'left her in charge'. One factor considered relevant in both *Winson* and *Vane* was whether the defendant was absent from the premises. However, the licensee's presence in another bar in *Howker* v *Robinson* [1973] did not prevent the court from holding that he had delegated to a barman who made an illegal sale in another bar. Vicarious liability was imposed in this case because the licensee had handed over 'managerial functions and responsibility' for part of the premises to his barman.

The principle only applies if the delegate acts within the scope of her or his authority but, just as with extensive construction, it is no defence that a delegator has expressly forbidden the activity. According to *Winson* the principle of delegation only applies where the statute uses a *mens rea* word. Another restricting factor is that the principle probably only applies to licensing offences or those concerned with the management of certain premises. This method of imposing vicarious liability therefore is of limited application to corporate bodies since a licensee will always be a natural person.

Participation in crime – corporate liability

In *Tesco Supermarkets Ltd* v *Nattrass* [1972] a branch manager in one of Tesco's stores had caused a false trade description relating to the sale price of washing powder. The question was whether Tesco could be held liable for his actions under the Trade Descriptions Act 1968. The company wished to rely on a statutory defence that it had taken all reasonable precaution and exercised due diligence and that the offence was due to the default of 'another person', the branch manager.

In *Meridian Global Funds Management Asia Ltd* v *Securities Commission* [1995] the investment manager and senior portfolio manager of Meridian Global invested in another company without making a disclosure required by statute. The company had no knowledge of the activities and the question was whether Meridian Global could be held liable for the breach of the securities legislation through the acts of its managers.

A corporation may incur personal or vicarious liability as indicated above. Moreover, assuming the conditions for the principles are satisfied, vicarious liability is incurred for the acts of all employees/delegates whatever their position in the company structure. However, vicarious liability cannot arise for traditional *mens rea* offences. There is a further doctrine which enables prosecution for more traditional fault-based (non-regulatory) offences which only applies to bodies corporate and not to human employers or unincorporated associations or partnerships. This is known as the doctrine of identification (or *alter ego*) whereby the company is identified with certain company officers such that their actions (and *mens rea*) are treated as the actions and states of mind of the company itself. This doctrine therefore enables a company to be found guilty of fault-based offences where a human employer could not be found guilty because of the limits of vicarious liability.

It has always been clear that a company is not identified with all those it employs. Liability used to be restricted to the actions of controlling officers rather than for those with less senior roles in the company hierarchy. The oft-quoted distinction between the 'brains' and the 'hands' of an organization is used to highlight the difference:

> A company may in many ways be likened to a human body. It has a brain and nerve centre which controls what it does. It also has the hands which hold the tools ... some ... are mere servants and agents who are nothing more than the hands to do the work ... others are directors and managers who represent the directing mind and will of the company and control what it does. DENNING LJ, in *Bolton* v *Graham* [1957].

A company is identified with its 'directing mind and will' and incurs corporate liability for almost any crime committed by such a person whilst performing his or her management function. Thus corporate liability could be incurred for crimes like fraud and those involving an intent to deceive: *DPP* v *Kent & Sussex Contractors Ltd* [1944], *ICR Haulage Ltd* [1944] and *Moore* v *I Bresler Ltd* [1944]. A company is not identified with its 'hands' and only incurs the more limited, vicarious liability for crimes committed by such employees. So, in trying to decide whether Tesco could be identified with its branch manager, the court examined the corporate structure to determine who carried out the functions of management. The shop manager was simply one of around 800 branch managers. He was not part of the 'nerve centre' and so was not identified with the company. Tesco therefore succeeded in its defence. It had a satisfactory system which meant it had acted with due diligence and since it was not identified with the manager, his default amounted to the 'default of another'.

The effect of *Tesco* was that only people like the managing director, the company secretary and members of the board of directors could be identified with the company. This decision limited corporate liability and made it easier for corporate liability to be avoided in larger organizations where it was unlikely that senior management would be involved in the daily activities of the company. As recognized in *National Rivers Authority* v *Alfred McAlpine Homes East* [1994] (a case involving pollution):

> in almost all cases the act or omission will be that of a person such as a workman, fitter, or plant operative in a fairly low position in the hierarchy of the industrial, agricultural or commercial concern.

The test was therefore out of line with the realities of modern corporate management structures and decentralized decision-making. It also failed to take account of the fact that the role of persons within a company may change such that they may be considered mere 'hands' in relation to one function but 'brains' in relation to another.

A more sophisticated approach was adopted in *Meridian*. The application of the *Tesco* test would have meant that Meridian was not liable for the actions of the investment manager because he was not a sufficiently 'superior' officer. After *Meridian*, identification ceases to be dependent on the status of the employee in the company hierarchy. Instead *Meridian* focuses attention on the language of the offence in question, its policy and content. It is necessary to determine who acts as the company for the purposes of the relevant statute such that their actions and states of mind can be attributed to it for that purpose. The purpose of the statute in *Meridian* was to disclose substantial investments to the company and to the Stock Exchange. Therefore the actions and states of mind of the manager, who had the company's authority to make such investments, were attributable to the company for that purpose (although not for other purposes) and *Meridian* was liable. The case of *Tesco Supermarkets* v *Brent London Borough Council* [1993] might also be interpreted as an application of the *Meridian* test.

Despite the recent widening of the responsibility of corporations, as employers, there is still dissatisfaction with the approach on corporate responsibility for crime. This is because liability still rests on identifying an individual within the corporate structure and establishing his or her personal liability before being able to attribute it to the company. Within larger companies, with complex organizational structures, it is often difficult to identify a responsible individual. Moreover, it is often the case that one individual cannot be singled out as blameworthy. Instead it is the actions or default of a number of individuals combined together that creates the elements of a crime. However, the possibility of basing corporate liability on aggregation in this way was rejected in *R* v *HM Coroner for East Kent, ex parte Spooner* (1989) and *R* v *P & O European Ferries (Dover) Ltd* (1991) (both cases arising out of the disaster of *The Herald of Free Enterprise*). Moreover it is often the culture, policy, procedures or systems of the company itself that are 'at fault' rather than individuals within the company. Whilst a model of liability focusing on the conduct of the company itself is the one adopted in the Health and Safety at Work Act, it is not currently possible to base liability for more traditional offences in this way. Liability for these offences is still parasitic. However, where, for example, the fault lies in failing to have a policy or a manager responsible for the particular activity, this prevents liability from arising. In this case, there is definitely no person to identify with the company and yet it is precisely the absence of such a person that gives rise to an offence.

FAULT-BASED CRIMES

What follows is a review of some of the fault-based offences that might be relevant to organizations either incurring liability corporately or as victim of the crime.

Manslaughter

In *R v P & O European Ferries (Dover) Ltd* (1991) the case arose out of the tragedy involving the sinking of the ferry *The Herald of Free Enterprise*. The ferry had set sail with its bow doors open. It capsized causing the death of 188 people. The assistant bosun who should have checked that the doors were shut was asleep. The chief officer had not checked the doors. The captain had no way of confirming they were shut from the bridge. Management had been informed that a warning light system was needed on the bridge but none was installed. P & O had no director solely in charge of safety and no clear policies or instructions dealing with safety measures for setting sail (or on open door sailing). There was a general communication failure within the company.

After criticizing the defaults of the assistant bosun, the Chief Officer and the Captain, the Sheen inquiry into the disaster reported in the following terms:

> the underlying cardinal faults lay higher up in the company. The Board of Directors did not appreciate their responsibility for safe management of their ships ... All concerned in management, from the members of the Board of Directors down to the junior superintendents, were guilty of fault ... From top to bottom the body corporate was infected with the disease of sloppiness (*The Sheen Report*).

In *R v Kite and OLL Ltd* [1994] a leisure company (OLL Ltd) and its managing director (Peter Kite) were prosecuted for manslaughter following the death of several canoeists during a trip organized by the company. The managing director was aware that there were inadequate safety standards.

The crime of manslaughter involves causing death either

- whilst intending to commit an unlawful act (a crime) which was likely to cause bodily harm; or
- realizing a risk of bodily harm however slight; or
- by breach of a duty of care that is so serious in the light of the risk of death that it amounts to gross negligence.

The *P & O Ferries* case established that a corporation could be prosecuted for manslaughter. However, liability could only be established through the doctrine of identification. The case occurred before *Meridian* and so it was necessary to show that a controlling officer within the management of *P & O* was personally liable for manslaughter. The assistant bosun, chief officer and captain were not sufficiently senior officers to be identified with the company.

P & O was found not guilty of manslaughter because it was not possible to prove the *mens rea* of manslaughter against anyone in senior management. The test for the *mens rea* at the time (recklessness) required proof that such a person had failed to appreciate that there was an obvious and serious risk that the ferry might sail with doors open when this would have been realized by a reasonably prudent ferry operator. Sixty-six witnesses, drawn from *P & O*'s employees, testified that they did not consider the risk to be obvious and serious. The fact that the ferry had sailed with its bow doors open previously had not come to the attention of senior management because of communication failures in the company. The case failed because of the doctrine of identification. It was precisely because the company had no proper system for safety and no director to monitor safety that no director could be identified as having the relevant state of mind. It was a failure in the corporate management systems that paradoxically prevented liability.

There has been a change in the *mens rea* requirement for manslaughter since the case but it is unlikely that the new test would be satisfied on the facts of *P & O* for the same reason the existing test failed. Nor is it likely that the *Meridian* test would have been satisfied because there was no person within the company with responsibility for safety whose state of mind could be attributed to the company for that purpose. It is the requirement that an individual be found before corporate responsibility can be established that caused the prosecution to fail. Moreover, the doctrine of aggregation was rejected by the court.

In *Kite and OLL Ltd* on the other hand, the company and the managing director were found guilty of manslaughter by gross negligence. The company was fined £60 000 and went into liquidation. Mr Kite was sentenced to 3 years' imprisonment (reduced to two on appeal). Liability was established using the pre-*Meridian* test of identification. The difficulties presented by the *P & O* case were not present in *Kite*. The managing director in *Kite* was grossly negligent and because it was a small enterprise it was easy to identify him with the company. No medium or large company has yet been convicted of manslaughter (although another successful prosecution for manslaughter was brought in *R v Jackson Transport (Ossett) Ltd* (1996) a case of a one-man business).

The difficulty in the *P & O* case might be overcome if liability were based on corporate or management failures as a whole. Similar issues have been highlighted in a number of other 'disaster' cases such as the Hillsborough stadium collapse, the Piper Alpha oil rig fire, the sinking of the *Marchioness* on the Thames, the Kings Cross fire and the Clapham rail crash. All cases where prosecutions for manslaughter were not brought. Moreover the continued application of the doctrine of identification based on individual responsibility was recently affirmed in *Attorney General's Reference (No 2 of 1999)* [2000] (above). The issue has been considered by the Law Commission (1996) which has recommended a new offence of corporate killing in the following terms:

> A company will be guilty of the offence (carrying a fine and order for remedial action) if
>
> (a) a management failure by the corporation is the cause or one of the causes of a person's death; and
> (b) that failure constitutes conduct falling far below what can reasonably be expected of the corporation in the circumstances.

A management failure is: 'a failure to ensure safety in the management or organisation of the corporation's activities.' Under (b) a jury would need to balance the likelihood of harm, the social utility of the activity and the practicability of precautions. It would also be necessary to take account of industry standards on levels of risk in the sphere of activity.

The Law Commission felt that the new offence would cover the *P & O* situation but is not certain that it would. If *P & O* had, as suggested in the case, acted as any experienced company in the same field of business would act they would not have been grossly negligent as defined unless a jury is prepared to find the industry standard grossly negligent in itself.

Theft

In *R* v *McHugh* (1976) the defendant put petrol in his car at a self-service petrol station. He did not intend to pay and he drove off without paying.

In *R* v *Kohn* (1979) an accountant used company cheques to draw money from the company accounts for himself. When he started to do so the accounts were in credit, later they went into overdraft but within an overdraft facility. Towards the end the accounts were in deficit in excess of the limit.

In *R* v *Ghosh* [1982] a surgeon claimed fees from a hospital for operations he had not carried out.

According to the Theft Act 1968 'A person is guilty of theft if he dishonestly appropriates property belonging to another with the intention of permanently depriving the other of it. (s.1).

Actus reus

- *Appropriation:* involves 'assuming any one (or more) rights of an owner': *R* v *Morris* [1984] where switching price labels on shop goods amounted to theft. It does not matter that the assumption occurs with authority (or consent): *DPP* v *Gomez* [1993]. Therefore it is possible to appropriate by, for example, simply moving goods and it makes no difference that the act is one that the defendant is permitted to do (although this might affect the *mens rea* of the crime by, for example, preventing the defendant from being dishonest). Mr McHugh appropriated the petrol when he put it in his tank.
- *Property:* this is defined as real or personal property, money (currency) and intangible property (e.g. credit balance in bank accounts, overdraft facilities and cheques). The petrol in *McHugh* was personal property and in *Kohn* the accountant was guilty of stealing from the accounts in credit and within the overdraft limit but not thereafter because there was no longer any property capable of being stolen.
- *Belonging to another:* the property must belong to another although it might also belong to the defendant. If Mr McHugh had been charged with theft on driving out of the garage, he would have been acquitted because by then the property in the petrol tank would have passed to him. However, property still belongs to another if the defendant has received it under an obligation to deal with it (or its proceeds) in

a particular way. For example, where money is given to a trader under a specific obligation to use that money to purchase goods for the victim, the money still belongs to the victim. Property also belongs to another where the defendant received it by mistake and is under an obligation to return it (or its proceeds or value). For example, where an employee is overpaid wages by mistake, the overpayment still belongs to the employer.

Mens rea

- *Intention permanently to deprive*: the defendant must intend not to return the property. If it is intended that it be returned, there is still an intent if the defendant 'treats it as his own to dispose of' or borrows or lends it in circumstances 'equivalent to an outright taking'. Mr McHugh and Mr Kohn, who were found guilty obviously intended to permanently deprive their victims of their property.
- *Dishonesty*: a defendant is not dishonest if he or she either honestly believe that he or she have a legal right to the property; or honestly believe that the victim would have consented in the circumstances (as in *R* v *Flynn* [*1970*]) or honestly believe that the owner cannot be found by taking reasonable steps. In all other cases, according to *R* v *Ghosh*, a defendant will be dishonest if (a) the behaviour was dishonest by the standards of reasonable people and (b) the defendant realized ordinary people would regard it as dishonest. On this test Mr Ghosh was dishonest and was convicted.

Fraud

In *DPP* v *Ray* [1974] the defendant ordered a meal in a restaurant, intending to pay for it. After having eaten it, he decided not to pay and ran off.

There are a number of crimes involving fraud. Most require proof of a false statement, such as the express one made by Mr Ghosh, above. A statement may also be implied from conduct. In *Ray*, by ordering the meal, the defendant implied that he would pay before leaving and that became a false statement after it had been eaten. It is then an offence if, as a result of a deliberate or reckless false statement, the defendant dishonestly obtains property belonging to another (Theft Act 1968 s.15); a pecuniary advantage (Theft Act 1968 s.16); a service (Theft Act 1978 s.1); or an evasion of liability to pay (Theft Act 1978 s.2). An example of the first offence would be obtaining the fee in *Ghosh* or, if he had deceived before eating it, obtaining the meal in *Ray*. The only examples of the second offence are where the defendant obtains an overdraft facility; an insurance policy or annuity contract (or an improvement in its term); the opportunity to earn remuneration in office or employment; or wins money by betting. An example of the third offence would be the cooking of the meal in *Ray* and an example of the fourth would be deceiving the restaurant into letting him leave without paying for the meal. This offence also covers cases where cheques are given in payment when the defendant knows they will 'bounce'.

There are a number of further offences involving fraud and malpractice including revenue and customs and excise fraud; stock exchange fraud and insider dealing.

Other offences

There are a series of other offences that may be relevant to business organizations including offences under the Computer Misuse Act 1990, the Data Protection Act 1984, the Criminal Damage Act 1971 and conspiracy under the Criminal Law Act 1977 and at common law.

CONCLUSION

The scope for organizational liability for criminal offences depends largely on the type of offence in question. Liability is more easily imposed on organizations where the offence is a strict liability, regulatory, statutory offence. Whether as a human or corporate employer, vicarious liability may arise for a number of offences but liability for more traditional fault-based crimes will only arise where the employer is a corporation and the doctrine of identification is satisfied.

The scope for organizations being the victim of a crime depends largely on the crime being of a type that does not involve injury of a personal nature. The types of crimes most likely to be committed against organizations are those involving property offences and fraud.

PROGRESS TESTS

1 Transit is a company which provides music equipment for hire. A firm of solicitors hires equipment from Transit for its Christmas party. Andy, Transit's store manager, loads the equipment into a Transit van and Billy, who works for Transit, drives the van to the solicitor's office. Unknown to any of the parties, the van has defective brakes, contrary to the Vehicle Regulations. Consider whether Transit could be successfully prosecuted for an offence under the Regulations of 'using, causing or permitting the van to be used' with defective brakes.

2 It has recently been discovered that Mixolite (a food colouring agent) is dangerous to health. Parliament passes the Mixolite Prohibition Act 2000 which provides as follows: 'It is an offence to cause or knowingly permit the use of Mixolite in the preparation or processing of any food intended for human consumption' (s.1). 'It is an offence to sell or supply any product intended for human consumption which contains Mixolite' (s.2). The offence is a summary offence, punishable by a fine. Carol runs a small catering company and she purchases from Doorway Stores several tins of tomatoes which she does not know contain Mixolite. These are used by Carol's cook in the preparation of lasagne which is then sold to a client. Consider the factors which would be taken into account in deciding whether any offence has been committed under the Mixolite Prohibition Act 2000.

3 Derek is the owner of a café and employs a manager, Elsie, to run it. Derek has been warned by the police about activities on the premises that may be in breach of s.44 of the Metropolitan Police Act 1839. This provides that it is an offence to 'knowingly permit or suffer prostitutes to meet together and remain in a place where refreshments are sold and consumed.' As a consequence, he expressly instructs Elsie not to allow prostitutes to congregate on the premises. Advise Derek of his liability, if any, when the police raid the premises and find prostitutes gathered there.

4 Gerrybuilt, a building company, is in financial difficulty. Harriet, the company's finance manager, misrepresents the financial position of the company in order to persuade traders to continue to supply Gerrybuilt with materials. She does so without the knowledge of the company's board of directors. Inda, the company accountant, draws money from Gerrybuilt's account and uses the money to book himself a holiday in the Bahamas. He hopes to be able to return the money to the company account when he is paid at the end of the month. Consider the criminal implications of these activities.

5 Costalot is a national chain of supermarkets. The company employs contractors to carry out repairs on faulty wiring in one of the stores. On advice from the director responsible for Health and Safety, the store remains open whilst the work is carried out. The contractors go for a tea break, leaving electrical cables exposed in an area near to the emergency exit of the store. It has become common practice for shelf fillers to pile emptied boxes near to the emergency exit prior to them being removed to the outside of the building. There is an accident during which the exposed cables cause a fire which spreads to the boxes. Two shoppers and one of the store's cashiers are trapped in the blaze and, unable to use the emergency exit, they die before they can be rescued. The branch manager has overall responsibility for running the store but no say in the management and control of the company. He had been warned by the branch health and safety officer of the danger posed by the unsafe piling of the boxes. Consider the factors that will be taken into account in determining any corporate criminal liability for the three deaths.

Part II
Transactions of the Business Organization

Trading with the consumer 8

Peter Wilding

WHEN IS A PERSON A CONSUMER?

A party to a contract deals as a consumer in relation to another party if:

  (a) he neither makes the contract in the course of a business nor holds himself out as doing so; and
  (b) the other party does make the contract in the course of a business; and
  (c) the goods ... are of a type ordinarily supplied for private use or consumption.

  Section 12 of the Unfair Contract Terms Act 1977.

Section 12 provides the best explanation of what the law means by 'consumer', though it is not always necessary for a person to be a party to a contract to be deemed a consumer. The Consumer Protection Act Part I creates a statutory tort and enables any person (whether or not a party to a contract) to sue for damages if injured by a defective product.

What is consumer law?

> In *Crowther* v *Shannon* [1975] Mr Crowther bought a second-hand Jaguar with 80 000 miles on the clock. The Jaguar exploded after he had driven the car 2,300 miles after purchase. LORD DENNING held that when sold the car was not reasonably fit for its purpose under the Sale of Goods Act 1979 and the sellers ought to have known this. Although the sellers said that they would repair the car, LORD DENNING ruled that repair was an inadequate remedy and the purchaser was entitled to be refunded the purchase price.

This case shows that a consumer has the legal right to get his money back and claim expenses if the seller sells a defective product. Thus consumer law is a fashionable name applied to a body of common law and statute which can be used to protect the person who buys a product or a service for private use.

HISTORICAL DEVELOPMENT OF CONSUMER LAW

Parties acting in the course of business have long been liable in contract to buyers – whether consumers or businesses – for unsafe or poor quality goods or services. In 1256 the Assize of Bread and Beer gave remedies to the purchasers of bad loaves and rancid beer. Even St Thomas warned sellers that it was sinful not to disclose a defect to the buyer. So, whilst *caveat emptor* (let the buyer beware) might well be considered the traditional common law position, history suggests a legal and moral responsibility has rested upon traders to take care of the products they sell and the people to whom they sell them.

Over the centuries litigation created common law rights and duties between seller and buyer. These were codified (i.e. put into statutory form) in the Sale of Goods Act 1893. This Act established that where a seller sells goods in the course of a business he or she was under a legal duty to ensure that the goods:

1 match their description;
2 are of merchantable (i.e. commercial) quality;
3 are fit for their purpose.

These conditions, which we will discuss in greater detail below, are still implied into every contract of sale of goods. They provide the foundation for consumer law, and are now to be found in the Sale of Goods Act as re-enacted in 1979.

Awareness of the needs and rights of consumers was strengthened in the 1950s by the development of lobbying groups, for example The Consumers Association. Up until then economic policy favoured the producers. Memories of the Great Depression persuaded governments to protect employment by erecting barriers to trade, fixing resale prices and turning a blind eye to anti-competitive practices.

However, the six governments which created the EEC in 1957 signed a Treaty which committed them to a common market without barriers to trade. The Common Market was to have a vigorous competition policy that would ensure anti-competitive agreements and behaviour would be punished. In the 1960s trade between EEC countries developed rapidly. By 1968 all tariff barriers and quotas were abolished. Nevertheless, trade in consumer goods was imperilled by the requirement to conform to differing national standards. Lobby groups sought trans-European legislation to assure consumers that goods imported from other countries would meet comparable standards. In 1961 the Commission Vice-President acknowledged that 'the general interests of consumers in the common market are not represented to the same extent as are those of the producers.' This provoked the second major development in consumer law – the European dimension.

In 1975 the first EEC Consumer Programme was adopted. It set out an action plan and five basic consumer rights:

1 *protection of health and safety*: goods must not present a risk under normal conditions of use;
2 *protection of economic interests*: the consumer must be protected against abusive practices like misleading advertising, unfair contract terms, and defective products and services;
3 *the right of redress*: the consumer is entitled to advice on defective goods and services, and rapid redress for any injury or damage suffered;
4 *the right to information and education*;
5 *the right of representation*: consumers' organizations to be consulted at local, national and European level.

Thereafter, consumer protection legislation deriving from Europe developed apace. Further consumer action programmes followed in 1981 and 1986. The 1986 programme complemented the British inspired Single Market project which was based on the need to get rid of so-called non-tariff barriers to trade such as differing national standards. Hand in hand with this 'new approach' to technical harmonization of standards came a far more vigorous consumer protection regime. This concentrated on quality and safety norms in the production and sale of consumer goods through the – by now twelve – member states of the European Communities.

In 1990 the first 3-year action plan produced a series of directives that had to be implemented in the United Kingdom, demonstrating that Europe had become predominant in the formation of consumer law. Directives regulating product safety, distance selling and comparative advertising headed a list of laws married to a vast number of harmonized standards. For business, Europe now offered the carrot of a new huge market of consumers as well as the stick of a regulatory minefield.

Although most of the legal activity derived from Brussels during the 1970s and 1980s, the United Kingdom swam with the tide of consumer law. New legislation extended the Sale of Goods Act type of protection to the sale of services, hire and hire purchase.

OF WHAT SIGNIFICANCE IS CONSUMER LAW TO A BUSINESS?

In *Harlingdon Enterprises Ltd* v *Christopher Hull Fine Arts* Ltd [1991] Mr Hull was asked to sell two paintings which had been described as being by the German Impressionist Gabriele Munter. The claimant bought one of the paintings for £6000 despite Mr Hull's statement that he was not an expert in the field. When the painting was discovered to be a forgery the buyer sued under Sale of Goods Act 1979 for the return of £6000. The buyer lost because, as an expert in his own right, he did not rely on the knowledge and skill of the seller – a pre-requisite for a Sale of Goods Act claim.

This case shows that where buyers are *consumers* they are not deemed capable of independent judgement: they are deemed to rely upon the knowledge of the seller. Business will therefore be liable to consumer law claims. The following types of businesses will be affected by consumer law:

- retailers selling goods or services under contract;
- producers and suppliers selling goods and services to retailers under contract;
- all business sellers under the tort of negligence and the Consumer Protection Act 1987.

CONSUMER LAW IN CONTRACT: WHICH ACT APPLIES?

In *Rogers* v *Parish (Scarborough) Ltd* [1987] Mr Rogers bought a Range Rover for £16 000. Although sold as new, defects arose in the gearbox and bodywork. Mr Rogers nevertheless used the car for 6 months, driving 5500 miles; during this period the garage tried unsuccessfully to rectify the defects. Exasperated, Mr Rogers demanded his money back plus expenses claiming breach of the Sale of Goods Act. Mr Rogers won. The Court of Appeal held that the car sold was not of merchantable quality.

In *Wilson* v *Best Travel* [1993] the Sale of Goods Act 1979 did not apply because Mr. Wilson did not buy *goods*. He bought a *holiday*. A holiday is regarded as a *service*. He was injured after falling through glass doors at a hotel. Mr Wilson claimed that Best Travel had breached an implied term in their contract which obliged them to exercise reasonable care and skill in their service, that is to verify that the hotel was reasonably safe. This term was implied by s.13 of the Supply of Goods and Services Act 1982.

These two cases show that if the consumer buys goods he or she is protected by the implied terms under the Sale of Goods Act 1979. If he or she buys a service he or she is protected by the implied terms under the Supply of Goods and Services Act 1982.

Sale of Goods Act 1979 (SGA)

The Sale of Goods Act 1979 applies only to contracts for the sale of goods for 'a money consideration called the price' (s.2(1)). The price can either be money or goods and money together, but not goods alone as, without the payment of a price, the contract would be one of exchange or barter.

Supply of Goods and Services Act 1982 (SGSA)

Part I of the Supply of Goods and Services Act deals with 'a contract for the transfer of goods'. This is defined as 'a contract under which one person transfers or agrees to transfer to another the property in goods'. In other words, the payment does not have to be in money form. This Act would apply to exchange or barter transactions.

Part I of the SGSA also deals with contracts of hire: these are defined as contracts 'under which one person bails or agrees to bail goods to another by way of hire'. The SGSA also deals with contracts which combine the sale of goods and services such as the sale and installation of double glazing. Part II of the SGSA implies terms into contracts for the pure supply of services. A contract for the supply of services is defined as 'a contract under which a person agrees to carry out a service'.

IMPLIED TERMS

In contracts for the sale of goods or services the buyer is protected by various legally binding terms which are implied or read into the contract. Although they may not feature expressly in the small print of a contract or a receipt they nevertheless form part of the contract because a remedy is given to the buyer if the following provisions of the Act are breached by the seller. The terms implied into a sale of goods contract are:

1 *Title*: Section 12 SGA states that there is 'an implied term on the part of the seller that ... he has the right to sell the goods.'
2 *Description*: Section 13 SGA states that 'where there is a contract for the sale of goods by description, there is an implied term that the goods will correspond with that description.'
3 *Satisfactory quality*: Section 14(2) SGA states that 'where the seller sells goods in the course of a business, there is an implied condition that the goods supplied under the contract are of satisfactory quality.'
4 *Fitness for purpose*: Section 14(3) SGA states that where the buyer makes it known to the seller an uncommon purpose for which he or she wants the goods and

the seller says the goods will fulfil that purpose then 'there is an implied condition that the goods supplied under the contract are reasonably fit for that purpose.'

Not only do these terms apply to sales of goods bought for a price as under the SGA; they also apply identically under the SGSA as section 2 (title), section 3 (description), and section 4 which covers both satisfactory quality and fitness for purpose.

As previously explained, Part II SGSA applies to contracts between buyers and sellers where only services are provided. The buyer obtains the benefit of implied terms to protect him or her against poor quality, late or extortionate provision of services in the following terms:

1 *Reasonable care and skill*: Section 13 SGSA states that 'in a contract for the supply of a service where the supplier is acting in the course of a business there is an implied term that the supplier will carry out the service with reasonable care and skill.'

2 *Reasonable time*: Section14 SGSA provides that if the contract does not specify a date for performance the supplier must perform the service within 'a reasonable time.'

In *Charnock* v *Liverpool Corporation* [1968] a car owner took his car to a garage for repair. A reasonably competent repairer would have taken 5 weeks. The garage delayed the work and took 8 weeks. The Court of Appeal held that they had failed to carry out the work within a reasonable time and were liable for breach of the contractual implied term.

3 *Reasonable price*: Section 15 SGSA provides that, in the unusual event that a price is not agreed at the time the contract is made, a 'reasonable price' shall be charged.

EXCLUSION CLAUSES

In *Chapelton* v *Barry UDC* [1940] Mr Chapelton hired a deckchair and collected a receipt. The deckchair collapsed and injured him. He sued Barry Council who sought to exclude their liability by referring to a printed exclusion clause on the back of the ticket absolving the Council from liability. The court held that the clause had not been brought to Mr Chapelton's attention at the time the contract was made and was void.

Consumer law benefits buyers by reading implied terms into contracts. However, sellers can incorporate into the contract terms which work to exclude or limit their liability to the buyer if they fail to fulfil an obligation in the contract. To prevent sellers avoiding their contractual obligations in this way the Unfair Contract Terms Act 1977 (UCTA) was enacted.

UCTA deals with attempts by the seller to avoid liability in the following areas:

- negligence;
- express contractual terms;
- implied contractual terms;
- guarantees;
- misrepresentation.

Negligence

Section 1 of UCTA defines negligence as the breach 'of any obligation ... to take reasonable care or exercise reasonable care and skill in the performance of the contract.' This corresponds most closely with the implied obligation of the seller of a service to perform his or her task with reasonable care and skill under s.13 SGSA.

Section 2 of UCTA provides that:

1 A person cannot by reference to any contract term ... exclude or restrict his liability for death or personal injury resulting from negligence.
2 In the case of other loss or damage (i.e. property damage or financial loss) a person cannot so exclude or restrict his liability except insofar as the term satisfies the requirement of reasonableness.

Section 2(1) imposes a complete ban on any exclusion clause giving the seller protection from liability for death or personal injury caused by their own negligence. Section 2(2) prevents the use of an exclusion clause to escape liability for other loss or damage caused by the seller's negligence, unless the clause can satisfy the test of reasonableness.

In *Philips Products* v *Hyland and Hamstead Plant* [1985] the second defendant (Hamstead) hired an excavator and a driver to the plaintiff. Condition 8 of the hire contract stated:

> where drivers and plant are supplied by the owner they are for all purposes in connection with their employment in the working of the plant to be regarded as servant or agents of the hirer ... who alone shall be responsible for all claims arising in connection with the operation of the plant by the said drivers or operators.

Philips sued for damage caused by the driver's negligence. The defendants argued that they were protected from liability by virtue of this condition. This condition, it was held by the court, would reverse a liability which would otherwise fall on the owner of the plant. It was not relevant that the clause was called a restriction or an exclusion. The court said 'the effect is beyond doubt. It is unreasonable': it breached s.2(1) of UCTA.

Breach of an express term

In *R&B Customs Brokers Ltd* v *United Dominions Trust* [1988] the claimants bought a Colt Shogun vehicle for personal and business use. The contract excluded the implied condition as to fitness for purpose. After engine leakage the plaintiffs claimed breach of SGA s.14(3). UDT relied on the exclusion clause. However, the Court of Appeal held that under UCTA s.3 the exclusion was unreasonable as the plaintiffs were dealing as consumers.

Section 3 of UCTA applies restrictions to exclusion clauses where one party *deals as a consumer* OR on the other's written standard terms of business:

As against that party, the other cannot by reference to any contract term:

(a) when himself in breach of contract, exclude or restrict any liability of his in respect of the breach; or

(b) claim to be entitled:
    (i) to render a contractual performance substantially different from that which was reasonably expected of him, or
    (ii) in respect of the whole or any part of contractual obligation, to render no performance at all,
except insofar as . . . the contract satisfies the requirement of reasonableness.

Where a seller sells goods, services or both under the same contract this clause prevents them from denying liability if they fail to fulfil all or part of their obligations under the contract unless the courts consider it reasonable for them so to do.

Implied contractual terms

Section 6 of UCTA deals with attempts by sellers to exclude or restrict the liability which would arise if they breached any of the terms implied into a contract by SGA or SGSA. Section 6 can be paraphrased thus:

1 section 12 of SGA regarding title can never be excluded;
2 where the buyer deals as a consumer ss.13, 14(2) and (3) can never be excluded.
3 where the buyer does not deal as a consumer ss.13, 14(2) and 14(3) can only be excluded if reasonable.

Guarantees

In *Adams* v *Richardson* [1969] LORD DENNING condemned a guarantee which effectively excluded the defendant's liability: 'If he wished to excuse himself from liability he should say so plainly. Instead of heading it boldly "Guarantee" he should head it "Non-Guarantee"; for that is what it is.'

Attempts by the seller to dress up exclusion clauses in the seductive guise of a guarantee were well-known before 1977. However, Section 5(1) of UCTA states:

In the case of goods of a type ordinarily supplied for private use or consumption, where loss or damage

(a) arises from the goods proving defective while in consumer use; and
(b) results from the negligence of a person concerned in the manufacture or distribution of the goods,

liability for the loss or damage cannot be excluded or restricted by reference to any contract term contained in or operating by reference to a guarantee of the goods.

For s.5 to be of effect the goods must be the type of goods consumers normally buy.

Misrepresentation

In *Walker* v *Boyle* [1982] a clause in the standard conditions governing conveyancing provided that there was no right to terminate the contract nor to seek damages for errors, misstatements or omissions in the description of the house for sale. The judge ruled that this clause which excluded liability for misrepresentation was unreasonable as it extended even to fraudulent misrepresentation.

A misrepresentation is a false statement of fact which induces a buyer to enter into the contract. The statements made which persuade the buyer to buy might not be expressly included into the final contract. If the representation is neither true nor included in the print of the contract the buyer will have no remedy under contract law. He or she will have a claim under the Misrepresentation Act 1967, but what happens if the seller excludes his or her liability for any pre-contractual statements which prove to be false?

Section 8 UCTA provides the answer. It states that any contract term which would:

1 exclude or restrict any liability to which a party to a contract may be subject by reason of any misrepresentation made by him before the contract was made; or
2 any remedy available to another party to the contract by reason of such misrepresentation

shall be subject to the requirement of reasonableness.

What is reasonableness?

While UCTA prevents the seller from excluding liability:

- for negligence which causes death or personal injury, and
- for breach of the implied terms,

in the case of exclusion of other forms of liability, UCTA leaves the final decision as to the validity of the clause to the courts. They are instructed to decide through the mechanism of the reasonableness test:

> In relation to a contract term ... the term shall be a fair and reasonable one ... having regard to the circumstances which were, or ought reasonably to have been, known to or in the contemplation of the parties when the contract was made (UCTA s.11(1)).

As this definition is less than clear, courts need to rely on the assistance of Schedule 2 which directs them to consider the following:

- the strength of the bargaining position of the parties taking into account alternative means by which the consumers' requirements could have been met;
- whether the consumer received an inducement to agree to the term, or in accepting it had the opportunity to enter into a similar contract with other persons, but without having to accept a similar term;
- whether the consumer knew or ought reasonably to have known of the existence and extent of the term;
- whether the term excludes or restricts any relevant liability if some condition is not complied with, whether it was reasonable at the time of the contract to expect that compliance with the condition would be practicable;
- whether the goods were manufactured, processed or adapted to the special order of the consumer.

The reasonableness test requires that attention should be paid to the *financial resources* of a party claiming the protection of an exclusion clause, for example which limits liability by reference to a specified sum of money, and also to the extent which he or she could *cover his or her liability by insurance*.

REMEDIES

So far this chapter has highlighted the protection available to the consumer from the terms implied by law into each contract the consumer makes with business. Business can seek to evade these implied terms but rarely with success through exclusion clauses or guarantees. In the event that the seller breaches the implied terms and cannot rely upon exclusion clauses the buyer will have a simple remedy: to repudiate the contract and/or seek damages. In other words, the buyer can demand his or her money back and seek further compensation if he or she has spent money because of the defective product. However, there is a limit to the amount of money the consumer can claim. The consumer must prove that the damages he or she seeks were reasonably foreseeable and not too remote a consequence of the breach.

Remoteness of damage

In *Hadley* v *Baxendale* (1854) a mill owner engaged the services of a carrier to transport a broken crankshaft for urgent repair. The carrier delayed the transport with the result that the mill lost more profits than were anticipated. The mill owner sued for the full amount. The case laid out two tests for determining what damages were recoverable:

1 was the damage expected in the 'normal course of things'; or
2 did the damage arise because of special circumstances.

In *Hadley* v *Baxendale* it was decided that the damages suffered arose from special circumstances because the mill owner had not told the carrier what the consequences would be if he delayed in performing his task. The mill owner lost. This result was enshrined in SGA s.53.

For buyers of goods or services it is critical to expressly state the anticipated financial consequences of the breach so that in the event of a breach the seller cannot claim that the damages the buyer seeks are too remote.

ACCEPTANCE

In *Bernstein* v *Pamson Motors* [1987] Mr Bernstein bought a new Nissan from Pamson for £8000. It was delivered on 7 December 1984. After one month and with only 140 miles on the clock the car broke down with a seized camshaft. Mr Bernstein tried to reject the car as the quality was not satisfactory. Pamson refused to pay back the £8000 on the grounds that Mr Bernstein had kept the car so long that he had accepted it. The Court held that the car did breach SGA s.14(2) but decided in favour of Pamson Motors that Mr Bernstein had accepted the car. He could only claim the cost of repair.

This case demonstrates that a problem particularly associated with a buyer's attempt to get his or her money back is the allegation by the seller that the buyer has held on to the goods for so long that it is unreasonable for the seller to take them back.

Section 35 Sale of Goods Act 1979 states:

> The buyer is deemed to have accepted the goods when he intimates to the seller that he has accepted them, or . . . when the goods have been delivered to him and

he does any act in relation to them which is inconsistent with the ownership of the seller, or when after a reasonable time he retains the goods without intimating to the seller that he has rejected them.

Section 35 SGA states that acceptance takes place either when the buyer intimates to the seller that he or she has accepted the goods, or when (after delivery of the goods to him or her) 'the buyer does any act in relation to them which is inconsistent with the ownership of the seller'. However, the buyer who has taken delivery of the goods without previously having examined them is not deemed to have taken delivery until he or she has had a reasonable opportunity to examine them to ascertain if they are in conformity with the contract.

Of course the buyer is still deemed to have accepted the goods if he or she has not (within a reasonable time after delivery) told the seller that he or she rejects them. But the question of whether a reasonable time has elapsed depends upon whether the buyer has had a reasonable opportunity of examining the goods. Furthermore, s.35 now provides that the buyer is not deemed to have accepted the goods merely because he or she asks or agrees for the seller to repair or arrange for their repair.

Finally, if a consumer is persuaded to accept a credit note or a replacement for the defective product has the consumer accepted the new product within the meaning of s.35? The answer is 'no' because by exchanging the old product for the new a fresh contract comes into existence based on the Supply of Goods and Services Act 1982.

If the consumer has not accepted the product under s.35 then any breach by the seller is called a breach of condition, that is a critical term in the contract. The buyer has the remedy of repudiation and/or damages – he or she can demand his or her money back plus expenses and any costs the court might give for distress and inconvenience. If the consumer has accepted the product by keeping it for too long or tampering with it the consumer loses the remedy of repudiation. He or she cannot treat the contract as void and demand his or her money back but can claim expenses, distress and inconvenience.

CONSUMER PROTECTION ACT 1987

In *Relph* v *Yamaha* [1998] the plaintiff was riding a three-wheeled all terrain vehicle manufactured by Yamaha in a hard field. Before attempting to ride the machine Relph claimed to have read the instruction manual carefully including the warning label on the back of the machine stating the machine should only be ridden by an experienced rider and that it could be dangerous for a novice. He claimed that if he had seen a warning that the machine might overturn he would not have ridden it in the first place. In fact the machine did overturn damaging the machine and causing him injury. He claimed damages for injury caused by a defective vehicle under the CPA 1987. He failed because he had read the warnings and instructions. Some he chose to ignore. Yamaha had sold a hazardous vehicle but had issued adequate warnings. It was not defective.

In *P&M Supplies (Essex) Ltd* v *Devon County Council* [1992] P&M imported 77 000 toys. Trading Standards Officers received a complaint concerning the safety of the goods. To avoid conviction under Part II CPA P&M had to prove that they took all reasonable precautions to test the goods. Of the 77 000 toys only 0.49 per cent were sampled. This was held to be inadequate and P&M were found guilty.

Proving breach of contract is difficult and expensive and the remedies are only available to the buyer. In order to make actions against the manufacturer of a defective product simpler the Consumer Protection Act 1987 (CPA) Part I provides a remedy not only for the buyer but also for anyone who suffers damage or injury caused the defective product. It also, in Part II, makes it a criminal offence to supply goods that are not safe. These two cases illustrate the difference between a claim under the civil and criminal parts of the CPA.

Civil liability is governed by Part I CPA

Section 2(1) provides:

Where any damage is caused wholly or partly by a defect in a product the following persons shall be liable for the damage:

- the producer of the product;
- any person who has held him- or herself out to be the producer of the product (e.g. with a trade mark); or
- any person who has imported the product into a member state from a place outside the member states in order, in the course of business, to supply it to another.

What is a defect?

Section 3 relates to the general safety of the product, not to its general quality, fitness for purpose or merchantability. Absolute safety is not required. The question is one of fact and degree in every case having regard to the general test: what are people generally entitled to expect in relation to a product.

There are four generic types of defect:

1 a lack of safety in design;
2 defects in construction or assembly;
3 inadequate warnings and instructions;
4 lack of conformity to express statement.

What is damage?

Section 5 defines damage as meaning death or personal injury and any loss or damage to any property including land. With the exception of economic loss, any form of loss or damage may be the subject of a straightforward claim in contract and/or negligence.

Liability

The Consumer Protection Act seeks to place primary liability on the producer, a person clearly defined under s.2(1) as the manufacturer of a finished product, the producer of any raw material or the manufacturer of a component part, any person who, by affixing their trade mark, presents him- or herself as a producer and the commercial importer of the product.

What defences are available?

The main defence that business has available to it is the development risks defence. This is an assertion that at the time of the supply of the product the state of scientific and technical knowledge was such that the defect which subsequently caused the personal injury or damage could not have been discovered.

Criminal liability

Whereas the central theme of the provisions relating to civil liability under the CPA is for defective products, criminal liability is for 'unsafe goods'. Section 10 of the CPA introduced a new general safety requirement stating:

> A person shall be guilty of an offence if he supplies any consumer goods which fail to comply with the general safety requirement. Consumer goods fail to comply with general safety requirement if they are not reasonably safe having regard to all the circumstances.

What is unsafe?

Section 19 carries a definition of 'safe' in relation to any 'goods' meaning that there shall be no risk or no risk apart from one reduced to a minimum that the goods will cause personal injury or death.

Who has a duty?

The duty is imposed on three categories of persons in relation to the supply of goods:

1 the producer;
2 the distributor;
3 other individuals.

The defences available are that the defendant has exercised due diligence and taken reasonable precautions. Due diligence requires the seller to have in place a system suitable to check product safety. Reasonable precautions requires that the system works.

The duties of both producers and distributors require that a system be in place and steps taken to maintain it. It is also very clear that the law envisages monitoring after the products have been supplied onto the market. Whereas previously precautions had to be taken only up to the time of supply, the test is now much wider and questions will be asked about post-supply cooperation.

The criminal liability of producers and distributors is now set out in the Product Safety Regulations 1994. These Regulations were made under the European Communities Act 1972, in order to implement an EC Directive.

THE CONSUMER AND CRIMINAL LAW

In *Lewin* v *Fuell* [1990] a stallholder at an open market was convicted of an offence under s.1 of the Trade Descriptions Act 1968 for selling cheap watches misdescribed by expensive brand names. His defence that nobody would be stupid enough to believe that they were buying top quality watches was not accepted!

It is important to note that the defendant was convicted of an offence at criminal law in this case. We have seen that so far the consumer's remedies for poor quality or unsafe goods have been available in civil law. On paper the buyer seems to be well protected. However the number of buyers who litigate to enforce their rights remains small. This is mainly because of the cost of litigation. Partly as a result of this, the practice has grown up of taking out insurance at the time of purchase of the goods. However, consumers also have the option of reporting sellers to Trading Standards Officers who have power under the criminal law to prosecute businesses.

The major legislation is the Trade Descriptions Act 1968. The two main offences are:

1 applying a false trade description to goods or supplying goods with such a description (s.1);
2 making a false statement as to the provision of services, accommodation or facilities (s.14).

Applying a false trade description means that the seller uses a false trade description which refers to the goods by words, packaging or advertisement.

The Act applies to business suppliers only and states that a trade description is false if it is false to a material degree (s.3(1)) or likely to be misleading to a material degree s.3(2)).

In *Denard v Smith and Dixons Ltd* [1991] a computer was offered together with a joystick and software. The deal was advertised at the counter and in a mailshot. After Miss Denard bought the computer she found that the software was missing. The defendants were convicted of applying a false trade description.

In relation to services an offence requires the proof of recklessness in the making of the statement.

In *Breed v Cluett* [1970] a buyer bought a new house from the builder plaintiff. Twenty days after the contract was signed the builder falsely stated that the house was covered by the NHBC 10-year guarantee. The court held that this was a recklessly made false statement as to services and was caught by s.14. The fact that the builder's statement did not induce the buyer to enter into the contract in the first place was irrelevant.

PROGRESS TEST

1 A consumer buys a second hand car from a dealer. The car is sold 'with all faults'. The consumer test drives the car and buys it for £3000. After delivery the car's axle breaks. Is the dealer in breach of the Sale of Goods Act implied terms? If so, which terms?
2 An architect works on the plans for an extension to X's house. The roof eventually leaks, partly for design reasons and partly because of poor materials used by the builder. Advise X.

3 'The seller accepts no liability for any loss caused by his negligence.' Is this exclusion clause valid?

4 X buys a new television set. A day after delivery it explodes, injuring X's wife. The shop X bought the TV from has closed down. What remedy will X's wife have and against whom?

5 Y falsely claims to be the window cleaner to Prince Charles. Is that an offence?

The employment relationship 9

David Lewis and Malcolm Sargeant

THE EMPLOYMENT RELATIONSHIP

In *Express and Echo Publications* v *Tanton* [1999] a delivery driver asked an employment tribunal for a declaration that he or she was an employee of the company and entitled to a contract of employment. The individual failed to obtain the declaration because he or she was not required to carry out all the duties personally. As a result the relationship could not be one of employer and employee.

In this chapter we examine an important aspect of employment law, which is the individual relationship between the employer and the employee. It is a relationship based upon the contract of employment. This contract and its contents have been regulated both by the common law and by statute. We look at how this has affected the contents of the contract and the duties owed by the employer and the employee to each other. There is also consideration of the ways in which the employment relationship can be ended as well as important issues related to the laws on discrimination.

RECRUITMENT

What category of worker?

In *Heasmans* v *Clarity Cleaning* [1987] a contractor engaged to clean offices (including telephones) was not vicariously liable when an employee dishonestly used the phones for his own purposes. Employees remain personally liable for their own acts and theoretically may be required to reimburse the employer for any damages paid out as a result of their failure to take care.

Perhaps one of the most important decisions to be made is whether workers are to be hired under contracts of service (i.e. employees) or contracts for services (i.e. independent contractors). Although some statutes apply to all workers, for example the Sex Discrimination Act 1975, there are still significant legal differences drawn between employed and self-employed persons.

Employees gain the benefit of a number of statutory rights and are subject to the unwritten general obligations implied in all contracts of employment. When employed, as opposed to self-employed, persons are engaged, employers are required by statute to deduct tax under Schedule E and social security contributions. In addition, employers are obliged to pay employers' national insurance contributions and to insure against personal injury claims brought by employees.

Perhaps the most significant difference at common law is that the doctrine of vicarious liability applies to employees but not to the self-employed. However, in exceptional circumstances employers will be liable for the tortious acts of their independent contractors, for example if they authorize the commission of the wrongful act or have responsibilities which cannot, by law, be delegated to someone else.

It should also be noted that in some cases the criminal law regards an employee's act as being that of the employer, in which case the latter will be responsible for the wrongs committed by the former. Before an employer can be held vicariously liable, some nexus has to be established between the employee's wrongful act and the circumstances of employment.

Distinguishing employees from other types of worker

In *O'Kelly* v *Trust House Forte* [1983] the Court of Appeal considered the case of casual workers who were regularly used to assist at banquets and functions. The Court stated that tribunals have to consider:

> all aspects of the relationship, no single feature being in itself decisive and each of which may vary in weight and direction, and having given such balance to the factors as seems appropriate to determine whether the person was carrying on business on his own account.

Given all the consequences of having an employee on the books, is it always possible to discern whether a contract is a contract of service or a contract for services? Unfortunately the answer must be in the negative, for the courts have ruled that the intention of the parties cannot be the sole determinant of contractual status; otherwise it would be too easy to contract out of employment protection legislation. It is the operation of the contract in practice that is crucial rather than its appearance.

Although the element of control is important, it may not be decisive in the case of skilled workers who decide for themselves how their work should be done. In such cases the question is broadened to 'whose business was it?'(see *Lane* v *Shire Roofing* [1995]). The fact that workers pay their own tax and national insurance cannot be conclusive in determining employment status. Cases, such as *McCleod* v *Hellyer Bros* [1987] show that people who perform work at home may be classed as employees so long as there is an element of continuing mutual contractual obligation. Of crucial importance is whether persons working for another are required to perform their services personally or not. In *Express and Echo Publications* v *Tanton* [1999] a contract allowed a worker to provide a substitute. This stopped the worker being defined as an employee because the obligation to do the work personally was, according to the Court of Appeal, an 'irreducible minimum'.

Temporary employees or agency staff?

In *McMeechan* v *Secretary of State for Employment* [1997] a temporary worker carried out a series of engagements supplied by an employment agency. For each engagement Mr McMeechan was given a job sheet which included a written statement of terms and conditions. There was no overall contract of employment. The Court of Appeal held that a temporary worker could have the status of employee of the agency for each assignment actually worked, even though he or she may not be entitled to employee status under the general terms of engagement.

Occasionally an organization may ask an agency to provide staff and if the worker engaged by the client organization is under a personal obligation to perform the work, a contract of employment may exist.

In deciding whether to employ on a temporary or 'permanent' basis, it should be noted that temporary staff have exactly the same statutory rights as other employees so long as they possess any necessary qualifying period of service. The only two exceptions to this proposition arise where an individual is employed on a temporary basis as a replacement for a woman on maternity leave or to replace someone absent from work under the statutory provisions relating to medical suspension.

Regulatory constraints

At common law, employers have the right to decide what policies to adopt in relation to recruitment, but this position has been altered by a series of statutory and non-statutory interventions designed to protect certain categories of job applicant. These interventions mostly concern discrimination on the grounds of gender, race, disability and membership or non-membership of a trade union (see below). Other issues include

- the rehabilitation of offenders;
- asylum and immigration;
- age.

The Rehabilitation of Offenders Act 1974

- The law does not require applicants to disclose facts about themselves which could hinder them in getting jobs (unless their silence amounts to fraud). Thus, if employers believe that certain information is important, they should seek it specifically before the job is offered.
- Section 4 of this Act relieves certain rehabilitated persons from the obligation to disclose 'spent' convictions to a prospective employer and makes it unlawful for an employer to deny employment on the grounds that the applicant had a conviction which was 'spent'. It is the policy of the Act that applicants should not be questioned about spent convictions, although if this situation does arise applicants are entitled to deny that they have ever been convicted.
- Under the Rehabilitation of Offenders Act (Exemption Order) 1975, protection is not afforded to those applying for a whole range of jobs, for example as a doctor, nurse, teacher, social worker or probation officer.
- Sentences of over 2½ years' imprisonment never become 'spent', otherwise convictions become 'spent' after periods which are related to the gravity of the sentence imposed. Thus for a sentence of imprisonment of between six months and 2½ years the rehabilitation period is 10 years. Imprisonment for less than 6 months requires a 7-year rehabilitation period and fines or community service orders take 5 years to become 'spent'.

Asylum and Immigration Act 1996

- Section 8 of this Act is concerned with restrictions on employment for persons subject to immigration control.
- According to s.8(1) employers commit an offence if they employ a person of 16 years or over if either the employee has not been granted leave to enter or remain in the United Kingdom, or if their stay in the United Kingdom is subject to a condition that precludes them from taking up employment. If, however, before the employment began, the potential employee produced suitable documentation and the employer retained it or kept a photocopy, then this may be a defence.
- It is not a defence if the employer knew that the applicant was not entitled to work in the United Kingdom. If this offence is committed by a corporate body, then that body will be liable to a fine, as well as those senior individuals in the corporate body that connived in the offence.

Age discrimination in recruitment

In 1999 the Government issued a Code of Practice on Age Diversity in Employment. One of the purposes of the Code is show how businesses and employers can take steps to ensure that they select, retain and develop the best person for the job by eliminating age as an employment criterion.

- The Code of Practice is a voluntary one, but the Government clearly hopes that employment tribunals will take it into account in their deliberations. Other countries, such as Ireland, Australia and the United States of America have adopted legislation to make discrimination on the basis of age unlawful. The UK Government prefers a voluntarist route aimed at persuading employers that it is their best interests to adopt the policies in the Code.
- It should be noted that discrimination on the basis of age is not unlawful in the United Kingdom, unless it amounts to indirect sex discrimination. It is not unlawful to place recruitment advertisements in the press which stipulate a required or preferred age range for applicants. The Government is hoping that it will become good practice not to do so.
- The Code of Practice considers the employment cycle and makes recommendations for good practice in each. The stages of the cycle are recruitment, selection, promotion, training and development, redundancy and, finally, retirement.

TERMS OF THE CONTRACT OF EMPLOYMENT

Contracts of employment may be oral or in writing. A contract of employment is like any other contract in the sense that it is subject to the general principles of law. In theory this means that the parties are free to negotiate the terms and conditions that suit them so long as they remain within the constraints imposed by statute and the common law. A significant section of the workforce does not negotiate on an individual basis. An important proportion is engaged on such terms and conditions as are laid down in currently operative collective agreements. In practice, these agreements are confined to the minority of employers as almost two-thirds of workplaces in the United Kingdom do not have any employees covered by collective agreements.

Express terms

> Where an employee begins employment with an employer, the employer shall give to the employee a written statement of particulars of employment.
>
> The statement may ... be given in instalments and ... shall be given not later than two months after the beginning of employment (Employment Rights Act 1996 (ERA), in ss.1–2).

The reasoning behind this is clear: if employees receive written statements of the main terms of employment, disputes over the nature and scope of their contracts will be minimized.

Express terms are those which are expressly stated to form part of the contract and they are binding irrespective of whether they differ from those contained in a job advertisement (as happened in *Deeley* v *British Rail* [1980]). Apart from statutorily implied terms, which cannot be undermined, express terms normally take precedence over all other sources, that is common law implied terms and custom and practice.

The following information must be given to employees individually, although, according to ss.2(2) and 3 of the 1996 Act, with regard to the matters mentioned in (6), (7), (8) and (9) below it is sufficient to make the information reasonably accessible to them by means of a document to which they are referred.

1 *The identity of the parties.*

> In *Secretary of State* v *Bearman* [1998] two individuals were placed, for work purposes, with another employer for a period of some 9 years. A dispute then arose as to who was the real employer. The correct approach was to look at the contract of employment and see whether this reflected the intentions of the parties.

Sometimes the identity of the employer can be in dispute, for example where people are 'hired out' to other organizations or where the employer consists of a management committee running a charity, as in *Affleck* v *Newcastle Mind* [1999].

2 *The date on which the employee's period of continuous employment began* (taking into account any employment with a previous employer that counts towards that period). Section 211 ERA 1996 defines the meaning of 'continuous employment'. It begins with the day that a person starts work for an organization, except any period worked before the age of 18 years will not count towards the length of service needed to qualify for a redundancy payment.

3 *The scale or rate of remuneration*, or the method of calculating remuneration, and the intervals at which remuneration is paid.

4 *Any terms and conditions relating to hours of work and normal working hours.*

> In *Ali* v *Christian Salvesen* [1997] a dispute arose over what happened to employees, working under an annualized hours contract of employment, if they left during the course of the year. The collective agreement that was incorporated into the contract of employment omitted to deal with the matter. The Court of Appeal concluded that the parties to a collective agreement might deliberately have omitted provisions dealing with termination of employment during the calculation period on the grounds that it was too complicated or too

controversial to include. So it was not for the courts to imply a clause dealing with it.

The concept of normal working hours is crucial, so in order to avoid confusion, employers should specify whether or not overtime is mandatory, that is whether it forms part of the normal working hours. Care is especially needed when considering annualised hours contracts, where it may still be advisable to define the working week for the purpose of calculating holiday entitlement and any overtime payments due to people leaving during the working year. The courts or tribunals will not necessarily be prepared to fill gaps left by agreements that are not comprehensive.

5 *Any terms and conditions relating to holidays and holiday pay.* Employees are entitled to be paid if holidays are taken in accordance with the terms of their employment during their period of notice (see ERA 1996 s.88(1)(d)). Those employees protected by the Working Time Regulations 1998 are entitled to four weeks paid holiday per leave year. The leave year can be the subject of agreement or, if there is no such agreement, it will commence on the day employment began and each subsequent anniversary thereafter.

6 *Any terms and conditions relating to incapacity for work owing to sickness or injury.*

7 *Any terms and conditions relating to pensions and pension schemes and a note stating whether a contracting-out certificate is in force.*

8 *The length of notice which the employee is entitled to receive and is obliged to give.*

9 *The title of the job or a brief description of the employee's work.*

10 *Where the employment is temporary, the period for which it is expected to continue or, if it is for a fixed term, the date when it is to end.*

11 *The place of work.* If the employee is required or permitted to work at various places, an indication of the employer's address. If an employee works in a number of different countries, the place of work has been defined by the European Court of Justice, in *Rutten* v *Cross Medical* [1997], as the place where the employee habitually carries out his or her work.

12 *Any collective agreements which directly affect the terms and conditions of employment.* This includes, where the employer is not a party to the agreement, the person by whom they were made.

13 *Where the employee is required to work outside the UK for more than a month the statement must specify the period of work outside the UK.* It must also specify the currency in which payment will be made, any additional pay and benefits to be provided by reason of the work being outside the UK, and any terms and conditions relating to the employee's return to the UK.

14 *Any disciplinary rules applicable to the employee.* However, where the employer has fewer than 20 employees on the date the employment commences, the statement need not refer to disciplinary rules or procedures.

15 *The name or description of the person to whom employees can apply if they are dissatisfied with any disciplinary decision or seek to redress a grievance.*

16 *Any further steps consequent upon an application expressing dissatisfaction over a disciplinary decision or grievance.*

If there are no particulars to be entered under any of the above headings, that fact must be mentioned in the written statement. It should also be noted that information relating to items (8), (9), (10), (11) and (12) may be given in instalments within the 2-month period. The other items must be dealt with in a single document called a 'principal statement'. Changes cannot be made to a contract of employment without the consent of the employee but, where there is a change in any of the details required by s.1, s.4 requires that written notification must be given to the employee within one month.

Implied terms

Terms implied by statute

- The equality clause – this is inserted by virtue of s.1 of the Equal Pay Act 1970 which states:

  > (1) If the terms of a contract under which a woman is employed at an establishment in Great Britain do not include (directly or by reference to a collective agreement or otherwise) an equality clause they shall be deemed to include one.

- The National Minimum Wage Act 1998 – this allows, in s.2, the Secretary of State to make provision for determining what is the hourly rate to be paid. Section 2(3) allows provision to be made with respect to when a person is to be treated as working and when they are not.
- The Working Time Regulations 1998 – these provide for maximum hours to be worked in various situations and occupations. They also deal with holidays, rest breaks and rest periods.

The above are examples of statutes implying terms into contracts of employment.

Terms implied by the common law

There are two distinct types of common law implied terms.

1 where there is a gap in the contract of employment it is possible to imply a term if a court can be persuaded that it is necessary to do so in the circumstances of the particular case (implied terms of fact);
2 there are terms which are regarded by the courts as being inherent in all contracts of employment (implied terms of law).

It is a basic principle that a contractual term can be implied only if it is consistent with the express terms of the contract. However, despite the increased use of written contracts and statements, it is not unusual for the parties to discover that they have failed to provide for a particular contingency. If there is a dispute over something that is not expressly dealt with in the contract of employment, a court or tribunal may be asked to insert a term to cover the point at issue. The party wishing to rely on an implied term must satisfy a court either that such a term was so obvious that the parties did not think it necessary to state it expressly (the 'officious bystander' test) or that such a term was necessary to give 'business efficacy' to the relationship.

Duties of the employer

In *William Hill Organisation Ltd* v *Tucker* [1998] the Court of Appeal considered an expert in spread betting and whether the employer had an obligation to provide work when the work was available. In this case the Court decided that there was such an obligation. This was partly because of the need to practise and partly because there was a contractual obligation on the employee to 'work those hours necessary to carry out his duties in a full and professional manner'.

In *University of Nottingham* v *Eyett* [1999] an employer failed to warn an employee who was proposing to exercise important pension rights that the way he was proposing to exercise those rights was not the most financially advantageous. This was not seen as breaching a duty of mutual trust and confidence.

In *Pickford* v *ICI* [1998] it was held that it was not reasonably foreseeable that a secretary spending 50 per cent of her time in typing would suffer, as a result, from repetitive strain injury. Indeed, it was assumed that a person of intelligence and experience would be able to intersperse typing with other activities without being told to do so.

In *Spring* v *Guardian Assurance plc* [1994] the complainant argued that a reference provided by a former employer was a malicious falsehood and/or a negligent misstatement and/or a breach of an implied term in the contract of employment that any reference would be compiled with all reasonable care. The House of Lords concluded that an employer did normally have a duty both to supply a reference and to take reasonable care in compiling it by ensuring the accuracy of the information upon which it was based.

To pay wages

This is the most basic obligation of employers and is normally dealt with by an express term. In certain circumstances, however, the law does not leave the parties entirely free to determine the amount of remuneration payable, for example in the application of the national minimum wage or if an equality clause operates.

To provide work

Employers are generally not obliged to provide work and most employees who receive their full contractual remuneration cannot complain if they are left idle. In certain circumstances the failure to provide work may, therefore, amount to a breach of contract:

- If a person's earnings depend upon work being provided: employees who are paid by results or commission or receive shift premiums must be given the opportunity to work, because the payment of basic wages alone would deprive them of a substantial part of what they had bargained for – the opportunity to earn more.
- Where the lack of work could lead to a loss of publicity or affect the reputation of an employee. In *Bosworth* v *Jowett* [1977] it was held that the higher a person is in the management structure, the more important it is for work to be given when it is available.

- Where employees need to practise in order to preserve their skills. The Court of Appeal, in *Langston* v *AUEW* [1974], has suggested that such employees should be given the opportunity of performing work when it is available. This is linked to the issue of 'garden leave'. This is the practice of continuing to pay an employee for a period, but not allowing them to work during that time. It has sometimes been used to stop a valuable employee leaving and immediately taking up employment with a competitor. A problem arises when such a period without work can have a detrimental affect on an employee's skills.

To cooperate with the employee

Originally this duty amounted to little more than an obligation not to impede the employees in the performance of their contracts. However, one of the effects of the unfair dismissal provisions has been that the courts have displayed a greater willingness to accept that employers have a positive duty to ensure that the purposes of the contract are achieved. Thus it has frequently been stated that employers must not destroy the mutual trust and confidence upon which cooperation is built, although there are limits as to how positive this obligation should be.

To take reasonable care of the employee

In addition to this duty implied by law, there are a number of key statutes in the area of health and safety. It is important to note that a person who is injured in the course of employment may be able to bring an action for damages based either on the common law duty or breach of statute or other regulations.

Recognizing that employers cannot guarantee that no employees will be injured at work, the standard of care which the law demands is that which 'an ordinary prudent employer would take in all the circumstances' (see *Paris* v *Stepney BC* [1951]). If a job has risks to health and safety which are not common knowledge, but of which an employer knows or ought to know, and against which he or she cannot guard by taking precautions, then, according to *White* v *Holbrook* [1985], the employer should tell anyone to whom employment is offered what those risks are. This is so, if, on the information then available, knowledge of those risks would be likely to affect the decision of a sensible prospective employee about accepting the offer. Thus, the common law accepts that employers should be held liable only if they fail to safeguard against something which was reasonably foreseeable.

Providing references

Strictly speaking this concerns a duty of care owed to ex-employees, but it is an issue on which employers need to take care. This duty is to provide a reference which is in substance true, accurate and fair (see *Bartholomew* v *LB of Hackney* [1999]). The provider of a reference must not give an impression that is unfair or misleading overall, even if the component parts of the reference are accurate. This can clearly mean the inclusion of matters not in the ex-employees favour as well as those that are. Failure to provide a reference for an ex-employee might, as in *Coote* v *Granada Hospitality* [1999], also be interpreted as coming within s.6(2) of the Sex

Discrimination Act 1975, which makes it unlawful to discriminate against employees by subjecting them to any detriment in relation to their employment.

Duties of the employee

To co-operate with the employer

This is concerned with the duty to obey lawful and reasonable orders and the duty not to impede the employer's business.

Fidelity

Employees must avoid putting themselves in a position whereby their own interests conflict with the duty they owe their employer or an employer to whom they have been seconded. Thus employees must not accept any reward for their work other than from their employer, (e.g. a gift or secret commission). However, employees have no contractual duty to disclose their own misconduct and whether there is a duty to report the misconduct of fellow employees depends on the individual contract of employment and the circumstances (see *Sybron Corporation* v *Rochem* [1983]). There are two particular aspects to this duty which we must now consider: the obligation not to compete with the employer and the obligation not to disclose confidential information.

The obligation not to compete with the employer

> In *Lancashire Fires* v *SA Lyons* [997] it was held that the renting and equipping of premises, in an employee's spare time, and arranging financial backing to set up in competition may be construed as a breach of an implied duty of fidelity. If the employer has reasonable grounds for believing that the employee has committed or is about to commit some wrongful act, dismissal may be justified (see *Adamson* v *B & L Cleaning* [1995]).

Generally the spare time activities of employees are no business of the employer, although an injunction may be granted to prevent employees working for competitors during their spare time if it can be shown that the employer's business would be seriously damaged. However, in *Nova Plastics Ltd* v *Froggat* [1982] the Employment Appeal Tribunal rejected the argument that there is a general implication that any work for a competitor should be regarded as being a breach of trust or a failure to give loyal service. It should be noted that the intention to set up in competition with the employer is not in itself a breach of the implied duty of loyalty, although there is a line over which the employee must not go.

The obligation not to disclose confidential information

The obligation not to use or disclose information might cover secret processes of manufacture or designs, or any other information of a sufficiently high degree of confidentiality as to amount to a trade secret as in *Lancashire Fires*. However, this obligation does not extend to information which is only 'confidential' in the sense that any unauthorized disclosure to a third party while the employment subsisted would be a breach of the duty of fidelity. In order to determine whether any particular item of information falls within the implied term thus preventing its use or disclosure after the employment has ceased, it is necessary to consider all the facts of the case.

Under the Public Interest Disclosure Act 1998, workers will be protected against victimization if they disclose information (whether confidential or not) in specified circumstances.

To take reasonable care

Employees must exercise reasonable skill and care in the performance of their contracts. If they do not do so, apart from any disciplinary action that may be taken against them, there is an implied duty to indemnify the employer in respect of the consequences of their negligence (see *Janata Bank* v *Ahmed* [1981]). In theory, therefore, if by virtue of the doctrine of vicarious liability (see above) an employer is required to pay damages to an injured third party the amount paid out could be recovered by suing the negligent employee. In practice, such embarrassing litigation is avoided because it is the employer's insurance company that actually pays the damages.

SEX AND RACE DISCRIMINATION

The Sex Discrimination Act 1975 and the Race Relations Act 1976

In *Mandla* v *Lee* [1983] the House of Lords held that 'ethnic origins' meant a group which was a segment of the population distinguished from others by a sufficient combination of shared customs, beliefs, traditions and characteristics derived from a common or presumed common past. This was so even if not drawn from what in biological terms was a common racial stock, in that it was that combination which gave them a historically determined social identity in their own eyes and in the eyes of those outside the group.

It is important to note that the titles of these two statutes do not fully reflect the matters that are covered. The Sex Discrimination Act 1975 (SDA 1975) outlaws, for example, discrimination against married (but not single) persons on the grounds of marital status. The Race Relations Act 1976 (RRA 1976) defines 'racial grounds' as meaning colour, race, nationality, national or ethnic origins. A racial group that is defined by colour may include people of more than one ethnic origin. Although a racial group cannot be defined by language or religion alone (see *Gwynnedd CC* v *Jones* [1986]), it has been accepted that Sikhs, Jews and gypsies all fall within the scope of the Race Relations Act 1976. In contrast, in *Dawkins* v *Department of the Environment* [1993] it was accepted that Rastafarians are a separate group with identifiable characteristics. But the Court of Appeal concluded that they have not established a separate identity by reference to their ethnic origins and are therefore not protected by the 1976 Act.

Both the Equal Opportunities Commission (EOC) and the Commission for Racial Equality (CRE) have issued Codes of Practice for the purpose of eliminating discrimination in employment. A failure to observe any of the provisions of these codes does not render a person liable to legal proceedings but the Commissions' recommendations are admissible in evidence before employment tribunals. Both statutes recognize that discrimination can be either direct or indirect.

Direct discrimination

Section 1(1)(a) of the Sex Discrimination Act 1975 describes direct discrimination:

> (1) A person discriminates against a woman in any circumstances relevant for the purpose of any provision of this Act if
> (a) on the grounds of her sex he treats her less favourably than he treats or would treat a man.

In *Weathersfield Ltd* v *Sargent* [1999] it was held that a white European woman was unlawfully discriminated against on grounds of race when she resigned as a result of being given an unlawful instruction to discriminate on racial grounds against black and Asian people.

Section 1(1)(a) of the Race Relations Act (RRA) 1976 has a similar provision concerned with treating people less favourably than others on 'racial grounds'. Thus, direct discrimination occurs where on the grounds of sex, marital status or race a person is treated less favourably than a person of the opposite sex, a single person or person not of the same racial group, would be treated.

Section 1(1)(a) RRA 1976 covers all cases of discrimination on racial grounds whether the racial characteristics in question are those of the person treated less favourably or some other person.

Sexual and racial harassment

In *Reed and Bull Information Systems* v *Stedman* [1999] the Employment Appeal Tribunal said that the essential characteristic of sexual harassment is that it is words or conduct which are unwelcome to the recipient. It is for the recipient for themselves to decide what is acceptable and what is unwelcome or offensive. Provided that any reasonable person would understand him or her to be rejecting the conduct of which he or she is complaining, then a continuation of that conduct would generally be regarded as harassment.

In *Jones* v *Tower Boot Co Ltd* [1997] an employee, whose mother was white and father black, was held to have been racially harassed as a result of a number of incidents at work, which included being called offensive names and having an arm burnt with a hot screwdriver. The employer was held to be vicariously liable for the harassment as the acts were carried out 'during the course of employment'.

Sexual harassment has been defined as 'unwanted conduct of a sexual nature, or other conduct based on sex affecting the dignity of women and men at work' (see *CC of Lincolnshire Police* v *Stubbs* [1999]).

The phrase 'in the course of employment' has been given a broad interpretation. It included, for example in *Stubbs*, actions that took place during a social event held immediately after work and during a leaving party for a colleague.

Indirect discrimination

Section 1(1)(b) of the Sex Discrimination Act 1975 defines indirect discrimination as where

> (b) he applies to her a requirement or condition which he applies, or would apply equally to a man but
>   (i) which is such that the proportion of women who can comply with it is considerably smaller than the proportion of men who can comply with it.

Section 1(1)(b) of the Race Relations Act 1976 has similar provisions which refer to the relative proportion of a racial group compared to the proportion not of that racial group that can comply with a requirement or condition.

Thus a person can complain of indirect discrimination where an employer applies a requirement or condition which would apply equally to a person of the opposite sex (single people or persons not of the same racial group) but which is such that the proportion of the applicant's sex (marital status or racial group) who can comply with it is considerably smaller than the proportion of persons of the opposite sex (single people or persons not of the same racial group). The applicant must also show that he or she suffered a detriment as a result of being unable to comply with the requirement or condition. Employers can avoid liability by demonstrating that the requirement or condition is 'justifiable' irrespective of the sex, marital status or race of the person to whom it is applied. Both statutes stipulate that when drawing comparisons the relevant circumstances must be the same or not materially different.

Lawful discrimination

The major exception, which is common to both statutes, is where sex or race is a genuine occupational qualification (GOQ). In the case of sex, this occurs, according to s.7 SDA, where the following criteria apply.

- The essential nature of the job demands a particular physiology (excluding physical strength) or for reasons of authenticity in entertainment.
- The job needs to be held by a particular sex to preserve decency or privacy because either it is likely to involve physical contact in circumstances where members of the opposite sex might reasonably object to its being carried out (e.g. searching for security purposes) or because people are in a state of undress or are using sanitary facilities.
- The nature or location of the employer's establishment makes it impracticable for the job holder to live anywhere other than on the employer's premises and the premises are not equipped with separate sleeping accommodation and sanitary facilities for one sex and it is unreasonable to expect the employer to equip those premises with separate facilities or to provide separate premises (e.g. where the employment is on a remote site). The words 'to live in' involve the concept of residence (either permanent or temporary) and do not cover the situation where the employee is obliged to remain on the premises for a limited period eating or resting (see *Sisley* v *Brittania Security* [1983]).

- The nature of the establishment demands a person of a particular sex because it is an establishment for persons requiring special care or attention and those persons are all of a particular sex and it is reasonable, 'having regard to the essential character of the establishment', that the job should not be held by a person of the opposite sex, as in *Lasertop Ltd* v *Webster* [1997].
- The job holder provides personal services which can most effectively be provided by a person of a particular sex (e.g. in a team of social workers).
- The job is one of two to be held by a married couple.
- The job is likely to involve the holder working or living in a private home and the job needs to be done by a member of one sex because objection might reasonably be taken to allowing someone of the other sex the degree of physical or social contact with a person living in the home or the knowledge of such a person's private affairs, which the job is likely to entail.
- The job is likely to involve the performance of duties outside the UK in a country whose laws or customs are such that the duties could not effectively be performed by a woman.

The only GOQs allowed for under the 1976 Act depend on authenticity in the provision of food and drink, in entertainment and modelling, and where the job holder provides personal welfare services which can most effectively be provided by a person of a particular racial group. Under both Acts, GOQs apply even though they relate to only some of the job duties, and, unless a duty is so trivial that it ought to be disregarded altogether, it is not for tribunals to assess its importance (see *Tottenham Green Under 5s* v *Marshall* [1991]). However, a GOQ will not provide a defence if the employer already has sufficient employees capable of carrying out those duties and whom it would be reasonable to employ in that way, as occurred in *Etam* v *Rowan*.

Disability discrimination

The Disability Discrimination Act (DDA) 1995 makes it unlawful for employers with fifteen or more employees to discriminate against existing or prospective staff for a reason relating to their disability. People are also protected if they have recovered from a disability that is covered by this Act. The DDA 1995 covers employees and contract workers, apprentices and those working under a contract to do any work. It excludes police and prison officers, firefighters, the armed services and people working on board a ship, aircraft or hovercraft.

According to DDA 1995 s.1(1), a person has a disability

> if he has a physical or mental impairment which has a substantial and long-term adverse effect on his ability to carry out normal day-to-day activities.

The definition covers impairments affecting the senses, such as hearing and sight, together with learning difficulties or a mental illness that is clinically well-recognized. For these purposes an impairment has a long-term effect only if it has lasted for at least 12 months, is likely to do so, or is likely to last for the rest of the life of the person affected. Long-term effects include those that are likely to recur. Day-to-day activities are normal activities carried out on a regular basis. Severe disfigurements are treated as disabilities although they have no effect on a person's ability to carry out normal day-to-day activities.

Medication or equipment is not taken into account when assessing whether an impairment has a substantial effect. One exception to this is when people wear glasses or contact lenses. Where a progressive condition has resulted in an impairment which has affected a person's day-to-day activities, but that effect is not yet substantial, it is to be treated as having a substantial effect if that is the likely prognosis. The examples given of progressive conditions are: cancer, multiple sclerosis, muscular dystrophy and HIV infection.

The proper approach to the question of whether a person has a disability, within the meaning of the Act, was considered in *Goodwin* v *The Patent Office* [1999]. The Employment Appeal Tribunal concluded that a tribunal should look at the evidence by reference to four different conditions.

1 *The impairment condition* – does the applicant have an impairment which is either physical or mental? If there is any doubt as to whether the impairment condition is fulfilled in a mental illness case, then reference should be made to the World Health Organisation International Classification of Diseases.
2 *The adverse effect condition* – does the impairment affect the applicant's ability to carry out normal day-to-day activities. This condition is concerned with the *ability* to carry out normal day-to-day activities whether at work or at home, for example a person may be able to cook, but only to do so with the greatest difficulty.
3 *The substantial condition* – is the adverse condition substantial? The tribunal will need to look at how the person's abilities were affected at the material time whilst on medication, and then try to deduce what they would have been like without medication. The question is then whether the actual or deduced affects on the applicant's ability to carry out normal day-to-day activities is clearly more than trivial.
4 *The long-term condition* – is the adverse condition long-term?

Section 5 provides that an employer discriminates against a disabled person if, for a reason relating to that person's disability:

   (a) it treats him or her less favourably than it treats or would treat others to whom that reason does not or would not apply; and
   (b) the employer cannot show that the treatment is justified.

Less favourable treatment can be justified only if such treatment is material to the circumstances of the individual case. Even so, employers must consider whether the reason could be overcome or made less substantial by making a reasonable adjustment. The rights of an employee to have these reasonable adjustments made are additional rights and do not depend upon an employee showing that discrimination has taken place under DDA 1995 s.5(1).

> In *Clarke* v *Novacold* [1999] the Court of Appeal concluded that the test of less favourable treatment is based on the reason for the treatment of the disabled person and not on the fact of the disability. It did not, unlike the SDA 1975 and the RRA 1976, need a comparator to show that discrimination had taken place.

Where any of the employer's arrangements or any physical feature of the premises place a disabled person at substantial disadvantage, the employer must take such steps as are reasonable in all the circumstances in order to prevent the arrangements or feature having that effect. There is a limit to the adjustments that an employer is required to make. They do not include the provision of personal carer services for a person that might need such help, as in *Kenny* v *Hampshire Constabulary* [1999]. They might, however, include the accommodation of such a carer if provided by others.

The duty to make adjustments does not arise until a disabled person is employed or such person applies or considers applying for a job. Applicants needs to make the employer aware of their disabilities and whether special interview arrangements are necessary.

> In *Ridout* v *T C Group* [1998] a candidate suffering from a rare form of epilepsy was interviewed in surroundings which, it was suggested, were unsuitable for someone with her disability. Although the Code of Practice for the elimination of disability discrimination in employment suggests that employers should think ahead in making arrangements for interviews, the Employment Appeal Tribunal concluded that no reasonable employer would be expected to know, without being told by the applicant, that the arrangements for an interview might disadvantage such an applicant.

It will be difficult to show that an employer is guilty of disability discrimination if they have not been told of the employee's condition.

> In *O'Neill* v *Symon & Co* [1998] an employee was dismissed after 15 months employment which contained a number of absences for a viral illness. The employee was diagnosed as suffering from ME/chronic fatigue syndrome and claimed discrimination on the grounds of her disability. The employer, however, did not know of this diagnosis, which meant that the reason for the dismissal was not the disability.

As with sex and race discrimination, anything done by a person in the course of employment is treated as also done by the employer, whether or not it was done with the employer's approval. However, employers will not be liable if they can show that they took such steps as were reasonably practicable to prevent the employee's action. Similarly, s.57 provides that anyone who knowingly aids another to do an unlawful act is to be treated as having committed the same unlawful act.

ENDING THE CONTRACT OF EMPLOYMENT – UNFAIR DISMISSAL

Section 94 ERA 1996 states:

> (1) An employee has the right not to be unfairly dismissed by his employer.

Those not protected

Age limits

No claim can be made if on or before the effective date of termination (see below) the individual had attained the normal retiring age for an employee in his or her position or was 65 years old. However, there is no age limit if the reason or principal reason for dismissal is 'inadmissible' (see 'Automatically unfair dismissal' below).

'Normal retirement age' is the age at which employees in a group (see *Barber* v *Thames TV* [1992]) can reasonably expect to be compelled to retire unless there is some special reason in a particular case for a different age to apply. In *Barclays Bank* v

O'Brien the Court of Appeal regarded a departure from the normal retirement age of 60 as being for a special reason. The exception was limited in time and was made for a relatively small category of employees in response to representations made on their behalf on the grounds of hardship.

The contractual retirement age does not conclusively fix the normal retirement age. Where there is a contractual retirement age there is a presumption that that age is the normal retirement age, but this presumption can be rebutted by evidence that there is in practice some higher age at which employees are regularly retired and which they have reasonably come to regard as their normal retirement age.

Continuous service

In order to complain of unfair dismissal one year's continuous service is required. This qualification does not apply if the reason or principal reason for dismissal was 'inadmissible' (see below). Continuity is to be calculated up to the effective date of termination in accordance with ERA 1996 ss.210–219. Employees who are wrongfully deprived of their statutory minimum entitlement to notice or receive a payment in lieu can add on that period of notice in ascertaining their length of service (see *Staffordshire CC* v *Secretary of State*).

The meaning of dismissal

Apart from the lay-off and short-time provisions, an employee is to be treated as dismissed if:

- the contract under which he or she is employed is terminated by the employer with or without notice; or
- a fixed-term contract expires without being renewed under the same contract; or
- the employee terminates the contract with or without notice in circumstances such that he or she is entitled to terminate it without notice by reason of the employer's conduct.

Constructive dismissal

The situation where the employee terminates the contract with or without notice in circumstances such that he or she is entitled to terminate it without notice by reason of the employer's conduct is commonly referred to as a 'constructive' dismissal. In these circumstances the employer's behaviour constitutes a repudiation of the contract and the employee accepts that repudiation by resigning.

Employees are only entitled to treat themselves as constructively dismissed if the employer is guilty of conduct which is a significant breach going to the root of the contract or which shows that the employer no longer intends to be bound by one or more of its essential terms. Whether the repudiatory conduct of a supervisor binds the employer depends on whether the acts were done in the course of the supervisor's employment (see *Hilton Hotels* v *Protopapa* [1990]).

If employees continue for any length of time without leaving they will be regarded as having elected to affirm the contract and will lose the right to treat themselves as discharged, as in *Wilton* v *Cornwall Health Authority* [1993]. However, provided that employees make clear their objection to what is being done they are not to be taken to have affirmed the contract by continuing to work and draw pay for a limited period of time (see *Rigby* v *Ferodo* [1987]).

Giving a reason for dismissal

Once employees have proved that they were dismissed, the burden shifts to the employer to show the reason, or, if there was more than one, the principal reason, for the dismissal and that it falls within one of the following categories.

- it relates to the capacity or qualifications of the employee for performing work of the kind which he or she was employed to do;
- it relates to the conduct of the employee;
- the employee was redundant;
- the employee could not continue to work in the position held without contravention, either on the employee's part or that of the employer, of a duty or restriction imposed by or under a statute;
- there was some other substantial reason of such a kind as to justify the dismissal of an employee holding the position which the employee held.

Automatically unfair dismissal

In certain circumstances a dismissal will be unfair because the reason for it was 'inadmissible'. Examples of 'inadmissible reasons' are:

- pregnancy or maternity;
- certain health and safety grounds;
- if the employee is dismissed for trying to enforce the national minimum wage.

Other unfair reasons for dismissal include those connected to the SDA 1975 and the RRA 1976 which stipulate that it is unlawful to discriminate on the prohibited grounds by way of dismissal; the Rehabilitation of Offenders Act 1974 which states that 'a conviction which has become spent ... shall not be a proper ground for dismissing'; and s.4(2) of the *Disability Discrimination Act* 1995 provides that it is unlawful to discriminate against disabled persons by dismissing them.

Potentially fair reasons for dismissal

Capability or qualifications

'Qualifications' means 'any degree, diploma, or other academic, technical or professional qualification relevant to the position which the employee held'. In *Blue Star Ltd* v *Williams* [1979] it was held that a mere licence, permit or authorization is not such a qualification unless it is substantially concerned with the aptitude or ability of the person to do the job.

According to ERA 1996 s.98(3) 'capability' is to be assessed by reference to 'skill, aptitude, health or any other physical or mental quality'. It has been held, in *Abernethy* v *Mott* [1974], that an employee's inflexibility or lack of adaptability came within his or her aptitude and mental qualities.

Measures should be taken to ensure that inadequate performance is identified as soon as possible so that remedial action can be taken. In all cases, the cause of poor performance should be investigated. Points to note include the following.

- An employee's incapability need only 'relate to' the performance of contractual duties; in *Shook* v *LB of Ealing* [1986] it was decided that there was no requirement to show that the performance of all those duties has been affected.
- Although employees who are sick will hope to remain employed at least until their contractual sick pay entitlement (if any) is exhausted, this does not mean that a person cannot be dismissed before the period of sick pay has elapsed. Equally, it will be unfair to dismiss simply because the sick pay period has expired.
- The employer's duty to act fairly is unaffected by considerations as to who was responsible for the employee's unfitness to work (see *London Fire Authority* v *Betty* [1994]).
- An employee who has become incapable of work may have to be treated as a person with a disability within the meaning of s.1 of the Disability Discrimination Act 1995.

In deciding whether an employer acted fairly in dismissing, tribunals must determine as a matter of fact what consultation, if any, was necessary, or desirable in the known circumstances; what consultation took place; and whether that consultation process was adequate in the circumstances. Thus, in *Eclipse Blinds* v *Wright* [1992] the Court of Appeal ruled that it was not unfair to dismiss without consultation where the employer was genuinely concerned about giving the employee information about her health of which she seemed unaware.

Conduct

In *Hamilton* v *Argyll* [1993] it was held that there is no necessary inference that, because an employee is guilty of gross misconduct in relation to his or her actual employment, they must necessarily be considered unsuitable for any employment whatsoever.

In *Lock* v *Cardiff Railway Company Ltd* [1998] a train conductor was dismissed for gross misconduct when he asked a 16-year old to leave the train because he did not have a valid ticket or sufficient money to pay the excess fare. The employer's disciplinary code did not specify which offences would be regarded as gross misconduct that would result in dismissal for the first offence. As a result the Employment Appeal Tribunal held that no reasonable tribunal properly directing itself could have concluded that the dismissal was fair.

In *Marshall* v *Industrial Systems Ltd* [1992] the Employment Appeal Tribunal held that it was reasonable to dismiss a managing director after discovering that, with another manager, he was planning to set up in competition and take away the business of their best client, and that he tried to induce another key employee to join them in that venture.

It is not the function of tribunals to decide not whether misconduct is gross or criminal but whether the employer has, in the circumstances of the case, acted reasonably in dismissing.

Clearly there will be cases where the misconduct is sufficiently serious that an employee can be dismissed without warning. Paragraph 8 of the ACAS *Code of Practice on Disciplinary Practice and Procedures in Employment* (2000) advocates that employees should be given 'a clear indication of the type of conduct that may warrant summary dismissal'. According to the Employment Appeal Tribunal, disciplinary rules that fail to follow the ACAS Code in specifying those offences constituting gross misconduct and justifying dismissal at the first breach will be defective.

Fighting is an example of an area where it is not necessary to state that such behaviour will be regarded very gravely, since the courts have decided that whether or not to dismiss for this reason is essentially a matter for the employer. The test is what would be the reaction of a reasonable employer in the circumstances. Thus, if without proper inquiry, an employer implements a policy of dismissing any employee who struck another there could be a finding of unfairness, as in *Taylor* v *Parsons* [1981], where the employee concerned had a good conduct record extending over 20 years.

The intention to set up in competition with the employer is not in itself a breach of the implied duty of loyalty. Unless the employer has reasonable grounds for believing that the employee has done or is about to do some wrongful act, dismissal will not be justified (see *Laughton* v *Bapp* [1986]).

Theft of an employer's property will amount to a fair reason for dismissal; far more difficult to handle are cases of suspected dishonesty. Where there is a reasonable suspicion that one or more employees within a group have acted dishonestly, it is not necessary for the employer to identify which of them acted dishonestly (see *Parr* v *Whitbread*). Thus, provided certain conditions are satisfied, an employer who cannot identify which member of a group was responsible for an act can fairly dismiss the whole group, even where it is probable that not all were guilty of the act.

Redundancy

For unfair dismissal purposes there is no presumption of redundancy, so it is up to the employer to establish this as the reason, or principal reason, for dismissal. Nevertheless, tribunals will not investigate the background leading to the redundancy or require the employer to justify redundancies in economic terms. A dismissal on grounds of redundancy will be unfair if it is shown that 'the circumstances constituting the redundancy applied equally to one or more other employees in the same undertaking who held positions similar' and either the reason, or principal reason, for which the employee was selected was inadmissible. A failure to comply with a procedural requirement to consult trade unions and to consider volunteers will not automatically be unfair (see *McDowell* v *Eastern BRS* [1981]). However, according to *King* v *Eaton* [1996], employers need to show that their method of selection was fair and applied reasonably and an absence of adequate consultation with the employees concerned or their representatives might affect their ability to do this. 'Last in first out' is frequently used as a criterion for selection and, in *International Paint* v *Cameron* [1979] it was assumed to be based on periods of continuous rather than cumulative service. Arguably, this form of selection indirectly discriminates against women and needs to be justified (see *Brook* v *LB of Haringey* [1992]).

It is now well established that employers have a duty to consider the alternatives to compulsory redundancy. Indeed, ACAS suggests the following methods of avoiding such redundancies:

- natural wastage;
- restrictions on recruitment;
- retirement of employees who are beyond normal retiring age;
- seeking applicants for early retirement or voluntary redundancy;
- reductions in overtime;
- short-time working;
- retraining and redeployment to other parts of the organization;
- termination of the employment of temporary or contract staff.

As regards alternative employment, 'the size and administrative resources' of the employer will be a relevant consideration here. However, if a vacancy exists, an employer would be advised to offer it rather than speculate about the likelihood of the employee accepting it. Nevertheless, only in very rare cases will a tribunal accept that a reasonable employer would have created a job by dismissing someone else. Finally, employers should consider establishing both redundancy counselling services, which would provide information on alternative employment, training, occupational and state benefits and hardship committees, which would seek to alleviate 'undue hardship'.

Some other substantial reason

In *Farrant* v *The Woodroffe School* [1998] an employee was dismissed for refusing to accept organizational changes. The employer mistakenly believed that the employee was obliged to accept a new job description and that the dismissal was therefore lawful. The Employment Appeal Tribunal held that dismissal for refusing to obey an unlawful order was not necessarily unfair. Of importance was not the lawfulness or otherwise of the employer's instructions, but the overall question of reasonableness. In this case it was not unreasonable for them to act on professional advice, even if that advice was wrong.

'Some other substantial reason' was included in the ERA 1996 so as to give tribunals the discretion to accept as a fair reason for dismissal something that would not conveniently fit into any of the other categories. It covers such diverse matters as

- dismissal for being sentenced to imprisonment (see *Kingston* v *British Rail* [1984]);
- being dismissed as manager of a public house because a partner had resigned from jointly holding the position (see *Alboni* v *Ind Coope* [1998]);
- refusing to sign an undertaking not to compete (see *RS Components* v *Irwin* [1973]);
- because the employer's best customer was unwilling to accept the particular individual (see *Scottpacking* v *Paterson* [1978]).

'Some other substantial reason' has frequently provided a convenient peg where employees have been dismissed as a result of a re-organization of the business. The Court of Appeal has taken the view that it is not necessary for an employer to show that in the absence of a re-organization there would be a total business disaster. It is sufficient if there is a sound business reason, which means only that there is a reason which management thinks on reasonable grounds is sound (see *Hollister* v *NFU*

[1979]). If the employer can satisfy a tribunal that a certain policy has evolved which was thought to have discernible advantages then dismissal in accordance with that policy can be said to be for 'some other substantial reason'.

Where an employee refuses to agree changes consequent upon a re-organization the test to be applied by tribunals is not simply whether the terms offered were those which a reasonable employer could offer. Looking at the employer's offer alone would exclude from scrutiny everything that happened between the time the offer was made and the dismissal, for example a potentially significant factor is whether other employees accepted the offer (see *St John of God* v *Brooks* [1992]). Equally there is no principle of law that if new contractual terms are much less favourable to an employee than the previous ones, dismissal for refusing to accept them will be unfair unless the business reasons are so pressing that it is vital for the survival of the business that the revised terms are accepted.

Tribunals will examine an employer's motive for introducing changes in order to ensure that they are not being imposed arbitrarily (see *Catamaran Cruisers* v *Williams* [1994]). The reasonable employer will explore all the alternatives to dismissal but, like consultation with trade unions and the individual concerned, such a consideration is only one of the factors which must be taken into account under ERA 1996 s.98(4).

Reasonableness in the circumstances

Section 98(4) ERA 1996 provides that where the employer has given a valid reason for dismissal the determination of the question whether the dismissal was fair or unfair

(1) depends on whether in the circumstances (including the size and administrative resources of the employer's undertaking), the employer acted reasonably or unreasonably in treating it as a sufficient reason for dismissing the employee, and

(2) shall be determined in accordance with equity and the substantial merits of the case.

Employment tribunals must take account of the wider circumstances. In addition to the employer's business needs, attention must be paid to the personal attributes of the employee, for example seniority and previous work record. Thus when all the relevant facts are considered a dismissal may be deemed unfair notwithstanding the fact that the disciplinary rules specified that such behaviour would result in immediate dismissal (see *Ladbroke Racing* v *Arnott* [1983]).

PROGRESS TEST

Answer these questions by drawing upon the text of this chapter and by referring to the cases and statutes mentioned.

1 What are the legal issues that need to be considered when recruiting employees? Are some of more importance than others?

2 Which items of information need to be included in the principal statement when employees are given a statement of their terms and conditions of employment? Can this statement also be a contract of employment?

3 Lynne attends a recruitment interview for a new job. After the interview she is told that she was not successful because the job required a great deal of energy as well as the ability to travel at short notice. She is told that her age counted against her and the fact that she is married might have stopped her being able to travel. Does she have a claim for unlawful discrimination?

4 Fiona is managing director of a wholesale supplies company. With another colleague she has been planning to set up a business in competition with her present employer. She has only done this in her spare time and there is nothing in her contract of employment about not competing with her present employer. The chairman of the company discovers what she has been up to and summarily dismisses her for gross misconduct. What are Fiona's legal rights in this situation?

10 Environmental responsibilities of the organization

Stephen Homewood

INTRODUCTION

What is the meant by the Environment?

> everything which isn't me (Einstein).

> all or any of the following media, namely, the air, water and land (Section 1, Environmental Protection Act 1990).

A fundamental question which arises when we seek to examine how far environmental law affects the business organization is, as the two quotations given here demonstrate, identifying what is actually meant by the term the 'environment'. This is not always an easy question to answer as the term is used in a number of different senses. This chapter is concerned with the legal responsibilities of the business organization in relation to environmental protection. The definition given in s.1 of the Environmental Protection Act (EPA), one of the most important pieces of legislation in this area is therefore very important.

This chapter will look at the law and regulatory system designed both to protect the environment, and to control or prevent its pollution. It is worth noting at the outset that other areas of law overlap with environmental law: the legal regimes relating to consumer protection and the health and safety of those at work are examples. However the law which it is proposed to discuss here is concerned with regulating those activities which might be detrimental to the interests of the wider community.

Such regulation has in the past been mainly enforced through planning controls. The increased concern about environmental protection and the failure of the existing common and statutory law has resulted in the introduction of complex new statutory controls. This chapter looks at key aspects of these controls, in particular:

- the role of the common law;
- land use and planning control;
- air and water pollution control;
- waste management and control;
- noise control and related problems.

It is a highly regulated system, but the law is clearly not the only means of protecting the environment and preventing pollution. Other approaches are being tried, including, for example:

- fiscal methods such as the landfill, petrol and emissions taxes;
- public persuasion or the pressure of publicity;
- providing public access to environmental information;
- Environmental Management Systems, for example ISO 14001.

This chapter will focus on certain areas of this vast and rapidly changing topic. It will not discuss some issues, such as the law in relation to countryside and wildlife protection, the protection of historic and architecturally important buildings, Genetically Modified Substances and certain aspects of waste, for example hazardous substances. Again it will only refer in outline to the requirements relating to contaminated land and to packaging waste: these areas are still evolving and there is much uncertainty about them. Further information must be sought on these topics from specialized sources.

Why is this topic of importance to business?

Over the last two decades there has been increasing concern at the harm caused to the environment by man's activities. Scientific debates and evidence have led to issues relating to environmental protection acquiring a higher political profile, and this has led to an explosion of new regulation, on international, European and UK levels. Thus, whether business organizations like it or not, they now have to comply with a wide range of licensing and permit systems in this country. If they trade abroad they may well be faced with similar controls of their activities in the other jurisdictions in which they operate. Failure to comply with these requirements may result in the business incurring criminal liability, civil liability and the loss of permissions needed to carry on with their business.

Of particular note are certain provisions that may not only cause loss to the organization but may also cause its managers to become *personally liable*. For example the EPA s.157 states that when an offence under this Act is committed by business and the business's 'directors, manager or similar person, consented, connived or was negligent' in relation to the offence, then they themselves can personally also be convicted, fined and possibly imprisoned!

Finally, it is suggested, people who work for commercial concerns also wish in their own personal life to enjoy a clean and healthy environment, and in that sense have a clear interest in ensuring that the environment is not damaged beyond repair.

Sources

The current law in relation to prevention and control of pollution has quite a long history, and in the past relied predominantly on the planning system and specific legislation related to public health. The common law played a limited role, based as it often was on the need for the plaintiff having a specified interest in the land concerned (e.g. tort of nuisance). However, following the political importance attached to protecting the environment in the 1960s and 1970s and specifically after the UK joined the EC, a major increase and change of focus occurred. A large amount of new legislation was introduced following the adoption of a number of EC Directives. Even though the original Treaty of Rome in 1957 contained nothing in relation to environmental protection, the Community developed a wide range of laws on, for example, air and water quality controls. Environmental conservation concepts such as 'Sustainable Development', and 'Polluter Pays' are now to be found amongst the main objectives of EC policy and law, and require the EC, following amendments to the EC Treaty at Maastricht and Amsterdam, to integrate environmental considerations into all other areas. The business community is likely to see more such controls from this source in the future.

The international community, in particular the United Nations at the famous 'Rio Summit' in 1992, has also developed a wide range of international legally binding treaties and conventions in relation to environmental law. An example is the Climate Change Convention in 1992, leading to restrictions on the amounts of global warming gases that may be emitted by states. Another example is the Vienna Convention on Ozone Layer Protection controlling the use of chemicals harmful to the ozone layer, or the Basel Convention in 1989 on the Transfrontier Movement of Hazardous Waste. The UK has agreed to abide by these treaties, and normally does so by incorporating changes in national law to reflect these agreements.

On the other hand, in this country, there has been the influence of the traditional common law. The common law tools most often used for protection of the environment are tort, contract and, to some extent, covenants in land law. The latter two have played a minor role, but tort has historically been significantly used, especially the areas of nuisance, trespass and riparian rights. Indeed it is still used to obtain civil compensation in some circumstances, or for the issue of an injunction to prevent harm from occurring or continuing. On the whole, however, the use of tort has been replaced by statutory regulation. There are a number of reasons for this, including the requirement (except in negligence) for some interest in the land before tort can be invoked by the claimant (See *Hunter* v *Canary Wharf* [1997]).

Another problem with the common law is that it is often control after the event. The common law has not been useful to prevent pollution, as injunctions derive from equity and are highly discretionary awards given somewhat reluctantly by the courts. Other problems concern the question of the burden of proof lying on the claimant, the difficulty of showing, for example, that someone acted negligently, or has been the direct cause of a nuisance. When the cost and risk of going to court are included there are considerable disincentives to using the common law. This has led to the rise of citizen action groups such as the Royal Society for the Protection of Birds, Greenpeace and Friends of the Earth, all of whom have used the common law and other statutory controls as part of their tactics.

Nevertheless, one area of the common law which has been used and is increasingly likely to be used, both by regulators and by those who wish to challenge their decisions, is that of judicial review. The procedure used in judicial review is authorized under s.31 of the Supreme Court Act of 1981, and Order 51 of the Rules of the Supreme Court. However, the basis of the jurisdiction of the High Court to review the legality of decisions of all kinds of public and quasi-public bodies is to be found in the common law. Thus companies, or others, may ask the court to check whether decisions of, for example, the Environment Agency, or the Secretary of State for a particular department, have been reached lawfully, observing procedural propriety (natural justice) and rationally and fairly. If applicants have a sufficient interest in the matter to be challenged, have acted promptly, and acted on one of the recognized reasons or has other good grounds to believe they have a right to challenge the decision taken, they may intervene. Although it is at their discretion, the judges may quash the decision and order the matter to be considered again, or issue an order to prevent some decision being carried out, or require a decision to be taken correctly, possibly with payment of damages to those harmed by the decision.

Enforcement agencies

> There shall be a body corporate to be known as the Environment Agency ... (in this Act referred to as 'the Agency'), for the purpose of carrying out the functions transferred to and assigned to it by or under this Act (Environment Act 1995 s.1).

In the UK's highly regulated system, major policy and regulatory initiatives come from the government departments most concerned with environmental issues, such as the Department of the Environment, Transport and the Regions, and to some extent the Ministry of Agriculture, Farming and Fisheries, and the Department of Culture, Media and Sport. It is important to note the wide powers that ministers possess in relation to the actual enforcement of the law. For example their jurisdiction in a range of planning appeals, such as under s.78 of the Town and Country Planning Act 1990. Similarly appeals may be made to the minister against pollution control powers exercised by the Environment Agency or local authorities, for example under EPA s.15. The minister normally delegates these appeals to the quasi-independent Planning Inspectorate, but the law still leaves very wide powers to the minister to make decisions. Equally environmental law is underpinned by many circulars, or 'guidance' issued by the Department: while these publications do not have the status of law they must be considered and understood by all those affected by the law. Companies will certainly find them useful in their dealings with this area of law.

The Environment Agency (EA), established under the Environment Act of 1995, has become the major agency over a wide range of environmental law. It has taken over the functions of a number of bodies, such as the National Rivers Authority, Her Majesty's Inspectorate of Pollution and the Waste Regulation Authorities.

The general aim or purpose of the EA is to be found in s.4 of the Environment Act 1995 which requires it to discharge its functions as to protecting, conserving or enhancing the environment. The objective is sustainable development. The EA must adopt an integrated approach giving consideration to the cost of its activities. Under ss.5 and 6, powers are more specific, reflecting its role as the main licensing and enforcement body in relation to integrated pollution control; the control of water pollution and dealing with the licences required for the management of waste. It can thus prosecute companies and individuals, and may in certain circumstances clean up the pollution and charge the persons causing it. It can, and does, charge for licensing (ss.41 and 42) and it should try to recover its costs from these charges. The EA has very wide powers of inspection and entry to premises under s.108, and it is an offence to intentionally obstruct the officers of the EA when carrying out its duties.

There are areas of environmental law which are not regulated by the EA. Other regulators include local authorities, who deal with planning issues, including contaminated land, air pollution, statutory nuisances and hazardous waste, and the privatized water companies who control what is placed into the sewerage system.

This chapter will focus on England. However, the recent creation of the Parliament and assemblies in Scotland, Wales and, hopefully, Northern Ireland is noteworthy, as all have certain powers to legislate on environmental law. There is also the issue of the English Regional Development Agencies and Assemblies, including the new Greater London Authority, which have, together with the new London Mayor, a number of powers in relation to planning, transport and air quality controls.

PLANNING LAW AND BUSINESS

> Planning permission is needed: 'for the carrying out of any development of land' (Town and Country Planning Act 1990 s.57).

The Town and Country Planning Act of 1990 (T&CPA) is the major piece of legislation determining whether, or to what extent, a business may develop or use its own land and buildings. The use to which land, a scarce resource, is put will have a number of environmental implications not least the loss of the land for agriculture and habitats, or for amenity. The impact of a new development can include traffic, air and water pollution and the waste produced. Controls are partially regulated under the land planning system. Thus many proposals which a firm may have, such as expanding its plant or offices or planning new commercial premises, will need to progress in compliance with the Local Planning System. This chapter therefore offers an outline of how such controls operate. It also outlines (under the law relating to waste and statutory nuisance) recent legislation relating to historically polluted land known as 'contaminated land' or more commonly 'brownfield' land.

Planning authorities (county councils, district councils or borough councils) are required to draw up development plans for their areas. County councils draw up the overall strategy called 'structure plans'; whilst district councils deal with details in local plans. There is a third kind of plan known as a 'unified development plan' for the Metropolitan areas. The new Regional Development Agencies also have a role affecting planning and the environment, in relation to their development strategies. All of these bodies, are required to have regard, when drawing up their plans, to environmental implications. These development plans are also important as planning permission must normally be granted in accordance with the development plan (see T&CPA 1990 s.54A).

When is planning permission needed?

> 'Development' [means] 'building, engineering or other operations in, on, over or under land or the making of any material change in the use of any buildings or land' (T&CPA s.55).

Planning permission, as noted above, is needed under s. 57 'for the carrying out of any development of land'. Section 55 clearly covers any substantial alteration of, or much more intensive use of, the land or of the use of buildings. The courts have taken a pragmatic view of the meaning to be attributed to this term: whether there is a development or not is a matter of fact and degree in each case.

However, there are certain exemptions from the need for planning permission.

- Developments covered by the General Permitted Development Order 1995 where permission is given automatically, for example buildings for agricultural use, small scale extensions or alterations to industrial premises, public service developments, such as the privatized utilities and local authorities.

- Proposals which count as a change of use within the same class under one of the sixteen classes of the Use Classes Order 1987. So the use of land for one of the purposes listed in the order means that any change provided it stays within the same category will not be considered to be a development. Thus for example, Class B1 covers premises used as an office, or for development and research, as well as the actual industrial process, which might be carried out in a residential area, without causing detriment to the amenity of that area because of things such as noise, smells dust and smoke. Changing from one such use to the other within this class will not be a development.
- Certain long-standing existing use of the land may not require permission.
- Special (and more liberal) planning regimes in areas such as the former urban development areas, and in enterprise zones and simplified planning zones.

On the other hand, developments in certain areas such as national parks, conservation areas and sites of special scientific interest are much less likely to be allowed. It may thus be unclear as to whether permission is actually needed. In addition to the common practice of businesses consulting the local planning officer, there are two other alternatives:

- making an application for outline planning permission, that is an application to the local planning authority to see whether they will grant permission in principle;
- using a procedure under s.192 of the Planning and Compensation Act [P and CA] 1991 that allows the applicant to ask the planning authority whether an existing or proposed development requires permission, and if it does not, to issue a certificate of lawfulness which is binding on the authority.

Application for planning permission

If it is clear that the business has to apply for planning permission it must submit an application to the local planning authority (district or borough), together with the fees, a plan and drawings, and notification must be made to the owner (if the owner is not the applicant). Some further publicity is required so that people are aware locally of the proposals.

The planning authority has the discretion to decide the application but must exercise that discretion in accordance with the development plan and in accordance with government guidance. This can be found in Department of Environment, Transport and the Regions (DETR) circulars and in planning policy guidance notes, both of which are publicly available. It is essential to consider such guidance when making an application.

The authority is obliged to consult widely with such bodies as the Environment Agency in relation to any waste and water pollution issues which may arise from the proposal, and with the local sewerage undertaker. It will consider also the particular facts of the application, any local objections and other material issues, such as transport and employment needs, and at this stage it may have to consider whether an Environmental Impact Assessment (EIA) (see below) is required or not.

The decision

The planning authority may take one of four courses of action.

Grant permission without conditions

This decision may only be challenged by judicial review, normally, of course, by those who oppose the development.

Grant planning permission with conditions attached

This is the norm and whilst the authority can decide which conditions are appropriate for the development, it must again have regard to government guidance which, amongst other things, requires that the conditions must be relevant, clear, precise and reasonable. Conditions might include, for example, limits as to noise, the aftercare of waste sites, time limits of work, etc. It is here that problems occur in relation to the overlaps in control which could arise between the planning conditions and conditions imposed by other regulatory bodies such as the EA. This issue of regulatory overlap means that it is not always clear who may authorize what, but government guidance (PPG 25) suggests that planning authorities should not duplicate conditions where controls are better left to the relevant environmental regulatory agency.

The imposition of conditions may be challenged by judicial review, for example on the basis that they are illegal in the sense of beyond the legal powers of the planning authority. However, it is far more likely that an applicant will use the appeals system under s.78 of the Town and Country Planning Act 1990. It is only the developer who may appeal and no third party. The appeal is a complete rehearing of the issues, normally by a Planning Inspector acting on behalf of the Secretary of State and conducted on the basis of written documentation: but there may be a public inquiry. There is a further statutory right of appeal from the Secretary of State's decision to the High Court under s.288 of the Act on similar grounds to the judicial review. Any 'aggrieved person', not just the applicant, may appeal. Thus there is a potential for challenge by objectors to the proposed development.

Refuse planning permission within 8 weeks

The refusal may be challenged on the same basis as that for challenging conditions attached to the planning permission above.

Not make a decision within the time limit of 8 weeks

An appeal may then be made as above.

Complaints may also be made to the Local Government Ombudsman against the granting or refusal of permission if it is claimed that maladministration has caused a person some injustice.

Enforcement

Assuming planning permission has been obtained (with or without conditions), the planning authority has a wide range of powers relating to supervision and enforcement of the permission granted. It is interesting to note that, first, there are some specific exemptions from enforcement action, for example where there is a certificate of established use or lawfulness (see above) or where it is 10 years since the breach and no action has been taken. Secondly, a development or use of land without permission is not by itself an offence. This is because the system of control is based on a two-stage procedure whereby various notices are served by the authority and it is the failure to comply with these notices that creates criminal liability. The methods of enforcement that can be used by the authority include the following:

- enforcement notice;
- stop notices;
- planning contravention notice;
- breach of conditions;
- injunctions;
- environmental impact assessment.

Enforcement notice

Under the T&CPA s.171, the authority may issue a notice whenever it believes there is some breach of planning control. It is not required to do so (s.172). Only planning authorities may issue such notices, and they have a very wide discretion, subject once again to government guidance. A notice will require the owner (or occupier) of the property to take steps to remedy the alleged breach and to do so within a specified time. Twenty-eight days' minimum notice must be given and failure to comply with the notice is an offence under s.179. Penalties may be up to £20 000 in the Magistrates' Courts, and unlimited fines in the Crown Court. In addition, if the required steps are not taken, or not taken in time, the authority can enter the property under s.178, do the necessary work itself, and then charge reasonable expenses to the owner or occupier.

The notice is subject to challenge by judicial review. It is also possible for the authority to vary or revoke the notice. More importantly, there is a right of appeal to the Secretary of State, (s.174) provided it is made before the notice comes into effect. The T&CPA 1990 lays down the grounds of appeal, for example that the time limits are too short, or that the matters complained of are not a breach, or that planning permission ought to be granted. The Minister decides the appeal and may do a number of things including granting permission, dismissing the conditions or adding new ones. Importantly, during the appeal the notice is suspended and has no effect. This has sometimes led to abuse, with appeals being made simply to delay enforcement.

Stop notices

As enforcement notices may take a considerable time, an authority is empowered to serve a stop notice under s.183. This has the effect of prohibiting the activity within a shorter time once the notice has come into effect. It is an offence to continue in breach of the notice and there is no appeal as of right. The problem with such notices is that the authority may have to pay compensation if the notice is withdrawn (a disincentive to the authority) and stop notices are only valid if there is also an enforcement notice in force at the same time. They are, therefore, little used.

Planning contravention notice

This new procedure in T&CPA 1990 s.171C was introduced by the Planning and Compensation Act 1991. It is a discretionary procedure enabling authorities to get information about activities on land when they suspect a breach of planning control. Failure to comply with the notice within 21 days is a summary offence.

Breach of condition notice

This was another new discretionary power under s.187A of the Act allowing an authority to take action against a breach of a planning condition. This is done by serving a notice requiring compliance within not less than 28 days. There is no appeal and failure to comply is a summary offence.

Injunctions

Whilst local authorities have a general power to obtain these court orders where necessary to protect or promote the interests of the local community, authorities also have the specific power to seek an injunction against an actual or proposed breach of planning control. These orders are discretionary, but if granted, failure to comply is contempt of court with the possibilities of unlimited fines and/or imprisonment. They are thus potentially very useful to an authority.

Environmental impact assessment

> Environmental information includes the environmental statement and any further information and representations duly made about the environmental effects of the proposed development (The Environmental Impact Regulations 1999).

This contains the essence of the legal requirement in certain situations that a developer must carry out a systematic process of considering the impact on the environment of the proposed development before planning permission is given. Although not an entirely new concept, United Kingdom regulations were originally passed in 1988 to implement a 1985 Environmental Assessment Directive, and have now been extended by the need to update the law as a result of the amending 1997 EC Directive on the same topic. The new regulations are to be found in the Town and Country Planning (Environmental Impact Assessment) (England & Wales) Regulations 1999 (the EIA Regulations 1999).

The system requires certain types of development to be subject to environmental impact assessment to provide a 'statement' of the effect of the proposed development on the environment. The assessment is it to be made available to the authority when considering a planning application. Such an assessment will always be necessary when there is planned any one of the major developments laid down in the 1st Schedule of the Regulations, for example oil refineries, power stations or landfill of special waste. The authority also has a discretion to decide an assessment is necessary where it judges that any project across a wide range of industrial, commercial and agricultural developments listed in the 2nd Schedule of the Regulations is 'likely to give rise to significant environmental effects' by virtue of factors such as its nature, size or location. An appeal against a decision to require an environmental impact assessment can be made to the Secretary of State. Guidance is available from both the Departments of Environment and Transport and from the region's circulars. The assessment is a statement drawing together the evidence on the anticipated effects of the proposal and ways of reducing its effects. If an assessment is required, it is usual to submit it at the same time as the planning application. A business will nearly always have to employ consultants to prepare this statement for them.

INDUSTRIAL POLLUTION CONTROL

> pollution of the environment due to the release (into any environmental medium) from any process of substances which are capable of causing harm to man or any other living organisms supported by the environment' (EPA 1990 s.1(2)).

> no person shall carry on a prescribed process after the date prescribed ... except under an authorization granted by the enforcing authority and in accordance with the conditions to which it is subject' (EPA s.6).

The above extracts give in outline the issues to be considered here. If a substance could cause harm or is capable of causing harm to humans or the environment, both the substance and the process of making it are normally to be subject to regulation. Whether, and by whom, such an authorization is required is considered below.

The process and its substances

The Environmental Protection Act 1990 now requires all who plan to introduce a new industrial process, or to expand their existing process and discharge substances into the environment, to be subject to some form of regulatory control and may well require consent before implementation. The bodies to be approached will vary according to the nature of the process, the substance to be discharged, and medium into which it is discharged. Here it is only intended to give an outline of the authorization system. The first step is to decide whether or not the activity is subject to Integrated Pollution Control (IPC). This involves considering whether or not the process is prescribed and whether it involves the discharge of a prescribed substance.

Prescribed process

The Environmental Protection (Prescribed Processes and Substances) Regulations 1991 provides lists of all processes and substances that are controlled. These lists are updated and amended regularly and they (as well as the Agency) should be consulted to check if proposed activities constitute a prescribed process. A prescribed process is one considered sufficiently harmful to the environment to require special permission before it can be released. For example, most processes undertaken by the chemical and metal industries are likely to be prescribed.

Schedule 1 of the current regulations divides industries into six sectors (i.e. energy; waste disposal; chemical; mineral; metal; and others). Certain processes are identified within each sector (e.g. halogen processes in the chemical industry and incinerating processes in the waste disposal industry) and are divided into two groups, namely Part A and Part B. If the process falls within Part A it is normally subject to IPC under EPA 1990. It will not be subject to IPC if a prescribed substance will not be released or will cause no harm, but it may still be subject to controls other than IPC (see below). If it falls within Part B it may not be subject to IPC (this depends on the substances used) but is likely to be subject to other regulatory controls, in particular local authority Air Pollution Control (LAAPC) (see below). If it falls within both Part A and Part B it is subject to IPC.

In fact IPC covers the 2000 or so processes which are likely to cause greatest pollution and are therefore subject to the most stringent controls covering all forms of releases into all the environment. If the process is subject to IPC, a business must obtain an authorization from the EA before beginning the process. Failure to do so may result in criminal prosecution under EPA 1990 s.23(1). New processes, substantial variations of existing processes and large combustion plants were subject to IPC from 1 April 1991. Other processes became subject to authorization in phased stages between 1 April 1991 and 31 January 1996.

However, all existing authorizations will be brought eventually within the new Integrated Pollution Prevention and Control (IPPC) system introduced by the Pollution Prevention and Control Act of 1999, (derived from the 1997 EC Integrated Pollution and Prevention Control Directive). As far as the UK is concerned it is essentially a consolidation process, but the tougher integrated system will be extended to a much wider range and number of industrial processes than before, some of which, such as agriculture, were not adequately controlled previously. Many of the new IPPC processes have been moved from local authority to central EA control. It remains to be seen how this large expansion of work will be managed by the EA. The new regulations have caused a great deal of controversy especially among those subject to these controls for the first time. Nevertheless they are likely to be introduced during the middle of 2000. After the commencement of the regulations, a business intending to start or vary an existing authorized process, and therefore making an application, will immediately be brought within the new system. In all other cases the scheme will be gradually implemented across the commercial sectors over a period of 5–7 years from 2000.

Prescribed substances

Both prescribed and non-prescribed processes may involve the use of substances that are prescribed. Thus, a business needs to consider whether or not the substances to be discharged are prescribed. A list of prescribed substances is given in Schedules 4, 5 and 6 of the 1991 Regulations. Schedule 4 prescribes certain substances released into air (e.g. sulphur and nitrogen oxides and compounds). Schedule 5 covers releases of substances into water (e.g. mercury and DDT). Schedule 6 covers substances released to land (e.g. organic solvents, oxidizing agents and pesticides). If a substance is prescribed, the activity in which it is used is subject to IPC (whether or not the process is prescribed) and again an authorization is needed from the EA.

Is an authorization necessary?

In considering these issues, it is possible to reach a number of positions:

1 a prescribed process (Part A) plus release of a prescribed substance(s);
2 a prescribed process (Part B) plus release of a prescribed substance(s);
3 a non-prescribed process plus release of a prescribed substance(s).

These three situations are governed by IPC and an EA authorization is necessary.

4 A prescribed process (Part B), and no prescribed substance(s) is released. This is not covered by IPC but could be governed by local authority Air Pollution Control (APC) and authorization must be obtained from the relevant local authority. If the substances involved may be discharged into water, it may also be necessary to obtain a water pollution consent and a Waste Management Licence, both from the EA. If trade effluent will be discharged to sewers, it is also necessary to obtain a consent from the local sewerage undertaker (see 5 below).
5 A prescribed process under Part A releasing no prescribed substances (or such trivial amounts as are not likely to cause any harm) will not be governed by IPC. Nevertheless the business may need water pollution consents and a waste management licence from the EA, and from the local sewerage undertaker, a consent to discharge to the sewers.
6 A non-prescribed process and no prescribed substance(s). Consents may still be required from the EA and local sewerage undertakers.

CLEAN AIR ACT 1993

Irrespective of the categories set out above, if the industrial process emits grit, dust or fumes from the furnaces, under s.4 of the Clean Air Act 1993 the local authority should be notified, since an authorization may be needed before carrying out the process. Under ss.6 and 7 prior approval of the furnace itself may be required. Failure, without good excuse, to have such an approval in advance may be an offence. Also if dark smoke, as defined under ss.1 and 2 of the Act, is produced the business may commit a criminal offence. Additionally, under s.16 of the Clean Air Act 1993, applications should be made for chimney height approval. It is an offence to operate without such an authorization or approval.

APPLICATIONS FOR AUTHORIZATION

Integrated Pollution Control (IPC): application to the Environment Agency

A business must make an application to the regional office of the EA covering the location of the process under the Environmental Protection (Applications, Appeals and Registers) Regulations 1991, as amended. In applying, the business must amongst other things, give details of: the location and description of the process; its components, purpose, category and the nature of any releases (and the medium into which discharges will occur); and assess its local, regional and global environmental decisions. Technical data on releases is vital and the business must also give details of techniques to be employed to prevent or minimize releases (this means providing information about BATNEEC (see below)). Reference to the qualifications of staff, and training and management of staff is required and it is probably necessary to refer to British Standards Institution procedures or total quality management systems. It is also necessary to advertise the application for authorization. Alternatively, since details of all IPC processes are kept by EA and the relevant local authority in public registers, the business could apply to the Secretary of State for exclusion from the register wherever it feels that the information in question is commercially confidential or a matter of national security. Such an application is unlikely to be granted.

Where IPC applies, no additional applications need to be made to the local authority (air pollution) or the EA. However, discharges of trade effluent still require a local sewerage undertaker (LSU) to consent. In addition to authorization, a waste management licence may be needed in respect of final disposal of waste from the EA itself (below).

Air pollution Control (APC): applications to local authority

For any prescribed process listed in Part B (or a substance prescribed in Schedule 4) that is not subject to IPC, application must be made to the relevant local authority covering the location of the process. The application covers authorization related to air pollution only. For other forms of pollution, other consents may be necessary. Applications in respect of new processes should be made during the design period. The information required is similar to that in EA applications and details are available in regulations. Again, the main issues are to provide information about pollution arrangements for monitoring air emissions and for assessing the impact on the atmosphere. Provisions relating to advertisement, public registers and confidentiality are similar to those for IPC.

Water discharges: application to the Environment Authority

The Water Resources Act of 1991 may require any of the processes or substances which are not subject to IPC, but which may give rise to discharges to the aquatic environment, to obtain EA consents as detailed below.

GRANT OF AUTHORIZATIONS AND CONDITIONS

Environment Agency Integrated Pollution Control authorizations

When granting an authorization, the EA may, under s.7 of the EPA, impose specific conditions such as monitoring, pollution abatement, analysis and quality assurance plans. Quite apart from specific conditions, it is implied, by s.7(2), that the authorization is subject to using Best Available Techniques Not Entailing Excessive Cost (BATNEEC) to control pollution. Even existing processes will have to comply with BATNEEC within 4 years of grant of authority and all authorizations are reviewed 4 years after grant. BATNEEC is not defined because it will depend on the different circumstances of each application. However, guidance is available from EA which has a large discretion in interpreting the conditions.

Applicants will have to show that the system they wish to use is the most effective available in controlling pollution in the light of all techniques in existence (even if these techniques are not being used). Effectiveness includes not only technology, but also training of staff, design of the plant, etc.

The best available techniques need to be balanced against the cost involved. What is excessive is considered in the light of the nature of the industry and the desired level of environmental protection. Where the situation is one of a prescribed process and prescribed substance(s), BATNEEC must be used to prevent the release of the substance or, if this is not practicable, to reduce the release to a minimum and render it harmless. Where the situation is one of a prescribed process, but non-prescribed substances, the requirement is simply to use BATNEEC to render the release harmless. The rise in standards must be considered because existing processes have to be upgraded as soon as possible (generally within 4 years of the date of the previous grant of consent and in any event before the year 2001).

Finally, where the discharge may affect more than one environmental medium, the EA will also take into account the Best Practical Environmental Option (BPEO). This means that the applicant must show that, given a number of techniques available at similar cost, the one achieving the best overall environmental result will be adopted.

Local Authority Air Pollution Control Authorizations

These authorizations under the EPA s.7 contain specific and other conditions and the residual BATNEEC condition. BATNEEC must be used to minimize the pollution and render it harmless. Particular emission standards may be imposed and account is taken of emission limit values and air quality limit values. Guidance notes are available from the Department of the Environment, Transport and the Regions.

Water discharge consents

These are normally needed for any discharge of trade effluent or sewerage effluent into controlled waters (see below) but are covered by the IPC authorization. It may be advisable to obtain a consent for any discharge of poisonous, noxious or polluting matter or any solid waste into controlled waters. Such consents may be a defence to the general water pollution offence under section 85 of the Water Resources Act 1991.

These consents are highly individual and the EA can impose conditions as it sees fit. For example, conditions relating to the nature, composition and volume of discharges may be attached to such consents and numerical limits imposed. National water quality objectives and standards are taken into account, along with relevant EU standards and directives. The EA will make appropriate charges.

Local sewerage undertaker consents

These undertakers normally have complete discretion over grant and conditions. However, if the sewers can cope with the discharge, the applicant will normally get consent, subject to conditions specifying such things as the place and time of discharge and payment of charges.

Refusal to grant

EA or local authority APC applications may be refused if required information is not supplied, or the fees are not paid. Grant will be refused under EPA s.6 if the regulator feels that the applicant cannot comply with the conditions.

After grant

- There is in addition to the application fee, also an annual charge for all authorizations and consents. Contravention of authorizations and consents is a criminal offence under EPA 1990 s.23 (see below).
- If a process subject to IPC or APC runs an imminent risk of causing serious pollution, s.14 requires that the EA or the local authority must issue a prohibition notice (even if the authorization is not contravened).
- EA may also impose new conditions.
- If conditions are breached or a breach is imminent, an enforcement notice may be issued.
- Both types of notice give details of the steps to be taken and the time limit for remedying the problem. In both cases it is a criminal offence under s.23 not to comply.

All the regulators have a wide range of powers of entry, inspection, sampling and monitoring. They also have the power under s.12 to revoke an authorization or consent and they can also under s.11 vary it to bring it up to date. An applicant can also apply for variation where plants are upgraded or processes change. A charge is required for substantial variation and where re-advertisement is necessary. EA and local authority consent is also required for any transfer of authorization to another operator (e.g. on sale of the business) by s.9. Failure to notify the transfer is an offence (see below). Transfers of water consents do not require EA permission.

Possible penalties

In relation to IPC and APC, s.23 of the EPA thus makes it a criminal offence to:

- operate prescribed processes without an authorization;
- contravene conditions of an authorization;
- fail to inform of a transfer of authorization;
- fail to comply with a prohibition/enforcement notice;
- fail to comply with a requirement from an inspector or to obstruct an inspector intentionally;
- fail to provide relevant information;
- give false or misleading information deliberately or recklessly;
- make a false entry intentionally.

Minor offences tried in the Magistrates' Court attract maximum penalties up to £20 000 or up to 6 months' imprisonment. All the offences are triable either way and therefore, if tried in the Crown Court, are subject to unlimited fines and/or imprisonment.

Generally, a company may be prosecuted for personally committing such offences, but unless it is a strict liability offence, a corporation may only be liable where a director or similar company officer had the necessary criminal intention.

As discussed earlier, under the Environmental Protection Act 1990 s.157, where the offence is committed by a body corporate with the consent, connivance or neglect of any director, manager or similar officer, that officer may be prosecuted and found liable as well as the company. Where the activity is due to the act or default of some other person, such as an employee or subcontractor, under s.158 that person may also be prosecuted as well as the company.

In addition to criminal liability, under s.26, a court may order the company to take relevant remedial action and the full cost of clean-up operations may be recovered from the company. This cost may well exceed any actual fines. Section 27 allows the EA, with the Secretary of State's permission, to arrange for reasonable steps to be taken to tackle the harm and clean up, and send the company the bill!

WATER POLLUTION AND THE WATER RESOURCES ACT 1991

> It is an offence to cause or knowingly permit any poisonous, noxious or polluting matter or any solid waste to enter controlled waters. (Water Resources Act 1991 s.85(1)(a)).

In a similar way to the previous regulatory systems, the control here requires that an offence will take place for each separate discharge by the company or entry of the above materials into controlled water, unless a consent exists or some other defence. Information supplied when applying for such a consent should include the nature of the discharge, quality and rate of flow.

The procedures under schedule 10 of the Water Resources Act for water discharge consents are more public than those for IPC and APC, with more extensive advertising and more information made available in the public register. As with IPC and APC, it is possible to apply for an exemption from the register where inclusion would prejudice a trade secret or be contrary to the public interest. Controlled waters are defined in the Water Resources Act 1991 s.104 and include inland and underground waters and in certain circumstances territorial and coastal waters.

Offences

Under the Water Resources Act 1991 s.85, offences are similar to those listed above in relation to breaches of the EPA. In the same way, the essential control is that of requiring a consent from the EA before the activity commences so that this will act as a defence provided it and conditions attached are complied with. Thus the three main offences are as follows.

1 Causing or knowingly permitting the discharge of trade or sewer effluent into controlled waters or any discharge where a prohibition is in force. This offence requires no proof of pollution, simply a discharge. The offence of causing the discharge is one of strict liability. Clearly knowingly permitting someone else to carry out the discharge does require some knowledge and is not strict liability.
2 Causing or knowingly permitting any poisonous, noxious or polluting matter or any solid waste to enter controlled waters. This offence, according to *R* v *Dovermoss* [1995], may also not require proof of pollution or harm, merely the likelihood of pollution or harm, and covers both deliberate and accidental (non-routine) escapes. The offence of 'causing' the matter to enter is one of strict liability and all that needs to be shown is a causal link between the action and the entry into the waters. The offence is also wider and it is perhaps easier to prove an 'entry' rather than that of a 'discharge'. The EA may thus have a choice as to which charge to bring in any

particular situation. Sometimes a business may find that it is held liable for causing the pollution even if it has not committed the offence itself.

3 To cause or knowingly permit the discharge trade of effluent into controlled waters without a consent or to breach the conditions of a consent.

The House of Lords held, in *Alphacell* v *Woodward* in [1972], and again more recently in *Empress Cars* v *NRA* [1998], that if a company actively operates a plant or process, and pollution occurs it will be liable unless the pollution is caused by an extraordinary event. If what has occurred 'is an ordinary and everyday event', even if it were unforeseeable that the particular incident would happen, it is possible for the business to be guilty. The issue then is what is meant by these phrases, and the court did not give a great deal of guidance, asserting that it was very much a question of the individual facts in each case! It is also clear following *Attorney General's Reference (No1 of 1994)* [1995] and *NRA* v *Yorkshire Water* [1995] that more than one person can be said to have 'caused' the event and could be liable, providing causation can be proven.

A person can be liable for 'knowingly permitting', where another person has actually committed the wrongful conduct. This is not an offence of strict liability as some degree of knowledge is required. In *Nuttall* v *Vehicle Inspectorate* [1999] this concept was considered in the context of the protection of road users and the use of tachographs, but the decision is understood to represent the law generally. The House of Lords took a wide view and found that the offence could be committed by failure to take such reasonable steps as were within one's power to prevent the prohibited situation occurring. Thus in order to avoid liability there seems to be a positive obligation for the defendant to take reasonable steps to stop someone else from polluting the water. The questions of how much knowledge is needed and who within a corporation must have this knowledge before liability is incurred raises difficult issues.

Defences

It is a defence to the first two offences that the discharge or entry is in compliance with a water discharge consent, an IPC authorization, waste management licence, or a statute or statutory order.

It is a defence to all three offences that the discharge was in an emergency to avoid danger to life of health and all reasonably practicable steps were taken to minimize the pollution and inform the EA.

There is a right of appeal to the Secretary of State against either the EA's refusal to grant the applications, or the imposition of unreasonable conditions.

DISCHARGES TO SEWERS: APPLICATIONS TO LOCAL SEWERAGE UNDERTAKER

The Water Industry Act of 1991 s.118 requires that, whether or not a process is subject to IPC, an application for a trade effluent consent will be necessary whenever any effluent (other than surface water) from trade premises is to be discharged into a sewer. A trade effluent notice must be served on the relevant local sewerage undertaker, who, usually after imposing certain conditions, may grant a consent.

Local Sewerage Undertaker (LSU) consent can be refused at the discretion of the regulator. Appeals from LSU decisions are made to the Director General of Water Services (OFWAT).

WASTE MANAGEMENT AND CONTROL

It is an offence to 'keep, treat or dispose of controlled waste in a manner likely to cause pollution of the environment or harm to human health' EPA 1990 s.33(1)(c).

The Environmental Protection Act 1990 Part 2, and the Waste Management Licensing Regulations 1994 deal with the major problem of waste products and materials. Normally having waste management licence and complying with it would be a defence to the above offence, but as will be examined, this very broad offence can be committed even if a licence has been obtained. The attempt to discourage the serious environmental consequences from waste materials lies behind this. However, the law's control of the storage, treatment and disposal of a company's waste raises a number of issues.

What is 'waste'?

Controlled waste is 'household, industrial and commercial waste or any such waste, including any substance which is scrap or is effluent or unwanted surplus from a process' (EPA 1990 s.75).

In *Kent CC* v *Queenborough Mill* [1990] waste building materials were being used to form the foundations of another building. Was this material waste? The court decided it was as it had been discarded by the former owner and was not being used for the same purpose.

In *Cheshire CC* v *Armstrong* [1995] a company took building waste from a site, reprocessed it and returned it to the same owner and site for new foundations. This was held not to be waste as the original owner had not intended to discard the material and it had been returned to him, although in a different form.

One man's waste is another man's raw material. It can thus be very difficult at times to correctly define when something is in law 'waste'. The judicial approach has been to look to the nature of the material when it is discarded even though it may be re-used. There are three different kinds of waste: controlled waste, special waste and hazardous waste. It is controlled waste that is of primary concern here. The latter two are regulated differently, and more strictly – see below and the Planning (Hazardous Substances) Act 1990. Following the 1975 EC Framework Directive on Waste, and more recently, Directive 91/156 amending the earlier Directive, and the Waste Management Licensing Regulations 1994, controlled waste is effectively what is defined in the Directive as being waste.

The Directive lists a series of categories of goods to be regarded as waste, with the final category covering 'any materials, substances or products which are not contained in the other categories'! In other words, virtually all substances can be waste. The directive requires that the goods in these categories must have been intended, or required to be discarded. It is therefore essential to determine if the articles have been discarded or not.

As the two cases cited above illustrate, problems arise in trying to determine if something has been discarded. The criteria are, essentially, as set out in government guidance circular 11 of 1994. According to this, something has been discarded by the owner when it has fallen outside the normal cycle of use or utility that he or she has for it. Thus, even materials being sent for recycling by a special recovery process could be regarded as waste until they have been reprocessed. Once something has been repaired or recovered it will then cease to be waste. The value of the goods seems also to be irrelevant. This is an area where specialist advice is needed and if any doubt one should check with the Environment Agency.

When granting a waste disposal licence, the EA could impose any conditions considered appropriate, including types of waste covered, duration of licence and steps needed for compliance with planning permission. Planning permission could also contain similar or more extensive conditions and therefore should be obtained at the same time. There are only two grounds on which the EA might refuse a licence. These were if satisfied that it is necessary to refuse to prevent pollution of the environment or harm to human health and if the applicant is not a fit and proper person. This is defined in s.4 and includes for example situations where the applicant has committed a relevant offence or the company does not have the appropriate technically trained management.

There are exemptions from the licensing scheme in Regulation 17, including temporary storage at the place of production of the waste until it can be removed, and a range of activities to do with recycling, such as washing and sorting specified amounts of goods for re-use. Even if exempt, if one recovers or disposes of waste it remains necessary to register with the EA under Regulation 18. Should controlled waste be transported from the premises by an outside contractor, the Control of Pollution (Amendment) Act 1989 provides that the carrier must normally be registered with the EA. Exemptions include a not-for-profit activity or normally, in the case of the producer of the waste. Failing to have the relevant registration is an offence.

With the introduction of the Waste Management Regulations and the EPA there are now four criminal offences under the EPA s.33. It is an offence:

1 either to deposit, or treat, or keep, or make a disposal of controlled waste without a licence;
2 to breach any condition of a waste management licence;
3 knowingly to permit or knowingly to cause the occurrence of any of the above activities;
4 to treat, keep or dispose of controlled waste in a manner likely to cause pollution or harm to human health, even though a licence has been obtained.

The first two offences are of strict liability. The third offence requires some knowledge for there to be liability. We have discussed the issues of causation in relation to water pollution offences and the same principles apply here, although here it is a requirement to have some knowledge as opposed to the situation with water offences. In *Shanks and McEwan* v *Environment Agency* [1997] it was held that for a conviction it wasn't necessary to prove knowledge of the breach of the licence conditions but simply that there was knowledge of the deposit of the waste. Equally some of the terms, such as 'deposit', are unclear but in *Thames Waste Management* v *Surrey CC* [1997] the court gave the meaning a wide interpretation: it may mean either temporary or continuing activities. In this particular case a condition required a cover on the waste. Failure to provide one was in breach of the licence as the meaning of 'deposit' extended to providing such a cover.

There are a number of defences available, including taking all reasonable precautions and exercising due diligence, or taking action in an emergency to avoid harm. The maximum summary penalty for such an offence is currently £20 000 or 6 months' imprisonment. On indictment the fine is unlimited and the maximum imprisonment is 2 years. It will therefore be important for the business to consider whether it needs to apply for such a licence. Civil liability may also arise either under the EPA 1990 s.73 or at common law if the company is in breach of the EPA 1990 and causes damage.

Obtaining a licence

Any applicant must demonstrate that he or she is a fit and proper person (technically, financially and without previous relevant convictions) or the agency may refuse the licence under s.74. If there is no planning permission in force the agency must refuse the licence. The EA may reject an application if rejection is necessary to prevent pollution or harm to human health under the regulations. Under s.35 conditions may be imposed on the grant of a licence in relation to activities and precautions. The EA will ensure compliance with the licence and may revoke and prosecute in cases of breach. There is a right of appeal to the Secretary of State under s.43.

It is important to note that IPC authorizations cannot cover the final disposal or deposit of controlled waste in or on to land, and therefore a waste management licence will be needed in addition to any IPC authorization. However, the treatment and keeping of controlled waste may be adequately covered by an IPC authorization, in which case a waste management licence is not also required.

Transfer, surrender and enforcement of the licence

If the company wishes to cease to operate a waste management licence, it may transfer it in accordance with s.40. Both transferor and transferee apply to the EA. If the EA do not consider the transferee a fit and proper person, no transfer is allowed. Where a suitable transferee cannot be found the transferor's only option is to surrender the licence. The EA will only allow surrender of a licence under s.39 if the premises do not present a risk of pollution or harm to human health. Thus it may be necessary to engage in clean-up activities before surrendering the licence. In addition, the agency may modify the conditions of the licence under s.37; suspend the licence or parts of it under ss.38 and 42. EA may revoke the licence under ss.38 and 42 if, for example, it considers the operator not to be a fit and proper person, or not technically competent.

Duty of care

Section 34 of the EPA 1990 introduced a new duty of care in relation to waste management. This applies to any holder, importer, producer, carrier, keeper, treater or disposer of controlled waste. Such a person is under a threefold duty to take all reasonable steps to:

1 prevent contravention of s.33 (see above) by any other person;
2 prevent the escape of waste from his or her control or that of any other person;
3 ensure that any transferee is an authorized person and that sufficient written detail is given to enable the transferee to avoid liability under s.33 (see above).

Guidance on discharge of the duty can be found in a code of practice. Any breach of this duty is a criminal offence and persons damaged by the activity may then also sue in civil law. As before, this gives rise to organizational liability but individual managers may also be liable. A conviction may adversely affect any future applications for a licence.

Special waste

Special waste is 'waste which may be so dangerous or difficult to treat, keep or dispose of that special provision is required for dealing with it' (EPA 1990 s.62).

See also the Special Waste Regulations 1996 and DETR Guidance in 1996, for further details. The kinds of waste dealt with here are those which are listed in the regulations or are dangerous in the sense of being, for example, toxic or highly inflammable. Controlled and special waste are both governed by Part II of the EPA 1990.

Packaging waste

The Environment Act 1995 imposed a new set of obligations on certain producers and others of packaging materials. Section 93 allowed for new regulations (the Producer Responsibility Obligations (Packaging Waste) Regulations (SI 1997 no.648)) to implement an EC Directive 94/62 on Packaging and Packaging Waste. This is a highly complex set of regulations, which have been amended a number of times, but the essential aim is to set targets for the re-use, recycling and recovery of different kinds of packaging waste, such as metals, plastics glass and paper. The Directive requires compliance with these regulations but permits a phase-in period so that the amounts so recovered, etc., are to be raised over 3–4 years to enable the UK to reach the targets. The system started in 1998, but it appears unlikely that the UK will reach the set targets, which were supposed to include 52 per cent of recovery and 26 per cent recycling of these products by 2001.

Organizations affected include those involved in manufacturing and converting of the raw materials used for packaging, or actually packing or selling packaging to the end user or consumer. Registration is only needed for those who deal with more than 50 tonnes per year and currently have an annual turnover of more than £5 million (to be reduced to £2 million in 2000, and subsequently to £1 million). Registration must be either directly with the EA, or by joining a compliance scheme, such as Valpak, which must itself be registered. These schemes are designed to carry out the obligations of the individual business under the regulations, for a fee. The obligation imposed on all is to produce recovery notes from those to whom they send the materials for recovery, again for a fee, showing the amounts they have sent, in order to comply with the set targets. It is an offence to fail to take reasonable steps to recover or recycle the specified targets for the particular items, or to fail to register with either the EA or a compliance scheme.

CONTAMINATED LAND

Contaminated land is land which appears to the local authority in whose area it is situated to be in such a condition, by reason of substances in, on, or under land, that either significant harm is being caused, or there is a significant possibility of such harm being caused, or pollution of controlled waters is being or is likely to be, caused (EPA 1990 s.78A).

From April 2000, the Environment Act 1995, Part II will come into affect, and the Contaminated Land (England) Regulations, made under this legislation will come into force. In fact the Act amends Part II of the older EPA 1990, by adding a new Part II A and new additions to s.78, dealing with Statutory Nuisance, so all the basic principles are to be found there. This again is a complex and large regulatory scheme and much detail is to be found in the regulations and in the statutory guidance and circulars issued at the same time as the regulations. There are also some confusing overlaps with other possibly relevant areas of the law, such as the clean-up powers under the Water Resources Act that will have to resolved. The scheme attempts to deal with land that has been historically polluted and so represents a risk of significant harm, and to bring it back into some 'suitable use'. Where possible the polluter of the land must pay for its remediation, but other persons, such as current owners, or occupiers may become liable for such costs. Under s.78F if a person causes or knowingly permits (see above) the contaminating substances to be on the land they are termed 'Class A' offenders. If no such person can be found after a reasonable enquiry, then owners or occupiers, and there can be more than one person, are termed in the guidance as 'Class B' offenders. They may be liable. There are a number of exclusions, including advisors, and those selling the land with information about its contamination. There are detailed rules about sharing liability.

The scheme is enforced by local authorities or if the land is so seriously contaminated that it is known as a special site, by the Environment Agency. The local authorities must inspect and carry out assessment of the sites to see if the site is causing harm. If harm is being caused they must set up procedures which in most cases will lead to the serving of a remediation notice on the person responsible to bring the land to a suitable condition for the use to which it will be put.

Failure to comply with the notice is an offence (s.78M) and default powers are available to the agencies to do the work and recover the cost from those responsible (s.78N and P). There remain major problems with the scheme, for example in relation to 'contaminated land' under s.78A, the meaning of 'significant harm' is unclear, but the definition does extend to harm to humans, wildlife, farm animals and crops, and ancient monuments. It remains to be seen also how much money is available to clean up these sites, particularly when there is no responsible person identified.

NOISE CONTAMINATION

Noise (and any vibration) from premises may give rise to actions in common law or statutory nuisance. These are dealt with above but is worth noting that under s.61 of the Control of Pollution Act 1974, an application can be made to the local authority, in advance, for a consent governing the times, duration, etc. of any building work.

Assuming a consent was granted and the conditions were complied with a local authority would be unable to serve a notice.

MANAGEMENT SYSTEMS

Of increasing interest to commercial organizations are the adoption and use of Environmental Management systems, such as the International Standards Organisation's ISO 14001. Registration and certification under this management system requires the firm to show that it has appropriate methods of dealing with its environmental issues. These methods relate to having an environmental policy and goals for the prevention of pollution, and ensuring that plant design, personnel training and monitoring of processes meets these goals. The adoption of such a management system may be beneficial for business in applying for consents and licences under the regulatory system. It may also be good for the company's image, may help the company in its dealing with its lenders and insurers, or be of assistance with a defence if action is taken in the civil or criminal courts against them.

PROGRESS TEST

1 If the company decides to change its operations, for example from running a 24-hour restaurant, to the operation of a new internet linked retail shop on the same premises, do you consider that the company would need to have planning permission before it makes these changes? What could it do if it were unsure? Has it committed any offences, if it does need permission, by failing to have the planning permission before commencing? Would it be advisable to contact any other regulatory agency before changing operations?

2 Imagine that James, an Environment Agency inspector, has been called in to examine the River Strange by Fred, a local resident. Fred had noticed that the river had turned an off-white colour and a number of dead fish were floating in it. James has checked the area and found that a small stream, containing the coloured water, entered the river, having flowed through a building site. It has become obvious to him that some cement has been allowed by the builders, Base Ltd, to get into the stream. What criminal charges might James bring against Base Ltd? Would the company have any defences and might Base Ltd be open to any action in the civil law?

3 The Small Company, who are general hardware retailers, has decided that it wishes to manufacture on the premises a small amount of the cleaning products which it sells rather than buying from its usual suppliers. In order to do this it will need a number of different chemicals, and to install a furnace to power the plant. It has received planning permission, but what else must it do before it begins to produce these cleaning products? To whom should it enquire? Would it commit any offences if it started to manufacture without taking any further steps?

4 The Middlefield Paper Company has decided that it wishes to increase its product range and the amounts that it produces. In order to do this it has bought a nearby disused warehouse for storage of the raw materials and to store the faulty manufactured products, before they are taken away by carriers or are given away to its employees. Advise the company whether or not it might have any liabilities in relation to the faulty products under the Environmental Protection Act 1990.

Protection of intellectual property 11

John Weldon

WHAT IS INTELLECTUAL PROPERTY?

In *University of London Press Ltd* v *University Tutorial Press Ltd* [1916] PETERSEN J said, 'there remains the rough practical test that what is worth copying is worth protecting'.

In *Chiron Corporation* v *Organon Telnika Ltd* [1994] ALDOUS J said, 'First it encourages research and invention; secondly, it induces an inventor to disclose his discoveries instead of keeping them a secret; thirdly, it offers a reward for the expense of developing inventions to the state at which they are commercially practicable and fourthly, it provides an inducement to invest capital in new lines of production which might not appear profitable if many competing producers embarked on them simultaneously'.

PETERSEN J was dealing with the protection of an author's copyright in examination papers and ALDOUS J was commenting on the benefits of a patent system but these two quotations illustrate the diversity of subject matter of intellectual property, and the common theme in this diversity of protecting the economic interests of innovators.

To understand a definition of intellectual property it is necessary first to examine the meanings of the words 'intellectual' and 'property', the latter being perhaps more problematic. 'Intellectual' means product of the mind, 'property' means a right to use and thereby exclude others from such use.

Colloquially the word 'property' refers to the thing a person 'owns'. Legally property means the right in relation to a thing not the thing itself. It is possible for different people to simultaneously enjoy different property rights in relation to the same thing as the chapter on land law has demonstrated. Similarly a student may have a personal property right in a book whilst the publisher retains the intellectual property right of copyright in the book. This means the student can do what he or she likes with the book but cannot copy it, whilst the publisher has the right to authorize copying it, yet has no other right in the book the student has purchased.

Over time the law has progressively recognized various products of the mind as being worth protecting or worth rewarding and encouraging by creating property rights in them.

Of what significance is intellectual property to a business?

The legal protection of innovation enables the creator to exploit his or her ideas free from competitors who would seek to gain unfair advantage by imitation.

- Intellectual property enables an innovator to give added value to products by differentiating them from those of competitors.
- State of the art technology in a patented invention gives an edge to new products over the out of date technology of competitors.
- Where technology in a range of products is mature, design can be the determinant of consumer choice.
- Where products are standard, the means of producing, marketing and pricing them may be secrets which create an advantage over competitors.
- Where the quality of goods or services is established, the name of the maker can be used to enhance market recognition. The name not only generates sales but may be traded to others in the form of licences to use or franchises.
- Intellectual Property Rights are valuable transferable assets which can be important in the valuation of enterprises in the context of mergers and takeovers. Such assets can also be used as collateral against loans.

Categories of intellectual property

There are a number of categories of intellectual property, each having common characteristics but encompassing a wide and varied field of subject matter. The remainder of this chapter will explain, in outline, the categories so far recognized in law:

- copyright;
- patents;
- trade marks;
- confidential information;
- design.

COPYRIGHT

Copyright protects authors' expression of ideas. It protects authors against having copies made of their works. One of the origins of the law of copyright was royal privileges granted to the Stationers' Company to print books. The kinds of works now afforded protection are itemized in s.1(1) of the Copyright, Designs and Patents Act 1988:

- original literary, dramatic, musical or artistic works;
- sound recordings, films, broadcasts or cable programmes; and
- the typographical arrangement of published editions.

Original works

In *Ladbroke (Football) Ltd* v *William Hill (Football) Ltd* [1964] LORD PEARCE said (finding that the authorship of a football coupon constituted originality albeit that the subject was mundane and common in the trade) that as the requirement of originality in subsection (a) does not require that the works be original in a sense of quality or inventiveness but it was necessary: 'only that the work should not be copied but should originate from the author'

A work must be tangible and fixed in some form to attract copyright, otherwise it would be impossible to test whether it has been copied or not.

Where an expression of an idea is fundamentally determined by the nature of the thing then there should be no copyright in such a work. Other exclusions from copyright include; work of minimal extent such as single words, or work constituting nothing more than a mechanical compilation of others' material lacking any skill, effort or judgement.

A database will attract copyright protection if it is the result of the author's own intellectual creation involving skill, effort or judgement. Under the EU Directive on the Legal Protection of Databases 1997 a database will also attract the sui generis protection of a database right if it is a collection of independent works arranged in a systematic way and accessible by electronic or other means. This gives protection to commercially valuable databases which may have not attracted conventional copyright protection in all EU States. Protection is for a period of 15 years.

Literary, dramatic, musical or artistic works

In *University of London Press Ltd* v *University Tutorial Press Ltd* [1916] PETERSON J said 'In my view the words "literary work" cover work which is expressed in print or writing, irrespective of the question whether the quality or style is high'.

Literary work includes, in addition to fine prose, commercially important material such as product manuals.

Dramatic work encompasses theatre works and dance pieces including all forms of physical art provided they can be fixed in some form such as an identifiable choreograph. Plots of TV programmes will only be copyright works if defined with precision.

Musical work exists as copyright as notated. Lyrics of songs carry literary copyright.

Artistic works include graphic works, photographs, sculptures and architectural works covering both buildings and models. Also included are works of artistic craftsmanship. In contrast to other types of copyrights, works of artistic craftsmanship must have some artistic quality in order to obtain copyright protection. This requirement apparently relates to some historical distinction between artists and artisans, whereby wokers who made furniture, jewellery and similar craft work were denied the protection of copyright law unless the work transcended into the heights of artistry.

Secondary copyright works

These are covered in subsections (b) and (c) of s.1. These need not be original: they are predominantly based upon some prior original literary, dramatic musical or artistic work such as a book, play, song or drawing. Sound recordings can be recordings of any sound, by any medium, but most typically are music recordings. Similarly films include the recording of moving images by any medium. Broadcasts (transmissions of visual images, sounds or other information by wireless telegraphy) include the traditional terrestrial channels plus satellite programmes. Cable programmes are distinguished in that they are not wireless but rely on fixed telecommunication lines. Both broadcasts and cable programmes should consist of presentations to the public. In the case of broadcasts they must be capable of being lawfully received by the public; encrypted broadcasts are regarded as being available to the public provided decoding equipment is also available. Cable programmes must be received at multiple sites. A website falls within the definition of a cable programme for the purpose of secondary copyright protection. A new typographical arrangement of a published edition has its own copyright in addition to the copyright in the literary content.

Duration

Literary, dramatic, musical and artistic copyright lasts for the life of the author plus 70 years from the end of the year in which the author dies. If there are joint authors the duration is calculated from the last of the authors' deaths. Computer-generated work lasts 50 years from the end of the year of its creation. Design Copyright lasts for 25 years from the end of the year of creation. Sound recording copyright lasts for 50 years from the year-end of creation or 50 years from release if released within 50 years of creation. Film copyright lasts for 70 years from the end of the year of the death of the last to die of the principal director, screenplay author, dialogue author and score composer. Broadcast and cable programme copyright lasts for 50 years from the end of the year of their transmission. Copyright in typographical arrangements lasts for 25 years from the end of the year of first publication.

Ownership

A work qualifies for UK copyright if it is:

- created by a UK citizen or by a national of a country recognized by the UK as giving reciprocal protection to copyright;
- first published in the UK or a reciprocating country.

By the Copyright, Designs and Patents Act 1988 s.11 the author of a work is presumed to be its owner subject to exceptions. Works:

- produced by Crown Officers in the course of their duties are Crown copyright;
- made by employees in the course of their employment belong to the employer unless the contract of employment provides otherwise.

In employment situations disputes often arise where there is lack of clarity in the contract. Disputes tend to involve two issues. First whether the person was an employee and secondly whether the work was produced in the course of employment. If the work is an integral part of the business and the employee holds a position in the firm in which that kind of work is expected of him or her, then the copyright is the employers. In practice employers should ensure that copyright issues are explicitly covered in contracts of employment.

Normally where the worker is not an employee, he or she will retain copyright in the work produced unless assignment is clearly intended. Hirers, like employers, should ensure that the contract specifies who has copyrights. Section 90 of the Act requires assignment of copyright to be written and signed by the assignor or his or her representative. Where royalties are payable in small sums over a large number of works, it is practice in some industries, particularly music, for the copyright owner to assign the function of collecting royalties to an agency who then distributes the income pro-rata to the participating copyright owners.

Where copyright is assigned by contract, the assignor retains moral rights set out in ss.77–85 of the Act. These are the right to:

- be identified as the author;
- object to derogatory treatment of the work;
- not have other work falsely attributed to another;
- privacy in photographs or films made for domestic and private purposes.

These are not economic rights, as copyright is, but are moral rights to be treated fairly in relation to creations after selling the work. They are subject to a number of exceptions. Literary, dramatic, musical or artistic works in newspapers or works of reference are not protected, nor are computer programs or computer-generated works. The right to be identified does not apply where the work is done in the course of employment. Where the work is done under a contract of hiring of services, it would not be unusual for the hirer to insist that the author waive the right to be identified.

Infringement of rights

In *Ladbroke (Football) Ltd* v *William Hill (Football) Ltd* [1964] LORD PEARCE said, 'Whether a part is substantial must be decided by its quality rather than its quantity. The reproduction of a part which by itself has no originality will not normally be a substantial part of the copyright and therefore will not be protected'.

In *Spectravest Inc* v *Aperknit Ltd* [1988] MILLET J said, 'In considering whether a substantial part of the plaintiff's work has been reproduced by the defendant, attention must primarily be directed to the part which is said to have been reproduced, and not to those parts which have not.'

The key question in infringement cases is the extent of copying needed to create liability. The test is whether the part taken is qualitatively substantial. To prove infringement it is necessary to prove two matters. First that the original work and the alleged infringing copy are objectively similar and secondly that there is a causal connection between the two. Most commonly this means showing that the defendant had access to the original work when producing the allegedly infringing copy. If access is shown, the defendant would need some explanation for the similarity other than copying. It is not uncommon for inert programming or bogus text to be incorporated into works as a means of revealing copiers.

The rights copyright gives to owners are not stated. The acts which persons other than the owner cannot do without infringing the copyright are those set out in the Copyright, Designs and Patents Act 1988 s.16 as the owner's prerogative. They are to:

- copy the work;

- issue copies of the work to the public;
- perform, show or play the work in public;
- broadcast the work or include it in a cable programme service;
- make an adaptation of the work;

or do any of the above in relation to an adaptation.

In addition ss.22–26 set out the types of 'secondary infringement' which exist. These can be categorized as culpable acts assisting primary infringement and include:

- importing infringing copies;
- possessing or dealing with infringing copies;
- providing the means for making infringing copies;
- permitting use of premises for infringing performance and providing apparatus for infringing performance.

To prove an act of secondary infringement it must be shown that the defendant knew or had reason to believe that he or she was dealing with infringing copies. Copying for the purpose of literary, dramatic, musical or artistic works means reproducing in any material form and includes storage in any medium, including by electronic means.

Infringement by issuing copies to the public means issuing copies that have been made without permission. However, copyright is exhausted in relation to a particular object once that object has been legitimately sold into the market. The Copyright and Related Rights Regulations 1996 allows educational establishments to lend without infringing and permits the commercial renting of copyright works subject to equitable remuneration.

Infringement by public performance to the public includes the playing of music, showing films or displaying TV programmes. The playing of ambient music in places of work, shops and restaurants constitutes infringement of copyright works if done without permission. Commonly the right to perform music in public is transferred by copyright owners to licensing agencies which collect royalties on the behalf of the owners for a share of the proceeds.

Infringement by adaptation is defined by s.21 of the Act and includes a number of important economic and artistic activities. Adaptation includes:

- translation of literary or dramatic work;
- translations, conversion to or from dramatic works;
- conversion into picture form of a written work;
- arrangements or variations of computer programs in other programming languages;
- translations and altered versions or arrangements of a database;
- arrangements or transcriptions of a musical work.

Unauthorized adaptations of adaptations are equally acts of infringement.

Remedies for infringement

There are a number of remedies available for infringement of copyright. Often a copyright owner cannot wait for a trial so applies for an interlocutory injunction to prevent harm from being done. After successful litigation the copyright owner will normally seek compensatory damages. He or she may seek additional damages to reflect the aggravated or flagrant nature of a breach. He or she may also seek the remedy of account for profits whereby the defendant must hand over profits made by infringement even though the copyright owner might not strictly have lost those profits him- or herself. This remedy exists to prevent unjust enrichment by infringement. To prevent further breaches the copyright owner might also seek the delivery and destruction of infringing copies.

Section 107 of the Act sets out a number of criminal offences related to copyright infringement. These include the production, importation, possession with a view to infringement, sale or distribution of infringing works in the course of business. Distribution other than in the course of business to such extent as would prejudice the copyright owner is also an offence.

Defences to copyright infringement

The defences to infringement are set out in chapter 3 of the Act. The general defences include the use of copyright material for research, private study, criticism, review, news reporting and incidental inclusion in an artistic work or a film or broadcast. Use for research and review must be in the nature of fair dealing. In practice educational publishers license limited reprographic copying of much of their material. There are a number of defences specific to educational establishments, libraries and archives. Certain acts done in the course of public administration such as parliamentary or judicial proceedings, activities under statutory authority and specified material communicated to the Crown in public business are not infringement of copyright.

There is a general but limited defence of acting in the public interest, for example, exposing criminal activity. There are some important defences in relation to software which have come into UK law by virtue of EU Directive on the Legal Protection of Computer Programs 1991. A legitimate licensee of software may make a back-up, may copy or adapt the program if necessary for the effective running of the program and may de-compile the program where this is necessary in order to achieve interoperability with other software.

Commercial value of copyright

The unusual characteristic of copyright allows for extensive commercial exploitation. The existence of primary and secondary copyright and the various rights which copyright confers enables authors of works to exploit their works to the full. An author of the lyric of a song will have original literary copyright in the song which he or she may license to a publishing company. When making a sound recording of the song he or she will come to some arrangement with the recording company as to ownership of the copyright in the sound recording. The author may also sell the right to broadcast the sound recording to a radio station who will own the copyright in the broadcast. He or she may make a video of the song which will have its own film copyright which in turn may be licensed to a cable TV company who will own the copyright of the cable programme when the video is shown. The author may license the right to adapt the song by translation and also license the right to adapt the song by cover version. Many of these licences can be non-exclusive so that they can be sold to different people at different times in different jurisdictions for different purposes.

PATENTS

> In *Hickton's Patent Syndicate* v *Patents and Machine Improvements Co Ltd* (1909) BUCKLEY LJ said: 'Every invention to support a patent must ... either suggest a new way of making something ... or it may mean the way of producing a new article altogether; ... It is much more true to say that the patent is for the idea as distinguished from the thing manufactured. No doubt you cannot patent an idea, which you have simply conceived, and have suggested no way of carrying out, but the invention consists in thinking of or conceiving something and suggesting a way of doing it'.

Section1(1) of the Patents Act 1977 sets out the requirements for patentability. These are that the invention must be new, inventive and industrially applicable but must not fall into any of the excluded categories of inventions.

Historically letters patent were given to craftsmen to permit them to carry out their trade. Later letters patent developed into Royal grants of monopolies over new methods in manufacture. A formalized structure of patenting recognizable in today's terms emerged in the nineteenth century. Today's patent system, whereby monopolies are granted in favour of proven new, inventive and industrially applicable inventions, is broadly similar throughout the world. The UK patent system, as governed by the Patents Act 1977, mirrors the requirements of the European Patent Convention. Although patent law is international in nature, patents themselves are not. There is no such thing as an international or European patent. Patents are granted by national patent offices for protection within the national jurisdiction. Bundles of national patents can be acquired through the European Patent Office covering most major European countries, or under the Patent Co-operation Convention which covers major world economies including the USA and Japan.

Novelty

The issue of whether an invention is new or has been anticipated arises in considering an application for a patent. It can also arise in an action for infringement where the defendant defends him- or herself by challenging the grant of the patent by producing evidence of anticipation. Where a patent application is rejected for lack of novelty, not only is no patent given, but, crucially the technology is given to the world and no one else can file for patent in relation to the same invention.

The novelty, or the anticipation, test requires that the invention be new. An invention fails the test if it has been made available anywhere in the world to the public either by use or in written form before filing a patent application. It is very important, therefore, that whilst developing an invention the innovator keeps the idea secret. If it is necessary to show the invention to others, such as potential investors, or technical collaborators, or suppliers of parts or tooling, this should only be done in private in circumstances where confidentiality is made explicit, and preferably after the third party has signed a confidentiality agreement. Use in public will prevent patenting if it discloses the means of operation. An invention is disclosed to the public if it is shown in public and could be replicated by a notional person skilled in the Art, irrespective of whether any given person realized at the time that the invention could be replicated from what was shown. Therefore the 'black box method' of using models or experiments which do not reveal the method may be used. Care should also be taken that the method is not disclosed incidentally in another patent application or by use of the product or inadvertently in use in another product which revealed the technology. Patenting will also be prevented if the invention has been disclosed in another patent literature.

Inventive step

To be patentable an invention must involve some inventive step, this is also known as the *obviousness test*. Section 3 of the Patents Act 1977 provides that an invention shall be taken to involve an inventive step if it is not obvious to a person skilled in the art, having regard to any matter forming part of the state of the art. The state of the art comprises (s.2(2)) all matter (whether a product a process, information about either, or anything else) which has at any time before the date of filing (priority date) of that invention been made available to the public (whether in the United Kingdom or elsewhere) by written or oral description, by use or in any other way but does not for these purposes include matters in patent applications having an earlier priority date but which have not been published at the time in question. The word 'obvious' does not have a particular legal meaning. A person skilled in the art is someone who has the knowledge of a skilled worker in the field. Such a person should be familiar with the generally expected level of knowledge of literature, patents and technology in the field without being inventive him- or herself.

Obviousness

In *Windsurfing International Inc* v *Tabur Marine (Great Britain) Ltd* [1985] OLIVER LJ set out a commonly used four-stage test of obviousness: 'The first is to identify the inventive concept embodied in the patent in suit. Thereafter, the court has to assume the mantle of the normally skilled but unimaginative addressee in the art at the priority date and to impute to him what was, at that date, common general knowledge in the art in question. The third step is to identify what, if any, differences exist between the matter cited as being 'Known or used' and the alleged invention. Finally, the court has to ask itself whether, viewed without any knowledge of the alleged invention, those differences constitute steps which would have been obvious to the skilled man or whether they require any degree of invention'.

The application of this test is largely a technical matter. Some broad principles may be drawn from the cases:

- to show something works will not necessarily be inventive nor will combining known albeit different technologies;
- expending considerable resources does not make something inventive nor will gaining considerable profit be necessarily evidence of non-obviousness though in both cases the failure of others to identify the need or supply the solution might tend towards a finding of non-obviousness;
- applying old technology to a new problem could be inventive if the application itself is inventive.

Industrially applicable

> an invention shall be taken to be capable of industrial application if it can be made or used in any kind of industry including agriculture (Patents Act 1977 s.4).

Methods of treating humans or animals by surgery, therapy or diagnosis are not regarded as being industrially applicable, though products for treatment, such as pharmaceuticals, are.

Excluded inventions

Section 1 (2) of the Patents Act 1977 sets out inventions excluded from patentability. These are: anything which consists of

1 'a discovery, scientific theory or mathematical method' – because they are not invented things having technical effects but are descriptions of natural phenomena and in the case of scientific theories are as yet unproven phenomena;
2 'a literary, dramatic, musical or artistic work or any other aesthetic creation whatsoever' – they are protected by copyright;
3 'a scheme for performing a mental act, playing a game or doing business, or a program for a computer' – to grant patents over these would be excessive in regard to things which are largely natural human mental acts;
4 'the presentation of information' – this is covered by copyright.

However, these matters are excluded only to the extent that a patent or application for a patent relates to that thing *as such*. Thus a discovery cannot be patented as such but if someone discovers something out of which he creates an unanticipated inventive technical effect then he or she can get a patent. This reflects the essential nature of patents in that reward comes from identifying something with a useful function.

Computer programs

> In *Vicom Systems Inc's Patent Application* [1987] it was held by the European Patent Office Board of Appeal that: 'a claim directed to a technical process which is carried out under the control of a program (be this implemented in hardware or software) cannot be regarded as relating to a computer program as such ... as it is the application of the program for determining the sequence of steps in the process for which in effect protection is sought. Consequently, such a claim is allowable'

> In *Fujitsu Limited's Application* [1997] a claim for a computerized system for modelling synthetic crystals (thus replacing cumbersome physical models) was rejected. ALDOUS LJ said: 'A claim to a computer program in a particular way is no more patentable than a claim to a computer program. A claim to a method of carrying out a calculation (a method of performing a mental act) is no more patentable when claimed as being done by a computer than when done on a piece of paper. Methods of performing mental acts, which means methods of the type performed mentally, are unpatentable, unless some concept of technical contribution is present'.

A computer program as such is not patentable. However, a computer program related invention could be patented if it has a technical effect. To add to the difficulty, computer related patents are challenged not just on the grounds that they are computer programs, but also on the basis that the underlying algorithms are methods of performing mental acts or mathematical methods or that the invention consists only of the presentation of information.

Further exclusions

A patent shall not be granted

(a) for an invention the publication or exploitation of which would be generally expected to encourage offensive, immoral or anti-social behaviour;

(b) for any variety of animal or plant or any essentially biological process for the production of animals or plants, not being a micro-biological process or the product of such a process (Section 1(3) of the Patents Act 1977).

Sub-category (a) means that the types of excluded matters could be extended on social grounds. Sub-category (b) does not exclude micro-biological processes: the technology behind creating a genetically modified mouse which would have the disposition to develop cancer was patentable. It was also found to be not against public order. Plants have separate legal protection under the Plant Varieties and Seeds Act 1964 as amended by the Plant Varieties Act 1983 whereby standardized, stable and distinctive plant varieties are given 30 years protection against unauthorized production or trading.

The European Union Directive on the Legal Protection of Biotechnological Inventions 1998 which requires implementation in 2000 provides that all member states should protect biotechnological inventions. It does not prevent states from excluding the patenting of animals or biological processes but it does appear to permit the patenting of isolated gene sequences which have a technical effect. It seems that cloning or gene sequences per se will not be patentable.

Application and duration

A patent comes into effect upon grant and lasts for 20 years from the date of filing the application. During the life of a patent renewal fees must be paid. Damages for infringement can be claimed for breaches after the publication date. A patent's life can be considerably shortened in commercial reality by the lengthy application procedure.

The initial application need only be the bare essentials of the patent, its description and administrative matters. Within 12 months from the original priority date, the applicant may re-file the application and file the application in other jurisdictions. The completed patent application consists of a request for grant of patent, a description including drawings which explains the invention's relationship with the prior art, and how the invention achieves its technical effect, plus the claims and an abstract. The claims are the key part of a patent in that they are the technical effects over which the applicant seeks a monopoly.

If the applicant wishes to proceed, a request is then made for a preliminary examination and search. This tests novelty and obviousness largely by searching and examining existing patent specifications. Following this the applicant may amend the claims but may not introduce claims not disclosed by the specification. Thus a patent and its claim may be refined but not be changed to the point of being a patent for different technology. After preliminary examination, the applicant may request what is known as publication.

Within 6 months of publication the applicant may request a substantive examination. This consists of a comprehensive scientific examination of the invention, testing that it complies with the requirements of the Patents Act. The application must disclose the method of replicating the invention. It may be for one invention or a group of inventions linked to form a single inventive concept. Subject to possible amendments the Patent Office will grant a patent when it is satisfied that the statutory requirements are satisfied. It is open for third parties to seek to have a patent revoked. A simple patent in the UK only may cost thousands of pounds to obtain. A complex patent applied for a number of European countries, through the European Patent Office, may cost tens of thousands. A complex patent applied for all the major economies, through the Patent Co-operation Treaty, will cost several tens of thousands, including high translation and legal costs. In total it can take about 4 years to gain a patent from the time of filing to grant. In 'high-tech', investment heavy industries this can mean that taking into account product development and testing, as well as the time for patenting, the length of the effective monopoly is cut short. This has been recognized in relation to the pharmaceutical industry. Under the Supplementary Protection Certificate for Pharmaceutical Products EC Regulations 1992 it will be possible to renew patents for medicines for up to 25 years. An accelerated procedure may be requested for examining a patent which is appropriate where the technology is straightforward.

Ownership

For the purposes of transactions, patents are treated as personal property. There is a rebuttable presumption that the applicant is the owner of a patent under s.7(4) of the Patents Act 1977. A claimant may apply under ss.8 or 12 to have a patent transferred to him or her where a better right to it can be shown. An inventor who is not the proprietor is entitled by s.13 to be mentioned in the patent form as the inventor. Typically the inventor is not the proprietor where the work is commissioned in the context of a contract. Section 39 provides that an employer shall be the owner of an employee's invention where the invention is made in the course of his or her normal duties or a specified task or in the course of his or her duties when there is a special obligation to further the employer's interests. An employee is entitled to claim compensation under the Patents Act 1977 s.40. In practice the claims are few and the amounts awarded are modest.

Transactions in patents such as assignment or mortgage are void unless done in writing by virtue of the Patents Act 1977 s.30(6). An assignee or licensee can act as though the grantee in pursuing infringement actions. Because of possible competing claims in the same patent, s.33 provides that a claim to a patent right shall prevail against other claims based on prior unregistered transactions. To protect oneself it is therefore necessary to register with the Patent Office any assignment, licence, sub-licence, mortgage, inheritance or transfer under a court order, of a patent.

Infringement of rights

Section 60 of the Patents Act 1977 s.30(6) sets out acts constituting infringement of patents in force. Section 60(1) provides that where the patent is for a product it is an infringement, if done without authorization, to make, dispose of, offer to dispose of, use, import or keep the product. Where the patent is for a process it is an infringement to use the process or to offer it for use in the UK where it is known or is obvious to the reasonable person that its use without the owner's consent would be an infringement. It is also an infringement in relation to a process patent to use, dispose of, offer to dispose of or keep any product obtained directly by means of that process. Thus the use or sale of a product is an infringement of strict liability but infringement of a process depends on actual or constructive knowledge. Section 60(2) provides a further infringement of, without consent, providing, to someone not entitled to work the patent, the means of putting the invention into effect when it is known or is obvious to a reasonable person that those means are suitable for putting the invention into effect. Providing a staple commercial product would not constitute an infringement under subsection 2, unless it were done to induce someone to carry out a subsection 1 infringement.

Infringements of patent are civil wrongs and do not involve criminal offences. Actions for infringement can be taken in the High Court or in the Patents County Court. Infringement must take place within UK jurisdiction. Thus it is necessary to obtain patents in those jurisdictions where infringements such as sale or manufacture are likely to take place if export markets are to be protected.

The scope of the patent

In *Catnic Components Ltd* v *Hill & Smith Limited* [1982] LORD DIPLOCK promoted the purposive approach as opposed to the literal approach. That is when determining whether the claim is infringed one asks whether the purpose of the claim rather than its literal wording has been infringed.

In *Improver Corp.* v *Remington Consumer Products Ltd* [1990] HOFFMANN J set out a model for purposive construction:

(1) Does the variant have a material effect upon the way the invention works? If yes, the variant is outside the claim. If no-

(2) Would this (i.e. that the variant had no material effect) have been obvious at the date of publication of the patent to the reader skilled in the art? If no, the variant is outside the claim. If yes-

(3) Would the reader skilled in the art nevertheless have understood from the language of the claim that the patentee intended that strict compliance with the primary meaning was an essential requirement of the invention? If yes the variant is outside the claim.

Whether a patent has been infringed depends on the construction of the claims in the patent. If the claims are too narrowly drafted (or interpreted) it may be possible that a variant on the invention might be regarded as being essentially different. On the other hand the Patent Office will not allow claims so broad that they constitute different inventive concepts or do not disclose all the methods in the invention. This problem indicates why professional assistance in patent drafting is advisable.

There has been much academic and judicial debate as to the better method of construing patent claims. Problems of construction also arise where the allegedly infringing article achieves the patented effect by a mechanically equivalent (but different) method. In *Improver Corp.* v *Raymond Industries Ltd* the patent concerned the 'Epilady' device for removing hair. The claimant's device used a helical spring to trap and cut hairs. The defendant's device used a rubber rod with slits. There was no infringement because the patent's claims did not make it clear that the use of the helical spring was not an essential requirement of the invention. The burden of proof of infringement lies with the patent owner. It may be impossible to prove breach where there are different expert opinions as to the technology concerned.

Remedies for infringement

Section 61 of the Act specifies the remedies available to a patent owner or a person such as an exclusive licensee. These are: injunction to restrain infringement; order to deliver up or destroy a patented product or a product in which a patented product is inextricably comprised; damages in respect of infringement; account of profits derived from the infringement; or declaration that the patent is valid and has been infringed. Action for damages or declaration can be brought before the Comptroller of Patents (with his approval) instead of court.

It is not possible to recover both damages and account of profits in respect of the same breach. Damages are not awarded where it is shown that the defendant was not aware and had no reasonable grounds to believe that the patent existed. Thus an infringer who can claim 'innocence' will have to stop the infringement and may have to account for his or her undeserved gain but will not suffer the penalty of damages.

Defences to patent infringement

The fundamental defence to an accusation of infringement is that the act does not come within the definitions of infringement in the Patents Act 1977 s.60(1). Though technically not a defence but of significance is a challenge to the fundamental validity of the patent which if demonstrated makes the allegation of infringement redundant.

The formal defences to patent infringement are in the Patents Act 1977 s.60(5). These include that the act is done:

- privately and for non-commercial purposes;
- for experimental purposes relating to the subject-matter of the invention;
- in the course of preparing medicine in accordance with a valid prescription;
- in connection with an aircraft or vessel temporarily in the jurisdiction.

The defendant may be able to show various contractual defences, for example:

- he or she is a licensee;
- at the time of infringement there was a contractual clause seeking a collateral advantage to the patent owner which is found to be void;
- there is an implied licence under a purchaser's right to repair, to do acts which would otherwise constitute infringement.

The following, while not strictly defences are nevertheless important.

- A person accused of patent infringement may bring an action alleging groundless threat of infringement proceedings. Unless the patent owner or person threatening proceedings can show that the patent is valid and has been or would be infringed then the remedies of declaration, injunction or damages may be awarded to the person threatened. This action is useful against patent owners who might seek to exaggerate their patent protection by using the threat of infringement proceedings.
- A good faith user of the invention before the priority date of the patent will not be liable for infringement. Such a person may continue to use the invention but may not license it.
- A demonstration that the patent owner's rights are exhausted.

Exploitation of patents

Major manufacturers can afford the considerable cost of patenting across a number of countries, but more importantly they cannot afford to lose the return on research and development investment. Private inventors cannot afford such considerable costs. This does not mean that patent protection is beyond the scope of the private inventor. The procedure for initiating patent protection in the UK is relatively cheap and easy. Once an application has been filed, the inventor has time to develop his or her ideas. He or she has established a priority date and most importantly has a defined technology which he or she may seek to exploit by selling or licensing it to manufacturers who have the money to develop and manufacture it plus the distribution chain to market it.

TRADE MARKS

Definition

> any sign capable of being represented graphically which is capable of distinguishing goods or services of one undertaking from those of other undertakings.

> A trade mark may, in particular, consist of words (including personal names) designs, letters, numerals or the shape of goods or their packaging (Trade Marks Act 1994, s.1).

The definition means that much more than traditional words and signs can be registered. It is possible to register signature jingles in the form of musical notations, perfumes in the form of chemical formulae, three-dimensional logos in the form of computerized images. The requirement that the sign is 'capable of distinguishing goods' means that the sign describes the origin of the goods but not the type of goods. For example, 'Round Football' would not distinguish one person's footballs from those of another. It also means that the name should be distinguishable from those used by another (e.g. my 'UmbroFootball' would not be capable of being distinguished from another pre-existing 'UmbroFootball') The inclusion of packaging means that previously unregistrable get-ups such as the shape of the classical Coca Cola bottle are now registrable.

Historically trade marks have been used by manufacturers to indicate the provenance of their products and thereby imply their quality. Early examples include silver makers' hallmarks. Trade marks became registrable in the late nineteenth century, the Bass beer red triangle being the earliest example. Trade marks can be registered or can be left unregistered. An unregistered mark cannot be protected by statutory actions for trade mark infringement. It can, however, be protected by the common law action for the tort of passing off. Registered trade marks can be protected by both the statutory and common law actions. Trade marks are registered in relation to one or more specified types of goods or services. There are 34 classes of goods and eight classes of services. UK law is presently governed by the Trade Marks Act 1994. Like other forms of intellectual property, registered trade marks are national rights even though the nature of trade marks worldwide is largely the same by virtue of widespread ratification of the Madrid Agreement Concerning the International Registration of Marks 1891 as revised. If one wishes to trade products or services internationally under the same name it is necessary to register and maintain marks in as many jurisdictions as is commercially necessary to prevent infringement. It is now possible to register a community trade mark to cover Europe. These will increase in importance but it is still true that enterprises owning significant marks must operate a sophisticated international trade mark protection strategy.

Section 2 of the Trade Marks Act 1994 Act confirms that a trade mark is a property right. As a property right it can be assigned, licensed or used as collateral thus giving legal foundation to various means of exploitation. Trade marks are not normally valued as assets of an enterprise except for the purpose of an actual transaction.

Excluded signs

Signs are excluded from registration on absolute grounds which relate to the nature of the mark applied for and relative grounds which relate to the relationship between existing marks and the mark being applied for.

Section 3 of the Trade Marks Act 1994 sets out the absolute grounds for refusal to grant a trade mark. In addition to signs not complying with s.1 these are trade marks:

- devoid of distinctive character;
- consisting exclusively of signs or indications which designate the kind, quality, quantity, intended purpose, value, geographic origin, time of production or other characteristics of the goods or services.

Signs or indications which have become customary are excluded unless the use of such marks has in fact become distinctive of the goods before application to register is made. These exclusions exist to ensure that marks are differentiated and do not deceive the public by attributing some (unproven) quality to goods.

Distinctiveness

In *British Sugar Plc* v *James Robertson* [1996] it was determined that the registration of the name 'Treat' in respect of dessert sauces and syrups was invalid because it lacked distinctive character.

In *Phillips Electronics BV* v *Remington Consumer Products* [1998] it was held that the registration of a mark consisting of a three-headed razor was invalid not only because it lacked distinctive character but also because the mark consisted exclusively of a shape which is necessary to achieve a technical effect.

The essence of a good mark is that it is distinctive but not descriptive. Common ways of achieving distinctiveness are to use made-up words such as Pepsi or acronyms of real names such as IKEA or foreign words lacking meaning in English such as Nike. Care, however, has to be taken in choosing new names, to avoid words having unfortunate meanings or connotations in other languages.

Section 3 also excludes absolutely:

- signs determined by the shape of the goods
- shapes necessary to perform a technical effect or shapes which give substantial value to the goods.

These are important because although it is possible to protect shapes and the get-up of goods, protection cannot be extended to using trade mark law as an indirect means of protecting the shape of goods themselves which should be dealt with by design law.

More general exclusions in s.3 are:

- trade marks contrary to public policy or accepted principles of morality;
- marks deceptive to the public in respect of the goods' nature, quality or origin;
- marks whose use is prohibited by UK or EU law;
- trade marks containing specially protected emblems;
- trade marks which have been applied for in bad faith.

This last exclusion helps to prevent speculative applications made where someone wishes to stymie a genuine application by another or made with a view to selling the name to another having need of it. Specially protected emblems include:

- representations of royal insignia including the flag;
- representations of members of the royal family;
- representations implying royal patronage;
- representations of national flags including those of reciprocating foreign countries and certain emblems of international organizations and representations of the Olympic symbol.

Section 5 of the Trade Marks Act 1994 itemizes relative grounds for refusal. These are if the mark is:

- identical to an existing mark in relation to identical goods;
- identical to an existing mark in relation to similar goods;
- similar to an existing mark in relation to identical goods;
- similar to an existing mark in relation to similar goods if there is a likelihood of confusion by the public including the likelihood of association with the existing mark.

These four exclusions are aimed to prevent confusion caused by imitation.

Identical or similar marks are not permitted in relation to dissimilar goods, if the existing mark has a reputation in the UK, and use of the mark without due cause would take unfair advantage of, or cause detriment to, the distinctiveness or reputation of the existing mark. This protects well-known trade marks against those who might inadvertently or intentionally take advantage of their repute.

Registration will not be refused if there has been already 'honest concurrent use of the mark' unless opposition proceedings are brought by the owner of the earlier mark. Other grounds for relative refusal in the Trade Marks Act 1994 s.5 are:

- marks which may conflict with earlier rights in unregistered trade marks;
- marks which may conflict with earlier rights in copyright works registered designs or design rights.

Application and duration

Section 32 of the Trade Marks Act 1994 provides the requirements for applying for a UK trade mark. The application must include:

- the request for the mark;
- details of the applicant;
- statement of the goods or services in relation to which the mark is to be used;
- a representation of the mark;
- a statement that the mark is in use or that there is a bona fide intention that it should be so used.

The 42 classes of goods and services include for example:

- class 1 for chemicals used in industry;
- class 15 for musical instruments;
- class 20 for furniture;
- class 38 for telecommunications.

Applications are lodged with the Registrar of Trade Marks in the Patent Office. An application in a reciprocating country gives the applicant a 6 month priority period in which to apply in the UK. An application is examined by the Registry to ensure compliance with the requirements of the Act and subsidiary regulations. The examination involves analysis of previously registered marks as well as examination of the mark itself. If the Registrar has doubts as to registrability, the applicant may make representations or offer amendments. If satisfied the Registrar will accept the application and publish it in the *Trade Marks Journal*. This gives others 3 months in which to oppose the grant of the mark. If oppositions are not forthcoming, or if they fail, and, subject to discovering errors in examination, the trade mark will be registered upon payment of a fee and a certificate of registration issued to the applicant. Registration may be subject to a disclaimer or limitation as to use, for instance, exclusive use may be partially waived or use may be geographically limited.

Frequently applications are for a series of marks in a variety of forms such as the name, plus the name in a particular typescript, plus the typescript in association with a logo. The procedure for obtaining a registered trade mark is relatively quick (months not years) and cheap (hundreds not thousands of pounds) especially in comparison to the fees brand designers charge and the time and money spent on developing and projecting brands.

Trade Marks are registered for an initial period of 10 years from the date of registration and may thereafter be renewed indefinitely for further periods of 10 years.

Registration of a trade mark may be revoked on the grounds that it has not been put into use within 5 years of registration or that its use has been interrupted without good reason. Marks may also be revoked if they have become deceptive. A mark may be revoked if it becomes the common name for the product or service such as Hoover. Registration may also be declared invalid if it becomes apparent that it did not comply with the requirements for registration in the Act. Any person may apply to the court or Registrar for a declaration of invalidity or revocation of registration.

There are two other specific forms of trade marks.

1 *Certification marks* such as the Woolmark are registered by bodies having objective criteria of quality for determining whether the mark can be used by others in relation to their goods.
2 *Collective marks* are registered by associations so that their members can use the mark in relation to their goods or services.

Ownership

Subject to assignment, the proprietor of a registered trade mark is the applicant to whom the registration certificate is issued. A trade mark is in the nature of personal property. The rights of trade mark proprietors are exclusive rights infringed by use of the mark in the UK without the owner's consent.

Trade marks are transmissible by assignment, will or operation of law, in the same way as other property. Transmission of a registered trade mark is not effective unless done in writing and signed. Transactions in registered trade marks including assignments, licences or the granting of a mark as security for a loan, may be entered on the Register of trade marks. If transactions are not registered, they are not effective against a person acquiring a conflicting interest in or under the registered trade mark in ignorance of the unregistered transaction.

Infringement of rights

The acts which constitute statutory infringement of registered trade marks mirror the grounds for refusal to register and are specified in the Trade Marks Act 1994 s.10:

(1) A person infringes a registered trade mark if he uses in the course of trade a sign which is identical with the trade mark in relation to goods or services which are identical with those for which it is registered.

(2) A person infringes a registered trade mark if he uses in the course of trade a sign where because
  (a) the sign is identical with the trade mark and is used in relation to goods or services similar to those for which the trade mark is registered, or
  (b) the sign is similar to the trade mark and is used in relation to goods or services identical with or similar to those for which the trade mark is registered,
there exists a likelihood of confusion on the part of the public, which includes the likelihood of association with the trade mark.

(3) A person infringes a registered trade mark if he uses in the course of trade a sign which

(a) is identical with or similar to the trade mark, and

(b) is used in relation to goods or services which are not similar to those for which the trade mark is registered,

where the trade mark has a reputation in the United Kingdom and the use of the sign, being without due cause, takes unfair advantage of, or is detrimental to, the distinctive character or repute of the trade mark.

Similarity

In *Wagamama Ltd* v *City Centre Restaurants Plc* [1995] the issue was whether the name Rajamama for an Indian restaurant was likely to confuse the public in relation to the name Wagamama for a Japanese restaurant. The court found that 'likelihood of association' was a possible example of confusion but was not a head of infringement in itself. LADDIE J found that there was confusion: 'I have come to the conclusion that the defendant's mark, in either form is so similar to the plaintiff's registered mark that in use there exists a substantial likelihood of confusion on the part of the relevant public. That confusion is likely to take the form that some members of the public as a result of imperfect recollection will think the marks are the same while others will think that they are associated in the sense that one is the extension of the other ... or otherwise derived from the same source'.

Signs can be similar visually, semantically or aurally, for instance Zn could be regarded as too similar to Zinc. The use of identical marks in comparative advertising became lawful under the Trade Marks Act 1994 provided it is done in accordance with honest practices in industrial or commercial matters. Whether goods are similar, can be tested by relation to the classes of trade marks, it can also be tested by reference to patterns of behaviour in commerce, for instance how products are marketed. Compact discs could be similar to computer systems because discs are used with computers and computers can be used to play music.

In subsection (2) similarity is not infringement in itself but must entail some likelihood of confusion. It seems that semantic similarity does not automatically make for confusion nor does mere association of one mark with another.

Section 10(3) is intended to protect well-known trade marks from unfair imitation. In *Baywatch Production Co Inc* v *The Home Video Channel* [1997] it was held that the subsection required the likelihood of confusion even though the wording of the section does not say this. Section 56 of the Trade Marks Act 1994 gives limited protection to foreign marks of reciprocating countries. The owner of a well-known foreign mark can obtain an injunction in the UK to prevent the use of a similar or identical mark in relation to similar or identical goods where the foreign mark is well-known in the UK, albeit not traded in the UK.

Use of a sign for the purpose of infringement includes in s.10(4) acts where an infringer:

(a) affixes it to goods or the packaging thereof,

(b) offers or exposes goods for sale, puts them on the market or stocks them for those purposes under the sign, or offers or supplies services under the sign;

(c) imports or exports goods under the sign; or

(d) uses the sign on business papers or in advertising.

Subsections (1), (2) and (3) require that such use must be in the course of trade but it has been judicially interpreted that such use need not be use in trade as a trade mark.

Section 92 of the Trade Marks Act 1994 creates a number of offences relating to the misuse of marks. Subsection (1) provides:

> A person commits an offence who with a view to gain for himself or another, or with intent to cause loss to another, and without the consent of the proprietor
>
> (a) applies to goods or their packaging a sign identical to, or likely to be mistaken for, a registered trade mark, or
> (b) sells or lets for hire, offers or exposes for the sale or hire or distributes goods which bear, or the packaging of which bears, such a sign, or
> (c) has in his possession, custody or control in the course of a business any such goods with a view to do anything, by himself or another, which would be an offence under paragraph (b).

Such offences can be tried in the Magistrates' Court or in the Crown Court where the applicable sentences can be severe.

Remedies for infringement

Civil actions for infringement are normally taken by the proprietor of the mark. Licensees may bring proceedings in the place of the proprietor if the proprietor refuses or fails to commence proceedings within 2 months of being called upon to do so. Subject to the terms of the licence, an exclusive licensee has the same rights as an assignee.

The remedies for infringement are the normal ones available in relation to infringement of property rights: damages, injunction and account for profits. The Trade Marks Act 1994 provides further specific remedies. The proprietor may apply for an order for erasure or removal of infringing marks from goods or, if removal of the offending sign is impracticable, destruction of the goods themselves. The proprietor may apply for the delivery up of infringing goods and for a further order that such goods be destroyed. Delivery up is not available after 6 years from manufacture of infringing goods or the application of infringing signs onto goods.

Defences to trade mark infringement

The defences to statutory infringement of trade marks, in s.12 of the Act, are described as limits on the effect of the registered trade mark. It is not infringement of a mark to use:

- a registered mark in relation to a different class of goods for which it is entered;
- a mark as an indication of kind, quality, origin, intended use or other characteristics provided such use is in accordance with honest practices in industrial or commercial matters;
- a mark where it is necessary to indicate the intended use of the product (such as identifying components) provided it is in accordance with honest practices.

A trade mark is not infringed where the goods concerned have been put on the European Economic Area market and thus the rights are exhausted. Though strictly not a defence, liability may be avoided by successfully applying to revoke or invalidate the trade mark registration.

A person against whom groundless threats of infringement proceedings are made can apply under the Trade Marks Act 1994 s.21 for remedies including damages, injunction or declaration.

Passing off

In *Erven Warnink Besloten Venootschap* v *J Townend & Sons (Hull) Ltd* [1973] LORD DIPLOCK enunciated a classical formulation of the tort of passing off: 'My Lords, *Spalding* v *Gamage* (1915) and the later cases make it possible to identify five characteristics which must be present in order to create a valid cause of action for passing off: (1) a misrepresentation, (2) made by a trader in the course of trade, (3) to prospective customers of his or ultimate consumers of goods or services supplied by him, (4) which is calculated to injure the business or goodwill of another trader (in the sense that this is a reasonably foreseeable consequence) and (5) which causes actual damage to a business or goodwill of the trader by whom the action is brought'.

The Trade Marks Act 1994 does not exclude the common law action of passing off to protect registered and unregistered trade marks. Passing off has been characterized as a means of protecting the business goodwill of an enterprise. In addition to registered marks it covers unregistered business names, the getup of products, the packaging of products including their colour and potentially any misrepresentation that goods or services offered originate from someone else.

Misrepresentation

In *J. Bollinger* v *Costa Bravo Wine Co Ltd (No 2)* [1961] it was held that the use of the name 'Champagne' in relation to sparkling wine was a misrepresentation likely to cause confusion even when qualified by the adjective 'Spanish'.

The misrepresentation must be some act creating a likelihood of confusion. It need not be exact copying but similarity causing confusion is sufficient. Misrepresentation can be direct impersonation of another's product to imply the goods are those of another, or it can be the false attribution of some quality in another's goods to imply that the goods offered have the quality of some more reputed manufacturer. A variation on this is where there is a false claim to authority or licence to use a name. Instances of misrepresentation include using similar names or wrappings in relation to goods in a common field of activity. The public is not expected to be especially astute. Research Surveys are often carried out to determine the extent of confusion amongst the public. A misrepresentation, including an obvious parody, which does not fool the public is not actionable on the basis that the claimant has lost nothing. The necessary element of confusion is also lacking where the claimant has acquiesced previously to the use of a name.

Use in the course of trade goes beyond normal trade and can include other economic activities such as carrying out a profession and the provision of services. The misrepresentation must be made to customers or consumers otherwise there would be no potential loss to the claimant. 'Calculation to cause injury' does not have its normal meaning because there is no requirement of intention.

Normally a common field of activity is required otherwise there would be no confusion. For instance Smiths the makers of crisps is not confused with Smiths the makers of car instruments. However, where a name is very widely known it may be that the common field of activity is unlimited because the wrongful use of the name in respect of any product would be potentially confusing. For instance if someone used 'Virgin' in relation to furniture it might create confusion that the real Virgin organization was involved.

UK law is moving towards a situation where the unauthorized use of a TV or cartoon character in relation to advertising goods (character merchandising) will be actionable in relation to any field of goods.

Remedies for infringement

In *Taittinger SA* v *Allbev Ltd* [1993] it was held that damage can also be inferred from loss of the exclusive right to use a name in the market. In that case the defendant had to desist from using the name 'Elderflower Champagne'.

As with most civil actions there must be some damage in order to justify a remedy. Normally damage is associated with loss of sales or loss of reputation caused by inferior products in the same name being on the market. Damage pre-supposes that the claimant has some reputation or goodwill which can be affected. This is typically demonstrated by public profile through sales or advertising.

The normal remedies for civil actions are available though in the case of passing off the most appropriate remedy is an injunction to stop the misuse of the name and put an end to the dilution of the claimant's reputation. The specific defences to actions of passing off are denials that one or more of the elements set out by LORD DIPLOCK have been met. General defences include acquiescence or delay.

Domain names

In *British Telecommunications Plc* v *One in a Million Ltd* [1999] injunctions were issued forcing the defendant to release the names he had registered on grounds of infringement of trade mark and passing off.

In *Pitman Training Ltd* v *Nominet UK* [1997] it was held that as between Pitman Training and Pitman Publishing, who were different companies owning the trademark 'Pitman' in different classes, the first to register the domain name pitman.co.uk was its owner.

In recent years use of the internet has created a number of difficulties in relation to trade marks. A domain name is the address by which a website is accessed by the public, for example bbc.co.uk. Whilst the same name can be registered in different jurisdictions in relation to different goods by different proprietors thus making trade marks 'shared', websites are unique. Smiths can co-exist many times as a trade mark but there can be only one 'smiths.com'. Domain names are issued by independent organizations without state regulation. The owner of 'smiths.com' will be first to register it. Normally when a name is registered the applicant vouches that no rights are being infringed. This represents little difficulty to the applicant who may have a legitimate interest in the name smith or smiths or variations thereof, or may simply take the (arguably legitimate) view that owning a domain name is not in itself an infringement of mark.

Two types of case have arisen: cybersquatting and legitimate conflicting use. Cybersquatting takes place where someone registers a number of domain names with a view to selling them back to persons owning a trade mark in the name registered.

Legitimate conflicting use happens where two organizations have registered trademarks in the same name albeit in different classes or jurisdictions.

Protection of rights

Enterprises should have a proactive strategy for securing and maintaining trade mark protection. This involves registration of marks in all the classes and jurisdictions necessary. It also requires careful maintenance of renewals, recording and registration of transactions and careful checks on threats of infringement. Nowadays it also involves maintenance of rights in domain names.

CONFIDENTIAL INFORMATION

In *Coco* v *A.N. Clark (Engineers) Ltd* [1969] MEGARRY J said: 'In my judgement, three elements are normally required if, apart from contract, a case of breach of confidence is to succeed. First, the information itself, ... must have the necessary quality of confidence about it. Secondly, that information must have been imparted in circumstances importing an obligation of confidence. Thirdly, there must have been an unauthorised use of that information to the detriment of the party communicating it'.

One unusual type of intellectual property is confidential information: colloquially one would call it trade secrets. These could be commercially valuable products of the mind which cannot be protected by more formal mechanisms, for example, a method of doing business is specifically excluded from patentablity by the Patents Act 1977 s.1(2)(c). Alternately they could be things which, although protectable formally are not thus given sufficient protection, for example, a client list when written down is copyright, but copyright law will not prevent someone memorizing the list rather than infringing copyright by copying it. Whilst a contract of employment contains implied terms of fidelity there are many situations where there are relationships short of employment in which it is important to maintain the secrecy of trade information, including relationships with former employees. In order to close such gaps in the statutory law, case law developed the tort of breach of confidence whereby the owner of confidential information takes an action for remedies for the unauthorized use of confidential information. Although there are earlier instances relating to breach of faith or contract and specific laws on official secrets, the law of breach of confidence developed largely in the latter half of the twentieth century. However there is no general law of privacy in the UK to protect private information.

The confidential quality of the information

In *Thomas Marshall (Exports) Ltd* v *Guinle* [1976] MEGARRY V-C set out a test for determining whether information had the necessary quality of confidence: 'First, I think that the information must be information the release of which the owner believes would be injurious to him or of advantage to his rivals or others. Second, I think the owner must believe that the information is confidential or secret, i.e. that it is not already in the public domain ... Third, I think that the owner's belief under the above two heads must be reasonable. Fourth, I think that the information must be judged in the light of the usage and practices of the particular industry or trade concerned'.

The owner's belief (and the reasonableness of that belief) in harm to him- or herself or benefit to others in losing the information would normally be demonstrated by how the owner treated the information. It is not sufficient to mark documents as confidential, it is necessary to treat them as confidential by, for instance, keeping them secure, restricting access, preventing copying and reference to legal obligations of secrecy. The belief in possible harm must be reflected in the nature of the information. The information need not be especially complex but it must represent some commercial benefit which it would be damaging to lose. The impossibility or expense of replacement would be factors in assessing this. The owner's (reasonable) belief that the information is in the public domain is assessed in the light of whether and how the information has been published. An owner may have collated information which is commercially useful but is in fact publicly available and only needs some effort to organize. Conversely an employer may have no way of knowing that information has already been stolen in which case its belief in its secrecy is still good. Where confidential information has been released into the public domain in breach of an obligation of confidence a person who owed an obligation of confidence cannot use the information personally even though it is now in the public domain. This is known as the 'springboard doctrine', that is people cannot use wrongly released information as a springboard for acts detrimental to the owner and of benefit to themselves. When determining the quality of confidentiality, account is taken of the practices in the trade concerned for example source codes for software are treated in the software industry as being highly confidential.

Obligation of confidence

The most common kind of obligation of confidence is a contract of employment. Other similar express contracts can be created, such as contracts with suppliers, buyers or distributors. In any situation where trade secrets need to be revealed to a partner in business it is advisable to use a confidentiality agreement. Obligations of confidence arise automatically in certain relationships such as solicitor and client. Obligations of confidence have been held to arise impliedly from certain circumstances such as when an idea for a TV programme was shown to producers, but it is not advisable to hope that courts will always be so generous. In principle a third party recipient of confidential information who is not under an obligation of confidence can use the information freely. One of the most difficult areas of obligation of confidence relates to former employees. Employers might wish to stop ex-employees giving trade secrets to their new competing employers. It is possible to place clauses in employment contracts which restrict the acts of ex-employees. However, such clauses cannot be so wide as to restrain a worker's legitimate trade or profession. Whether a clause is valid depends on the circumstance. A lifetime ban on competing would normally be ineffective but could be valid if it applied to only a small geographic area. Conversely a countrywide ban might be effective if it relates to a very short period such as the completion of a project. Where the contract of employment is silent as to the behaviour of ex-employees there can be an implied term of confidentiality which is less than an employee's implied term of fidelity. Even where there is an obligation of confidence it may be a defence to release information if it is in the public interest to do so.

Unauthorized use

Whether use is unauthorized depends upon the terms (express or implied) of the obligation of confidence. It does not depend on the belief or motivation of the person using the information. The usual remedies for civil actions are available, though an injunction is often the most appropriate remedy to prevent the further harmful use of information. Breach of confidence is a relatively weak action in that in most cases the damage is done by the time action is taken and is often in commercial reality irretrievable. It is therefore necessary to ensure that confidential information is protected by practical measures.

DESIGN

There are two methods of protecting designs. Registration of designs may be used to protect the aesthetic appearance of a manufactured product. Design rights protect the functional aspect of the shape or configuration of an article. The earliest design legislation in the UK goes back to the late eighteenth century. During the twentieth century there has been considerable overlap between the law governing design and artistic copyright creating considerable confusion not least from the transitional arrangements which are partly to blame for the low level of applications made for design registration. Registered designs are governed by The Registered Designs Act 1949 as amended by the Copyright, Designs and Patents Act 1988. Design rights were created by and are governed by the latter Act.

Registered design

In this Act 'design' means features of shape, configuration, pattern or ornament applied to an article by any industrial process, being features which in the finished article appeal to and are judged by the eye, but does not include

(a) a method or principle of construction, or
(b) features of shape or configuration of an article which
   (i) are dictated solely by the function which the article has to perform, or
   (ii) are dependent upon the appearance of another article of which the article is intended by the author of the design to form an integral part (Section 1 of the Registered Designs Act 1949).

A registered design is thus meant to protect the 'look' of a manufactured article. The requirement of industrial process excludes individually made artistic pieces. 'Article' means a separate, individually sold object and it is not intended that individual components of a machine having no self-standing purpose are covered. It is possible, though, to protect a series of articles such as a furniture collection. One area of difficulty in design law is the status of automobile spare parts. It seems that a spare part is not protectable as a registered design unless it consists of, for example, an alternative panelling design. The requirement of appealing to the eye means that the look of the article must influence the purchasing decision from the perspective of the notional consumer (not the designer, commentator or distributor). The utility or convenience of the design is not the issue. It seems that the eye-appeal can be material in two senses. First where the choice of a particular product out of a range is determined by aesthetic appeal, or secondly where the choice of a product from a selection is not usually determined by appeal, but the design in question does have some specific aesthetic appeal.

The exception to registrability that the design should not be a method of construction or be determined by function, is to prevent design law from being used to gain monopolies over functional designs. If something has a novel technical effect it may be patentable but it must go through the rigorous test for establishing patents.

Another exception is that a design cannot be registered where the shape is dependent upon the appearance of another article of which it is intended to be an integral part. This is meant to prevent manufacturers from controlling the supply by third parties of spare parts (to the extent that spare parts can be protected). This is known as the 'must-match' exception. The Registered Designs Rules 1995 also exclude particular types of work of a copyright character including sculptures, dress patterns, maps and postcards.

To be registered a design must be new in that it is not anticipated by a prior application for registration or by prior publication in the UK. The proprietor of a design is presumed to be its author unless its creation is done in the course of employment or is commissioned. Upon application, the Designs Registry of the Patent Office carries out searches to determine whether the design is new. The Registrar may reject the application if it fails the statutory requirements. He also has a discretion to refuse, which may be used on public policy grounds. When an application is accepted it gives the proprietor the exclusive right to make and sell the design. Registration is for an initial period of 5 years and may be extended for up to four further 5-year periods. Assignments should be in writing and should be entered on the Register. Infringement consists of doing these acts without authorization or making something without licence to enable the design article to be made. Defences fall into two categories: those relating to denying that some element of the requirements for registration was satisfied; and those relating to the nature of the alleged infringing article. These include that the design is substantially different or that the design does not relate to details of design claimed in the registered design. The usual remedies of injunction and account for profits are available but damages are not recoverable if the defendant was not aware, and had reasonable grounds for not being aware, that the design was registered. Compulsory licences to use registered designs are possible where the proprietor abuses registration by not working the design without good cause.

Design right

(2) In this Part 'design' means the design of any aspect of the shape or configuration (whether internal or external) of the whole or any substantial part of an article.

(3) Design right does not subsist in
  (a) a method or principle of construction,
  (b) features of shape or configuration of an article which
    (i) enable the article to be connected to, or placed in, around or against, another article so that either article may perform its function,
    (ii) are dependent upon the appearance of another article of which the article is intended by the designer to form an integral part, or
  (c) surface decoration (Section 213 of the Copyright, Designs and Patents Act 1988).

Whereas a *registered design* protects the look of a design, a *design right* protects the way an article is configured. Registered designs have some characteristics of patents, design rights are more akin to copyright. In particular they do not require registration but come into being by being created and recorded. A design right can relate to the internal or external shape of an article and can apply to the whole or parts of an article subject to exceptions. As with registered designs, methods of construction are excluded and the must-match exclusion exists. In addition there is the must-fit exception to prevent design rights being acquired in relation to designs which enable articles to be placed together so that either can perform. The exception applies to the design of the connection and so may leave scope to gain design right over the non-connecting part of a component.

A design must not be commonplace in the industry. This means that it must be more than simply not copied: it must be a departure from common designs in the field. Additionally the design must be original in the sense of not being copied. The design must be fixed in some tangible form either in a design document or by being made in an article.

The designer will be the first owner of the design unless done in the course of employment or a commission. Where neither the designer, employer or commissioner are qualified to own a UK design right, the person who with authority first markets the design in the UK will be the first owner presuming he qualifies by citizenship of the UK or a reciprocating country. A design right lasts for 15 years from the end of the year of creation but is only protected for 10 years of exploitation. Assignments and exclusive licences of design rights should be done in writing. A design right confers the exclusive right to make articles to the design and make design documents enabling manufacture of the article. Infringement consists of doing these exclusive acts without authorization. Primary infringement would be the copying of the design by making articles to the design which are exactly or substantially the same. Secondary infringement consists of importing, possessing, selling or offering to sell in the course of business infringing articles which the infringer knows or has reason to believe are infringing articles. As with registered designs the defences to infringement fall into two parts; those relating to the qualification for protection of the design being copied and those relating to whether the alleged copy matches those aspects of a protected design. The remedies of injunction, including delivery up and account for profits, are available but damages are not recoverable where the defendant did not know and had no reason to believe that a design right subsisted.

There is a further particular type of design right governed by the Design Right (Semiconductor) Regulations 1989. This protects original patterns (topography) of semiconductors (such as silicon chips).

Harmonization of design law across the EU is pending.

CONCLUSION

It is important that enterprises are aware of the importance of intellectaual property in achieving competitive advantage. To that end enterprises should have a structured strategy for identifying, acquiring, protecting, maintaining and exploiting their intellectual property rights.

PROGRESS TEST

1 Can you identify which types of intellectual property are protected in the products you regularly purchase?
2 Can you identify the price difference between products with novel technology and those with mature technology?
3 What instances of infringement of copyright are you aware of? What impact do you think this has on copyright owners?
4 What kinds of trade mark do you think are valuable and why?
5 What kind of business information do you think would be regarded as confidential and what measures should be taken in an organization to protect such information?
6 Can you think of any products which have added value derived from their design? Can you distinguish between whether the relevant design protection is a Design Right or a Registered Design?

12 The taxation responsibilities of the organization

Martin Kleyman

INTRODUCTION

> every person who is chargeable to Income Tax ... for any year of assessment ... shall ... give notice to an officer of the Board that he is so chargeable. (Taxes Management Act 1970 s.7(1)).

> every company which is chargeable to Corporation Tax for any accounting period ... shall ... give notice to the inspector that it is so chargeable (Taxes Management Act 1970 s.10(1)).

> Value Added Tax shall be charged ... on the supply of goods and services in the United Kingdom (Section 1 Value Added Tax Act 1994 s.1).

As earlier chapters have explained, anyone wishing to start in business will have to decide whether to trade as a sole trader, a partnership, or through a limited company. While it will be clear that tax is by no means the only consideration to be taken into account when deciding the legal form under which the business operates, in making this decision attention must be given to the tax consequences. A vitally important factor is likely to be maintaining cash flow in the formative years of the business. Whichever trading vehicle is chosen, either s.7 or s.10 of the Taxes Management Act (TMA) 1970 will apply, thus ensuring that the business is responsible for informing the Inland Revenue of every tax liability.

Tax may be due on a number of different bases: on profits; on staff costs; on turnover; and on the eventual sale of part or all of the business. Most businesses will be liable to the first three of these taxes in each year. The entrepreneur needs to consider each of these, and the purpose of this chapter is to outline the tax implications of trading through each of the vehicles mentioned above.

It is important for any business to keep records which will satisfy the various taxing authorities when they come to check up that the correct tax has been paid, and also that the right amount of tax is paid by the due date. It could be fatal to a business to suddenly be faced with a large tax bill (plus a variety of penalties).

Therefore this chapter seeks to set out the requirements under each of the taxes which may apply to a business in the UK. In relation to each tax, it will be explained how the tax is calculated and reported, and who is responsible for the collection. The chapter will also outline what happens if insufficient tax is paid.

The body responsible for the administration and collection of income tax, capital gains, and national insurance contributions is the Inland Revenue, while Customs and Excise are similarly responsible for VAT.

TAX ADMINISTRATION

The Inland Revenue Regulation Act 1890, and the Customs and Excise Management Act 1979 provide that although tax legislation is set by Parliament, it is administered by the Inland Revenue and Customs and Excise as appropriate. The law is laid out in taxes statutes, which are regularly amended by the Finance Acts (FA) which follow each Budget, and Statutory Instruments which are introduced from time to time to correct mistakes, or make minor changes in, or add detail to, the law. In addition, there are many reported tax law cases, most of which concern interpretation of what the tax legislation actually means. Reference will be made to some of the more important sections and cases through the remainder of the chapter.

The Inland Revenue and Customs and Excise are therefore not responsible for making tax law, they merely interpret Parliament's intents. In recent years businesses have seen the need for constant rationalization and re-organization in order to maintain efficiency, and even the taxing authorities have not been immune from the current demand for efficient business operation. The Inland Revenue has therefore been going through its own revolution.

Allocation of responsibilities

It is now the responsibility of the taxpayer to assess how much tax is owed, and to pay it, without waiting for a demand from the Inland Revenue. It is has therefore become far more important for the taxpayer (and the taxpayer's agent) to calculate tax due, and arrange for it to be paid by the due date. The taxpayer should also keep sufficient records to convince an inspector that the correct amount of tax has indeed been paid.

In the new regime, the Inland Revenue's responsibilities are largely concerned with checking that the taxpayer is complying with the law. Inspectors of Taxes thus concentrate their time on performing spot checks on businesses to ensure that the correct amount of tax has been paid, and in conducting detailed investigations.

By making random inspections of businesses the inspectorate seeks both to satisfy itself that the correct income tax or corporation tax has been paid, and to verify the salary and other sums paid to staff, and the income tax and national insurance contributions deducted, as well as whether the correct amount of VAT has been paid over.

Some investigations are carried out at random, and others are undertaken where the Inland Revenue or Customs and Excise has reason to believe that the taxpayer may have understated his or her liability to income tax. These reasons will include evidence that taxpayers are living beyond their means (i.e. someone living in a large house, driving expensive cars, going on foreign holidays, while their income is too low to support such a lifestyle); comparisons with income in previous years; and information received from the public.

Apart from carrying out inspections and investigations, the inspectorate's work is entirely clerical, recording tax paid for each business and employee, and making any repayments or chasing any underpayments as the case may be.

Dispute resolution

Procedures are in place for resolving differences in interpretation between taxpayer and taxing body. The easiest and cheapest method to resolve a dispute is through the Commissioners. This is a body of independent people, employed on a part-time basis, to act as arbitrators, and most cases are resolved to the satisfaction of both parties at this stage.

Either party can normally appeal against the Commissioners' decision to the High Court, and thence to the Court of Appeal and the House of Lords. Going through this route is likely to be expensive, and is normally only followed where the amount of tax involved is significant and the matter contentious.

Case law, which is widely reported, helps establish the rules for other taxpayers, who can then determine whether the facts in their situations are similar to decided cases before deciding how far to proceed with the case. However a decided case may cease to be a precedent because subsequent legislation has changed the rules. On the other hand, as cases are decided according to the laws in force when the events under consideration occurred, a party's case may be determined according to law no longer in force at the time of the trial. Sometimes new legislation changes the rules precisely because judicial interpretations of the earlier laws have given them a meaning the legislature considers inappropriate.

Assistance for business

The Inland Revenue publishes extensive material on how to self assess, and how to operate a PAYE scheme, including booklets on such topics as statutory maternity pay, and statutory sick pay. It also runs courses to explain new innovations and changes, and operates help lines that business persons or employers can call if they come across a situation where they do not know what to do.

It is noteworthy that the employer is not paid for acting as collector and administrator for the tax deducted and paid over to the Inland Revenue through PAYE, and the responsibility can be quite onerous. The rules are also quite complicated, and it is easy to go wrong. Fines and penalties will be levied if the employer gets it wrong, while the employee is under no obligation to advise the employer if something has gone wrong.

THE VAT SYSTEM – FINES AND PENALTIES

Customs and Excise have much more wide-ranging powers than the Inland Revenue. They have to deal with drug trafficking and smuggling, and this is one reason why Customs and Excise were given the responsibility of administering VAT. Additionally, they were already heavily involved in imports and exports and were therefore ideally placed to charge VAT, where appropriate, on imports and exports.

The potential severity of the offences, explains why the penalties for VAT evasion are more harsh and the powers that Customs and Excise have to enforce compliance with the legislation are more extensive than those applicable for other tax offences. Most penalties are financial, but imprisonment is possible in some situations.

CORPORATION TAX

> Corporation tax shall be charged on profits of companies, (Income and Corporation Taxes Act 1988 s.6(1)).

Most of the rules regarding corporation tax come from the Income and Corporation Taxes Act (ICTA) 1988. Corporation tax is the main tax that a company will pay. It is a tax on the profits that a company makes, and is comparable to the income tax that an individual pays on his or her income.

Determining liability for corporation tax

> Section 74 of ICTA 1988 provides that 'in computing the amount of the profits or gains to be charged ... no sum shall be deducted in respect of ...' various expenses as detailed below.

It will first be necessary for the company to determine the profit made during a year, which will be from the profit and loss account prepared under the various accounting rules. In a simple world, the company would then be taxed on this profit figure.

However, (as s.74 demonstrates) the statute has decreed that accounting profit and taxable profit are not quite the same thing. The Inland Revenue has to be satisfied that the company has been totally honest in calculating certain parts of its profit acting in the knowledge that tax could be reduced by artificially reducing its profits. The statutory provisions also allow the Government to use tax as an incentive to persuade companies to act in a certain way, for example by encouraging them to invest in capital equipment by giving such expenditure favourable tax treatment.

Disallowable expenditure

Section 74 ICTA sets out the main types of expenditure not allowable for tax. The system therefore starts with accounting profit, as shown in the profit and loss account, and then the necessary adjustments are made, starting with additions back to profit, and then making certain deductions.

Section 74(1)(a) ICTA 1988 disallows 'any disbursements or expenses, not being money wholly and exclusively laid out or expended for the benefit of the trade'. This subsection has been interpreted very widely to disallow many expenses that might be considered by a business person to be genuine trade expenses, for example, a barrister's clothing in *Mallalieu* v *Drummond* [1983].

The statutory rules provide:

1 *Depreciation*: depreciation is not a cash flow. Depreciation is an arbitrary figure in the accounts, as companies may choose whichever rate/(s) they wish, for example 20 per cent straight-line or 25 per cent reducing balance basis. The basis chosen would directly affect the accounting profit. Depreciation is therefore not allowed for taxation, and is replaced by capital allowances (see below).

2 *Profit/loss on disposal of fixed assets*: the profit or loss on disposal is determined by the company's depreciation policy which we know to be arbitrary. Any profit or loss is therefore disallowed, and once again capital allowances will be given instead.

3 *Entertaining*: s.577(1)(a) provides that 'no deductions shall be made in computing profits or gains chargeable to tax under Schedule A or Schedule D for any expenses incurred in providing business entertainment.' Entertaining a company's staff is allowable, but entertaining anyone else is not. Therefore, while it may be considered that providing entertainment for a business's customers and suppliers is necessary in order to ensure favourable trading positions for a company, there can be no deduction for such expenditure. It could also be argued that there is a personal benefit in providing expenditure (e.g. taking a client/supplier out to dinner) and it would therefore fail the 'wholly and exclusively' test laid out above in s.74 ICTA.

4 *Fines and penalties*: where a company has been fined for failing to meet its legal obligations, the Inland Revenue will not compensate the company by reducing its tax liability. It does not matter whether the fine is for late payment of tax, or for any other reason, such as for breaching environmental regulations, or for parking.

5 *General provision for bad debts*: s.74(1)(j) disallows all debts except 'a bad debt', 'a debt or part of a debt released by the creditor wholly and exclusively for the purpose of his trade, profession or vocation', or 'a doubtful debt'. It is accepted that some customers will not pay the company the amount that they owe for their purchases, and the company will therefore make a loss. At the end of each accounting period, the company's accounting staff will consider which debtors will not pay, and make a specific provision against each one. This is allowable for tax deduction. However, if an organization makes a general provision (e.g. it supposes that 2 per cent of debtors will not pay) this will not be allowed for tax: this rule is to prevent organizations from making large provisions to reduce their taxation liability.

6 *Capital expenditure*: 'any capital withdrawn from, or any sum employed or intended to be employed as capital in, the trade, profession or vocation'. It is usual for companies to exclude capital expenditure from the profit and loss account, but if the company decides that it is appropriate to put capital expenditure through the profit and loss account, it will have to be added back to reach the taxable profit.

7 *Dividends from UK companies*: these have already been subjected to corporation tax, and it would be harsh to tax them again simply because the profits have been moved from one company to another. This is known as Franked Investment Income, where 'franked' means 'already subjected to Corporation Tax'.

Capital allowances

> where a person carrying on a trade has incurred capital expenditure on the provision of machinery or plant wholly and exclusively for the purpose of the trade, and in consequence of his incurring that expenditure, the machinery or plant belongs or has belonged to him, allowances and charges shall be made to and on him (Capital Allowances Act 1990 s.24).

Capital allowances, which are based on very strict calculation rules set out in the Capital Allowances Act (CAA) 1990, are given in place of depreciation and profits/losses on disposal of capital allowances. Not only do the rules prevent companies manipulating their profits, the rates can be changed by Parliament in order to persuade companies to invest in capital expenditure. For example, the 2000 Budget has introduced a 100 per cent profit deduction for certain expenditure on computers and computer equipment.

In order to qualify for capital allowances, the expenditure must come within the definition of plant and machinery. It is beyond the scope of this chapter to provide a detailed analysis of what would constitute plant and machinery, but it would include most fixed assets under the headings of plant and machinery, motor vehicles, fixtures and fittings, and equipment. The law is very vague as to what constitutes plant and machinery, and hence there is a lot of case law on this subject.

There have been numerous cases, the upshot of which are that capital allowances will be granted for expenditure which is functional, but not on expenditure which relates to setting. The leading case is *Yarmouth* v *France* (1887), in which it was determined that a horse could qualify as plant and machinery.

Other cases on this matter include the following. While it is only possible to give the briefest account of each of them here, it will be apparent that each made some contribution to the development of the meaning of the statutory words:

CIR v *Barclay Curle & Co Limited* (1969): A dry dock used to help in the repair of ships was plant, as it played an important role in enabling ships to be repaired.

Cooke v *Beach Station Caravans Limited* (1974): A swimming pool in a caravan site was plant, as it added to the enjoyment of the site.

Schofield v *R & H Hall Limited* (1975): A grain silo was plant because it enabled the grain to be moved.

Leeds Permanent Building Society v *Proctor* (1982): Display boards in the window of a building society were plant, as they served the function of enabling the building society to advertise its products and services.

Jarrold v *John Good & Sons Limited* (1963): Partitions were plant, so long as they were movable, and were regularly moved. This was because they were not part of the setting.

Cole Brothers v *Phillips* (1982): Specialist lighting in a shop was plant (e.g. in displays), but not general lighting. Specialist lighting encourages people to buy the products by making them look desirable.

Inland Revenue Commissioners v *Scottish and Newcastle Breweries Limited* (1982): A painted mural, and sea items such as an anchor, which create an ambience were plant, as this was what attracted people into the pubs.

St John's School v *Ward* (1974): A science laboratory in a school was not plant, as the laboratory played no direct role in providing science education, or in the experiments that took place. It merely provided a warm and dry setting for science lessons to take place.

Benson v *The Yard Arm Club Limited* (1979): A ship used as a floating restaurant was not plant, as the ship was simply the setting in which the restaurant functioned.

Dixon v *Fitch's Garage Limited* (1975): Canopies over the petrol pumps at a service station were not plant, as they only provided shelter for purchasers, and did not actually help in the transfer of petrol from pumps to cars.

Brown v *Burnley Football and Athletic Club* (1980): A football stand was not plant, as it had no bearing on a game of football.

Hampton v *Fortes Autogrill Limited* (1979): A false ceiling in a fast food restaurant was not plant.

Allowable expenditure

The expenditure is then divided into one of three main headings:

1 motor cars costing less than £12 000 (known as the *'Car pool'*) (CAA s.41);
2 motor cars costing more than £12 000, each one of which is kept separately (CAA s.34(1));
3 plant and machinery – broadly all other qualifying expenditure (CAA s.24(2)(a)(i)).

The annual allowance is then 25 per cent on the reducing balance basis (CAA s.24(2)(a)(i)), subject to the provision that each expensive motor car cannot be written down by more than £3000 per annum (CAA s.34(3)).

Disposal proceeds are deducted from the appropriate headings. For expensive motor cars, the calculation must now come to an end, and a balancing allowance or balancing charge is given so that the company has received allowances over the period of ownership exactly equal to the capital cost to the company of owning that car. (CAA s.24(5) and (6)).

In addition, in recent years, the Chancellor of the Exchequer has sought to encourage expenditure on plant and machinery (but not motor vehicles) by allowing a 40 per cent write-down in the year of acquisition (e.g. CAA s.22). In the 2000 Budget, the Chancellor also proposed a 100 per cent first year allowance on expenditure on computers and periphery equipment for small companies.

Expenditure on buildings will not qualify for capital allowances, which might appear strange, since this is likely to be a company's most expensive acquisition. Industrial Buildings Allowances, at the rate of 4 per cent on cost for buildings erected since November 1962 (2 per cent previously), are allowed on any building used for an industrial process (CAA ss.3–4). This is therefore aimed at factories and manufacturing processes, as offices and shops are specifically excluded from being able to obtain this particular allowance.

Rates of tax

Once the company has determined its taxable profit, it will be necessary to decide what rate of tax to apply. This depends on the size of the company, and size is determined by the company's profits. The rates are set each year by the Finance Act.

For the year ended 31 March 2001, trading companies will pay Corporation Tax at the following rates:

£0–£10 000	10%
£10 000–£50 000	22.5%
£50 000–£300 000	20%
£300 000–£1 500 000	32.5%
£1 500 000 upwards	30%

Due dates

Corporation tax is normally due 9 months and 1 day after the end of the accounting period. Therefore, if a company's year-end is 31 December 1999, the tax will be due by 1 October 2000. If it is paid late, even by one day, the company will be charged interest. (ICTA s.10(1)).

Companies whose profits are above £1 500 000 have to pay their tax in instalments during the year. The main purpose of this is to increase the government's cash flow. It will have to pay one-quarter of the total tax bill on three occasions, making three-quarters in total. The final payment will be a balancing payment, once the actual profits are known, to bring the payments on account up to the actual liability. The instalments are based on the company's own estimates of the tax liability for the year, and are due on the 14th day of the 7th, 10th and 13th months of the year, with the balancing payment due on the 14th day of the 16th month. This means that large companies are paying their tax far in advance of their smaller counterparts (TMA s.59E).

Section 11(4) TMA 1970 provides that 'the final day for delivery of any return ... shall be ... the first anniversary of the last day of the period to which the return relates'.

Tax rates run on financial years, which run from 1 April to 31 March. If a company's year-end does not coincide with this year, then it will have to use rates from two different financial years. Suppose that a company's year-end is 31 December 1999: it will then be taxed from January to March 1999 using the rates for the 1998/99 financial year, and from April to December 1999 using the 1999/2000 rates.

INCOME TAX

Introduction

If the business is operating as a sole trader or partnership, corporation tax will not apply, and the profits will be subjected to income tax.

The rules for calculating taxable profits are almost identical to the rules for corporation tax. The main difference concerns the money paid to the people running the business. For companies, payments to directors (which must be made under PAYE – see below) are allowable expenses in calculating the taxable profits.

Section 74(b) ICTA provides that 'any disbursement or expenses of maintenance of the parties, their families or establishments, or any sums expended for any other domestic or private purposes distinct from the purposes of the trade profession or vocation' are not allowable.

Year end

Fiscal years run from 6 April to 5 April, although in practice, the Inland Revenue is prepared to accept 31 March as being the year-end for tax purposes. A business can choose to have any year-end that it likes, which need not be a month end (although it almost always is).

Basis of assessment

The rules for allocating taxable profits, arising from a set of accounts, into tax years, in the business's early years are set out by ICTA s.61.

- In its first tax year, the owner is assessed on profits from the day the business started to trade until 5 April.
- In its second tax year, the owner is assessed on profits of a 12-month accounting period ending in that year. If there is no such accounting period, the first 12-months' profits are assessed.
- From the third year onwards, the assessment is based on profits for the 12-month period ending in that year (ICTA s.60).
- In the final year, the profits assessed are those made from the day after the profits assessed for the penultimate year, until the date of cessation (ICTA s.63). The owner may then deduct any profits assessed twice in the past (known as overlap profits) caused normally by some profits being taxed in both years 1 and 2 (ICTA s63A).

System for making tax payments:

- Section 8(1) TMA 1970 provides that a person may be required 'to make and deliver to the officer . . . a return containing such information as may reasonably be required in pursuance of the notice,' which means that a taxpayer may be required to complete and submit a tax return.
- Section 8(1)(a) TMA 1970 states that the deadline for filing the tax return is normally 'the 31st January next following the year of assessment.' E.g. the return for 1999/2000 is due by 31 January 2001.
- Section 9(1) TMA 1970 provides that 'Every return under section 8 or 8A shall include a self-assessment'. As well as filing the return, the taxpayer will need to calculate the amount of tax he or she is liable for that year.
- 'A person shall not be required to comply with subsection (1) above if he makes and delivers his return for a year of assessment on or before the 30th September next following the year' (TMA 1970 s.9(2)). If the owner wishes the Inland Revenue to calculate the tax due, the return must be filed by 30 September after the end of the tax year.
- 'The taxpayer shall be liable to a penalty which shall be £100' (TMA 1970 s.93(2)) for failure to deliver his or her tax return on time. The deadline is strictly enforced, and there are few acceptable excuses for failure.
- 'If the failure by the taxpayer to comply with the notice continues after the end of six months beginning with the filing date . . . the taxpayer shall be liable to a further penalty which shall be £100.' (TMA 1970 s.93(4)). Once the return is more than 6 months late, the Revenue can then start to press for more charges on a daily basis.
- 'the taxpayer shall be liable to a penalty of an amount not exceeding the liability to tax which should have been so shown' (TMA 1970 s.93(5)). The fine cannot be greater than the tax due under self-assessment, so that if the tax due is only £40, the fine cannot be more than £40.

- Self-assessment tax is paid in three instalments:
  1. 'the first on or before the 31st January in that year' (TMA 1970 s.59A(2)(a)): 50 per cent of last year's self-assessment liability.
  2. 'the second on or before the next following 31st July' (TMA 1970 s.59A(2)(b)): 50 per cent of last year's self-assessment liability.
  3. 'the difference shall be payable or repayable on or before the 31st January next following the year of assessment' (TMA 1970 s.59B(4)): the balance of tax due after deducting the first two instalments.

- Interest is charged automatically on all late payments (FA 1995 s.110):

   Where any of the tax remains unpaid on the day following the expiry of 28 days from the due date, the taxpayer shall be liable to a surcharge equal to 5 per cent of the unpaid tax (TMA 1970 s.59C(2)).

   Where any of the tax remains unpaid on the day following the expiry of 6 months from the due date, the taxpayer shall be liable to a further surcharge equal to 5 per cent of the unpaid tax (TMA 1970 s.59C(3)).

NATIONAL INSURANCE CONTRIBUTIONS

Self-employed people also have to pay two classes of National Insurance Contributions. The law here is provided mainly by the Social Security Contributions and Benefits Act 1992 (SSCBA).

- 'Every self-employed earner who is over the age of 16 shall be liable to pay Class 2 Contributions at the rate of £2.00 a week' (SSCBA 1992 s.11(1)). The trader can choose to pay this monthly by direct debit, or quarterly by cheque.
- 'Regulations may provide for an earner who is otherwise liable for Class 2 contributions in respect of employment as a self-employed earner to be excepted from the liability in respect of any period in which his earnings from such employment are, or are treated by the regulations as being, less than £3825 a tax year.' (SSCBA 1992 s.11(4)).
- 'A Class 4 contribution for any tax year shall be an amount equal to 7 per cent of so much of the profits . . . as exceeds £4385 and does not exceed £27 820' (SSCBA 1992 s.15(3)). It is paid together with income tax, as if it were part of the income tax liability.

PAY AS YOU EARN (PAYE)

This system is another reason for identifying whether those working for an organization have the status of employees (on the common law rules for identifying employees see the *Ready Mixed Concrete* case cited in Chapter 5 on Tort). However, the common law rules have in some situations been amended by regulations to ensure that some categories of worker (e.g. external examiners employed by universities) are classified as employees for taxation purposes.

Most employees are paid on a monthly basis, but the Inland Revenue also provides rules for payment of wages on a weekly or annual basis. The PAYE scheme is so designed that employees need have no contact with the Inland Revenue, unless they have other sources of income which have not been fully taxed.

The following are the major factors governing the operation of the system:

- The employer of employees is responsible for making deductions of Income Tax from employees' gross wages before making salary payments to them.
- Employees have different personal circumstances and their tax liability will vary accordingly. For example some are married: some are single. The age of the employee is also relevant (i.e. whether they are aged under 65, 65 to 74, or 74 plus), and these factors help to determine the amount of tax to be deducted (See Regulation 6 of IT (Employments) Regulations 1993 SI No. 1993/744).
- In order that the employer may collect the correct tax, without divulging too much information on each employee to the employer, each employee is given a coding number, the higher the coding, the less tax the employee will have to pay. The employee will be informed how that coding number is calculated, but the employer will only be given the number. This number will show how much pay the employee can receive tax-free over the course of the year (which runs from 6 April to 5 April). One-twelfth of this amount is then given to the employee each month over the year, and is called free pay (See Regulation 10 of IT (Employments) Regulations SI No. 1993/744).
- Income tax is calculated on a cumulative basis, that is, after each month, the total pay for the year to date is added up, and the free pay to date is deducted to arrive at taxable pay. (Regulation 14 of IT (Employments) Regulations SI No. 1993/744).
- Tables provided to the employer then enable the calculation of how much tax the employee should have paid to date on taxable pay for the year so far. By deducting tax already paid this year, the tax due for the month can be calculated.
- The tax tables assume that the employee will continue to earn the same amount throughout the tax year, but the system works reasonably well even for those whose pay may vary, perhaps because of bonuses or overtime. For employees who are on a constant salary, the tax deducted will be the same each month, varying only by a few pence caused by the rounding in the tax tables.
- The employer is responsible for paying tax deducted over to the Inland Revenue, usually on a monthly basis. Each PAYE month runs to the 5th, and the deductions are due by the 19th of that month. Therefore for the month from 6 May to 5 June, deductions taken from employees during this period must be paid to the Inland Revenue by 19 June (Regulation 40 of IT (Employments) Regulations 1993 SI 1993/744).
- The Inland Revenue is aware of the total amount of PAYE received from each company, but will not know how much has been deducted in respect of each employee. It will once again be the employer's responsibility to provide this information.
- 'The employer shall render a return to the inspector or, if so required, to the collector, not later than 44 days after the end of the year, in such form as the Board may approve or prescribe, containing the particulars specified in paragraph (2) in respect of each employee in respect of whom the employer was required at any time during the year to prepare or maintain a deductions working sheet in accordance with these Regulations' (Regulation 43 of IT (Employments) Regulations 1993 SI 1993/744). This means that shortly after the year-end of

5 April, the employer will have to produce form P60 for each employee who has worked for the business during the year. This will record full personal details of the employee (name, address, national insurance number), and the tax details (gross pay, income tax, and both types of national insurance contributions deducted). The P60 is a three-part form, with one copy going to the PAYE department of the Inland Revenue, a second copy going to the National Insurance department of the Inland Revenue, and the third copy going to the employee.

- Form P35 summarizes the details on the P60s for all employees, and shows the total income tax and national insurance contributions deducted and paid over. This will therefore immediately show if the company has underpaid any of its deductions for the year, and the Inland Revenue will be able to follow up such underpayments, with interest charges and legal action where appropriate.

- The penalty for failing to file these forms on time (by 19 May) is £50 per 50 employees (or part thereof) per month (or part thereof) late (TMA 1970 s.98). So if a company has 51 employees and is just over one month late, they will be fined £200.

- 'where in any year a person is employed in employment to which this Chapter applies and by reason of his employment there is provided for him, or for others being members of his family or household, any benefit to which this section applies; and the cost of providing the benefit is not (apart from this section) chargeable to tax as his income, there is to be treated as emoluments of the employment, and accordingly chargeable to income tax under Schedule E, an amount equal to whatever is the cash equivalent of the benefit' (ICTA 1988 s.154). Some employees will receive part of their pay in kind, rather than in cash, for example, company cars, private health care, or free accommodation. These benefits are still taxable, and it is the responsibility of the employer to report these to the Inland Revenue.

- Some employees change jobs during the year, and will be included within two (or more) different PAYE schemes. In order that the new employer has all the necessary information, the old employer will have to complete form P45 for the employee leaving. This form has four parts: one for the old employer's tax office; one for the employee; one for the new employer; and the final one for the new employer's tax office (Regulations 23 and 29–31 of SI 1993/744).

- The P45 will contain personal details of the employee (name, national insurance number), both tax offices (those of the old and new employers), total pay to date, total tax to date, and the tax coding number used. The new employer can then continue to deduct the correct amount of tax.

Employed or self-employed?

It is normally advantageous for a person to be considered as self-employed rather than an employee, at least from a tax viewpoint. Not only do the self-employed pay their tax later than employees, they are also normally able to deduct more expenses in calculating their taxable income.

The Inland Revenue has tried to enforce strict interpretations on the determination of a worker's status so that more people will be considered employees. It has announced this through a leaflet, IR 35.

VALUE ADDED TAX (VAT)

> 'Value added tax shall be charged in accordance with the provisions of this Act' (Value Added Tax Act 1994 s.1).

Most businesses will also be registered for VAT, if they make taxable supplies, and here again the company will be responsible for collecting VAT, and passing it on to Customs and Excise.

Companies tend to think that VAT is a very simple area, and consequently tend to allocate few resources to VAT planning. In fact, VAT legislation is extremely complicated, and the amounts involved can be very large, especially where land and buildings are involved. As a result, many companies have found themselves insolvent through their unexpected liability to Customs and Excise which could have been avoided if proper planning and thought had been brought to bear.

Rules governing liability for VAT

- A business will need to be registered if its taxable turnover in any 12-month period exceeds the threshold (currently £52 000), although it can choose to register even if it does not reach the threshold (Value Added Tax (VATA) 1994 s.3).
- Once registered, a company will have to account to Customs and Excise for all output tax (VAT on taxable supplies of goods and services made by the business) less recoverable input tax (VAT on purchases of goods and services made by the business).
- A company may wish to register voluntarily either because it does not want its business contacts to know how small it is, or maybe because most of its customers are VAT registered. The customers will be indifferent to the additional VAT charge (as they will be able to claim it back), but it will allow the company to reclaim some or all of its input tax which would otherwise be an expense (Schedule 1 of VATA).

Taxable and exempt supplies

Once registered, a company will have to charge its customers VAT on all its taxable supplies of goods and services. All supplies of goods and services are taxable unless they are exempted by VATA, which provides for twelve groups of goods and services to be exempted, including insurance and financial services.

Rates of VAT

If a supply is not exempt, it must be taxable, but there are currently three rates of VAT:

- The rate of 5 per cent applies only to the provision of fuel for domestic purposes, and this has little effect on most businesses (VATA s.2(1A)).
- The other two rates are 0 per cent and 17.5 per cent. Supplies which are zero-rated are detailed again in VATA and include most food, but if not so described as zero-rated, the supplies must be standard-rated.
- The current rate in all other cases is 17.5 per cent (VATA s.2(1)).

The company will need to charge VAT at the appropriate rate to the customer, and pay that amount over to Customs and Excise.

ACCOUNTING PERIODS

Accounting is normally performed on a quarterly basis, and the company has the right to choose which quarters to use, so long as the quarters finish at the end of a calendar month. Companies usually decide to align their VAT accounting periods with their accounting year-end, but this is not compulsory.

> Every person who is registered or was or is required to be registered shall, in respect of every period of a quarter or in the case of a person who is registered, every period of 3 months ending on the dates notified either in the certificate of registration issued to him or otherwise, not later than the last day of the month next following the end of the period to which it relates' (Regulation 25 Value Added Tax Regulations 1995 SI 1995/2518).

After the end of each quarter, the company will have one month to complete a one-page VAT return (form VAT 100), and send it to Customs and Excise together with the net VAT due for the quarter.

Customs and Excise role will be to process the VAT returns received from traders, and to visit traders on a regular basis to ensure that each trader has been correctly paying VAT.

Small businesses

A small business is one whose annual taxable turnover does not exceed £350 000. There are two concessions for small businesses, and both concessions are optional.

- Small traders are allowed to prepare one annual VAT return, instead of four. This is particularly useful where the company does not have an internal accountant, and uses a professional accounting firm instead. Rather than having to engage the accountant four times a year, the company can pass the accounting records at the end of the year to the accountant, who will prepare the annual VAT return at the same time as producing the company's financial statements and corporation tax return. In order that Customs and Excise do not lose out from a cash flow view, the company will be required to pay nine instalments, with each instalment being equal to 10 per cent of the total VAT liability of the previous year. The tenth instalment is due one month after the year-end, and the company will have to pay the balance of the VAT due (if any) at this time (Regulation 49–55 Value Added Tax Regulations SI 1995/2518).
- Small companies are allowed, if they choose, to account for VAT on a cash basis, that is they account for output VAT when it is received from customers, and may deduct input VAT when paid to suppliers. This is in contrast to the general position. Most companies are forced to account for VAT on an accruals basis. This means that they have to account for output VAT based on the date of the sales invoice, yet the customer may not pay for many months, long after the company has had to pay the VAT over to Customs and Excise. While they are also able to account for input VAT on the same basis, most small companies are very much at the mercy of their larger business contacts. This means that while they may have to pay suppliers very quickly, they may get paid very slowly (Regulation 57 to 65 Value Added Tax Regulations SI 1995/2518).

Large companies

Large companies (those where annual VAT liability exceeds £2 000 000) have to make payments on account of VAT during the quarter. The first instalment is due after the second month of the quarter, and the second instalment at the end of the quarter. Each instalment is 1/24th of the previous year's VAT liability. The final balancing payment is due on the normal due date – one month after the end of the VAT return quarter (VATA s.28).

Bad debts

If a company is not doing business on a cash basis, they may well have a VAT problem with bad debts. If they make a sale to a customer who, it transpires, will never pay them, the output VAT is still payable to Customs and Excise. In order to get the VAT back, the company will have to achieve the following:

1 wait at least 6 months from the date of the sales invoice;
2 write to the customer, and advise them that the VAT is to be reclaimed (VATA s.2(1A)).

This procedure is to ensure that Customs and Excise do not have to refund output VAT to the supplier, while simultaneously having to refund input VAT to the customer.

Disallowable input tax

No input VAT can be reclaimed on:

● entertaining, except staff entertaining (Regulation 5 of VAT (Input Tax) Order Regulations 1992 SI No. 1992/3222). This is one of the few cases where income tax and VAT legislation are similar.
● the purchase of a motor car, except for companies in the motor trade, which will include car dealers, taxi firms, and some car hire companies (Regulation 7 of VAT (Input Tax) Order Regulations SI 1992/3222).

Exempt input tax

Further complications arise where a company makes taxable and exempt supplies.

● No input VAT may be reclaimed on purchases which relate entirely to exempt supplies, while full input tax may be reclaimed on purchases which relate directly to taxable supplies (VATA s.26).
● There may be inputs which cannot be identified as relating directly to any sale, for example electricity charges, and the audit fee. A proportion of this input tax may be reclaimed according to the formula:

$$\text{Unattributable input tax} \times \frac{\text{taxable supplies (net of VAT)}}{\text{total supplies (net of VAT)}}$$

Any other reasonable formula may be used, but this is the standard.
● If the total disallowed input VAT is less than £7500 per annum, and less than 50 per cent of all input tax, then it may be reclaimed regardless on a *de minimis* basis.

International trade

Special rules also apply to imports and exports, and here it is important to determine whether the trade is with someone in another EU state, or with someone outside the EU.

- Where the goods are imported to the UK from outside the EU, VAT is charged usually at the point of entry into the UK, and the company will be able to reclaim this input VAT on their next VAT return in the usual way.
- Imports from the EU will not have VAT charged by the supplier. However, the UK company will have to record both output and input VAT on the purchase. While this has no affect on cash flow, it is an additional responsibility on the trader, and very easy to get wrong.
- Exports to outside the EU are largely outside the scope of VAT, and the few that are within VAT are zero-rated, so that no VAT is chargeable. This helps to make UK exports competitive with the rest of the world, as otherwise VAT would be effectively an additional cost to the overseas purchaser.
- Exports to the EU are zero-rated.

Penalties

Late registration fine

If a business fails to advise Customs and Excise that it should be registered for VAT, it will be fined a percentage of the VAT which should have been declared from the date that the business should have registered to the date that the business did register. The percentage depends on how late the business is, ranging from 5 per cent to 15 per cent. As the amount of VAT involved is likely to increase the longer times goes by, a business will still gain by admitting neglect early rather than trying to carry on the deception. Customs and Excise also have discretion to reduce the penalty where there are mitigating circumstances, and even the fact that the business approached Customs (rather than Customs catching them out), has been considered sufficient to reduce the penalty (VATA s.67).

Errors on the VAT return

It is extremely easy for a business to make a mistake on its VAT return. Where the error is small (less than £2000), the business is permitted to simply correct the next VAT return, and there will be no penalty. If the error is greater than £2000, it must be notified separately to Customs and Excise. In either case, where the business discloses the error, no penalties will be levied, and the only downside will be an interest charge for the larger errors (VATA s.63).

However, if the errors are spotted by Customs and Excise, which normally occurs on one of their regular control visits, then the repercussions may be more serious.

Criminal fraud

Being found guilty before a magistrate can lead to up to 6 months' imprisonment and a fine of up to £5000 or three times the tax evaded whichever is the greater. If the conviction is by a jury, the prison term can be up to 7 years plus an unlimited fine (VATA s.2).

Serious misdeclaration

This occurs where the VAT return is substantially inaccurate to avoid paying VAT or to obtain a VAT refund. A misdeclaration becomes serious if the amount of tax lost is greater than 30 per cent of the total input tax plus total output tax for the quarter concerned. The penalty is up to 15 per cent of the tax so lost (VATA s.64).

Default surcharge

Where a company fails to both file the VAT return and pay the resulting tax by the end of the month following the return period, this is known as a default. The only consequence of a first default is that the company is put on notice. If the company manages to complete all VAT returns and payments for the next year on time, the default notice is removed, and the matter is finished. The company could then be late again, with the only consequence that they would be put back on notice for another year. If the company makes a second default while on notice, the notice period is extended to a year from the date of the end of the new default period. In addition, a surcharge is levied as a percentage of the VAT on the late return ranging from 2 per cent to 15 per cent (VATA s.59).

CAPITAL GAINS TAX

> Tax shall be charged in accordance with this Act in respect of capital gains, that is to say chargeable gains computed in accordance with this Act and accruing to a person on the disposal of assets (Taxation of Chargeable Gains Act 1992 s.1(1)(1)).

The Taxation of Chargeable Gains Act 1992 (CGTA) provides that individuals have to pay tax on their capital gains, while companies will pay corporation tax thereon.

This may happen where a person or company owns a building or shares for example, and sells these for a profit. If this is in the course of the business (e.g. the company buys and sells shares as a trade) then normal income/corporation tax rules will apply as set out above. However, where it is not a part of the trade, but merely incidental thereto (perhaps where the company sells its factory), then the rules are different. In this case there will be liability for capital gains tax (for an individual) or corporation tax (for a company) on the gain, calculated according to the rules provided in CGTA.

Unindexed gain

The first stage in calculating a chargeable gain is to calculate the unindexed gain, and this is simply the difference between the purchase and selling price, after allowing for any costs the company may have incurred on acquisition or disposal of the asset (e.g. solicitor's fees) (CGTA s.38).

Inflation

> if on the disposal of an asset there is an unindexed gain, an allowance ("*the indexation allowance*") shall be allowed against the unindexed gain. (CGTA 1992 s.53).

If the asset has been owned for a period of years, part of this gain will probably be due to inflation. Indexation allowance may be deducted from the unindexed gain based on the Retail Price Index (RPI) for any period of ownership since March 1982 (when indexation was introduced). Where the asset was purchased before March 1982, the value of the asset at 31 March 1982 may be substituted for cost in calculating the unindexed gain shown above and the indexation allowance (CGTA 1992 s.55).

Rollover relief

If the company is selling its factory in order to help finance the purchase of a new, bigger factory it is likely to be facing a negative cash flow position even before the charge to corporation tax based on the capital gain. All of the proceeds from the sale of the old asset may be needed to purchase the new asset.

In such cases, the company may make use of rollover relief (CGTA s.152). Rollover relief allows the gain on the disposal of the old asset to be deferred until the new asset is sold. This is achieved by calculating the gain on the sale of the old asset as normal, and then deducting this gain from the cost of the new asset, thereby increasing the unindexed gain the company will make on the eventual sale of the new asset.

The legislation also recognizes that there may be a timing problem in replacing the asset. The new asset may be purchased up to 1 year before the old asset is sold, or up to 3 years afterwards, and rollover relief can still be applied. This means that the company can purchase the new factory and get it ready to move into while still operating out of the old factory, or can move into temporary accommodation having sold the old asset but before the new asset is ready for use.

The relief is available on a variety of assets, including land and buildings, space stations, and potato quotas. There is no need to replace like with like, so that rollover relief may be utilized where a building is sold, but the company reinvests in machinery.

However, the relief is only available in full if the company reinvests all of the proceeds. Where only some of the proceeds are reinvested, the amount held back is fully taxable now. Therefore, if a company sells one asset for £100 000, realizing a gain of £20 000, but only spends £95 000, the amount still held (£5000) is taxable immediately. The remaining gain of £15 000 may be rolled over.

Holdover relief

A further similar relief is available for plant and machinery, which is a wasting asset. Where the new asset is a wasting asset, the gain may only be held over until either the new asset is sold or scrapped, or the expiration of 10 years. This delays the payment of the tax for some while, but not indefinitely. This is known as holdover relief (CGTA s.154).

Of course, it would be possible to hold over a gain by replacing the first asset with plant and machinery, and then rolling over the gain by replacing that plant and machinery within 10 years with land and buildings.

CONCLUSION

Tax law is an extremely complex and ever-changing area. What is set out above constitutes a mere grain of sand in a desert full of rules and regulations, laws and cases, situations and exceptions. It is therefore advisable always to take professional advice. But it is just these points that make tax such an interesting area – both for study and practice.

PROGRESS TESTS

1 Who sets the rules for Income Tax and Value Added Tax, and who administers them?
2 What are the purposes of the Finance Acts?
3 Why does s.74 ICTA 1988 disallow certain items of expenditure that have been deducted in arriving at a business's trading profit?
4 Why are capital allowances given in place of depreciation?
5 What is meant by the function test?
6 How can a taxpayer avoid having to calculate the amount of tax he or she owes for a tax year?
7 What is the main advantage of the PAYE system?
8 Why do the Inland Revenue often try to show that a person is employed, rather than self-employed?
9 Why would a business choose to be registered for VAT, even though its turnover is below the threshold for registration?
10 What is the difference between exempt supplies and zero-rated supplies?
11 What is the purpose of the indexation allowance?

Part III
Coping with Change

Organizational change: Reconstructions and transfers of undertakings

13

Elvira Rubin and Malcolm Sargeant

RECONSTRUCTION OF THE COMPANY

What is a reconstruction of a company?

A reconstruction of a company is a transfer of the whole or part of a company in liquidation to a new company under the Insolvency Act 1986, or a reconstruction or transfer of a company to another company through a scheme of arrangement or amalgamation of companies under the Companies Act 1985.

- A reconstruction of the first type happens when a company voluntarily reorganizes itself into a structure more likely to survive commercially.
- Reconstruction of the second type could occur when two companies agree to unite, merging their assets and liabilities in order to operate more effectively. It could also occur where a company splits itself in half, so that each half can operate more effectively.
- A third type of reconstruction occurs where a single company re-allocates its share capital and hence the relative voting power of its shareholders or reaches a compromise with its creditors.
- A fourth type of reconstruction occurs where one company takes over another and merges with it.

Reasons for merger or take-over

Companies are merged or taken over for a variety of reasons, such as: guaranteeing a steady supply of raw materials or market for their output, diversification of activities, tax reasons, acquiring much needed assets or believing that the performance of the other company can be improved.

Legal and self-regulatory control

Legal

This may involve common law rules, British statutory rules under the Companies Act 1985, Insolvency Act 1986, Financial Services Act 1986 and Competition Act 1998, or under EC law.

Self-regulatory

Self-regulatory provisions are to be found in the City Code on Takeovers and Mergers, the Yellow Book of the Stock Exchange.

Official inquiry

The conduct of companies may also be investigated by:

- UK Competition Commission;
- Securities Investment Board
- other self-regulatory organizations;
- Bank of England;
- EC Commission.

Reconstruction or mergers under the Insolvency Act, s.110

Reconstruction

This procedure can be used by a company proposed to be or being wound up voluntarily by its members. It may however also, with the sanction of the court or the liquidation committee, apply to companies in a creditors' voluntary winding up. The aim here is to transfer or sell to the transferee company part or the whole of the transferor company's business or property in exchange for cash or shares, policies or other like interests in the transferee company. The result will be a new company with the same shareholders. There would be a merger if the assets of the transferor were sold to an existing company.

Merger

Section 110 may also be used to dissolve two companies and transfer their assets to a new company. The shares in the new company could be distributed to the respective shareholders of the former companies.

Procedure

The members of the transferor company pass a resolution that the company is to be wound up, appoint a liquidator and give him or her the authority to transfer the company's assets to the transferee company (either a new or existing company) in return for shares. These shares will then be distributed amongst the members of the old company as far as possible according to their shareholding in the old company, although the new shares may confer different rights.

Dissenting members who did not vote in favour of the resolution may, within 7 days, serve written notice on the liquidator asking him or her not to effect the scheme or to purchase their shares at an agreed price. The company may not be wound up until the dissenting shareholders and any creditors have been paid in cash. The drawback to this procedure is finding the required cash.

Reconstruction or merger under the Companies Act 1985, s.425

This procedure may be used with the approval of the company, for reaching a compromise or arrangement between the company and its creditors or members or class of members or for a take-over without going into liquidation.

Procedure

An application is made to the court by the company or any member or creditor to convene and direct the conduct of meetings of members, classes of members and creditors to consider the proposed scheme. Notices calling the meetings must be accompanied by explanatory information regarding the proposed scheme and a statement of the interests of the directors, such as possible compensation for loss of office. The scheme needs the approval by each class affected of a majority in number representing 75 per cent in value present and voting either in person or by proxy.

> In *N.F.U. Development Trust Ltd* [1972] BRIGHTMAN J said that the purpose of majority in number and value is to prevent a numerical majority with a small stake to outvote a minority with a large stake.

The court will only approve the scheme if it is satisfied

> the procedural requirements have been satisfied, there is no fraud on the minority and the scheme is one which can reasonably be supported by sensible business people (*Re Alabama, New Orleans, Texas and Pacific Junction Ply Co* [1891]).

Although the court cannot alter the terms of the scheme, it can correct mistakes. The scheme will be approved by an order of the court and will take effect only once a copy of that order has been sent to the Registrar of Companies. The scheme then has a binding effect on all parties concerned. The advantage of this procedure is its binding effect on *all*. It is assumed that the approval by the majority is sufficient evidence of its merits.

Where the scheme is 'for the purpose of, or in connection with, a scheme for reconstruction of any company or companies, or the amalgamation of any two or more companies, and under the scheme the whole or any part of the undertaking or the property of any company concerned in the scheme is to be transferred to another company' the court may make the following orders:

- transfer of assets of the transferee company;
- allotment of shares, debentures, policies or other similar interests to members or debenture holders of the transferor company;
- continuation of legal proceedings pending by or against a transferee company by or against a transferor company;
- dissolution of transferor company without winding up;
- provision to be made for dissentients from the scheme (s.427).

Reconstruction and mergers of public companies

Section 427A divides the proposed schemes of public companies into three categories. The court cannot sanction a scheme unless the additional requirements imposed by Schedule 15B of the Act have been complied with. What is needed is the approval by each class of members of the transferor as well as the transferee company.

Take-over and compulsory acquisition of shares

Take-over offer

'A takeover offer' means an offer to acquire all the shares, or all the shares of any class or classes, in a company (other than shares which at the date of the offer are already held by the offeror), being an offer on terms which are the same in relation to all shares to which the offer relates or, where those shares include shares of different classes, in relation to all the shares of each class (Companies Act 1985 s.428).

When the directors of a company (target company) do not favour a bid for the shares in their company the bidder (offeror company) may directly approach the shareholders and make a take-over bid for all the shares on the same terms for all the shares of the same class. This is called a 'hostile take-over'. But it may be a 'friendly' takeover as well. The offer to buy the shares in a company is 'investment advice' and subject to the provisions of the Financial Services Act 1986 and the Rules of the Stock Exchange.

The terms of the offer may be varied, should that be necessary to comply with the laws applying to shareholders in other jurisdictions. Some jurisdictions may not permit accepting consideration for shares in the form it is offered. Such a variation does not constitute a new offer for the purposes of this section.

'Shares already held by the offeror' includes also the shares not yet acquired but contracted for at the date of the offer and the shares already held or contracted for by an associate to the offer.

Compulsory acquisition

Once the bidder (offeror) has acquired the required percentage of shares (90 per cent threshold) within the prescribed time, that is within four months from the date of the offer, he may give notice to the remaining shareholders who have not accepted the bid that he desires to acquire those shares on the terms of the offer. The notice must be given within two months of having acquired the required 90 per cent acceptance. The bidder then 'shall be entitled and bound to acquire those shares on the terms of the offer' (Companies Act 1985 s.429).

The 90 per cent threshold

The 90 per cent threshold does not include the shares held by the bidder. It only applies to 90 per cent in value of the shares of any class to which the offer relates and not to the total share capital. If the bidder already holds say 15 per cent of the issued share capital he or she must acquire at least 90 per cent of the remaining 85 per cent.

Any shares the bidder has acquired after having made the offer for all the shares will be calculated within the required 90 per cent provided:

- the consideration given for those shares does not exceed the consideration stated in the offer; or
- if the consideration given exceeds that of the offer, the offer price must be raised to at least that level.

Two or more persons may join together to make a joint offer and may then jointly acquire the necessary acceptance of 90 per cent but must also have joint rights and joint liabilities.

Procedure for acquisition

Six weeks after the notice has been duly served on the dissenting shareholders the bidder must send to the target company:

- a copy of this notice;
- a transfer instrument executed on behalf of the shareholders by a person nominated by the bidder; and
- the consideration for the shares being acquired.

The consideration could be either cash or allotment of shares. The target company must keep the consideration on trust for the former shareholders and register the successful bidder as owner of the shares.

Untraceable shareholders

In the event that some shareholders cannot be traced the court may nevertheless allow the acquisition of the dissenting shareholders' interest provided the untraceable and accepting shareholders combined make up the 90 per cent threshold. The consideration of untraceable shareholders will, after 12 years, be paid into court.

Application by dissenting shareholders to block the acquisition

Within 6 weeks of having received the bidder's notice of the desire to acquire their shares, the minority may make an application to the court for an order:

- to prevent the acquisition; or
- to specify different terms for acquisition.

No acquisition by the bidder will take place until the court has disposed of the application. The applicant/s will only be liable for costs when the application was unnecessary, improper or vexatious, has caused unreasonable delay or his or her conduct was unreasonable. The burden of proof is on the applicant unless the bidder was an insider (see *Re Bugle Press Ltd* [1961]).

Right of minority shareholders to be bought out by offeror

If, at a time, when the offer is still open, the bidder has acquired 90 per cent of the shares (NB the 90 per cent now applies to the total share capital) any shareholder who has not accepted the offer may, in writing to the offeror, require him or her to acquire his or her shares. Since shareholders may not know when the 90 per cent have been acquired the offeror is obliged to inform those who have not accepted the offer of their right to require the offeror to acquire their shares. The shareholders have 3 months from the end of the offer to exercise this right (s.430A). Any disputes between offeror and shareholders will be settled by the court.

Notification of interests in shares in public companies

Shares may be held beneficially by nominees whose identity is not revealed in the share register. In order to avoid any unpleasant surprises of ownership, shareholdings must be disclosed to the company in certain circumstances.

Material interests

A 3 per cent interest of any class of voting shares must be disclosed to the company within 2 days of acquisition and thereafter, of any acquisition of a whole percent or a disposal to below 3 per cent.

Not-material interests

A 10 per cent interest, considered not-material must be disclosed as above; this would apply for example to holdings by investment managers. 'Interest in shares' is defined in the Act and includes 'an interest of any kind whatsoever in shares'.

Two or more persons acting together, otherwise known as a 'concert party', are treated together. If one of them acquires or disposes of an interest in shares it is treated as an acquisition or disposal of others in the party. Public companies have a statutory right to require that the identity of beneficial owners be revealed (Companies Act 1985 ss.198–220).

City Code on Takeovers and Mergers

> The Code and the panel operate principally to ensure fair and equal treatment of all shareholders in relation to takeovers. The Code also provides an orderly framework within which takeovers are conducted. The Code is not concerned with the financial or commercial advantages or disadvantages of a takeover. These are matters for the company and its shareholders. Nor is the Code concerned with those issues, such as competition policy, which are the responsibility of the government'. (City Code on Takeovers and Mergers, Introduction).

This is a self-regulatory code of conduct for application during take-overs and mergers.

The actual take-over bids are regulated by the law of contract. The Companies Act itself does not contain any provisions for the conduct of take-over bids but the Code does. The Code was first formulated in 1968 on the initiative of the Stock Exchange to prevent suspicious behaviour during take-overs and mergers.

Administration of the Code

The Code is administered by a *Takeover Panel* instituted by the Bank of England. Its 18 members, appointed by the Governor of the Bank of England, include practitioners as well as representatives of major city institutions, such as the Stock Exchange. The day-to-day administration lies with the 'Executive' under a Director General. The full panel meets only for appeals against decisions by the executive. It is only possible to appeal to an Appeal's Committee against the Panel's decisions if disciplinary actions are proposed or if the Panel's jurisdiction is questioned.

The function of the Executive was explained in the following case.

In *R* v *Panel on Take-overs and Mergers, ex parte Guinness Plc* [1989] 'It is the executive which takes the lead in examining the circumstances of take-over bids and, if thought necessary, referring them to the Panel for consideration and adjudication according to the rules ... It acts as a sort of fire brigade to extinguish quickly the flames of unacceptable and unfair practices'

Legal position of the Panel

Since the Panel is a non-statutory body its decisions do not have the force of law. That they are nevertheless open to judicial review has been established:

The panel is an unincorporated association without legal personality. It has no statutory, prerogative or common law powers and it is not in contractual relationship with the financial market or with those who deal in the market ... Lacking any authority de jure, it exercises immense power de facto by devising, promulgating, amending and interpreting the City Code on Take-overs and Mergers, by waiving or modifying the application of the code in particular circumstances, by investigating and reporting upon alleged breaches of the code and by the application or threat of sanctions. These sanctions are no less effective because they are applied indirectly and lack a legally enforceable base ... The issue is thus whether the historic supervisory jurisdiction of the Queen's courts extends to such a body discharging such functions, including some which are quasi-judicial in their nature ... The Panel is without a doubt performing a public duty and an important one ... The rights of citizens are indirectly affected by its decisions ... At least in its determination of whether there has been a breach of the code, it has a duty to act judicially and it asserts that its raison d'etre is to do justice between one shareholder and another ...

I wish to make it clear beyond a peradventure that in the light of the special nature of the panel, its functions, the market in which it is operating, the time scales which are inherent in that market and the need to safeguard the position of third parties, who may be numbered in thousands, all of whom are entitled to continue to trade upon an assumption of the validity of the panel's rules and decisions, unless and until they are quashed by the court, I should expect the relationship between the panel and the court to be historic rather than contemporaneous (SIR JOHN DONALDSON, MR in *R* v *Panel on Take-over and Mergers, ex parte Datafin Plc* [1987]).

And it was later stated in *R* v *Panel on Takeovers and Merges, ex parte Guinness Plc* [1989]:

And when it comes to disciplinary action by the Panel, which necessarily will be taken in retrospect and with all due deliberation, the court will find itself in its traditional position of protecting the individual from any abuse of power.

Sanctions for breaches of the code

Those who have acted in disregard of the Code may find themselves severely criticized. An important function of the Panel is to supervise the professional conduct of those involved in the securities industry. Any breaches of the code may result in them being reported to other self-regulatory bodies of the securities industry and they may be denied access to the facilities of the securities markets in the UK.

The Panel, however, may and does impose financial penalties as was shown in the Guinness case. Here a false market in the offeror's shares was created and the Panel ordered the offeror company to compensate the shareholders of the target company.

The scope of the Code

The Code applies to public companies and to certain classes of private companies:

- those who were listed on the Stock Exchange during the previous 10 years;
- those who have made offers of shares to the public through advertising;
- those whose shares have been subject to marketing arrangements of a recognized Stock Exchange;
- those who have filed a prospectus for the issue of shares.

It must be observed by all those involved in the merger or take-over.

The parties involved are

- offeror company (bidder);
- offeree company (target);
- shareholders of both companies;
- merchant bank;
- solicitors;
- stockbrokers;
- accountants.

The Code consists of

- ten general principles and
- 38 specific rules.

Its main purpose as stated in the general principles is:

- all shareholders of the same class of shares of the offeree company must be treated equally and fairly;
- all shareholders should have the opportunity to decide whether or not to accept the offer.

Duty of directors

The boards of directors of both offeror and offeree companies, and their advisers have a duty to act in the best interests of their respective shareholders. Consequently they must exercise their power of control in 'good faith' and not to the oppression of the minority and must not create a false market in the companies' securities. Shareholders must be given all the relevant information and sufficient time to be able to make up their minds. Shareholders must be informed at once, by a notice in the press, of a serious intention to make a take-over bid. The timing of such notices is crucial; early announcement may result in a withdrawal of the offer, one made too late may give rise to insider dealing. The announcement has to be made by the target company and must contain the terms of the offer. If a formal offer is not made to the target company within 28 days of the notice of intention to make a bid the Panel may ask for explanations in the delay and may enforce the making of the offer. The issue of 'Insider dealing' is addressed by precluding anyone other than the offeror, with price sensitive information, from dealing or recommending dealing, in the offeree's shares between the time of the take-over offer and the public announcement.

Mandatory offer

Anyone who acquires 30 per cent of the voting rights of a public company or anyone, who, together with others, holds no less than 30 per cent but no more than 50 per cent of the total voting rights, wishing to make an offer must make a cash offer to acquire all the equity shares in the company. The price that must be offered for these shares is the highest price paid during 12 months preceding the time when that holding reached 30 per cent. A mandatory bid may only be conditional on achieving a 50 per cent acceptance and lapsing when referred to the relevant competition authorities. Mandatory offers are relatively rare.

Voluntary offer

The majority of offers fall into this category. Here, conditions other than those for mandatory offers may be introduced. For example, the bidder might want to make the bid conditional on achieving a higher percentage of acceptance, approval by the shareholders or some other condition. A bid becomes 'unconditional' once the required acceptance level and/or other conditions are met.

Conduct during the offer

All shareholders must receive the same information in sufficient time to enable them to reach a properly informed decision. All documents from the board of the offeror and offeree companies must be prepared to the same standard of care as is required for a prospectus. The board of the offeree company, before giving any advice to its shareholders, must consult with independent advisors. Any recommendations, by the board of the target and bidder company, made to the shareholders must be in the interest of the shareholders – who are now owed a duty of care – and not in their own personal interest. In case of rival bids the shareholders must be free to choose the best offer. The directors of the target company may not in any way frustrate a bona fide bid such as by increasing the share capital, disposing of the company's assets or entering into any contracts otherwise than in the ordinary course of business.

Timing of the offer

The posting day of the offer document (which must occur within 28 days of announcement of interest in making an offer) is deemed to be day one of the offer.

Within 14 days of receipt of the offer, the board of the target company must provide their shareholders with the relevant advice. The offer must remain open for at least 21 days. Any amendments must be made within the first 46 days and offers close after 60 days. Consideration for the offer (cash or shares or a choice between the two) must be given within 14 days of it becoming unconditional. An offer that has not reached the required level of acceptance may not be repeated within the following 12 months. The Panel may, under certain circumstances, grant exceptions to this rule.

Competition policy

A merger of companies may put these companies into an extremely strong position in the market, giving them an unfair advantage due to their newly gained strength, especially if they now constitute a monopoly. Thus distortion of competition may occur. To ensure that every player in the market has a fair chance and the public is not unfairly disadvantaged, mergers may be subjected to investigations by the competition authorities, either at domestic level or EC level.

United Kingdom dimension

> In a merger inquiry the Commission is asked to investigate and report on whether a merger situation exists or is in contemplation and, if so, whether it operates or may be expected to operate against the public interest. If there is an adverse public interest finding, the Commission may recommend remedies to the Secretary of State's consideration.
>
> The main parties (those persons most likely to be seriously affected by the outcome of the investigation) to an inquiry, i.e. those most directly affected by the outcome, such as the parties to a merger, will be asked to provide detailed information about their activities, often by means of a questionnaire. Questionnaires may also be sent to other interest parties. In some inquiries expert consultants may be commissioned to undertake surveys or other work relevant to the investigation and the main parties are consulted when this is done (Commission's Chairman Guidelines, 7 February 2000).

The relevant Act used to be the Fair Trading Act 1973. This Act has now been repealed and was replaced on 1 March 2000 by the Competition Act 1998. The former investigating authority, the 'Monopolies and Mergers Commission', has been dissolved and is replaced by the 'Competition Commission'.

Any actual or prospective mergers are under the scrutiny of the Secretary of State for Trade and Industry and the Director General of Fair Trading. Upon reference of a merger being made, the Competition Commission investigates the proposed or actual merger on the basis of whether or not it is against 'public interest'.

If the Commission's report is adverse:

- the Secretary of State may make orders to remedy the situation;
- the Director General of Fair Trading may seek to take an undertaking from the affected parties to eliminate the monopoly situation on a voluntary basis.

Investigations are normally dealt with within 3 months.

EU dimension

Cross-border mergers with a Community dimension may become subject to investigation by the European Commission under the provisions of the Council Regulation 4064/89, as amended by Council Regulation (EC) 1310/97 according to fixed criteria and thresholds. Qualifying mergers must be pre-notified to the Commission within one week of the agreement or announcement of the bid. A decision is normally reached within one month but may take up to four. Under certain circumstances the member state may intervene.

European Economic Interest Grouping (EEIG)

This is a creation of the EC and is a new legal form for cross-frontier cooperation between individuals, companies, firms and other legal bodies to facilitate or develop the economic activities of its members. Its existence is based on a contract between the members of the grouping. In the UK an EEIG has been given corporate status with a separate legal personality but with unlimited liability. It needs to be registered and is subject to a number of disclosure requirements. The management is in the hands of one or more persons, appointed either by the contract or the members. The authority of the manager is based on principles of agency law.

TRANSFERS OF UNDERTAKINGS

> a relevant transfer shall not operate so as to terminate the contract of employment of any person employed by the transferor in the undertaking or part transferred but any such contract, which would otherwise have been terminated by the transfer shall have effect after the transfer as if originally made between the person so employed and the transferee (Transfer of Undertakings (Protection of Employment) Regulations 1981, regulation 5(1)).

The purpose of the Transfer of Undertakings (Protection of Employment) Regulations 1981 (SI 1981/1794; (TUPE)) is the protection of employees' contracts of employment when there is a change of employer.

The result is that those who are protected by the Regulations have their whole employment relationship transferred when there is a relevant transfer. It is as if they originally agreed their contract of employment with the new employer.

The TUPE Regulations are the result of the Acquired Rights Directive (Directive 77/187). This Directive had its derivation in the Community's Social Action Programme of 1974. There was a concern that the development of the common market, and the subsequent internal market, would lead to important changes in employment patterns within the Community. There would be an increasing number of amalgamations and take-overs as industry and commerce became more European and international, rather than just national based. This would have consequences for the workers involved in these enterprises.

In order to make this change more acceptable, the European Commission put forward a number of proposals for safeguarding employee rights. These concerned the protection of workers with insolvent employers: rules on consultation in collective redundancy situations; and the protection of the rights of employees who experienced a change of employer. This latter proposal became the Acquired Rights Directive, intended to transfer the contracts of employment and the employment relationship of workers where there was a transfer of the undertaking, business or part of a business for which they worked. The Directive has been amended (by Directive 98/50), but the effect of these amendments are unlikely to be felt in the United Kingdom until the second half of 2001.

Who is protected by the TUPE Regulations?

In *Foreningen Arbejdsledere i Danmark* v *A/S Danmols Inventar* (sometimes referred to as *Mikkelson*) the Court of Justice stated that 'It follows that Directive 77/187 may be relied upon only by persons who are, in one way or another, protected as employees under the laws of the Member State concerned. If they are so protected, the directive ensures that their rights arising from a contract of employment or an employment relationship are not diminished as a result of the transfer'.

The Acquired Rights Directive extends those national laws that already exist for the protection of employees to include also protection against dismissal by reason of a transfer. There is no intention to create any protection for other groups of workers. In the United Kingdom this means that, according to Regulation 8(1) of the TUPE Regulations:

> Where either before or after a relevant transfer, any employee of the transferor or the transferee is dismissed, that employee shall be treated for the purposes of Part X of the 1996 [Employment Rights] Act ... as unfairly dismissed if the transfer or a reason connected with it is the reason or principal reason for his dismissal.

It seems, therefore, that there is a strict interpretation and that only those employees with a contract of employment will be protected by the Regulations. Those working under a contract for services, such as self-employed workers and consultants, will not receive any protection with regard to employment protection during a transfer. They may, however, have other recourse against the transferor if their contracts have been breached.

The conclusion is, therefore, that only those workers who are currently treated as employees, and who receive employment protection under existing national laws, will be protected by the TUPE Regulations and if such employees are dismissed for reasons connected to a relevant transfer, they will be treated as being unfairly dismissed.

What is a relevant transfer?

> This Directive shall apply to the transfer of an undertaking, business or part of a business to another employer as a result of a legal transfer or merger (Article 1(1) Acquired Rights Directive).

In order for employees to be protected by the TUPE Regulations there needs to be a relevant transfer in terms of the Regulations.

There is no further definition of what constitutes a 'transfer' or what constitutes an 'undertaking, business or part of a business'. The TUPE Regulations, in Regulation 2(1), offer the following as a definition of a 'relevant transfer':

relevant transfer means a transfer to which these Regulations apply and transferor and transferee shall be construed accordingly.

Undertaking is defined as including 'any trade or business'. As a result of the lack of adequate definitions the matter has been the subject of interpretation by the courts and especially by the European Court of Justice. The Court of Justice has been given the freedom to interpret the Directive liberally and, for a time, widen its scope of application in a way not altogether expected by its authors.

In Case C 144/87 *Berg and Busschers* v *Besselsen* the Court of Justice held that the Directive applied as soon as a 'change occurs of the natural or legal person operating the undertaking who, in that capacity, has obligations *vis-à-vis* the employees employed in the undertaking, and that it is of no importance whether the ownership of the undertaking has been transferred'.

The test, therefore, is whether there has been a change in the natural or legal person running the operation, as in a change of contractors or being merged into a larger organization. Actual ownership is not important, so merely transferring the shares in an organization will not be enough.

The types of situations in which there may be a relevant transfer of an undertaking, include:

- *Going concern transfers* – these include the transfer of a business which is then continued as a business entity or becomes part of a much larger business. This will also include the transfer of 'non-business' concerns, such as charitable bodies.
- *Insolvency transfers* – these are one of the commonest type of transfer and occur when an undertaking becomes insolvent and its business is disposed of by an administrator; see *Kerry Foods Ltd* v *Creber*.
- *Licence transfers* – these concern the transfer of a business via a licence or franchise and where one holder of a licence or franchise transfers that licence or franchise to another person.
- *Public service transfers* – these are about the applicability of the Regulations to the public sector, especially concerning outsourcing of activities by the government.
- *Part transfers* – these take place when an undertaking transfers part of its operations to another undertaking.

Spijkers

the decisive criterion for establishing the existence of a transfer within the meaning of the Directive is whether the entity in question retains its identity.

The case of Case 24/85 *Spijkers* v *Gebroeders Benedik Abattoir* is perhaps the seminal case for defining the approach to be adopted in deciding what constitutes a relevant transfer. The case was a reference from the Dutch Supreme Court and concerned an abattoir that was sold by a company which became insolvent. The abattoir was closed for a period and Mr Spijkers was not employed by the new owners. The Court of Justice looked at the purpose of the Acquired Rights Directive and concluded that its purpose was to ensure the continuity of existing employment relationships. It then stated the approach (cited above) that has been followed extensively in subsequent decisions in the Court of Justice and in the UK courts.

Thus, if the operation that is transferred is an identifiable entity before and after the transfer then a relevant transfer is likely to have taken place. It is difficult to conceive, in retrospect, how such a definition could not have been held to apply to most outsourcing situations. The Court of Justice then gave further guidance as to factors that would help in the decision as to whether a transfer had taken place. It was necessary to take all the factual circumstances of the transaction into account, including

- type of undertaking or business in question;
- transfer or otherwise of tangible assets such as buildings and stocks;
- value of intangible assets at the date of transfer;
- whether the majority of staff are taken over by the new employer;
- transfer or otherwise of customers;
- degree of similarity between activities before and after the transfer;
- duration of any interruption in those activities.

The Court of Justice stated that each of these factors was only part of the assessment. One had to examine what existed before the transfer and then examine the entity after the change in order to decide whether the operation was continued. This helpful clarification proved to be a stepping stone to a series of cases that further defined and expanded the applicability of the Directive.

In Case C 209/91 *Rask and Christensen* v *ISS Kantineservice* the Court of Justice considered a situation where a company had outsourced its internal catering operation. The arrangement was that the company, Philips A/S, would pay the contractor a monthly fee as well as providing the premises, equipment, electricity and various other services. Mrs Rask and Mrs Christensen were two of the catering workers who were taken over by ISS, the contractor. Some of their conditions of employment were changed against the wishes of the employees. They were dismissed and subsequently claimed that their contracts of employment were protected by the fact that a relevant transfer of an undertaking had taken place.

The Court of Justice relied upon the decision in *Spijkers* and the various factors that had been listed in that case. It also held that these were only single factors and there had to be an overall judgment as to whether a transfer had taken place. It decided that, even though the activity transferred was ancillary to the company's main business, it was still capable of being a relevant transfer. It was argued that control still rested with the company, for example on price fixing, and that all that was being transferred was a service which could not be called an 'undertaking' within the meaning of the Directive. The Court responded by stating that the fact that it was an ancillary service, and only a transfer of a service, did not stop it being a relevant transfer because the decisive criterion, as in *Spijkers*, was whether the business retained its identity.

In Case 29/81 Dr *Sophie Redmond Stichting* v *Bartol* [1992] this interpretation also meant that the transfer of the task of looking after drug dependants of Surinamese ethnic origin in the Netherlands from one charitable body to another was also an event in which the entity retained its identity and thus was a relevant transfer.

Schmidt

Case C 392/92 *Schmidt* v *Spar und Leikhasse der Fruheren Amter Bordesholms* was a case concerning one cleaner in one branch of a bank. The cleaning work was put out to contract and the contractor made some minor changes to Mrs Schmidt's contract of employment. The Court relied upon *Spijkers, Sophie Redmond* and *Rask* to decide that a transfer had taken place. The Court concluded that the Directive could be applied to a situation 'in which an undertaking entrusts by contract to another undertaking the responsibility for carrying out cleaning operations which it previously performed itself, even though, prior to the transfer, such work was carried out by a single employee.'

This approach of the Court of Justice probably reached its apex in the *Schmidt* case. The size of the contract was not the issue, but the fact that an economic entity retains its identity is of importance.

New doubts were subsequently raised by a number of decisions of the European Court of Justice imposing restrictions on the scope of the Directive.

The case of Case C 48/94 *Ledernes Hovesorganisation, acting for Rygaard* v *Dansk Arbejdsgiverforening, acting for Sto Molle Akustik* [1995] concerned the transfer of work between contractors on a construction site. The work concerned had a limited duration before completion. The Court of Justice introduced a new test to show that there had not been a relevant transfer. The test presupposed that 'the transfer relates to a stable economic entity whose activity is not limited to performing one specific works contract'. It did not appear to be a problem for the Court that one could equally apply this definition to a term contract for cleaning a bank branch office, as in *Schmidt*, or a term contract for providing in-house catering facilities, as in *Rask*.

The *Rygaard* decision concerned the transfer from one contractor to another of uncompleted building work and was specific to the particular facts. It was, however, a precursor to the far more restrictive decision in Case C 13/95 *Süzen* v *Zehnacker Gebaudereinigung GmbH Krankenhausservice*.

Süzen

The *Süzen* decision concerned a second-generation competitive tender for a school-cleaning contract. The Court of Justice considered whether a transfer of an undertaking had taken place and whether one could distinguish between an entity and an activity. The transfer of an activity only may not be a relevant transfer. The Court concluded:

The Directive does not apply to a situation in which a person who had entrusted the cleaning of premises to a first undertaking terminates his contract with the latter and, for the performance of similar work, enters into a new contract with the second undertaking, if there is no concomitant transfer from one undertaking to the other of significant tangible or intangible assets or taking over by the new employer of a major part of the workforce, in terms of their numbers and skills, assigned by his predecessor to the performance of the contract.

This case appeared to state that if there were no transfer of assets, then there needed to be, at least, a transfer of the major part of the workforce in terms of their numbers and skills. Although the effect of this decision was watered down somewhat by Case C 127/96 *Francisco Hernandez Vidal SA* v *Gomez Perez* it still led to different courts in the United Kingdom giving apparently conflicting judgments.

> In *Betts* v *Brintel Helicopters* [1997]-, which applied the *Süzen* decision in the Court of Appeal, it was stated that 'the decision in *Süzen* does represent a shift of emphasis, or at least clarification of the law, and that some of the reasoning of earlier decisions, if not the decisions themselves, may have to be re-considered'.

In the *Betts* case there was a change of contractors supplying helicopter ferrying services to North Sea oil rigs. The new contractor had neither taken on any of the transferor's employees nor any of their assets. Applying *Süzen* the Court of Appeal decided that there was no relevant transfer.

> In contrast, the Court of Appeal, in *ECM Ltd* v *Cox* [1999], decided that, in a case concerning the transfer of a car delivery contract where there was also no transfer of assets or employees, that there was a relevant transfer. In this case they were concerned that no one was taken on in order to try and get round the Regulations.

Were the applicants employed in the undertaking immediately before the transfer?

> a relevant transfer shall not operate so as to terminate the contract of employment of any person employed by the transferor in the undertaking or part transferred (Regulation 5(1) TUPE).

The result is that the contract is transferred to the new employer and it is as if that contract was first agreed with that new employer. According to Regulation 5(3), however, this only applies to those persons employed in the transferred undertaking immediately before the transfer.

The question here is whether it is possible to dismiss people before the time of the transfer and argue that they were, therefore, not employed at the time of the transfer. If they were not employed at the time of the transfer then there would be no obligation to transfer their contracts of employment. This was tested in the Court of Appeal.

> In *Secretary of State for Employment* v *Spence* [1986] the workforce of an insolvent company was dismissed 3 hours before the transfer took place. The Court held that the contracts of employment of the workforce were not subsisting at the time of the transfer and so were not protected.

Subsequently:

> in *Litster v Forth Dry Dock & Engineering* [1989] the House of Lords distinguished *Spence* on the grounds that the dismissals were not in connection with the transfer. Here the old owners agreed with the new owners to dismiss the workforce one hour before the transfer, so that they were not employed at the time of transfer and protected by Regulation 5(3). The House of Lords found the argument that they were not employed at this time to be unconvincing and relied on Case 101/87 *Bork* at the European Court of Justice.

In *Bork* the Court of Justice considered the closing and subsequent re-opening of a beech wood veneer factory where there was a gap of 8 days between closure and opening. The conclusion was, however, that the dismissals were by reason of the transfer which was not permitted by Article 4(1) of the Acquired Rights Directive. As the dismissals were unfair in terms of the Directive, the workforce were considered as being still employed with the result that their contracts of employment should have been transferred. In *Litster* the House of Lords followed this approach and construed Regulation 5(3) as applying:

> to a person employed immediately before the transfer *or who would have been so employed if he had not been unfairly dismissed before the transfer for a reason connected with the transfer* (emphasis added).

Economic, technical or organizational reasons

> The transfer of an undertaking, business or part of a business shall not in itself constitute grounds for dismissal by the transferor or the transferee. This provision shall not stand in the way of dismissals that may take place for economic, technical or organisational reasons entailing changes in the work force (Acquired Rights Directive, Article 4).

The words 'economic, technical or organisational reasons (ETO reasons) entailing changes in the work force' are repeated verbatim in Regulation 8(2). Thus a dismissal that can be justified for an ETO reason entailing changes in the workforce will not be stopped by a transfer of an undertaking. It will not be an unfair dismissal and will be held to be a 'substantial reason of a kind to justify the dismissal' as in the Employment Rights Act 1996 s.98(1).

The words have been considered in a number of cases.

> *Berriman* v *Delabole Slate Ltd* [1985] concerned a quarryman in Cornwall working in a quarry which was transferred to a new employer. He was offered employment at a lower rate of pay in order to bring his earnings into line with their other employees. The Court of Appeal subsequently ruled that standardization of pay was not an ETO reason entailing changes in the workforce. The objective needs to be to achieve changes in the workforce and not merely the standardization of pay rates.

The possible constructive dismissal of one employee could not be construed as such a change.

> In *Wheeler* v *Patel,* [1987] Mrs Wheeler was dismissed by the transferor and not employed by the transferee. The dismissal was held to be to obtain a better price for the business, so an economic reason was claimed. The Employment Appeal Tribunal did not accept this because the terms economic, technical or organizational should be considered together, rather than as separate factors.

> In *Trafford* v *Sharpe and Fisher* [1994] an individual was dismissed because the new owners of a company wanted to reduce numbers. The dismissal was held to be an economic reason entailing changes in the workforce. The Employment Appeal Tribunal stated that the 'rights of workers not to be dismissed on the transfer of an undertaking must not stand in the way of dismissals which take place for economic

reasons entailing changes in the workforce. In such cases the rights of workers may be outweighed by the economic reasons'.

This shows a somewhat more relaxed approach than was apparent from earlier cases.

In *BSG Property Services* v *Tuck* [1996] the company won a contract in a competitive tender to provide Mid-Bedfordshire District Council with housing maintenance services. Two days earlier the Council dismissed its housing maintenance staff for reasons of redundancy. The company had tendered on the basis of using self-employed staff to do the work. This method of working had led the parties to conclude that there was no transfer and that, in any case, there was an ETO reason entailing a change in the workforce, namely the change to self-employed status. The Employment Appeal Tribunal dismissed this argument and concluded that there was no ETO reason. They stated that when looking at the reason for the dismissals, one needed to look at them at the time they took place. There may have been a subsequent re-organization but, at the time of the dismissals, the reason for those dismissals was the transfer and not any ETO reason.

If the customer makes a decision that, as part of a tendering exercise, the number of employees working for the contractor should be reduced, then this has been held to be an ETO reason and not because of the transfer, as in *Whitehouse* v *Chas Blatchford* [1999].

The problem is, therefore, to show that the dismissals are for an ETO reason entailing changes in the workforce and are not for a reason connected to the transfer.

When taking on a contract and a group of employees it is not always the case that a transferee wishes to employ all of those previously employed by the transferor. As the *Wilson* v *St Helens* [1998] case shows it is possible to re-organize or, possibly, reduce the number of employees involved in a transfer, providing the reason for the dismissal is not connected to the transfer. It is often not easy to separate the reasons for dismissals in order to show that they were for another reason. Nor is it necessarily possible for the transferee to avoid responsibility for actions carried out by the transferor.

Consultation

In *Kerry Foods* v *Creber* [2000] the Employment Appeal Tribunal approved the approach of the employment tribunal in awarding the maximum 4 weeks' pay to each worker for the failure of the Receiver to consult the employees about the transfer. The EAT stated that there was a difference between the passing on of information and consultation. In this case there were no trade unions involved, but there was still a duty to consult employee representatives.

Regulation 10 of the TUPE Regulations is concerned with the duty to inform and consult employee representatives and Regulation 11 with the consequences of failing to do so. The rules are that:

1 the appropriate representatives of all employees must be informed of

- the fact that a relevant transfer is to take place,
- when that transfer is to take place,

- the reasons for the transfer,
- the legal, economic and social implications of the transfer for the affected employees,
- the measures which the employer envisages that he or she will take, in connection with the transfer, in relation to the affected employees or the fact that there are in such measures envisaged;

2   there is an obligation upon the transferor to inform its affected employees of the measures that the transferee envisages it will take in relation to those employees. There is also an obligation upon the transferee to provide the transferor with such information as it will need to carry out this duty;
3   this information will be given 'long enough before' a relevant transfer in order for there to be opportunities for consultation;
4   this information is to be given to the representatives or sent to them by post;
5   if measures are envisaged, then the employer must consult the appropriate representatives of the affected employees with a view to seeking their agreement to the measures to be taken. In the course of those consultations the employer will consider the representations made by the appropriate representatives and reply to them. If the employer cannot accept any of the representations it must give its reasons.

The obligation in the TUPE Regulations is to begin the process 'long enough before a relevant transfer' to enable consultation to take place.

In *South Durham Health Authority* v *Unison* [1995] the Health Authority started the process on 7 February when it wrote to the trade union informing them of a transfer to trust status on the following 1 April. On 24 February the union replied asking for more information and complaining that not enough time had been allowed to comply with Regulation 10 of the TUPE Regulations. The employer replied on 11 March and suggested a meeting in the near future. The unions presented an application to an industrial tribunal complaining of the breach of Regulation 10 by the Health Authority on 16 March, that is 2 weeks before the transfer was to take place. Regulation 11 provides that complaints must be made within 3 months of the date of the relevant transfer, or another date if the tribunal agrees that this was not practicable. The Health Authority objected, but the Employment Appeal Tribunal held that although the Regulations specified an end date for complaints, they did not specify a start date.

This was also the case in *Banking Insurance and Finance Union* v *Barclays Bank* [1987] where the Court concluded that 'the transfer was not an essential element' before a complaint could be made about lack of consultation. It is possible, therefore, to complain about lack of consultation prior to a transfer, although it is arguable whether such a complaint would be successful unless there were a definite transfer planned and underway.

The High Court in *Institution of Professional Civil Servants* v *Secretary of State for Defence* [1987] decided that the words 'long enough before "a transfer" to enable consultations to take place' means as soon as measures are envisaged and *if possible* long enough before the transfer. The Court held that the words did not mean as soon as measures are envisaged and *in any event* long enough before the transfer. The case concerned the introduction of private management into the Royal

Dockyards at Rosyth and Devonport to which the trade unions were opposed. Before consultation can take place there need to be some definite plans or proposals by the employer around which negotiations can take place. There was a failure of consultation in this case because, according to the court, the unions were so opposed to the introduction of commercial management into the dockyards that they failed to take the opportunities to negotiate. The Court commented that 'effective consultations cannot take place with those who do not wish to be consulted.'

PROGRESS TEST

1 How can a company be reconstructed under the provisions of the Companies Act 1985 or the Insolvency Act 1986?
2 How does the City Code on Takeovers and Mergers apply to the reconstruction of a company?
3 What is the legal status of the City Code on Takeovers and Mergers?
4 Consider the different types of transfers described and make up examples for each of the categories.
5 Compare the decisions in *Schmidt* and *Süzen* or *Betts* and *ECM*, in order to identify the differences in approach.

What law will there be in the future? 14

Brenda Barrett

WHO WILL CHANGE THE LAW?

In *McLoughlin* v *O'Brian* [1983] LORD SCARMAN asked: 'Why then should not the courts draw the line, as the Court of Appeal manfully tried to do in this case? Simply, because the policy issue as to where to draw the line is not justiciable. The problem is one of social, economic and financial policy. The considerations relevant to a decision are not such as to be capable of being handled within the limits of the forensic process.'

In *Morgans* v *Launchbury* [1972] LORD WILBERFORCE said: 'The respondents submitted that we should depart from accepted principles and introduce a new rule, or set of rules, applicable to the use of motor vehicles, which would make the appellant liable as owner . . . Any new direction, and it may be one of many alternatives, must be set by Parliament.'

McLoughlin v *O'Brian* demonstrated that there are times when even the judges realize that the law is not clear because there is no precedent sufficient and appropriate to guide them. In this case the claimant was the mother and wife of road accident victims. It was foreseeable that witnessing her relatives at a hospital immediately following the accident would cause her to suffer nervous shock. Nevertheless their Lordships were concerned that requiring compensation to be paid to her by the negligent lorry driver who had caused the accident could open the floodgates to much litigation. However they considered that it was not appropriate that the courts rather than the legislature should make the decision that she should be denied damages.

Morgans v *Launchbury* also concerned a road accident causing death and serious personal injury. The car involved belonged to, and was insured by, a woman. She had lent it to her husband, authorizing him to drive it between their home and his workplace. The accident occurred when a friend of the husband was driving it. The husband was, at the time, too drunk to drive but at the time of the accident the friend was driving the husband away from, rather than towards, the matrimonial home. The question before the court was whether the driver could be deemed the agent of the wife. If he were not the vehicle would not be insured. In this case their Lordships declined to extend the meaning of agency to ensure that the victims were compensated.

The floodgates that might have been opened by *McLoughlin* have been firmly secured again by their Lordships as a result of *Alcock* v *Chief Constable of South Yorkshire Police* [1992] and *White* v *Chief Constable of South Yorkshire Police* [1999]. As a result of these two cases, bystanders (secondary victims) of catastrophe, who are in no personal danger of physical injury cannot rely on *McLoughlin* to found a claim unless they have close ties of love and affection with the primary victims and were present at the scene of the catastrophe either at the time it occurred or immediately afterwards.

The two cases have in common that the highest appeal court did not perceive its role as being to change the direction of the common law. If radical change were necessary they considered it should be brought about by Parliament.

DEVELOPMENT OF LAW THROUGH STRATEGIC LITIGATION?

In *Tai Hing Cotton Mill Ltd* v *Liu Chong Hing Bank Ltd* [1985] LORD SCARMAN said: 'I do not believe that there is anything to the advantage of the law's development in searching for a liability in tort where the parties are in a contractual relationship.'

This case concerned the respective liabilities of bank and customer when neither had noticed that, over a period of time, forged cheques had been drawn on the customer's account. The Privy Council maintained the view that the relationship between banker and customer was well established to be a contractual one and it was therefore not appropriate to allow the issue to be determined according to the rules of tort. LORD SCARMAN's speech continued by noting that it was particularly important that there should be certainty in commercial relationships:

> their Lordships believe it to be correct in principle and necessary for the avoidance of confusion in the law to adhere to the contractual analysis: on principle because it is a relationship in which the parties have, subject to a few exceptions, the right to determine their obligations to each other and for the avoidance of confusion because different consequences do follow according to whether liability arises from contract or tort.

Similarly in *Marc Rich & Co* v *AG Bishop Rock Marine Co Ltd (The Nicholas Heron)* [1996] the House of Lords held it would not be just fair and reasonable to make the marine surveyor liable in tort to the cargo owners as the Hague Rules provided appropriate remedies in contract.

These two cases provide further evidence that even in the last century the courts were not prepared to accept responsibility for bringing about fundamental changes in the framework of the law. The first two cases cited in this chapter showed that the courts would not take this initiative themselves, these later two demonstrate that they will not be led by the litigation strategy of the parties into being the agents of such change.

Apart from any questions about democratic process requiring change to be made by Parliament, there is an overwhelming reason why the courts should leave the task to Parliament. Theoretically judges do not make the law: they declare it. This means that judgments have retrospective effect. In three, at least, of the cases cited here, (*McLoughlin* is the exception) if the judges had been the agents of change, there would have been major back-dated implications, particularly in these cases, for the insurance industry. Insurance premiums are calculated on the basis of potential liability. Had, for example, the House of Lords in *Morgans* v *Launchbury*, extended the concept of agency, insurance companies would have been faced with many unexpected claims in respect of road accidents that had occurred prior to the date of the judgment. On the other hand while Parliament can, it rarely does, legislate with retrospective effect. Most legislation is brought into effect at a commencement date some time after the statute has received the Royal Assent. The period of time between the enactment and its being brought into effect may be used by organizations to adjust their commitments to enable them to operate within the new law. Had Parliament legislated for the concept of agency to be extended in the context of motor vehicle insurance no doubt there would have been an appropriate increase in motor insurance premiums to coincide with the commencement of the legislation.

Generally, if there are to be major changes in the legal framework within which business organizations operate they will be introduced by Act of Parliament.

HUMAN RIGHTS

By way of exception to the general situation, there is one area in which the judiciary may play a major role in changing the law to meet the needs of society. This is by interpretation of the Human Rights Act. It is now widely accepted that the implementation of this Act is likely to have very important effects upon practices in circumstances as disparate as the use of police and inspectoral (e.g. the Environment Agency) powers, the compensation of the victims of pollution, and the relationship between employer and employee. It is, of course, possible that the implications of this Act will be so widely understood that litigation will not occur. However this seems highly unlikely: it is much more likely that litigation will produce case law that will bring about fundamental changes in the British Constitution, in the relationships between business organizations and those with whom they come into contact, and in the relationships between individual citizens.

The judges will also have the novel task of evaluating legislation in relation to the Act. While the courts will not have the power to declare an Act of Parliament invalid they will have the duty to declare, if such be the case, that the Act before them cannot be reconciled with the Human Rights Act. Parliament could ignore the ruling of the court (which could lead to a reference to the European Court of Human Rights at Strasbourg) but it is most unlikely that Parliament would not respond to the declaration of the court.

WILL THERE BE LESS OR MORE LAW IN FUTURE?

(1) If, with respect to any provision made by an enactment, a Minister of the Crown is of the opinion
  (a) that the effect of the provision is such as to impose or authorise or require the imposition of, a burden affecting any person in the carrying on of any trade, business or profession or otherwise, and
  (b) that by amending or repealing the enactment concerned and, where appropriate, by making such other provision as is referred to in sub-section (4)(a) below, it would be possible, without removing any necessary protection, to remove or reduce the burden or, as the case may be, the authorisation or requirement by virtue of which the burden may be imposed,

he may, subject to the following provisions of this section and sections 2 to 4 below, by order amend or repeal that enactment (Deregulation and Contracting Out Act 1994 s.1).

Anyone who has worked through this book will realize how much the activities of business organizations are subject to law.

It is unlikely that there will be less law in future! Successive Governments in the UK have promised to reduce the role of the state and even to reduce the burden of regulation on businesses, but have failed to do so.

Notably the Conservative Government in the 1990s privatized a number of industries that had previously been run as state enterprises, for example water, gas, electricity and telecommunications. However these industries have arguably been more heavily controlled by the state since privatization than they were when run as nationalized industries. The pattern of the legislation bringing into effect the privatization has been to create a Director General whose responsibility it is to monitor the performance of the company. The Director General's duties have included protecting the interests of the general public, as consumers.

The Conservative Government also enacted the Deregulation and Contracting Out Act 1994 and New Labour did not repeal it. However there is little evidence that the burden of regulation has been reduced as a result of this or other legislation. A supposedly important feature of the Act was s.37 which gave special powers to repeal occupational health and safety provisions. This was deemed necessary because the Health and Safety at Work Act 1974, the principal Act concerning health and safety, did not permit outdated regulations to be repealed or revoked unless they were replaced by new laws. However, while s.37 enables the removal of obsolete British laws, the European Union has more than compensated for any reduction in the burden of national regulatory initiatives in this area. Directives on occupational health and safety could be made by the qualified majority procedure, under what was then Article 118a of the Treaty of Rome. Therefore this Article was relied on heavily; not least for controversial (to the British!) measures such as the Working Time Directive introducing the 48-hour week.

WHY SHOULD THE LAW CHANGE?

> What happens if you slice the problem up a different way and say that the future will be made up of a heady mix of things which can be extrapolated, things which stay endlessly constant throughout history and things which are discontinuous and which cannot be predicted? (Preface, *Britain towards 2010: the changing business environment*).

This quotation is taken from a report published in 1999 by the Department of Trade and Industry and the Economic and Social Research Council. It represents the findings of research conducted under the UK Foresight programme whose intention is to build bridges between business, science, government and the voluntary sector. The research represented in the publication is presented by Richard Scase. The outcome of research by Foresight is used by companies to re-shape their business strategies and build sustained competitive advantage.

The report identifies areas in which there is likely to be change impacting upon business organizations and upon society more generally. The following subheadings represent the major findings of the report and have here been related to the legal framework covered in this book.

- *The development of regional government within the UK.* Already there are legislative assemblies for Wales and Scotland; devolution to regions is likely to be extended. The outcome may be more local variations in the legal framework within which businesses have to operate and could, in the extreme, influence the siting of organizations.
- *Demographic change.* Ageing of the population will have major consequences, both as to the needs for health care and other social services and to the kinds of products and services the consumer will require from business organizations. Another consequence, in relation to the law presented in this book, may be changing patterns of employment.
- *The utilization of new technologies.* Particularly important will be the spread in the use of information and communications technology (ICT). This may lead to changes in the marketing of products and also in work patterns. Possibly an increasing number of people will work from home using ICT to communicate with their employer and other colleagues. If this is so then the employment status of homeworkers (already recognized as being capable of being employees – see *Nethermere (St Neots) Ltd* v *Taverna and Gardiner* [1984]) – may become more important. It will also mean that workers so employed will have an increased responsibility for ensuring their own working conditions are satisfactory – this again has already been acknowledged in, for example, the Health and Safety (Display Screens Equipment) Regulations 1992. However enforcement of satisfactory working conditions in a domestic environment has always been almost impossible as the history of the sweat shop industries (e.g. machine sewing) has established.
- *A more demanding population.* The population is already educated to a much higher level than it was in the middle of the last century. This trend will increase as an even greater proportion of the population undertakes higher education, and, having graduated, continues with a programme of life long learning. Greater use of the internet will place information at the disposal of a population equipped to find it and use it. These trends will impact both on the competencies and skills of workers and on the critical expectations of consumers. Already public service providers are expected to provide 'best value' to meet the needs of their stakeholding clients. The ensuing change in climate will surely impact on business organizations operating in the private sector.
- *Changes in family structure.* On the one hand the greater employment of women, that has already occurred, may result in the normalization of shared parental responsibility. The introduction of paternity leave (albeit unpaid) is a move in that direction. On the other hand the breakdown of marriages and other partnerships may mean that the one parent family remains commonplace. Either way the accommodation of domestic commitments within the relationship between the business organization and its workers is likely to increase rather than decline. Another factor, so the report suggests, will be the increase in single people and a consequential increase in people living alone. This is likely to change the demand for living accommodation and for the products required when setting up home.
- *Globalization.* The expressions 'global market' and 'global village' had already found their way into the vocabulary before the end of the last century. The more general use of ICT will increase this trend. The world may become even more

extremely divided between the under developed and the developed economies, the former contributing manual labour and the later, in which the UK must be ranked, competing to become leading edge information economies.

This brief summary is very much a gloss on a valuable report, which ought to be read in full by anyone intending to enter management.

The successful business organization will have a rolling plan in which is set out its aims and objectives for the future. Very often such plans are 5-year plans, subject to annual review. In making such plans the business will need to have a realistic vision of the environment in which the organization will be operating in the future.

As will have become apparent by now, any business that does not observe the legal rules is at risk of prosecution in the criminal courts and/or litigation in the civil courts. Before some suggestions are offered as to the ways in which the law may change to meet changes in society and the business environment there is another important factor that must be taken into account.

THE IMPACT OF THE EUROPEAN UNION

PART I

PRINCIPLES

Article 1

By this Treaty, the HIGH CONTRACTING PARTIES establish among themselves a EUROPEAN COMMUNITY

Article 2

The Community shall have as its task, by establishing a common market and an economic and monetary union and by implementing common policies or activities referred to in Articles 3 and 4, to promote throughout the Community a harmonious, balanced and sustainable development of economic activities, a high level of employment and of social protection, equality between men and women, sustainable and non-inflationary growth, a high degree of competitiveness and convergence of economic performance, a high level of protection and improvement of the quality of the environment, the raising of the standard of living and quality of life, and economic and social cohesion and solidarity among Member States.

So begins the Consolidated Version of the Treaty Establishing the European Community; in other words the outcome of the Treaty of Amsterdam.

The United Kingdom remains a member state of the European Union fully committed to its jurisdiction and its principles. This is in spite of some popular opposition to continuing membership of the Union and uncertainty about when, if indeed at all, the UK will adopt the euro as its currency. It is clear that legislation from the European Community has become an important, indeed perhaps the major source of UK legislation in recent years. There is no reason to expect that this will change. Since the Union is a grouping of states in close geographical proximity, and all forming part of the developed world, there is every likelihood that others who are currently member states of the European Union will be experiencing many of the social and technological changes predicted for Britain between now and the year 2010.

The question for the future development of law in the UK is the extent to which Europe will introduce new community-wide measures in the face of the changing social and economic environment; and if it is minded to facilitate change, the extent to which it will do this through legislation.

The indications are that the question of enlargement will dominate European Community policy in the next few years. Political changes in Eastern Europe in the last decade of the twentieth century have meant that the list of potential applicants for community membership has grown to include most of Eastern Europe and Turkey, Malta and Cyprus. Negotiations have started with Hungary, Poland, Estonia, the Czech Republic, Slovenia and Cyprus. The Treaty of Amsterdam did not address the institutional changes that will be needed: some politically difficult decisions will have to be made, for example over the number of Commissioners. These decisions could result in changes in the balance of power within the Community. Arguably if the number of states increases the influence of the UK may diminish.

The inclusion within the Union of Eastern European states is likely to impact on the economic and social development of the Union. Already it has been seen that the inclusion of Eastern Germany in the Union, following the collapse of the Berlin Wall, has impacted on the development of Germany. Broadly Eastern Europe is less economically and socially developed than Western Europe. New entrants to membership will, in any case, have a taxing task in assimilating the laws which the Western member states have implemented over time.

Enlargement of the Union will bring both social and economic diversity into the Union and make it more difficult to harmonize the laws of the member states. In the long run such expansion may strengthen the power of the Union as a trading bloc and as a force in world politics. In the short run it may retard the integration of member states into the superstate. Nevertheless reform of the Common Agricultural Policy will be necessary both because of the incorporation of new entrants from the east, and because of world trade liberalization.

Expansion will lead to the incorporation of states where the tradition of democracy is less well established. Fundamental rights have received stronger emphasis in each revision of the Treaty. Recent additions in the Treaty of Amsterdam can be seen as being a preparation for future enlargement.

It is difficult therefore to speculate whether the Union will push forward with harmonization at the risk of overwhelming new member states, or slow down the pace at the risk of widening the gap between the existing members states and the new entrants. Moreover any relaxation of the pace of harmonization could widen the gap between the existing states themselves: there already is clearly a mismatch between the state of the British economy and the economies of other major Western European member states.

Whatever the pace of developments in the EU, there is already a considerable agenda for the UK of legislating to introduce and working to assimilate EU law into the British system. In particular now that the UK has signed up to the Social Chapter there may be expected to be Directives under this chapter. Already the Transnational Information and Consultation of Employees Regulation 1999 have been introduced to implement the EU Directive on European Works Councils. They set out the procedure in Community-scale organizations for the purposes of informing and consulting employees. They are indicative of the worker participation culture that is already normal in other member states, but somewhat novel in Britain.

Work in hand in the EU includes proposals for Directives to combat racial discrimination and to broaden the protection against discrimination in employment. The later Directive is intended to cover disability, age, sexual orientation and religion. If adopted, this Directive could require current British legislation to be strengthened. The Government, for example, is currently encouraging employers not to discriminate by reason of age, but has stopped short of legislating to prohibit this kind of discrimination. British case law on discrimination by reason of sexual orientation is not at all clear.

WHAT CHANGES WILL THERE BE IN BRITISH LAW AND PRACTICE?

> The Citizen's Charter programme follows on and brings together the radical changes in government and ideology ... Both in theory and in practice, the charter has had the effect of rewriting the relationship between state and citizen in contractual terms (*Law and Administration* Carol Harlow and Richard Rawlings, Butterworths 2nd edn, p. 144).

This chapter began with the speculation that the judiciary would not be responsible for bringing about radical changes in the legal framework within which business organizations operate. On the other hand nothing in those cases prevents the State, or citizens from using well-recognized legal tools, such as contract, in novel ways to regulate their activities.

The stakeholder society

A major change in the public sector in recent years has been the move from detailed regulatory control to a framework within which state services, such as the National Health Service, are required to operate to contractual principles. The supply of goods and services between departments within the particular public service, for example between general practitioners and hospitals, and between the public service and the general public has come to be modelled on the law of contract. Strict competitive tendering (employing the lowest bidder) has given way to the concept of 'best value'.

In the 1940s and 1950s, when the National Health Service and the Welfare State more generally were first introduced, the general public, attuned by the years of the Second World War, to bureaucratic and highly intrusive regulation by the state, was happy to accept state support, as a discretionary gift, in times of personal crisis. Fifty years on members of the public now consider they have a right to services for which they have paid through taxation. Moreover they require that the services received should be of a standard and at a price that is acceptable. The new style is regulation by audit, through Ombudsmen and more especially investigation, followed by report to Parliament by the National Audit Office (see National Audit Act 1983). There is no reason to suppose that this system of regulation through quasi-contract and audit will not be maintained and even strengthened in future.

People power

Politicians, quoted by the media, have highlighted the role of 'The People' as stakeholders in, and, to a large extent determinants of, what is socially acceptable. Notably, in death, Princess Diana was hailed as 'The People's Princess'.

The role of 'people' in the workplace has long been acknowledged by the European Community, which has stressed the importance of the social partnership between employers and workers. Articles 137–139 of the Treaty of Amsterdam (the Social Chapter) enable certain social regulations to be formulated by the social partners and brought into effect by collective agreement rather than by Directive. In these situations the member states are not required to legislate to introduce the collectively agreed provisions into the law of their states: at state level the changes needed may be brought about by collective agreement.

In the UK the Select Committee on Health and Safety at Work (Robens Committee) reported in 1972, and its recommendations were reflected in the Health and Safety at Work Act 1974. It stated 'the promotion of safety and health at work is first and foremost a matter of efficient management.' It proposed only that workers should be consulted on matters of health and safety at their workplace. The Health and Safety Representatives and Safety Committees Regulations 1977 implemented this proposal for employees at workplaces where there was a recognized trade union. It was not until 1996 with the Health and Safety (Consultation with Employees) Regulations that similar rights were given to those who worked at non-unionized workplaces.

The Health and Safety Commission is now committed to fundamental review of the 1974 Act, feeling that after 25 years it may be showing signs of age. Closely related to this review, the Commission has published a consultative document suggesting a particular need to review the two sets of regulations on worker involvement and identifies a number of ways in which more power might be given to the workforce to produce change and monitor workplace standards. Possibly the Health and Safety Commission is influenced by the provisions in the Treaty. However the Treaty envisages quasi-legislation through collective agreement: the most that revised safety representative regulations in the UK would be likely to achieve would be to define what the organization and its workers considered the acceptable level of risk at the particular workplace. It is unlikely that a collective agreement at national level would determine legally enforceable national standards.

Intellectual property

ICT makes it increasingly difficult for the owners of copyrights to protect their works. The internet makes unauthorized copying and exploitation quicker and easier. It is not obvious, however, how changes in the law can prevent this happening. The relatively small scale pirating of material through the use of the home-based video and other media equipment, has already demonstrated this difficulty; though prevention of publication on a large scale of material illicitly acquired is possible, with constant vigilance and at considerable expense. It is not clear that the public would be sympathetic to legislation introducing expensive policing through a dedicated state inspectorate.

It is interesting to note that the new Regulation of Investigatory Powers Act 2000 now makes provision for and about the interception of communications. It covers postal communications but is clearly directed at misuse of the internet. It prohibits unauthorized interception of messages but gives wide powers of authorized interception, primarily by the Security Service, the Secret Intelligence Service and Government Communications Headquarters. It envisages international agreement to facilitate prevention of misuse of telecommunications systems on a super-national scale. If enacted this Bill may go some way towards preventing computer 'viruses'. The operation of the scheme would be likely to impose considerable financial burdens on providers of internet services: they will be required to cooperate with the operation of the scheme. Any powers to intercept e-mails will have to be reconciled with the right of individual privacy granted by the Human Rights Act. Employers wishing to monitor the conduct of their employees' use of the telephone or e-mail at work must bear this in mind.

The trend towards patentability of software related inventions might continue even though it may concentrate too much power in the hands of monopoly holders. However the litigation in the USA against Bill Gates over the monopoly position exercised by Microsoft may be indicative of the direction in which frustrated competitors will respond in the future. It is possible that business organizations may utilize the Community trade mark; but in the global market it may not be valuable. It is also possible that arbitration procedures will be utilized for resolving domain name disputes. Again there would need to be an international forum.

There is scope for interesting litigation to determine issues such as: determining the responsibility for material published on the internet. Should it be the organization providing the server, or the person who enters the material on the site? English law of defamation suggests that both would be deemed to have published the material. But on the analogy of defamation, the provider of the server might have a defence if 'innocent'. However, failing to monitor the situation, so that the offensive material continued to be available for an unduly long period of time, might be deemed negligence.

There is another problem to be resolved. If an internet publication is unlawful, where in the world will it be deemed to have been published? In the jurisdiction where it was entered on the server, in the jurisdiction where the server is located, or in the jurisdiction where the message is read? The situation is further compounded because some publications, e.g. pornographic, may potentially be the subject of prosecution, whereas others may lead to litigation, possibly as the tort of defamation.

'Forum shopping' – the practice of looking for the most favourable jurisdiction in which to open proceedings – is already practised on a small scale in personal injury litigation. The potential for this appears to be much greater in relation ICT.

KEEPING UP WITH TECHNOLOGICAL CHANGE

There are four areas in which continuing legislation is almost certain:

1 *Intellectual property.* Given the growing important of ICT it seems probable that, at least at European level there will be legislation aimed at harmonization of design law. Perhaps, given that this is an area where globalization is significant, there may be an international treaty with significance beyond Europe.
2 *Product safety.* Standards for numerous products are determined for adoption across Europe, partly as a matter of harmonization and partly as a matter of safety.

The standardization goes beyond the member states of the EU, but within the EU it is authorized by Articles 94 and 95 of the EC Treaty. The European Standardisation Committee (CEN) carries out the work of determining standards for products and a similar special Committee (CENEL) is responsible for the standardization of electrical goods. Products are of an acceptable standard throughout Europe if they are stamped with the 'CE' kite mark. It is certain that producers and suppliers will have to have regard to changing standards brought about by these bodies. However this will occur without legislation.

In addition to this the EU has, over a number of years, adopted many Directives on product standards and on the protection of people from exposure to dangerous substances. These Directives are aimed at protecting both the workers and the consumer. Notable in this context is the Control of Substances Hazardous to Health Regulations (COSHH) and the Chemicals (Hazard Information and Packaging) Regulations (CHIP). These two sets of Regulations represent the British response to EC Directives. COSHH aims to control the exposure of workers to dangerous substances. CHIP protects both the worker and the public. Each set of Regulations contains Schedules listing particular substances that have to be controlled. A year does not go by but that, in the light of new knowledge, the EU adopts supplementary directives and UK Regulations have to be updated.

3 *Environmental protection.* It has been seen that business organizations already have considerable legal responsibilities to control pollution brought about by their activities. Just as advances in scientific knowledge and technical expertise lead to a constant flow of EU Directives on the control of products and substances, so it is to be expected that there will be further Directives on environmental standards, such as have already been seen on the quality of water, and the quality of beaches. British law may require organizations to carry out strategic environmental assessments in relation to new projects.

Related to environmental protection, but relevant also to human health and safety, regulation of genetic modification of organisms is likely.

4 *Regulation of transport.* While no UK Government has had the stomach to legislate radical measures for the control of the use of the motor vehicle, it seems almost certain that there will be at least some measures – even if only at a local or regional level – to make the use of the motor vehicle less attractive. Possibilities are tolls on use of vehicles in urban areas and restrictions on the lay out of roads. Parking charges are also likely to be increased. Further taxes on the licensing of heavy goods vehicles or on the price of petrol may not be practical unless a policy of penalizing (or even economically charging) for the use of heavy goods vehicles is adopted at EU level.

It is noteworthy that many of the major catastrophes of recent years have involved public transportation, by rail or by sea. It is therefore possible that there may be higher regulatory standards imposed on the standards and operation of public transport vehicles and systems.

THE ORGANIZATION AND ITS CONTRACTORS

The 1990s saw the development of the practice of organizations 'contracting out' the provision of services. Many people were made redundant only to continue with providing the service they provided as employees, often to the very organization by which they were previously employed.

There are already indications that the law is not sympathetic to large organizations using the system of contracting out work to escape the legal responsibilities that are a consequence of hiring employees. The EC does not make the same distinction, as does British law, between employees and other workers. Traditionally UK legislation and case law has distinguished the employed from the self-employed. Employment protection legislation has imposed on the employer duties in respect of employed persons but had less concern with organizational responsibilities for the self-employed.

Already there are indications that the British custom and practice (backed by legislation) of categorizing workers is of declining importance. Recent legislation tends to favour the word 'worker' rather than employee when creating rights and responsibilities in the employment relationship. Thus the Working Time Regulations 1998 set out the rights and duties between the employer and 'workers'.

It is significant that s.3 of the Health and Safety at Work Act, has been interpreted very broadly in a number of prosecutions. The section imposes on employers the duty to do what is reasonably practicable to secure the health and safety of persons who are not employees of the employer, in situations where such people might be put at risk by the 'conduct of his undertaking'. Thus, in *R* v *Board of Trustees of the Science Museum* [1993] the Court of Appeal found the Museum in breach of the section when it allowed bacterium to escape into the street where it might have endangered the public. In *R* v *Associated Octel Co Ltd* [1998] the House of Lords upheld the conviction of Octel following an accident caused by its subcontractor failing to follow Octel's permit to work system when carrying out maintenance work at Octel's plant. These cases do more than demonstrate the extent of the organization's responsibility to operate to a safe system. They indicate a tendency to impose a wide ranging social responsibility on large organizations for the training and supervision of those who carry out work on their behalf.

THE BALANCE BETWEEN CRIMINAL AND CIVIL LAW

Much of the history of the twentieth century was of the decriminalization of conduct. Two very different examples are the reduction of the use of the criminal law as a regulator of trade disputes and the decriminalization of homosexual activity. The current discussion about the legalizing of certain drugs, such as cannabis, indicates that this trend is likely to continue.

An alternative regulatory method has been to legislate providing rights that individuals may, at their own election, choose to enforce. Discrimination in employment is an example. This tendency may continue with legislation against ageism in employment and in society more generally.

There are indications that the EU will adopt a Directive imposing strict civil liability on organizations that cause damage to the environment.

The principal area in which the criminal law is likely to be strengthened is in matters concerning the protection of personal safety. As long ago as 1994 the Law Commission published Consultation Paper No 135 on *Involuntary Manslaughter* in which it advocated the creation of corporate liability for causing death by the operation of defective systems. The continuing incidence of fatal catastrophes, such as the *Marchioness* collision in the Thames and a number of rail crashes have kept the issue in the forefront. Legislation to create this new offence therefore seems likely.

TAXATION

British tax laws are much in need of reform and simplification. This need is widely accepted but it seems unlikely that the present Government will address this matter.

CONCLUSION

It is not possible to predict with any certainty the detail of what the future will hold. All the trends are, however, that business organizations will be increasingly expected to demonstrate social responsibility. They will be expected to assess risk (as occupational health and safety law already requires and environment law is likely to require!), monitor performance and close the loop by improving their systems. In doing this they will have to have regard to all the stakeholders: that is the state, their workers, their customers and the general public – as well as their shareholders.

Further reading

Bainbridge, D. (1999) *Intellectual Property*, 4th edn, Financial Times/Pitman Publishing.

Bell, S. (2000) *Bell & Ball on Environmental Law*, 5th edn, Blackstone Press.

Clarkson, C.M.V. (1998) *Criminal Law, Text and Materials*, 4th edn, Sweet & Maxwell.

Cornish, W.R. (1999) *Intellectual Property Patents, Copyright, Trade Marks and Allied Rights*, 4th edn, Sweet & Maxwell.

Elliott, C. and Quinn, F. (2000) *English Legal System*, 3rd edn, Longman.

Gravells, N. (1999) *Land Law: Text and Materials*, 2nd edn, Sweet & Maxwell.

Keenan, D. (1999) *Smith & Keenan's Company Law for Students*, 11th edn, Financial Times/Pitman Publishing.

Kent, Penelope (2000) *Law of the European Union*, 3rd edn, Longman.

Lewis and Sargeant (2000) *Essentials of Employment Law*, Institute of Personnel and Development.

Mackenzie, J.-A. and Phillips, M. (1999) *Textbook on Land Law*, 8th edn, Blackstone Press.

Mckendrick, E. (2000) *Contract Law*, 4th edn, Macmillan.

Megarry, R. and Thompson, M. (1993) *Megarry's Manual of the Law of Real Property*, 7th edn, Sweet & Maxwell.

Morse, G. (1999) *Charlesworth and Morse on Company Law*, 16th edn, Sweet & Maxwell.

Nightingale, K. (2000) *Taxation, Theory & Practice*, 3rd edn, Prentice Hall.

Richards, P. (1999) *Law of Contract*, 4th edn, Financial Times/Pitman Publishing.

Ridall, J.G. (1997) *Introduction to Land Law*, 6th edn, Butterworths.

Rogers, W.V.H. (1998) *Winfield & Jolowicz on Tort*, 15th edn, Sweet & Maxwell.

Sealy, L.S. (2000) *Cases and Materials in Company Law*, 7th edn, Butterworths.

Slapper, G. and Kelly, D. (1999) *English Legal System*, 4th edn, Cavendish.

Smith, J.C. (2000) *Smith & Thomas A Casebook on Contract*, 11th edn, Sweet & Maxwell.

Thomson Tax Limited (2000) *Thomson Tax Guide*, Thomson Tax Limited (updated annually).

Weir, T. (2000) *A Casebook on Tort*, 9th edn, Sweet & Maxwell.

Wells, C. (1993) *Corporations and Criminal Responsibility*, Oxford University Press.

Wolf and White (1997) *Principles of Environmental Law*, 2nd edn, Cavendish.

There is also a wealth of information on the EU website: www.europa.eu.int

Index